HISTORY OF
NICHOLAS COUNTY
WEST VIRGINIA

WILLIAM GRIFFEE BROWN

Southern Historical Press, Inc.
Greenville, South Carolina

This volume was reproduced
from a personal copy located in
the Publishers private library

All rights reserved. No part of this publication may be reproduced,
stored in a retrieval system, transmitted in any form, posted
on the web in any form or by any means without the
prior written permission of the publisher.

Please direct all correspondence and book orders to:
SOUTHERN HISTORICAL PRESS, Inc.
1071 Park West Blvd.
Greenville, SC 29611

Copyright 1954 by:
 W.G. Brown
New Material Copyright 2025 by:
 Southern Historical Press, Inc.
ISBN #978-1-63914-648-2
Printed in the United States of America

Dedication

This book is dedicated to the school boys and girls of Nicholas County, with the earnest wish of the Author, that from its pages they may catch something of the unconquerable spirit of their ancestors, and be thereby inspired to emulate the noble character and patriotism of their forefathers, and to strive to make Nicholas County the ideal community of which its founders dreamed.

AUTHOR'S PREFACE

SINCE boyhood the author has had a keen interest in the settlement and development of Nicholas County, and in the course of a long and busy life has studied its records and learned the traditions of its people. For the past ten years careful research has been made of our written history as it appears of record, and to supplement much that is lacking from other reliable sources. In this quest the State Department of Archives and History, the Virginia Historical Society, and National Archives and the Library of Congress have been searched for any event or person of note of the century and a half of our history.

In the Chapter on Pioneer Families the nationality of the pioneers has been gathered from government records, family tradition and such sources. The notes of Colonel Edward Campbell, deeds, wills, marriage records, family papers and traditions are relied on in the personal sketches. Care has been taken to secure accuracy, but doubtless some error may have escaped notice.

In this arduous work my wife, Evie Cutlip Brown, has tirelessly aided me in gathering data and preparing the manuscript. My daughters, Dama Langley and Mabel Rowe have been of great assistance in correcting and arranging the subject matter and directing publication. Others to whom I am indebted for assistance are Mrs. Roy B. Cook of the State Department of Archives and History, Mr. Sterling M. Craig for supplying old papers and records, Mr. P. N. Wiseman, Mr. L. O. Bobbitt, Mr. Harrison Groves for their help and suggestions in the preparation of the Chapter on Education. My thanks are also extended to County Superintendents James Creasy and Harry Straley and to Agent John M. Curry for information given from their respective offices.

My dominant purpose has been to preserve the early history of Nicholas County in so far as possible at this date and to enlist the interest of the coming generation in the character and labors of their pioneer families to whom they are so deeply indebted.

W. G. Brown
Summersville, West Virginia

August 5, 1954.

FOREWORD

THE history of our County of Nicholas and its people has been too long delayed. We are fortunate indeed that the superior knowledge and the ability to clearly record possessed by the author have been utilized to the end that a more complete history than has ever been attempted is now finished.

Such a history is important as a matter of keeping the facts of our past in workable form for future generations. It is more important as an instrument to arouse and keep alive an interest among the people in and of the county who are the descendants of those pioneer families which organized the county. The descendants of these families, and other families who came to this county in the footsteps of the pioneers, are now our leaders; and many of them bear family names recorded by the author.

During a long and busy life, it has been my privilege to know many leading citizens of our State, nation and other countries of the world. Our own people of Nicholas County compare favorably with these leaders in native intelligence and ability, in strength and breadth of character, and in a lofty desire to serve their fellow-men.

Our pioneer ancestors found Nicholas County a wilderness. They, and those who have followed them, have made it into a community of homes, of productive farms and thriving industry.

They hewed down forests and made their homes.

They had no government—they organized government.

They had no schools—they created schools.

They had no roads—they built roads.

They had no churches—they built and maintained churches.

These examples are sermons for those of us who follow.

What we of later generations now need is a keener desire to do the utmost of which we are capable in the worthwhile activities of life. This would be expected of us by those stalwart people who were our ancestors and who themselves represented the best in American citizenship.

This foreword must not be closed without a special reference to the author of this history. His life is an example of service and success in many fields; but his greatest contribution, in my judgment, to the citizens of our county and surrounding counties was made as a teacher. He not only taught hundreds of students, he taught teachers who in turn taught others. Those of us who were privileged to sit in his classes, or in the classes of the teachers he trained, may properly give credit to him for a large part of any success attained in life.

He taught the basic principle that the very foundation of a good and serviceable education was the ability to make a wise choice in any situation; and that true wisdom consists of disproving and disarming falsehood with truth. He was not responsible for the failure of any; he has contributed immensely to the success of a great family.

Arthur B. Koontz

Charleston, West Virginia
August, 1954.

CONTENTS

	Page
DEDICATION	v
AUTHOR'S PREFACE	vii
FOREWORD	ix
WILSON CARY NICHOLAS	xv
PIONEER FAMILIES	xvii
BACKGROUND	xix

Chapter

I.	GENERAL DESCRIPTION	1
II.	EARLY SETTLEMENTS	22
III.	ORGANIZATION AND ADMINISTRATION	46
IV.	TRANSPORTATION, POST OFFICE, MAILS	67
V.	LOCAL GOVERNMENT—VIRGINIA AND WEST VIRGINIA	84
VI.	NICHOLAS COUNTY IN THE WARS	101
VII.	HOME LIFE, 1818-1861	126
VIII.	HOME LIFE AFTER THE CIVIL WAR	155
IX.	MUNICIPALITIES AND VILLAGES	205
X.	EDUCATION, SCHOOLS, TEACHERS, TEXTBOOKS	223
XI.	PIONEER FAMILIES	281
XII.	PRODUCTS, FUTURE POSSIBILITIES	392

APPENDIX	409
Dedication Address—Unveiling of Morris Monument	409
Gauley River	416
Brown Waters of Gauley	419
Teaching Local History	421

LIST OF ILLUSTRATIONS

The Author . . . . *Frontispiece*

                                                    Facing Page

Wilson Cary Nicholas xv
Colonel Edward Campbell 278
Bethel Methodist Church 165
Zoar Baptist Church 168
Alderson Baptist Church 169
Old County and Circuit Court Clerk's Office, 1824-1898 46
Scene on Gauley River 416
Morris Monument 409

Maps

Map of Nicholas County Showing Boundary Changes   2
Map of Magisterial Districts 4
Map of Cross Lanes Battlefield 103
Map of Carnefix Battleground 104

GOVERNOR WILSON CARY NICHOLAS
The county was named in his honor.

Wilson Cary Nicholas

WILSON CARY NICHOLAS was born at Williamsburg, Virginia, January 31, 1761. He was the son of Robert Carter Nicholas and Anne Cary Nicholas. He left his class as a student in William and Mary College at the age of eighteen to join the Continental Army and served as Commander of Washington's Life Guard till the close of the war. He married Margaret Smith, daughter of John Smith of Baltimore and lived at Warren in Albemarle County. In 1784 he represented his county in the General Assembly and held his seat there till 1799 when he was appointed to the U. S. Senate to fill the unexpired term of Henry Tazewell. In 1807 he was elected to Congress and held this office two terms. He was Governor of Virginia from December 11, 1814 to December 11, 1816.

As a member of the General Assembly he was the leading advocate for the adoption of the Constitution. Jefferson declared he was the most influential man in leading Virginia to adopt the Constitution. He also supported Jefferson's "Statute for Religious Freedom"; was a member of the Committee that laid off the District of Columbia; and had the statue of Washington placed in the Capitol at Richmond.

In the Senate he advocated Jefferson's Louisiana Purchase, and the adoption of the Constitutional Amendments. As Governor his able messages had a strong influence in Virginia legislation.

He was a cousin of Sir Robert Walpole, the English

statesman, and a blood relation of Talleyrand, the noted French statesman.

He owned land on Birch River in Nicholas County and assisted in the formation of the new county.

He died at the residence of his son-in-law, Thomas Jefferson Randolph, on January 10, 1820, and was buried at Monticello.

PIONEER FAMILIES

ALDERSON	DOTSON	HUTCHINSON
AMICK	DRENNEN	HYPES
BACKUS	DUFFY	JOHNSON
BAILES	DUNBAR	JONES
BAKER	EVANS	KEENAN
BAUGHMAN	EWING	KESSLER
BELL	FITZWATER	KINCAID
BENNETT	FOCKLER	KING
BOBBITT	FOSTER	KOONTZ
BOLEY	FRAME	KYLE
BROCK	GIVEN	KYER
BROWN	GRAY	LEGG
BURDETT	GROSE	LEMASTERS
BRYANT	GROVES	LILLY
CALLAGHAN	HALSTEAD	MALCOLM
CAMPBELL	HAMILTON	MARTIN
CARNEFIX	HAMRICK	MASON
CAVENDISH	HANNA	MILLER
CHAPMAN	HARDWAY	MORRIS
COPENHAVER	HENDERSON	MORRISON
CORRON	HEREFORD	McCLUNG
COTTLE	HEROLD	McCOY
CRAIG	HICKMAN	McMILLION
CROOKSHANKS	HILL	McNUTT
CUTLIP	HINKLE	McCUTCHEON
DAVIS	HORAN	McCUE
DIETZ	HUFF	MURPHY
DODRILL	HUFFMAN	NEIL
DORSEY	HUGHES	NUTTER

PIONEER FAMILIES

NICHOLLS	SEBERT	STEPHENSON
ODELL	SHAWVER	STICKLER
PATTERSON	SHELTON	SUMMERS
PERKINS	SIMMS	TYREE
PIERSON	SIERS	VANBIBBER
PITTSENBERGER	SKAGGS	VAUGHAN
RAMSEY	SMITH	WALKER
RADER	SPARKS	WILLIAMS
RENICK	SPENCER	WISEMAN
RIPPETOE	SPINKS	WOODS
ROBINSON	STANARD	YOUNG

BACKGROUND

THE background in a landscape painting—mountains in the distance, the forests, the clouds and clear sky—gives meaning and character to the picture. So the earliest history of the land and its inhabitants, gives us a better understanding of its later history. Let us glance at the background of Nicholas County.

Sebastian Cabot, sailing under the English flag in 1498, had visited the eastern shores of North America and given basis to England's claim in the newly discovered continent. Almost a century later Sir Walter Raleigh's luckless venture at planting an English colony on Roanoke Island, gave the name "Virginia" to a vast and uncertain territory.

No further attempt at English settlements followed Raleigh's failure till the year 1606, when King James I granted to the London Company the charter for all the territory in this Virginia lying between the 35th and 40th parallels of north latitude, and later extended the grant to all the country lying between the mouth of Cape Fear River on the south, that of the Hudson River on the north, and from the Atlantic Ocean on the east, westward to the Pacific.

From this vast wilderness two hundred years later our County of Nicholas was to evolve.

At the beginning of English settlements in Virginia, the whole vast country from the Atlantic westward to the prairies of the Mississippi Valley was one unbroken forest. Only along the streams flowing to the sea from the Appalachian Mountains were to be found clearings in which the Indians were growing corn and the vegetables they cultivated. In the fertile valley of the Shenandoah River, between the Blue Ridge and the Alleghanies, there were extensive natural meadows, open grass lands and Indian cornfields. Beyond the rugged mountain barriers, where the "western waters" found their way to the Mississippi, stretched the "Big Woods". Here giant poplars, chestnuts, oaks, maples, hickories, beeches and walnuts grew side by side, with many other species of trees, and lifted their towering foliage in a dense roof of verdant leaves that shut out the sunlight. Only from the highest points of the mountain ridges, where dwarfed mountain oaks, pines and laurel grew less densely, could a view be had of this seemingly limitless forest.

The only passages through this labyrinth of mountains, valleys and rushing streams were the game trails and Indian warpaths, hedged in by thick underbrush of rhododendron, mountain laurel and other shrubbery. The early settlers of the coastal plain, only knew of this western region from legends of their boldest hunters and trappers, who had ventured over the mountains, and they thought of it only as the home of wild animals and savages.

For a century after the settlement of Jamestown the English colonists had only partially occupied the lands along the James, Rappahannock and Potomac rivers, to the foot of the Blue Ridge. By conquest and barter they had forced the most of the Indians to remove west of the mountains. In this manner they made bitter and lasting enemies of the displaced tribes, and especially had they aroused the hatred of the Shawnees and Delawares, who had been driven from east of the mountains, and who now violently and savagely opposed the further westward progress of the colonists.

At this juncture a new and powerful factor in the future settlement of Virginia was coming into play—the coming of the *"Scotch-Irish"* and the *"Pennsylvania Dutch"* to the frontiers.

About the time King James I granted the London Company's Charter, he had begun the settlement of Ulster in North Ireland with colonists from Scotland, Wales and North England. His plan was to locate these Protestants,—followers of Calvin and Knox,—in Ireland with the purpose to ultimately outnumber and control the Catholics of Ireland. Fiske, in his "OLD VIRGINIA AND HER NEIGHBORS", says: *"These settlers were picked men and women of the most excellent sort. They were intelligent artisans, and most could read and write. By 1650 300,000, were in Ulster, and they had transformed its bogs and fens into a garden, and their manufacture of woolens and linens had become famous throughout the world. Their flourishing manufactories aroused the jealousy of rival merchants in England, and by 1700 English laws had been passed restricting their trade and closing their schools and churches".*

Such treatment these sturdy people would not brook, and by 1719 they had begun to migrate to America in volume. One week in 1727, six ship loads came to Philadelphia, and between 1730 and 1770 a half-million had come from Ulster to America. They settled largely in the Shenandoah, Yadkin and Catawba river valleys, and from these centers they later moved over the mountains.

Next in importance to the Scotch-Irish settlers were the Germans from the Palatinate of Germany, who also were Protestants fleeing from religious persecution, and coming to Pennsylvania in large numbers.

Soon this flood of emigrants found it difficult to get cheap lands from the Quakers in Pennsylvania, and the overflow poured into the Valley of Virginia and the Piedmont region of North Carolina. They were generally known as "Pennsylvania Dutch", from the incorrect translation of *"Pennsylvanische Deutsche"*. These Germans were excellent farmers, and in the open lands of the Shenandoah Valley and on the South Branch of the Potomac, soon were growing wheat and raising cattle, hogs and sheep. This great influx of Scotch-Irish and German settlers at once aroused the Indians to violent opposition, and Valley settlements especially felt the brunt of savage ferocity.

The colonial government of Virginia had by prior treaty agreed with the Indians to limit settlement to the country east of the Alleghany Mountains, but the press of settlers overran this boundary, and the Colonial Governor in an effort to pacify the Indians, had by the Treaty of Fort Stanwix, November 5, 1768, bought from the Six Nations their claim to the vast area between the Ohio and Tennessee Rivers. This powerful Indian Confederacy, known as the "Six Nations", had by conquest of the other tribes, established title to all the country lying between the Alleghany Mountains and the Great Lakes; and the Shawnees, Delawares, Mingoes, Wyandots and parts of other tribes, were allowed to occupy this territory as their tenants.

Although the Six Nations had been paid a large sum for their claim and had by formal writing deeded the territory to the King of England, the tribes named, living mostly north of the Ohio River, denied the right of the Six Nations to sell their grounds, refused to be bound by the Treaty of Fort Stanwix, and continued their savage warfare against settlers till they were forced, after their defeat by General Wayne, to sign the treaty of Greenville in 1795. This treaty bound them to occupy certain territory north of the Ohio River and left the Trans-Alleghany region open to settlement.

For two generations the resolute Scotch-Irish and the sturdy Germans had been slowly and painfully planting their cabin homes in this disputed area. At first they fell easy victims to the tomahawk and scalping knife, but their sons and daughters, trained in this fearful struggle for existence, had become skilled in woodcraft and matched the savage warriors in the relentless battle for the land. At Brushy Run, under Colonel Bouquet, and at Point Pleasant under General Lewis they defeated the chosen warriors of the red men. And in many minor engagements, and in the single-handed defense of their cabins, they slowly but steadily advanced into the hills and valleys of the "Western Waters" and possessed the land.

Before the coming of the white men, many Indian trails led from the Ohio Valley through what is now West Virginia and over the mountains to Virginia. Throughout the period of the Indian wars these paths or trails were used by the war parties. From the country of the Shawnees, whose principal town was located in the vicinity of the present Chillicothe, Ohio, a trail led to the mouth of the Great Kanawha, up its north bank to Gauley River, thence up that river to the mouth of Rich Creek, where it divided. One branch led up Rich Creek over Gauley mountain, passing the site of Ansted, followed the general direction of the present U. S. Route 60, through the site of Lewisburg and over the mountains and down Dunlap Creek into Virginia. This was the route of General Lewis's army to Point Pleasant. The other branch followed Gauley River to Little Elk Creek, up that Creek, and through the low gap to Otter Creek, down Otter and up Peters Creek by the site of Summersville, to Muddlety, and from the mouth of Muddlety up Gauley to Cherry River and over the mountains to Greenbrier River, and the South Branch of the Potomac. Until recently evidences of an Indian camping ground, on this trail were to be found near the mouth of Muddlety Creek.

Over these trails the first hunters, traders and land surveyors came to what is now Nicholas County.

In the dozen years from the close of the French and Indian War to the Revolution, the English Government opposed settlement of the Trans-Allegheny region. King George III by proclamation in 1763 forbade the Virginia Colony to grant land warrants, surveys or patents in that area, but the land hungry emigrants were determined to occupy the country despite King George and the Indians.

Especially after the Treaty of Fort Stanwix, in 1768,

BACKGROUND

the daring Scotch-Irish and German yeomanry pushed over the mountains to the Greenbrier, New and Kanawha rivers, up the Potomac and down the Monongahela and Ohio to the region around Wheeling. These first settlements in what is now West Virginia were made on the middle stretches of the Greenbrier, New and Great Kanawha, and on the Cheat, Tygarts Valley, Buckhannon, and West Fork, all branches of the Monongahela, and down that river and the Ohio to Graves Creek. These small, disconnected settlements formed an irregular circle around a great wilderness on the waters of Gauley, Elk and Little Kanawha, that was practically untouched till a quarter of a century later.

The second generation of Scotch-Irish and Germans held no remembrance of Europe and European ways of life. "They had become as emphatically products native to the soil as were the tough and supple hickories out of which they fashioned the handles of their long, light axes".

From their savage foes they had learned, at fearful cost, skill in woodcraft, the growing of Indian corn, and the primitive methods of wresting food, clothing and shelter from the forest. In short they had developed that inimitable type ever after to be distinguished as *"American Backwoodsmen"*.

Their red foes were fierce and strong, superlatively cunning, dreadful in battle and merciless in victory. The woodsmen did not encounter cowards and dispossess a weak adversary. They boldly met and overcame the stout hearted savages, and firmly held every acre of ground and every cabin home by the rifle and ax. The trained soldiers of England could not withstand the red warriors in their forests. Only these pioneer woodsmen could wrest possession from savages and replace the wilderness with meadows and harvest fields, supplant wigwams with farm houses, and transform game trails and war paths into highways.

The progress of settlement was slow. At first traders with Indians, hunters and surveyors penetrated the Wilderness. Occasionally some of these adventurers would locate a desirable site for a future home. All along the frontier young men were venturing to secure a home a little deeper in the forests. In the early Spring the young backwoodsman, alone or with one or two companions would proceed to mark out his claim by blazing trees around it with his tomahawk, and marking corners with his initials. This gave him what was termed a "tomahawk right".

Armed with rifle and ax, and a few meager supplies, he would build a "brush camp", sometimes called a "half-faced camp", near a spring, and around it begin his "clearing" by cutting away the smaller timber, girdling or brush burning the larger trees, and then planting his "patch" of Indian Corn. While cultivating and guarding his crop from the wild things of the woods he would go on with his clearing and the building of a cabin.

The cabin built of small straight logs was usually eighteen by twenty feet, high enough for the low ceiling living room and a loft or attic reached by ladder from the outside. The floor was the solid earth, a huge chimney built on the outside of logs, sticks and clay, and a stone fire place. The single strong door on deerskin

BACKGROUND

hinges had a wooden latch lifted from the outside by a leather string passing through a small hole, called the latch string, that could be pulled inside at night or in time of danger. A window was made by a small opening in the wall, over which greased paper was sometimes stretched, in place of glass. The roof was made of rough boards split from oak or chestnut and held in place by "weight poles",—not a nail or iron spike was used in the building.

Sometimes the sturdy young wife would come with her husband and share the "brush camp" and clearing, and cabin building, but usually the wife came after a cabin had been reared and a crop of corn raised. At best the cabin was furnished with blocks of wood or a few three-legged stools, for seats, a bedstead made of poles against the wall, the outside corners held up by forked stakes driven in the ground. Leaves, moss, deer and bearskins were mattresses and covers. The table was a large split log or "puncheon" on four legs; a pot or skillet and perhaps a few tin or pewter dishes completed the furnishings. Often for lack of table ware, wooden plates, noggins and bowls made from knots, and gourds or squash shells were used.

This was the pioneer home till twenty or thirty years later a hewed log or frame house could be built.

The dress of the backwoodsman was very similar to that of the Indians. Both men and women wore moccasins made of deerskin. In cold weather dry leaves stuffed in the moccasins and leggings served for stockings. Men wore buckskin leggings and hunting shirts made of the same material, reaching below the knees and drawn in around the waist with a broad belt, with sheathes for tomahawk and scalping knife. A coonskin cap was the usual headgear. A woman wore buckskin leggings, and in place of the hunting shirt a closefitting buckskin skirt. This primitive clothing obtained till flax and wool could be produced to furnish the homespun linen and "linsey-woolsey", woven by the pioneers during our early history.

Food, until the first crop of corn could be grown, was supplied by the wild game and the wild fruits and nuts of the woods. Corn was the prime dependence of the early settlers. It was a product of the New World and the principal crop grown by the Indians. Without this wonderful food white men could hardly have survived in subduing the wilderness. In the virgin soil it produced "roasting ears" by mid-summer; while the kernels were still soft a coarse meal for "journey-cakes" was made by grating the ears; and in maturity meal was ground with crude hand mills or made by "pounding mills". It furnished when roasted, rations for the knapsack of hunter or soldier. The husks provided rude mattresses and the stalks and blades were provender for cattle and horses until meadows gave them hay.

Turnips, beans, pumpkins and melons were grown along with the corn crop and to these, sometimes meager products, together with nuts and wild fruits from the forest, they must add a store of meat from the game abounding in woods around them. On food thus produced by their own skill and labor, they slowly and laboriously built their cabins, cleared the land, planted their corn, and hunted the wild game, with the danger of the tomahawk and scalping knife ever impending.

Only in severe winter weather did they have respite from this fear. Even in mild weather, sometimes coming after early winter storms, they could expect Indian forays. This gave name to "Indian Summer", still descriptive of such weather.

Many other hardships and dangers beset the lonely pioneer. The gloomy woods sheltered fierce bears, panthers and wolves, that preyed on their domestic animals, and even attacked settlers. Rattlesnakes and copperheads infested the country. In warm weather swarms of deer flies, buffalo gnats, and mosquitoes preyed on men and animals. This hard life continued until the Indians were driven out, the wild animals subdued and homes and highways built.

From Braddock's defeat in 1755 to Wayne's victory in 1795, the merciless border warfare raged on over what is now West Virginia. The famous chieftains Cornstalk, Logan and Killbuck led their fierce warriors in a determined effort to exterminate the whites or drive them back across the mountains. Thousands of cabin homes were burned and families murdered or taken captive. Settlements in the Greenbrier Valley were twice wiped out. Captives were taken for torture or enslavement. Donnally's Fort in Greenbrier and Hughes's Fort on the Kanawha offered the only refuge to our earliest settlers.

The complete subjugation of the Shawnees and Delawares by General Wayne brought peace to the white settlers south of the Ohio. The saddened survivors with unabated courage and energy returned to the ashes of their cabins, and unmarked graves of relatives and friends to restore their homes and lay the foundation of our civilization. The story of how they and their descendants transformed the wilderness and gave us our "goodly heritage" is presented in subsequent pages.

CHAPTER I

General Description

THE laws of England followed the settlement of Jamestown Colony in Virginia. In 1634 the colony was divided into eight counties, modeled after those in England. As the settlements moved westward new counties were formed. In 1734, just one hundred years after the county system was adopted, Orange County was established and embraced all of Virginia west of the Blue Ridge. In 1738 Augusta County was formed; it included "all of the utmost parts of Virginia", and extended from the Blue Ridge on the east to the Mississippi River on the west. From this vast area have been carved the states of West Virginia, Kentucky, Ohio, Indiana, Illinois and Michigan. In 1769 Botetourt County was taken from the southern part of Augusta, and in 1776 Montgomery County was formed. In 1777 Greenbrier County was erected from that part of Augusta, Botetourt and Montgomery lying west of Rockbridge and Rockingham Counties and extending to the Ohio River; and in 1789 Kanawha County was formed from the Counties of Greenbrier and Montgomery, and included the territory of those counties lying south of the Little Kanawha River.

By act of the General Assembly of Virginia, January 29, 1818, Nicholas County was formed mainly from

Kanawha but included a small area from Greenbrier and Randolph Counties. By this act the boundaries of the county were so indefinitely defined that by the Act of January 29, 1820 they were entirely changed and fixed as follows: "Beginning at the mouth of Gauley River on the east bank thereof; thence up said river and binding thereon one mile and a half; thence to the mouth of Back Camp Fork on Bell Creek; thence to the mouth of Otter Creek; thence up the west side of Otter Creek to the dividing ridge between Little Kanawha and Elk Rivers; thence with said ridge to a point where a due south course from the upper end of a tract of land now claimed by John Mollohan including Hackers Lick, will strike said line; thence with the reverse of said course to the upper end of said tract; thence to Miller's old improvement on Elk River; thence to Spice Bottom on Williams River; thence to the Forks of Cranberry; thence to the Sixteen Mile Tree on the Wilderness Road; thence crossing the State Road on Dogwood Ridge, so as to include the inhabitants between said ridge and Gauley Mountain, to New River; thence down the same to the beginning, instead of the boundaries heretofore prescribed for said county." By another act of the Assembly in 1823 almost 150 square miles more were added to the western part of the county, taken from Kanawha.

The map shows the original area of the county, which was approximately 1800 square miles, and the present area after the loss of territory to adjoining counties. The original area included more than one hundred miles of the Elk River valley.

In 1831 the County of Fayette was established giving

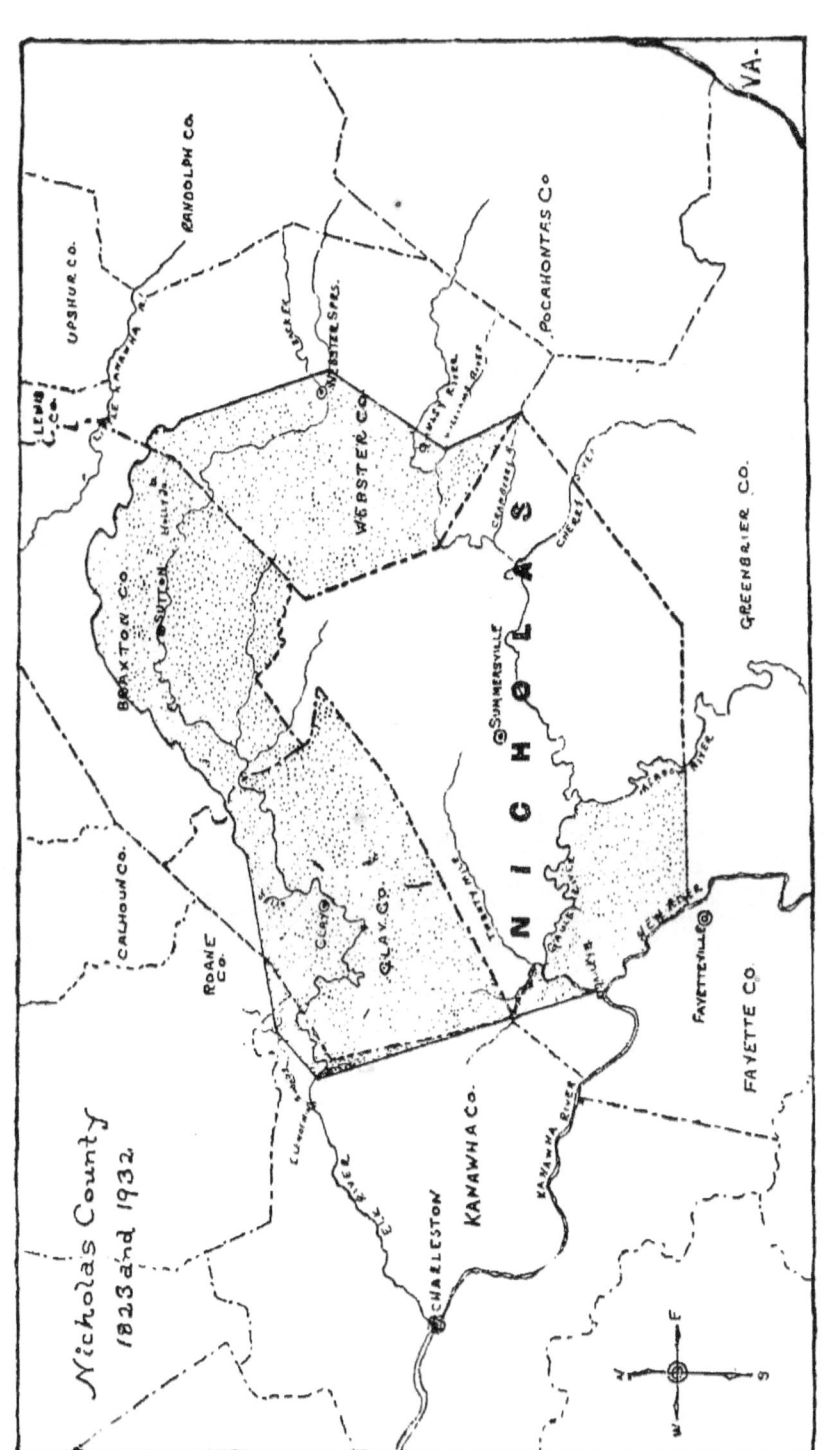

Map of Nicholas County Showing Boundary Changes

General Description 3

to the new county that part of Nicholas included by Meadow River, Gauley and New River, making almost one-sixth of its area.

In 1836 Braxton County was formed taking from the north of Nicholas about two-thirds of the area of Braxton.

In 1858 Clay County was erected from Nicholas and Braxton and about seven-eighths of the new county was cut from the west of Nicholas.

In 1860 when Webster County was created Nicholas was made to give about one-half the area of that county. All these territorial losses are shown on the map.

A dispute having arisen over the boundary line between Nicholas and Clay—both counties claiming the village of Bentree—a commission was authorized in 1908 to locate the true division line. The commission was composed of L. W. Herold and M. B. Mason representing Nicholas and S. T. Wilson and M. W. Murphy representing Clay County. James Ballenger of Braxton County was chosen as umpire, and R. M. Cavendish and O. G. Robinson were employed as surveyors. G. W. Springston, Prosecuting Attorney of Clay and W. G. Brown, Prosecuting Attorney of Nicholas, represented their respective Counties in presenting the evidence required. The Commission reported its finding as follows: "The division line between Nicholas and Clay Counties begins at the "Ruffner Oak" on Bell Creek; thence runs 1519 poles to a point on Rock Camp Branch of Twenty Mile Creek; thence 4528 poles to a point on the land of B. Grose; thence 2523 poles to a point on Strange Creek on Braxton County line." A plat was filed with the report showing the line on a scale 300 poles to the inch.

The report, by neglect, was not filed in Nicholas County, but is of record in the office of the Clerk of the County Court in Clay County in "Plat Record 1" at page 89.

Some time prior to the Nicholas-Clay controversy, a dispute over the line between Greenbrier and Nicholas from the Forks of Cranberry to the Sixteen Mile Tree on the Wilderness Road had been settled, but no record appears of this settlement in Nicholas County. Thus the boundaries of the county have been changed as shown, seven times by legislative action and twice in the courts.

The counties of Kanawha, Fayette, Nicholas and Clay have a common corner on Bell Creek. Richard Ramsey's house was built on the line separating Fayette and Kanawha. When a boy, the writer spent a night at the Ramsey home; dined in Fayette, slept in Kanawha, stabled his horse in Nicholas and watched "Uncle Dick" grind corn at his mill in Clay the next morning.

The old gentleman delighted to tell that he sometimes milked his cow in Fayette while she was chewing her cud in Kanawha County and switching flies into Clay and Nicholas.

MAGISTERIAL DISTRICTS

Area	Square miles	Population, 1950	
Jefferson	78.54	Jefferson	2,488
Grant	48.95	Grant	1,467
Summersville	64.25	Summersville	3,026
Hamilton	148.94	Hamilton	3,347
Beaver	109.15	Beaver	10,675
Kentucky	118.03	Kentucky	4,326
Wilderness	88.9	Wilderness	2,365

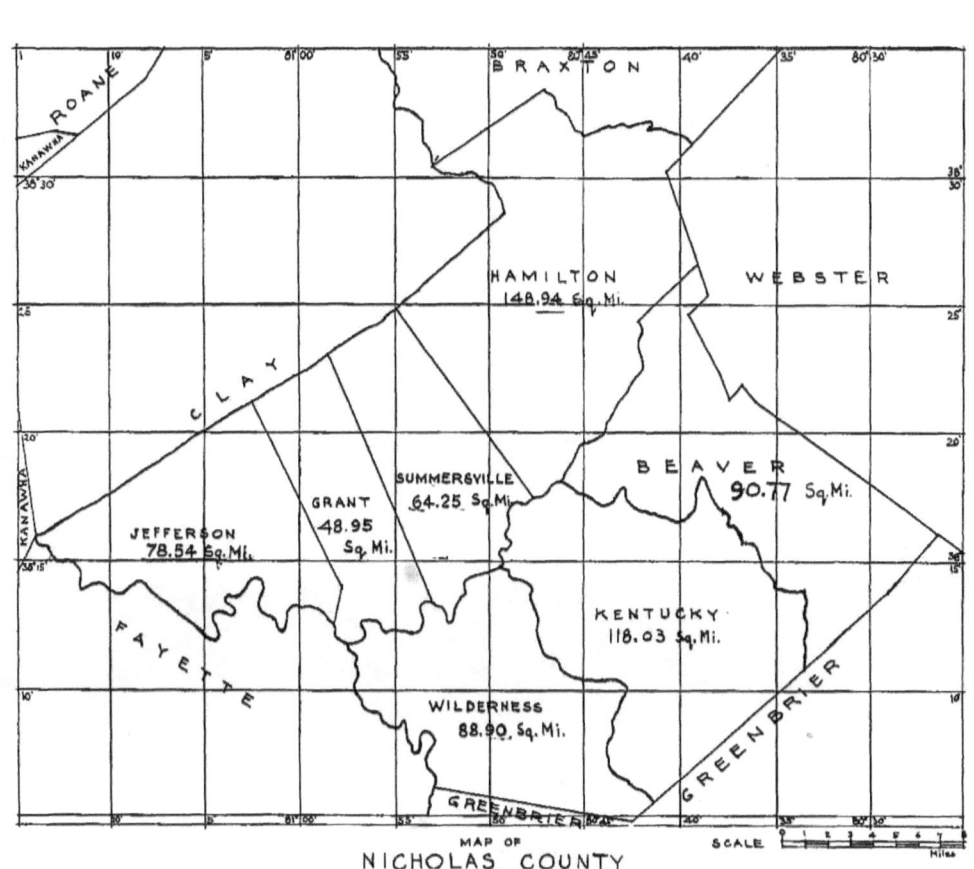

MAP OF
NICHOLAS COUNTY
SHOWING DISTRICTS

General Description 5

The County was not divided into magisterial districts until after the Civil War. Under the Constitution of 1863 they were named as "Townships". The six townships were first named Jefferson, Grant, Summersville, Mumble-the-Peg, and Number Five and Number Six. Later Wilderness took the place of Number Five and Kentucky was the name given to Number Six.

Under the Constitution of 1873 the "townships" became "districts", Mumble-the-Peg was changed to Hamilton and in 1887 Beaver District was formed from parts of Hamilton and Kentucky.

The geographical situation of the county is in the south central part of the state. It is bounded on the north by Clay, Braxton and Webster; on the east by Webster and Greenbrier; on the south by Greenbrier and Fayette; and on the west by Fayette and Clay Counties.

In longitude Nicholas County lies between 80 degrees, 26 minutes and 12 seconds west, and 81 degrees, 14 minutes and 45 seconds west, from the Meridian of Greenwich. In latitude it extends from 38 degrees, 4 minutes and 45 seconds north to 38 degrees 33 minutes and 27 seconds north. The longest north and south line across the county from the Braxton line to the Greenbrier line is 33 miles; and the longest west and east line from the "Ruffner Whiteoak," where the four counties, Kanawha, Fayette, Clay and Nicholas meet to the common corner of Webster and Greenbrier Counties is 44 miles.

The lowest point is at Belva, 675 feet above sea level, and the highest point, on the Webster line near Richwood is 3850 feet. The elevation of the Court House is 1894 feet, at the front door, and Lone Tree Mountain, west of Summersville rises to 2550.75 feet above sea level. The undulating character of the surface appears when the altitude of Snow Hill, 3392 feet, Craigsville, 2288 feet, Richwood, 2200 feet and Mount Lookout, 2069 feet is compared with the lowest and highest elevations. The mean elevation is a little above 2000 feet. The area of the county is 656.77 square miles or 420,333 acres. The population by the census of 1950 is 27,696 of which only 1190 are foreign born.

The climate varies considerably with the elevation. At the highest points south of Gauley River, the summer or growing season is on an average three weeks shorter than at the lowest points north of the river.

The average mean temperature of the county is about 50 degrees; the maximum temperature about 95 degrees and the minimum about 15 degrees below zero. Killing frosts in the higher altitudes rarely occur after May 20th, nor before September 20th. The average rainfall is about 53 inches. The main course of the winds is from west and northwest, and the rain and snow is usually from that direction, though occasionally from the east.

The surface may be described as hilly, the eastern portion even mountainous; the central part as an undulating plateau, divided by Gauley River canyon; with hills and ridges in the west and north. The entire surface is cut up with numerous streams flowing to Gauley and Elk Rivers.

The soil in the narrow valleys of these streams is a sandy loam; on higher ground it is usually clay with

General Description 7

more or less sand. On the north sides of the hills and in the hollows the dense forests had formed a rich humus which the pioneers generally utilized in growing their chief crop—Indian corn. This accounts for the worn out and brush covered hillsides often seen in the county.

The principal watercourse is Gauley River which practically bisects the county and drains about 82 per cent of its surface. The Gauley rises in the western part of Pocahontas County, at an elevation of 4000 feet, enters Nicholas at Allingdale, and flows in a southwestern course for a distance of 62.7 miles through the county, to the Fayette line at Belva. Its stream cuts a deep, tortuous channel through the Great Conglomerate Sandstone, and its numerous shoals and low falls are caused by thousands of boulders fallen from the huge sandstone cliffs that overhang its course. The current is rapid, dropping about 21.5 feet to the mile or a total of 4347 feet in its length through the county.

The principal tributaries of Gauley on the south are Cranberry River, Cherry River, Panther Creek, Hominy Creek, Collison Creek and Meadow River; on the north, Strouds Creek, Beaver Creek, Persinger Creek, Muddlety Creek, McKees Creek, Meadow Creek, Peters Creek, Little Elk Creek and Twenty Mile. These streams are fed by a multitude of branches and branchlets that gush in springs from almost every hillside. The water is usually free from mineral deposits, but there are occasional chalybeate springs having their source in the sandstone strata. From the same source wells in many parts of the county furnish this type of mineral water.

The tributaries of Elk River are Sycamore, Leatherwood, Buffalo, and Strange Creeks, rising in the western part of the county, and Birch River that rises in Webster County and flows through Nicholas for about ten miles.

Taking up the description of the main branches of Gauley River: Cranberry River rises in Pocahontas County, flows through Webster and for about seven miles through Nicholas to Gauley River at Woodbine. It is a swift shallow stream, with a narrow valley, mostly in forests. Its principal tributaries are Jakeman Run, Barrenshe Run, Dogway Run and North Fork. Cherry River is formed by the confluence of the North and South Forks at Richwood. The South Fork rises near Cold Knob in Greenbrier, and the North Fork rises in Pocahontas about one mile west of Kennison Mountain. Cherry flows northward from Richwood to Curtin, a distance of 10.6 miles. Its principal tributaries in ascending order are, Curtin Run, Coal Siding Run, Mill Branch, Morris Creek, Big Laurel and Little Laurel. Only a small portion of its valley is farm land. Panther Creek rises near the Greenbrier line, flows northward through forests a distance of 9.5 miles to Gauley River about two and a half miles below Curtin. Its tributaries in ascending order are, Bear Run, Adkins Lick Run, Geho Run, Jims Branch, North Run, Nettle Run and Cranes Nest Run. Hominy Creek rises at Grassy Knob in Greenbrier, flows southwestward a distance of 21.8 miles to Gauley River about one and a half miles above Hughes Bridge. Its chief tributaries in ascending order are, Mouse Creek, Deer Creek, Chestnut Camp Run, Middle Branch, Grassy Creek, Hellroaring Branch, Sugar Branch and Prices Fork. There is some cleared farm land along the upper stretches but the lower valley is mainly woods. Collisons Creek rises in Wilderness District about three-fourths of a mile from McMillion School, flows northwestward about ten miles to Gauley River two and a half miles above Carnifax Ferry. There is some farm land along its course but much of the way is through cut-over woodland.

Meadow River, the largest southern tributary of Gauley, rises at Keeny Knob in Summers County, flows northward into Greenbrier, then northwestward partly along the Greenbrier-Fayette line to the common corner of these counties with Nicholas; thence in the same general direction with the Nicholas-Fayette line to its confluence with Gauley River at Carnefix Ferry, a distance of 11.4 miles on this line. There is some cultivated land in its valley near Nallen, but its course from there is turbulent, filled with large boulders fallen from the great sandstone cliffs along its way. Anglins Creek and Miller Creek are its main tributaries from the Nicholas side. Beaver Creek, the first important northern tributary of Gauley, rises in Webster County, about three and a half miles northwest of Cowen. Its general course is southwestward entering Nicholas County near Tioga and flowing a distance of 17 miles into Gauley River. From Tioga to Beaver Mills is a wide fertile valley and a thickly settled farming community. From Beaver Mills to the mouth its valley is narrow and its course is rapid with heavy sandstone cliffs and steep wooded hillsides. Going up stream its principal tributaries are, Wyatt Run, Little Beaver, Hannah Run, Left Fork, Horse Run, Bear Pen Fork, Board Fork, Old-He Fork and O'Brien Fork. Persinger

Creek rises near Wild Cat Knob, flows northward a short distance, turns sharply southwestward and flows into Gauley River just below the old "Persinger Ford." The total length is less than 5 miles. Above Persinger Post Office its valley is cultivated, below its current descends rapidly in a narrow channel cut out of the sandstone cliffs.

Muddlety Creek, another important tributary, rises in Hamilton District about two and a half miles northwest of Tioga, flows southward about three and a half miles, then veers directly westward to Hookersville, then from this point southward into Gauley River at Brocks Bridge, a whole distance of 20 miles. The upper course is through cut-over woodlands, but from the former site of Opal to Duffy Branch is a wide valley that was once thickly settled with farms cleared halfway to the hill tops, but now with little cultivation. Below Duffy Branch the sluggish current takes on a rapid flow through a narrow valley lined with sandstone cliffs. Ascending the main tributaries are Arbuckle Branch, Glade Creek, Duffy Branch, Phillips Run, Fockler Branch, Trout Run, Pearson Branch, Enoch Run, McMillions Creek, Brushy Fork, Little Creek, Clear Fork, Laurel Fork, and Harris Fork. McKees Creek rises against Lone Tree Mountain just west of Summersville, flows southward and empties into Gauley River at Hughes Bridge. Its total length is 4 miles, and most of the course is through farm lands, but near the mouth it plunges through a deep gorge into the river. Meadow Creek rises in the western edge of Summersville District one mile west of Gad, flows southward and empties into

Gauley River two miles below Carnefix Ferry, a total length of nearly 6 miles. Its upper course is nearly base level through a large savannah or natural meadow, surrounded by good farming lands, but in the last mile and a half of its course it flows rapidly through woodlands. Peters Creek rises in the corporate limits of Summersville, flows in a general westward direction to Lockwood, where it veers to the south and empties into Gauley River about three miles below Woods Ferry. Its total length is 17.5 miles through a narrow valley, but with farm land along the creek and on the upland on either side, except the last mile where it plunges into the canyon of Gauley River. Its main tributaries in ascending order are, Otter Creek, Line Creek, Laurel Creek, Jerrys Fork, Jones Branch, Whitewater, Bucks Garden Creek, Rock Camp Fork, McClung Branch and Pine Run. Little Elk Creek rises in Jefferson District about two and a half miles northwest of Lockwood and flows northwestward to Gauley River at Swiss. Its entire course of 3.5 miles is through cut over woodland. Twenty Mile, an important tributary, rises in Summersville District about one mile southwest of former Muddlety Post Office, and follows a general southwest course through Summersville, Grant and Jefferson Districts to Gauley River at the Fayette County line at Belva. Its total length is 27 miles, with a narrow valley of sandy loam soil, most of which has been in cultivation from the early history of the county, but the sides of the steep mountains on either side are cut-over lands. Below Vaughan the bottoms are wider and in good cultivation. Twenty Mile is one of the most beautiful streams in the county, with a smooth bed and pools of cool, clear water. Ascending the main tributaries are, Bell Creek, Rock Camp Fork, Ash Fork, Robinson Fork and Rader Fork.

Birch River, chief tributary of Elk River in Nicholas County, rises in Webster County just west of Cowen, flows northwestward across the northern edge of Nicholas County and empties into Elk River at Glendon in Braxton County. The length of its course through Nicholas County is 9.5 miles. Through most of its course it is a swift, shallow stream flowing between steep hills, and having only narrow bottom land. Its main tributaries in Nicholas County are, Mill Creek on the South, and Powells Creek, Mill Creek, Anthony Creek and Poplar Creek on the north. Strange Creek rises on the western slope of Powells Mountain and flows in a northwestern direction, for more than 7 miles through the county and empties into Elk River at Strange Creek Station in Braxton County. Buffalo Creek rises against Powells Mountain and flows northwestward a distance of 4.5 miles to the Clay County line and thence to Elk River at Dundon. Its tributaries in Nicholas County are, Lilly Fork, Beech Fork, Robinson Fork and Taylor Creek. Leatherwood Creek rises in the western part of Grant District, flows about 2 miles to the Clay County line, and empties into Elk River at Upper Leatherwood Station. Sycamore Creek rises in Jefferson District about 2 miles northeast of Vaughan, flows about two miles through cut-over woodlands in Nicholas County, and empties into Elk River at Big Sycamore Station.

When the first settlers came to what is now Nicholas County, the streams and mountains had no names save

General Description 13

those the Indians may have given them. In course of time names were given them of necessity. From the few records available and from tradition we know the origin of these names.

Gauley River, that the Shawnee Indians had appropriately called *To-ke-be-lo-ke*, meaning falling creek, was given no name in the earliest surveys but was described as a branch of Woods River, which later was named New River. The name spelt "Gawly" first appears in Henning's Statutes. The most plausible theory is the river takes its name from a French trapper and trader named *Galois* who was known to visit Kanawha River and tributaries.

Bell Creek is named from the legend that marauding Indians took bells from cows and hung them on the branches of shrubs to lure the settlers into an ambush when the bells sounded from the swaying limbs.

Twenty Mile took its name from the scouts in the army of General Lewis on his march to Point Pleasant, who reported they had gone twenty miles up stream to recover straying horses.

Little Elk took its name from the numerous elk found there.

Peters Creek was named for Peter, a slave of Henry Morris, who left alone by his master had spent a winter in a camp on the creek.

Line Creek is so named because it formed the beginning line of the 600 A, survey of Henry Morris.

Meadow Creek, once called Coopers Creek, was so named from the wild meadows through which it flows in the Cross Lanes area.

McKees Creek was named from William McKee who was granted a large tract of land on it and lived there a short time.

Muddlety Creek was first called "Mumble-the-Peg", and was so named from the Indian game of mumble-the-peg played there in a camp occupied by a company of surveyors engaged in laying off the Hudson-Martin lands. The name Mumble-the-Peg occurs on our early records as the name of the creek, and later as the name of a township. It was corrupted first to "Muddlety-peg" and then became Muddlety.

McMillion's Creek was named in honor of Joseph McMillion, the first permanent settler on the creek.

Glade Creek took its name from the savannahs or glades on its course, first known as the "Lower Glades".

Persinger Creek was named for James Persinger, an early settler on it.

Beaver Creek has its name from the beaver dams found on it and from a large beaver dam on Gauley River at its mouth.

Strouds Creek has its name in commemoration of the Strouds family massacred by the Indians there. This was the family of George Strawn, whose name was incorrectly recorded "Stroud".

Cherry River readily took the name from the fine cherry trees growing in Cherry Tree Bottom, now the site of Richwood.

Panther Creek was named by the early hunters from the numerous panthers found there.

Hominy Creek is so called from the story that a party of hunters, who had camped under a cliff at its mouth,

General Description 15

were snowed-in there and subsisted for a time on hominy, furnished them by a nearby settler by the name of David McColgin.

"*Hell-Roaring Branch*" took its name from the families that lived on this branch and were always quarreling and fighting.

Callison Creek was named from an early settler on its waters.

Meadow River received its name from the natural meadows near its source in Greenbrier County.

Bucks Garden Creek from the deer lick on that stream. The lick was in an open grassy plot that the hunters called "Buck Garden", and thus the name attached to the creek.

Sammons Creek was named for Henry Sammons who was said to have camped under a cliff near its mouth and gathered saltpeter and made gunpowder for the early settlers.

Birch River was given the name from the abundant growth of birch trees along its course.

Strange Creek takes its name from the tragic story of a lost member of a party of surveyors. The only record of his fate was found on a beech tree below the forks of the creek. Cut in the bark was the date: "January 20, 1794. Wm. Strange on strange ground, lost, never to be found".

Powells Creek has its name from William Powell, noted hunter, and early settler on Peters Creek.

Sycamore Creek was named from the trees along its course.

Leatherwood Creek was given its name from a small

shrub growing along its course that pioneers called by that name.

Buffalo Creek had a herd of buffaloes when first visited by hunters.

Williams River was named from Williams, a surveyor who was employed by the grantees of several large tracts of land in that part of the county.

Anglins Creek was named from Isaac Anglins who patented a tract of three hundred acres on Meadow River including part of the creek.

Laurel Creeks are found in almost every section of the county named of course from the big laurel or rhododendron found on the banks of the streams.

Many small streams take their names from early settlers or hunters, or from some event that characterized them.

Prominent mountains likewise took their names from early settlers or from some circumstance connected with the place.

Cottle Knob was named for C. W. Cottle, a man prominent in the settlement of the county. He had a cattle farm in the glades near by.

Powells Mountain was named for William Powell who first hunted there.

Hinkle Mountain was named from the pioneer family living there.

Panther Mountain had its name from an adventure of Captain George Fitzwater in killing two panthers there that were attempting to get the deer he had killed and hung up while hunting.

Originally the entire area of the county was covered

with a dense forest, except where an occasional swamp, glade or natural meadow broke the monotony of the great woods. Cottle Glades, Lower Glades on Glade Creek, "McClung's Meadows", in the Cross Lanes community and "McKee's Meadow" on McKees Creek, were such openings in the primeval forest. Only from the highest hills could an extended view be obtained.

Both vegetable and animal life were remarkable in variety and extent. The woods originally had little undergrowth. The underbrush that came later was caused by frequent fires and cuttings. The forests were made up of the great variety and species of trees native to the Appalachian Region. The following lists the most important native trees: oaks, half dozen species, poplar, chestnut, maples, both sugar and soft, black and white walnut, beech, elm, linn, birch, hemlock, pine, spruce, cedar, cherry, ash, hickory, sycamore, locust, black gum, sweet gum, buckeye, and magnolia, were the principal large trees; sassafras, sourwood, dogwood, holly, serviceberry, persimmon, mulberry, crabapple, ironwood, papaw and willow were smaller trees. Many shrubs as alder, witchhazel, hazlenut, chinquapin, haw, thornbush, elder, spicewood, sumac, chokecherry, red bud, rhododendron, mountain laurel, buckberry, mountain ash and huckleberry were found in the undergrowth. Wild grape vines festooned the trees and shrubs along the streams and on the hillsides. Virginia creeper, wreathing dead trees in the forest, glowed with crimson leaves in autumn. Native medical plants were numerous and in general use by the settlers: Boneset, bloodroot, ginseng, calamus, dandelion, elecampane, everlasting, mullen, comfrey, goldenseal, ground-ivy, Indian physic, lobelia, May-apple, mountain tea, pennyroyal, horsemint, pipsisiway, red puccoon, sarsaparilla, snakeroot, spignet, witchhazel elm bark, wormwood, and squaw vine, were the principal. The medicinal value of many of these plants is still recognized. A few poison plants, as poison ivy, poison sumac, swamp ash, greenbrier berries, nightshade and jimson weed were common.

Many plants now seen everywhere were from the old world and came with the early settlers. Catnip, peppermint, mullen, yarrow, groundivy, bouncingbet, ragweed, spanish needles and thistles are examples of these imported plants.

Wild flowers flourished from early spring to late autumn. Among many species may be named trailing arbutus, a dozen varieties of violets, wind-flowers, spring beauties, ladyslipper, jack-in-the-pulpit, wild geranium, redbud, serviceberry, and dogwood, in the early spring; brier rose, orchis, mullen, ox-eye daisy, blackeyed-Susan, and silkweed, in summer; and in autumn, goldenrod, ironweed, wild sunflower and joe-pie-weed grew all around. The crowning beauty of the woodlands was displayed in the flaming beauty of the azaleas, redbuds, rhododendrons and dogwoods.

The woods sheltered and fed a world of animal life. Bears, deer, panthers, wolves, foxes, wildcats, raccoons, otters, minks, beavers, weasels, skunks, groundhogs, squirrels, rabbits, and muskrats abounded. Elk and buffaloes were found occasionally in the early days.

Bird life was prolific. Eagles, owls, hawks, buzzards, turkeys, ducks, pheasants, woodpeckers, sapsuckers, yellowhammers, and wood pigeons were the most common. Of the song birds blue jays, catbirds, wrens, sparrows, bluebirds, cardinals, thrushes, goldfinches, and whippoorwills were native. Crows, blackbirds, robins came with the pioneers from over the mountains. Opossums, rats, and mice also followed the settlers from the east where they had their natural *habitat* or had been imported from Europe. The red fox, brought from England by the Virginia sportsmen, soon became an associate of the native gray fox.

The streams were alive with fish. Gauley River and its largest tributaries literally teemed with catfish, trout, eels, suckers, chubs, sunfish and minnows. Bass and pickerel were not brought into these waters until many years after the country was settled. Even the small branches were filled with trout, chubs, sunfish and minnows. Turtles, tortoises, frogs, toads, and lizards were found everywhere.

Snakes were also common everywhere. Rattlesnakes, copperheads, and occasional water moccasins or "cottonmouths" were the only poisonous species. Rattlesnakes were the most dreaded by the early settlers. Children bitten by them, and adults struck about the face seldom survived. Horses and cattle, usually bitten on the head, frequently died. The "razorback" hogs were the only snake-proof animals. If a rattler struck a "razorback" the event ended by his snakeship becoming a lunch for the pig. The thick skin of the hog kept the poison from reaching the blood and the poison was ineffective. These hogs roaming the woods for mast then so plentiful had much to do in ridding the country of snakes.

The cliffs along Hominy Creek were noted for "dens" of rattlesnakes. Copperheads were more generally distributed than the rattlers, and while very poisonous were not so deadly as the rattlesnakes. Hunters and surveyors protected themselves in the woods by wearing heavy deerskin leggings. Blacksnakes, garter snakes, common water snakes, house snakes, vipers and the little green tree snakes were harmless.

Swarms of insect pests annoyed the early settlers. Mosquitoes, buffalo gnats, chiggers, deerflies, hornets, yellowjackets, wasps, woodticks infested the land. In the clearings and before their cabin doors they built "gnat-smokes" to protect themselves, and when hunting or at work in the woods often greased their face and hands with bear's oil to shield themselves from the vicious swarms of deer flies and gnats. The deerflies and a large buffalo fly preyed on the horses and cattle. It was often necessary to shield them by greasing their ears and necks with bear's oil or rubbing them with the crushed leaves of certain plants, such as penny-royal, or covering them with cloth or leaves.

The common house flies and fleas were not native to the forests but came with the settlers, as did also bees. The wild bees found in the woods had escaped from the colonies and spread through the woods ahead of the settlements.

Appalachian America, in which Nicholas County is situated is thus described by Nathaniel S. Shaler, a distinguished naturalist: "We find there a climate resembling in its range of temperature those which characterize the most favored regions of the world; and it is there, perhaps, we may look for the preservation of our race's best characteristics. It has a finer climate, better water, and a higher condition of health than any other region of which I have any knowledge; and is withal one of the most beautiful regions in the world."

CHAPTER II

Early Settlements

"The Pioneer was a rugged seer,
　　As he crossed to the Western River,
　Where the Copper Man, called the Indian,
　　Lay hid with bow and quiver."

THE settlement of Nicholas County differed in many ways from that of the older counties, in that it was not subject to sudden and violent attacks by the Indians, was less isolated from the older communities and was made by men who came with their families to establish permanent homes.

On the South Branch of the Potomac, in the valleys of the Monongahela and its branches, and along the Ohio and the Kanawha, hardy frontiersmen had built their camps and cabins and were traversing the rivers and forests and clearing fields in the very thick of the struggle with the Shawnees for possession of the land. The bloody conflict had continued for more than a quarter of a century and was drawing to a close when the settlement of our county was commenced. After the Battle of Point Pleasant in 1774, there had been a lull in Indian forays, till the murder of Cornstalk at Point Pleasant in 1777, incited the Shawnees to renewed hostilities. This continued until Wayne's victory at Fallen Timbers in 1794 completely subdued the Shawnees and their allies.

Early Settlements 23

Washington's western trip in 1770 and the published reports of his journey aroused great interest in these western lands. Speculators in the colonies east of the mountains formed companies and sent their surveyors to select and lay off great tracts of land. The war of the Revolution had interrupted their plans, but as soon as the war was over the land grabbing was renewed. The land book records of Greenbrier and Kanawha Counties show the numerous grants of the Commonwealth to lands that were later to be included in Nicholas County. Even before the Revolution surveyors had penetrated this wilderness and located desirable lands. In the period from 1783 to 1795 a major part of the land in our county had been thus patented in large tracts, and some of the earliest are here given: Warder and Parker, 16,000 acres on Gauley and Beaver; William Henshaw, eight 1,000 acres tracts on Gauley and Beaver; Robert Morris, 24,630 acres on Birch and Gauley; Tupper and Prior, 14,500 acres on Twenty Mile; William Wilson, 93,000 acres between Elk and Gauley; Skyles, 32,000 acres on Gauley and Twenty Mile; McClung, Moore and Welch, something over 135,-000 south of Gauley, are a few of these earliest grants.

After 1795 settlers from Greenbrier and Monroe mainly, but also from other parts of Virginia and Pennsylvania began rapidly to occupy the lands that in 1818 were formed into the new county of Nicholas.

Sometime before this, however, a few families of German descent, had ventured to seek homes in the glades on Gauley River near the present Camden-on-Gauley. They had come over the mountains from the South Branch of the Potomac. Soon after they came, the family of

George Strawn, living at the mouth of Strouds Creek, was murdered and the cabin burned by Indians. This, according to Virgil A. Lewis, was in the summer of 1774; Governor Atkinson in his history of Kanawha County states that the event occurred in 1772, and claims that George Strawn was the first settler in what was later Kanawha County. Strawn was away from home at the time. On his return, joined by some of his neighbors, he followed the trail of the savages, who had driven off his cattle, to Bulltown on the Little Kanawha River. This small village of friendly Indians was so named from their chief, Bull. Although no trace of the cattle was found, and these friendly Indians denied all part in the raid, they were all slaughtered by the enraged whites and their bodies thrown into the river. This wanton act was never admitted by the avengers of the Strawn family, but was later fully established. George Strawn was drowned in Gauley River some years later and his body buried at the mouth of Little Elk River. Some years later a writer gave the name Strawd, which later appeared as Stroud, and the error is retained in the name of the creek.

Among the families living in the "Glades" at the time of the Strawn massacre, appear the names, Given, Hamrick, Cutlip, Doyle and others who are identified as among the refugees to Donnally's Fort in Greenbrier at the time of the Stroud tragedy and later they fled to this fort again when alarmed by the killing of the Morris children.

Captain George Fitzwater was perhaps the first white man to make his home in this wilderness. He was in the country with a party of surveyors prior to the Revolu-

Early Settlements 25

tion. A cliff on the hillside fronting Gauley River near Arnett Church, was one of his camping places. "Pen Knob" on the tract of land on Laurel Creek sold by Captain Fitzwater to Alexander Brown is named from the "bear-pen" still marked by a depression on the hill, where Fitzwater trapped for bears and wolves. He was associated with a surveyor named Henry Stockwell, and they marked off several tracts of land along Gauley River from the Cross Lanes community to Panther Mountain. His first land warrant was not issued until 1783. Fitzwater was living in a camp near the Hamilton Farm at Cross Lanes when Edward McClung and family appear on the scene. On the day of the Morris massacre, Captain George Fitzwater and Edward McClung were hunting and heard shooting in the distance. They returned to their cabins and kept guard for fear of the Indians. About midnight Mathias Young came from Peters Creek and told of the killing of the Morris children. Next morning Fitzwater and McClung with his wife and three children went with Young and assisted in the burial of the little girls, and then proceeded in safety to Hughes Fort. The settlers in the "Glades" and on Peters Creek and at Cross Lanes remained where they had taken refuge in the forts, until the Indians were subdued in 1794.

Edward McClung while at the fort sold his land to Edward Hughes and John Campbell. The same year he was drowned in the Kanawha River.

The exact date of the Morris Massacre is not known. The date fixed by Colonel Edward Campbell in his letters, is the spring of 1792. He stated, however, that he fixes the date by reference to the deed of Edward Mc-

Clung to Edward Hughes and his father John Campbell, and that the massacre may have been earlier than 1792.

Henry Morris, a son of William Morris who had settled on the Kanawha in 1774 had doubtless visited the Peters Creek country several years before his settlement. According to the Morris family tradition, he had a hunting camp on the creek and his negro servant, Peter, had passed a winter there alone some time before the cabin was built and the family moved in. Morris had marked off and established a "tomahawk right" to a tract of 600 acres lying on Peters Creek at the mouth of Line Creek.

His cabin was built near the banks of the creek just below the Paul Summer's residence. The spring that supplied the cabin was on the bank of the creek and the path down the bank may still be traced.

A path led from his cabin through the woods to the cabin of Conrad Young, about one mile up the creek.

At the time Henry Morris located on Peters Creek, Conrad Young built his cabin just above him on what was later the Samuel Neil farm; and Edward Hughes and family were living at the "Meadows", now Cross Lanes, a distance of about eight miles from the Peters Creek settlement. Captain George Fitzwater who had not yet married and located his cabin, was surveying lands in the vicinity and hunting with Edward Hughes. It is not established whether the Simms and Johnson families had yet come to the mouth of Little Elk, as they are not mentioned as going to Hughes's Fort. There were at least these three families named that we know were living in their cabins at the time of this Indian foray.

On a Spring day in 1792, Henry Morris was out hunting on Line Creek. He killed a young bear and divided it among his team of dogs, and with his usual caution concealed himself in a thicket. Soon the dogs came to him "with their bristles up". Morris, alarmed at this action of his dogs, hurried home and told his wife that he suspected the dogs had scented Indians. It was late in the afternoon and soon would be "milking time". There were no fences, and his cows were separated from their calves by driving them some distance up the creek and the calves taken in opposite direction down the creek.

Morris believing that any Indians that might be skulking near would not show themselves in the day time laid aside his gun and started to the spring for water. His wife called and asked if he thought it safe for Betty and Peggy to go for the cows. He replied that he thought there was no danger. The children started for the cows, following the path to the Conrad Young cabin. Hardly had they disappeared from the cabin when the mother heard their screams and called to Morris, who was still at the spring, that the Indians were after the children; running to the cabin he seized his gun and rushed up the path the girls had taken. He found Peggy lying in the path almost in sight of the house tomahawked and scalped. As he stooped over her she gasped, "a yellow man killed me". Hurrying on to find Betty, he saw an Indian crossing the creek and attempted to shoot but his gun failed to fire. Seeing nothing of Betty, and believing she had been carried away, he carried Peggy to the cabin just as she expired. Conrad Young was notified; his son, Mathias, sent to warn Edward McClung; and Morris and

Young stood guard until dawn. In the early morning Edward McClung and family and Captain George Fitzwater came with Mathias Young. Further search discovered Betty's body that had been scalped and thrown into the underbrush. A rude coffin was shaped from slabs of wood, and the two little bodies were buried in one grave.

When the fugitives reached Fort Hughes a company from the fort set out to search for the Indians. They found that the murderers had been sitting at a "gnat smoke" beside the path connecting the Young and Morris cabins. The exact location is at the point where State Route 39 comes to Peters Creek about one-half mile east of Lockwood. The savages were in the little ravine at this point, still covered with undergrowth as it was on that fateful day. The party finding no other traces of the Indians went on to McClung's cabin and found that it had been entered, the bed tick emptied of contents and carried away, and three horses that were in pasture in the savanna had also been taken. The trail of the Indians was plain, but they had so much the start, pursuit was hopeless.

It appeared that Peggy had eluded the Indians at first and was running for the cabin, but when just in sight of home her foot was tripped by a vine and she was caught by her merciless pursuer. Henry Morris planted an apple tree where Peggy fell. Grafts from this tree in orchards of neighbors preserved the "Peggy Apple" for many years. A dogwood marked the burial place of the children and for nearly a century bloomed over their grave. It has been replaced by a marble headstone, which

Early Settlements 29

may be seen from the marker standing on State Route 39 near Fairview Baptist Church. This marker commemorates the tragedy, and a small concrete monument erected to their memory in 1916 stands on the Court House grounds in Summersville.

Henry Morris always maintained that the renegade, Simon Girty, had led the Indians in this raid. Soon after Morris had moved his family to Peters Creek, a stranger had come to the cabin as a hunter, and had remained through the winter hunting with Morris. In the spring, Morris on a trip to Fort Clendennin mentioned this fact, and some one in the fort suggested that his visitor was perhaps Simon Girty and that Girty was identified by a scar covered by his forelock. On his return Morris confronted the stranger, pushed back the hair from his forehead, and saw a vivid scar. He angrily denounced him as the renegade Girty, and ordered him to leave at once on pain of death. Bitterly denying the charge the man left. Later when Morris was away he came back and attempted to take one of the bear dogs, but the little girls held the dog and the man left cursing and threatening them. Some years later a drunken Indian at Fort Clendennin exhibited two red-haired scalps and boasted he had taken them. Morris then at the fort was told this, and it is reported that when the Indian left the fort Morris followed and killed him. Many different versions of the massacre have appeared by imaginative writers. The foregoing statement is the story as handed down by the Morris family. Lineal descendants of Henry Morris still live on the original grant of 600 acres, and own the land where his cabin stood.

When white men first saw the region now embraced in Nicholas County, it was a part of Augusta County. In 1777 Greenbrier County was formed from Augusta, Montgomery and Botetourt Counties, and the future County of Nicholas was a part of Greenbrier for the twelve years from that date till Kanawha was formed from Greenbrier and Montgomery in 1789.

The first grants of land were in Greenbrier County and later ones in Kanawha. Usually the first settlers selected land and afterwards had it surveyed and obtained grants. The date of the patent consequently does not show the time of the settlement.

James Simms settled on Gauley at the mouth of Little Elk. His claim was first by "tomahawk right", and his grant was dated in 1789, though his settlement may have been later. He was a gunsmith and brought the first negro slaves to Nicholas County. William Johnson, a Revolutionary soldier and his son, John Johnson, were also among the first settlers near James Simms and Henry Morris. John Campbell, who had bought Edward McClung's land built his cabin near the head of Whitewater Creek in 1792. He had married Nancy Hughes, the daughter of Edward Hughes, while in the fort on Hughes Creek and after the danger from the Indians passed, he moved to his land and spent his life there. His grave may be seen near where his cabin stood, just off the public road that leads from Route 39 on Peters Creek to Cross Lanes. Thomas Hughes, brother of Edward Hughes, had a hunting camp on Laurel Creek near where Bethel Church stands. He was the leader in building the fort at the mouth of Hughes's Creek and the fort and creek were given his name. He owned land in Nicholas, but never located on it. Isaac Foster and his family came from Monroe and located about the same time on what was later known as the John R. McCutcheon farm, but the Fosters soon settled in the bend of Gauley. Other settlers that came between the years 1794 and 1798 were Jeremiah Odell and his brother Silvanus, who bought land from Captain George Fitzwater and made their homes near him; David Robinson, who came first with a party of surveyors, selected his land on Hutchinson's Creek, and brought his family there in 1795; Mathias Van Bibber, who had been associated with Daniel Boone in Kanawha County, moved to Camp Fork of Peters Creek about this time; Eleven Nicholas came to Peters Creek and built the first mill in the county near where Gilboa Church stands; Benjamin Lemasters came from Pennsylvania in 1798, and located on Bucks Garden; the same year Thomas Bailes and Robert Martin settled in this community; Jesse Childers built his cabin about this time on Twenty Mile on land after occupied by Spencer Hill; and the same year, Jesse James came from Bath County, married a daughter of Henry Morris, and located on Otter Creek; James a little later moved to the Elk River settlement, where he spent his life. Some of his family moved to Missouri several years later, and are supposed to be the ancestors of the notorious outlaws, Frank and Jesse James.

After the year 1800 settlement increased rapidly. George Rader came that year from Shenandoah County, bought land on Bucks Garden, and besides farming he operated the first blacksmith shop in the County. His son-in-law, Samuel Bell settled on Camp Fork. Joseph Backhouse came from Pennsylvania, bought fifty acres of land on Bucks Garden, but soon sold and moved to Twenty Mile where he acquired much land. Many of his descendants still live on these lands on Twenty Mile. Jonathan Dunbar came from Monroe County, bought a tract of land from James Foster on Backus Branch, lived there for a time, then moved to Laurel Creek. Alexander Brown came from Monroe, and bought land on Laurel Creek from Thomas Hughes and Captain George Fitzwater. Near this time Elverton P. Walker came from King George County and bought the farm of John Hess on Laurel Creek. Edwin Bell now owns the land where Walker built his cabin. Colonel Edward Campbell says in his letters on the early settlements: "The coming of Brown and Walker made quite an addition to the population of the County, as each had a family of fourteen children".

About this time the first tannery was set up on Line Creek, by John Bird, a brother-in-law of Henry Morris. He sold to Jacob Koontz; and he and his brother, John carried on the business successfully for many years. John, who was a skillful shoemaker maintained a shoe shop. The Koontz brothers moved to Fayette County where their descendants still live.

In 1805 John Hamilton came to Cross Lanes from Rockingham County. He was a man of means and built the first substantial dwelling house in the County. It was two stories in height, with a dressed stone chimney still retained in the old Hamilton residence. Hamilton is credited with bringing the first wagon to the County, and the appraisement of his estate showed him at that time the wealthiest man in the County.

In 1816 Henry Koontz came from Monroe County, purchased the farm of Edward Ryan near Cross Lanes, which remains in the possession of his descendants.

In 1809 Samuel Neil came from Monroe County, bought Conrad Young's land, and was later granted several large tracts in that section. He was a wagon-maker and owned the second wagon used in the county. Many of his descendants followed his trade as wagon makers and carpenters.

In 1810 Edward Ryan came from Monroe, purchased a mill site from Samuel Neil, and being a mill wright built the first good mill in the County. He soon had many customers and added a saw mill to his plant. The mills later fell to the heirs of Samuel Neil; Grimes Neil, grandson of Samuel, last operated a mill on this site.

C. W. Cottle had come to Strouds Glades at an early date. The natural meadows furnished abundant pasturage and hay for his stock, and he became the first successful cattleman in the county. The Glades were soon known as Cottle Glades and the high hill to the west became Cottle Knob. He was an energetic business man, widely and favorably known, and was Sheriff of Kanawha County a short time before Nicholas County was organized.

John D. Sutton, coming from Pendleton County, some time before Nicholas County was formed, had settled on Elk River, near the location of Sutton, which was named for him. Other settlers in the Elk Valley about this time were the Hamricks, Givenses, Mollohans, Duffields, Frames, Friends, Skidmores and Dyers, all prominent in the early history of Nicholas. Few settlements had been made at this time, south of Gauley River.

The settlers in the mountains and upper Elk Valley, were compelled to go to Charleston to transact their legal business and to vote. This meant much hardship in travel as it was made in that time, as they were from fifty to one hundred miles from their County seat.

In 1814 the population of Kanawha County was about five thousand. The law of Virginia provided that a new County must have a population of one thousand or more. In 1815 a committee consisting of C. W. Cottle, Samuel Neil, Edward Ryan, and others, had drafted a rough outline of a new County, containing the requisite population.

Their petition asking for the new County was refused by the General Assembly of Virginia, at its session in 1816, on account of the opposition of the members of Kanawha County. However our energetic pioneers knew how to "play politics", even in that early day. When John Hansford and Lewis Summers announced themselves as candidates for the General Assembly, a committee of leading citizens from the proposed new county, conferred with these candidates and pledged the vote of the mountaineers, if they would assist in erecting the new County. The proposition was accepted, Hansford and Summers were elected, and by the added influence of Wilson Cary Nicholas, ex-governor of Virginia, the new county was promptly established at the session of 1818. In honor of Wilson Cary Nicholas the new county was named Nicholas, and the County seat was given the name Summersville for Lewis Summers. The act further provided that John Hansford, one of the delegates to the General Assembly who had voted for the new county, should meet with the justices, who at that time should be selected for the county. The meeting was fixed at the residence of John Hamilton, to be held April 7, 1818.

More than a quarter of a century had elapsed from the first settlement in the county up to the time of its organization. Few records exist of the struggle of the pioneers of this period in establishing their homes in the mountain wilderness. The nearest store and post office was at Fort Union. To reach this point from any place in the present County of Nicholas, the journey must be made over the trails that led to the mouth of Rich Creek, thence by the "Baggage Trail" to Fort Union, afterwards named Lewisburg in honor of General Lewis.

Colonel Edward Campbell who was born in a cabin in 1800 thus pictures life in his boyhood in going to market and post office: "They had to go down to the ford of Gauley River, at the mouth of Rich Creek, and when there they were further from their destination than when they left home. They went up Rich Creek and over Gauley Mountain following the Baggage Trail to Lewisburg. This was done on pack horses and mules and they had to camp out at night and furnish their own provisions—a hard way to market 65 miles distant. Salt that cost four dollars a bushel was carried from Lewisburg on pack horses. What did we do for bread? We had none till corn could be grown. Until we had mills, roasting ears took the place of bread; when too hard for roasting ears, it was grated on a tin grater, and when too hard to be grated, we used the hominy pounder, and beat the grains into a coarse meal. This method of getting bread was continued for more than ten years after the first settlements, and until we had the first water mills".

The romancers who in their fiction have often attempted to describe the character and habits of our pioneers, usually picture them as ignorant and ruthless adventurers, who had left the older communities because of some grievance or crime, or perhaps they had wanted to get away from the restraints of orderly living. Indeed some of the early traders and hunters may have merited this description to some extent; but the pioneers of Nicholas County, coming largely from the older counties in Virginia and Pennsylvania, were in the main the descendants of the Scotch-Irish and Germans who had come to America in quest of religious freedom and liberty in civil rights. They were not ignorant; and usually had been given the rudiments of an English education. Many of them were artisans, and had experience in the common trades of that day, and had in their home communities enjoyed civilized life. Their fathers and mothers were Presbyterians or Mennonites, and had reared them in the observance of the forms of religious worship. They came to the wilderness deliberately, soberly and thoughtfully in search of homes. They brought with them wives and children, believing that this new country could be subdued, and that it promised them not only subsistence, but by determined effort they would be able to build a government that would bring freedom and prosperity to them and their children. And history proclaims that they toiled not in vain.

The selection of land and the building of his cabin was the first objective of the home seeker. The site of the cabin was chosen near a spring, with the surroundings suited for his building material and with fertile soil for prospective crops. The cabin was constructed on a well developed plan that had grown up from experience in the backwoods. The usual dimensions were twenty feet by twenty-four feet. Unhewed logs of a size readily handled were selected for the walls and carefully notched and fitted at each corner. When the proper height was reached to provide a one-story building with a low loft or attic, provision was made for the roof by shortening the end logs until a single log formed the comb of the roof. On these logs the roof was laid of clapboards rived with a froe from suitable timber, and held in place with weight poles, as nails were not to be had. The floor was formed from puncheons eighteen or twenty inches wide made by splitting timber of the necessary size and hewing the faces smooth with the broadax. A door was made by cutting an opening out of the wall, framing it with slabs and fitting a shutter of hewed slabs, on wooden hinges, and with a wooden latch worked with a buckskin strap from the inside. A similar opening though wider was cut in the end of the building for a chimney, which was built of logs like the walls of the cabin and made large enough to allow a lining of stones and mortar to form a large fireplace and the jambs. Flat stones formed a hearth, and the chimney was topped out with "cat and clay" work. The cracks between logs in the wall were "chunked and daubed" by filling them with splits of wood and mortar. The mortar was simply clean clay mixed in water to the right consistency.

The furniture inside also followed a general pattern. A table was made from wide slabs hewed smooth and set permanently on round legs fitted in two-inch auger holes. Some three legged stools were fashioned in the same way. Wooden pins set in the wall at the back of the house supported clap board shelves for any table ware. In one corner a rude bedstead was framed by four stakes with forked tops set in auger holes in the floor. Rails of smooth saplings were laid in the forks, and slabs, or strips of bark or deerskin held up a sort of mattress of deerskin filled with dry leaves or cornshucks, with bear skins or deer hides for covers. Pegs driven in the walls served as a wardrobe for articles of clothing; and the antlers of a deer fixed in the joist over the door way held the ever ready rifle and shot pouch.

The clothing of the men was a fur cap, moccasins, buckskin leggings, and a fringed hunting shirt of deerskin or home spun. The women and girls wore about the same garments as the men, except the buckskin or home spun skirt took the place of the hunting shirt.

The food of the earliest settlers was often only meat from the wild game, and with wild fruits and nuts, until the corn crops and "truck patch" could furnish roasting ears, corn meal and such vegetables as beans, pumpkins and potatoes grown with corn. Journey cake and pone in the early days were the only forms of bread used for breakfast and dinner. For supper corn meal mush or hominy was eaten with bear's oil or gravy from fried

Early Settlements 39

meat, till later milk could be had. On the table food was served in trenchers, noggins, and wooden bowls; even gourds and the hard shells of squashes were so used. Maple syrup and maple sugar were in common use in the spring. Coffee and tea could not be had in the early settlements, and tea made from dittany, spicewood and sassafras was frequently served. After bees had been introduced in the settlement, metheglin was made from honey.

Medicines and medical treatment were lacking—wounds and snake bites were common and poorly treated. Poultices from various plants, applications of salt and gunpowder, and cupping were resorted to in treating wounds; and "sucking" the wound and applying the raw flesh of the snake, was about the only treatment for snake bite. Constant exposure in bad weather and the arduous toil of the frontier brought on such ailments as rheumatism, pleurisy and tuberculosis, for which the sufferers found little remedy. Fevers, flux, diphtheria and croup took heavy toll of the children. Severe labor, exposure, and lack of medical aid shortened the life span of the pioneers.

Sickness and death saddened many a lonely backwoods home. Often the parents must look after the burial of a dead child, fortunate if even a solitary neighbor was present; and children often had to perform the last sad rites for a parent. In the earliest settlements the only casket for the dead was a shield of rough slabs laid around and over the body. Later rude coffins could be made.

Morality and religious sentiment was not wanting.

Theodore Roosevelt, in his "Winning of the West", speaking of our early settlers says: "At the bottom they were deeply religious in their tendencies; and although ministers and meeting houses were rare, yet these backwoods cabins often contained Bibles, and the mothers used to instil into the minds of their children reverence for Sunday, while many even of the hunters refused to hunt on that day".

Amusements, even in the toil and hardships of these early years, were not wanting. In connection with social gatherings for log rollings, house-raisings, corn-huskings, and other social affairs, there was fiddling and dancing at the close of the meetings. Men and boys had diversion in wrestling, jumping and shooting at marks. Playing the game of mumble-the-peg and tomahawk throwing were boyish sports. Weddings were occasions for neighborhood jollification. The wedding dinner at the home of the bride followed by the "infare" at the groom's home gave opportunity for relaxation with pranks and dancing.

The tools of the first settler were very primitive and limited. He went into the wilderness with rifle, ax and fire to clear his fields. To build his cabin he needed beside his ax, a large auger and a broadax. If he lacked the auger and broadax, a neighbor could perhaps loan him these tools. A saw, an auger, a froe and a broadax would supply a whole settlement and were used as common property in the erection of the log cabin and its furniture.

Fortunately there were a few of the earliest settlers who came with equipment and means to at once set up comparatively comfortable homes, and who did not un-

Early Settlements 41

dergo all the privation and hardships of those who must start almost empty handed.

James Simms and his sons, among the first to come, brought negro slaves, and equipment for his home and to set up a shop to carry on the work of gunsmith and blacksmith. The Simms rifle soon won a great reputation. John Hamilton, who had bought the Edward Hughes land at Cross Lanes, was a man of property and employed workmen to erect a substantial dwelling house and make improvements before he came with his family. In the first wagon to reach Nicholas County he brought equipment for his home. Samuel Neil, a wagon maker, bought the improvement of Conrad Young on Peters Creek, and had ample means to develop it. George Rader and Benjamin Lemasters also purchased lands on Bucks Garden, and had money to build and improve their farms. Other men came with means to purchase and improve the clearings of discouraged or restless owners. These new arrivals, who erected better buildings and bought better tools and equipment set a pattern for their neighbors, and raised the standard of living in their communities. As a result advances were made in buildings and home life. Wheat, oats and flax were now grown; more cattle and horses were in use and hogs, sheep and poultry were to be seen on almost all farms.

After food, clothing was the prime necessity in the new country. The cornfields soon provided suitable soil for other crops. Wheat, oats, flax, and the tame grasses were cultivated. Small flocks of sheep that could be penned at night and protected from panthers and wolves produced wool. Flax easily raised, could, by a tedious process, be made to furnish linen.

The Scotch-Irish had been the famous weavers of linen and woolen cloth in Ireland and they brought the art of weaving in their emigration to America. Their descendants learned to construct rough looms, and with the few tools the backwoodsmen had looms were now made to furnish clothing. Some few of the first settlers had brought spinning wheels, but these now were made by local artisans.

The women were the weavers and tailors in every cabin. Place was made for the loom and the spinning wheels in the one room cabin or a special building provided, if it could be afforded. The women clipped the wool from the sheep, washed, carded, spun it and wove it into "linsey-woolsey" and jeans. They usually took care of the crop of flax from the field, "watered" the stalks, braked and scutched the "sholes" or woody fiber out of the stalks, hackled this tow into silken, glossy fibers for spinning, and spun it into threads for sewing and weaving. Only rare specimens of this lost art of "home-spun" weaving exist today.

From the woolen yarn, stockings, mittens, "comforts" and other articles of clothing were knitted by the housewife and the girls of the family. Cloth was cut and fitted into clothing for adults and children; and women's work in addition to this was milking, churning, manufacturing soap and dyeing and washing clothes, while all the time preparing food for the table, nursing and training the children.

The men were engaged in clearing and fencing the

fields, planting and harvesting crops, improving their buildings, making the farm implements—harness for horses, yokes for the oxen, sleds, plows, harrows, rakes, forks, mauls and furniture for the cabins, mostly of wood and rough tanned leather, save perhaps an iron share for a plow. They dressed and tanned skins for leather, made moccasins and shoes for their families and the harness and saddles for the horses. The "pack-saddle", made from sapling forks and side-boards, was a special product of the backwoods. Venable in his "Footprints of the Pioneers", tells of the preacher in an outdoors meeting, who paused in his sermon as he pointed to a sapling and exclaimed: "Brethren, I have just noticed one of the best forked limbs for a pack-saddle that ever grew; after meeting we will go and cut it."

The growing of wheat took time. It did not flourish on the raw soil, but after a crop or two of corn, it was sowed between the corn rows in the fall, and dug or plowed in. At harvest it was cut with sickles, stowed under shelter, threshed with flails, and the chaff removed by pouring in the wind, until an ingenious pioneer devised the fanning mill.

The growing crops must be guarded from the deer, squirrels, crows and other animals that preyed on them. The little flock of sheep and the few hogs must be kept out of the woods and kept in pens to protect them from bears, panthers and wolves. Chickens and geese must also be housed and continually guarded against hawks, owls, wolves, foxes and other prowlers. In this the children usually aided by watching the crops, and caring for the sheep, pigs and poultry. With all this care often a bear or a wolf would invade the clearing and carry off a sheep or hog.

Some time was also required that the man supply venison or other wild meat for food, and to join with his neighbor in cutting out and widening the game trails into passable roads for pack animals and sleds and by slow degrees to be made fit for wheels.

Turning away from all these hardships, the pioneer life had its compensations. Although there were no electric lights, pine knots, tallow dips and candles lighted a sturdy and happy family; though there were no tropical fruits and nuts, chinquapins and filberts were plentiful and the chestnuts, walnuts and hickories showered down delicious nuts that could be gathered by the bushel to be feasted on around the cabin hearths on winter nights; though there was no fancy fishing tackle, fish could be taken from any stream at any time with a pole and line. And although money was scarce it was of little need in providing the food and clothing that must be wrested from forest and field. While there was no newspaper, almost every home had a Bible and hymnbook, and it appears from appraisement lists of record that the leading settlers had books that had come with them to the wilderness. It is worth noting that the appraisement of Captain George Fitzwater's estate listed books as follows: Two Bibles, a hymnbook, dictionary, grammar, arithmetic, History of the United States, History of the World, Acts of Congress and a few volumes of poetry and fiction.

The transformation from pioneer life that has occurred in the six generations of our history is astonishing.

No one now living has witnessed this change, which was slow for the first century. Few persons living today can recall the virgin forests, the clear streams alive with fish, the legions of squirrels and flocks of pigeons and grouse that swarmed in the woods. Few public men can now boast of birth in a log cabin. The coming generation has no memory of the problems of their pioneer ancestors, and can only learn and know of their heroic struggles in conquering the wilderness from fading family traditions and the scant records they have left us. They were too much engaged in making history to record its details. They lie in many unmarked graves in the soil they loved, and the paths they trod and the sites of their cabin homes have long since been lost and forgotten.

CHAPTER III

Organization and Administration

THE County of Nicholas was organized at the residence of John Hamilton in the residence still standing at Cross Lanes. Somewhat modernized, it is owned and occupied by descendants of the original builder. The record of this meeting is found in County Court Record "Book A" in the office of the Clerk of the County Court. Written with quill pen on the rough unlined paper, of that day, it is remarkably clear and legible after the lapse of more than one hundred and thirty-five years.

It will be of interest to let Colonel Edward Campbell tell us in his own words of the set-up of the county organization, and the following is taken from his memoirs published in 1883:

> "The organization was on the second Tuesday in April, 1818, and according to an act of the Virginia Legislature. John Hansford, Esq., of Kanawha County was appointed to be present on that day and administer the oath of office to one of the justices who was appointed a member of said court. He (Hansford) administered the oath to Samuel Neil, and then Esq. Neil administered the oath of office to his associates, to-wit: Thomas Masterson, William Simms, Samuel Hutchinson, C. W. Cottle, Isaac Gregory, John Hamilton, Joseph McNutt, John Campbell, Mathias VanBibber, James Robinson, John Skidmore, A. P. Friend, David Frame, James Given and John Duffield."

Old County and Circuit Court Clerk's Office, 1824-1898

Organization and Administration

"John Duffield presented a commission from the Governor by which he was appointed the first "High Sheriff". He gave bond and qualified, and John McKey Hamilton and Robert Hill qualified as his deputies. This being done there was an announcement made by a crier that "Silence is now commanded while the Honorable County Court is setting for the transaction of business".

Election of a Clerk of the County Court was the first business in order—voting was done at that time by ballot. There were three candidates for the clerkship, Robert Hamilton, Felix G. Hansford and John Given. When the ballots were counted it was found that Given had a majority of the votes. He was therefore declared duly elected, given bond and qualified. The Court then appointed William Smith, Esq. as Commonwealth Attorney. Perry Wetherd qualified to practice law in this Court. The Court then adjourned to the following morning, as it was the day to hold the State election for members of the Legislature. Each County was entitled to two delegates to represent it in the General Assembly and there were four candidates: E. Rian, C. W. Cottle, Thomas Masterson, and Andrew P. Friend. When the election closed and the votes were counted E. Rian and C. W. Cottle were found to be elected. It becoming late the people had to disperse and scatter out through the neighborhood to get lodging for the night, as there was no house of entertainment. The snow was two inches deep and many who had no further business with the Court left for their homes".

"On the second day Court convened at 9 o'clock a.m. and proceeded to business. William Given was appointed Commissioner of Revenue, with John Bowyer Assistant Commissioner. Samuel Hutchinson was appointed Surveyor of the county. The Court then proceeded to appoint various Road Overseers, and to recommend the various militia officers to the Governor for his appointment and commission. This must be done before the 126th Regiment of Virginia Militia could be organized. The following were recommended for commissions: Robert Hamilton for Colonel; Isaac Gregory for Lieutenant Colonel; William Hamilton for Major; William Simms, E. Rian and John G. Stephenson for Captains.

"After transacting some other business the Court adjourned to meet in May at the house of James Robinson, on Muddlety, until some cabins were built on the Groves Farm and then the Court met there until the first court house was built at Summersville".

As soon as the new County had been assured, a group of citizens headed by Archibald Hutchinson planned to have the county seat located at Hutchinson's farm on Muddlety later owned by John M. Hutchinson. This plan was approved by Wilson Cary Nicholas, and Hutchinson sure of its success had laid off town lots and sites for public buildings. For some reason not given, John Hansford, who had been appointed by the act creating the county to qualify the justices that would take office at the organization, notified Samuel Neil, one of the justices, to call the meeting at the residence of John Hamilton at Cross Lanes, and accordingly the organization was perfected there. When on April 8th the question came up for adjournment to the May Term, Justices Samuel Neil, Thomas Masterson, William Simms, Samuel Hutchinson, John Hamilton, John Campbell, Joseph McNutt and Mathias Van Bibber voted to meet at the Hamilton residence. The other justices angrily protested, and James Robinson, C. W. Cottle, Isaac Gregory, John Skidmore, Andrew P. Friend, David Frame, James Given and John Duffield voted to meet at "our county seat" on the Archibald Hutchinson farm. It was a complete deadlock, and there was much feeling. Finally James Robinson proposed a compromise by offering to furnish a building to be used as court house, and in this way the county seat

Organization and Administration 49

was duly located. The Court met for the May Term at Robinson's house and after that at the residence of John Groves till the public grounds and buildings were regularly established according to law.

The Virginia law required that all officials must subscribe to four oaths as follows: The oath of fidelity; the oath to support the Constitution of the United States; the oath to suppress dueling; and the oath to faithfully discharge the duties of the particular office. The record shows that all officers of the new county took these several oaths in qualifying for their duties.

The County Court was made up of the sixteen justices above named. Strange as it seems no quorum was fixed for attendance at the monthly terms, and no penalty prescribed for failure to attend. After the first meeting a full attendance of the sixteen members never appears of record and sometimes as few as four members held court.

The Court under the early Virginia law exercised almost unlimited jurisdiction in the county. The court made up of justices commissioned by the Governor was allowed to name all succeeding justices and was thus self-perpetuating. The Court appointed all county officials, except the Clerk of the Circuit Court who was named by the judge, and the Delegates of the General Assembly and Overseers of the Poor who were elected by popular vote.

The Court laid the levy for taxes, fixed the rates for ferries and ordinaries, and the salaries and fees for all local officers, thus controlling the finances of the county without responsibility to any authority. Its jurisdiction extended to all criminal cases, and once or twice a year, a grand jury term was held at which indictments were found and tried. It had jurisdiction in most civil actions as trespass, ejectment, condemnation under eminent domain and others now within the jurisdiction of our circuit courts only. Indeed it occasionally invaded the realms of chancery and issued injunctions, and restraining orders. The Court approved all deeds, wills and other writings before they could be recorded. The appointment of fiduciaries, appraisers and the settlement of estates was entrusted to this court. All public improvements as roads, bridges and public buildings were determined by this body. It issued license for ferries and ordinaries and authorized the building of mills.

An examination of its records from 1818 to 1861, now in the office of the Circuit Clerk, will show the tremendous amount of work of this court in the exercise of its broad jurisdiction. And this work was done without salary or even mileage and necessary expenses. It was held a high honor to sit as a member of the County Court, though the position was without remuneration and involved considerable personal sacrifice to give several days each month to the discharge of the onerous duties involved. Jurors also served without any compensation. It was considered a duty to give such service freely for the general welfare of the new government.

The Constitution of 1850 changed the manner of selecting the members of the County Court and enlarged the rights of suffrage, giving more voice to the selection of officers by the electorate. The justices were now elected for a term of four years; the county clerk and the county surveyor were elected for a term of six years; the sheriff was elected for a term of two years; and jurors allowed payment for their services.

At the May Term, 1818, Samuel Neil, William Cottle, John Hamilton, Mathias Van Bibber, Thomas Masterson, John Campbell, William Simms, James Robinson and Joseph McNutt were the justices attending. The Court was in session only one day and after appointing four constables—Samuel Grose, Joseph Prior, Benjamin Duffield and Robert Martin—entered the following orders:

"William Simms, Joseph McNutt, Samuel Neil, Edward Rian and David Lilly are by the Court appointed to view a way for a road from the mouth of Twenty Mile Creek down Gauley to intersect the road at the mouth of Scrabble Creek, who are to make their report of the conveniences and inconveniences thereof at the next Court."

"Samuel Wiseman, James Scaggs, Ephraim Simmons, James Lykins and Samuel Masterson are appointed to view a way for a road from Kincaid's Ferry to Dogwood Knob, the shortest and best way, and report the conveniences and inconveniences thereof to the next Court."

At the June Term the first levy for taxes was laid in a very simple way compared with modern methods. An owner of property was a "titheable" and the brief order: "Three Dollars is the County Levy for the present year for each titheable" was the authority given the "Commissioners of the Revenue" for collection of the taxes. It was in fact a capitation tax. The record fails to show the number of titheables in the County at this time or the amount of taxes collected for the year.

"The first grand jury was called and qualified as follows: "David Stuart, foreman, Jonathan Dunbar, John McClung, Jacob Hutchinson, Edward McClung, David Murphy, Israel Brown, David McCoy, William Lilly, Elverton P. Walker, Alexander Brown, Samuel Bell, George Hardway, John G.

Stephenson, David McCue and John Fitzwater were sworn as a Grand Jury of Inquest for the body of this County and having received their charge retired from the bar to consult of their presentments, and returned into Court and presented as follows, to-wit: Within six months last past William Dodrill for swearing a profane oath, on the information of Jacob Hutchinson and David Murphy, two of our own body, a true bill. And the Said Grand Jury having nothing more to present were discharged. Joshua Stephenson came into Court and paid the fine to the Clerk."

"Ordered that the rates of McClung's Ferry be as follows: For every man eight cents, for every horse the same as a man, for every head of neat cattle the same as for a man, and for every hog, sheep or goat one-fifth part of eight cents."

At the July Term there was much routine business in approving and certifying deeds for record, settlement of claims against the County.

An attorney was admitted to practice by the following order:

"James Wilson, Gentm. on his motion is admitted to practice law in this Court, whereupon he took the oath of an attorney, the oath of Fidelity, the oath to support the Constitution of the United States, and the oath to Suppress Dueling."

At the August Term the first civil action, a suit in debt brought by William McClintic against Thomas Legg was docketed and set for trial.

The act establishing the county provided that a commission composed of John Hansford and John Wilson of Kanawha County, Samuel Brown and John Welch of Greenbrier County and William Marteny of Randolph County should locate the county seat for the new county. The report of the commission made at this term was entered as follows:

Organization and Administration 53

"Agreeable to an act entitled an Act to Establish the County of Nicholas, John Wilson, John Welch and William Marteny, three of the commissioners names in the foregoing act, made the following report, to-wit: We the undersigned, being appointed by an act of the General Assembly, passed the 30th day of January, 1818, for establishing the County of Nicholas, etc., having met in said county for the purpose mentioned in said act, *viz* to ascertain the most proper place for erecting the public buildings and for holding courts in said county, have taken the same into consideration and are of opinion that the buildings aforesaid be erected on a tract of land known as Arbuckle's Tract of five hundred acres, adjoining the land of John Groves on the southeast side, and near a large double whiteoak about 4 or 5 poles on the southeast side of a new road leading from Kanawha to Randolph; and on the tract aforesaid, the whiteoak aforesaid to be marked with the letter "N" on the side next the road.

Given under our hands this 5th day of August, 1818, Signed:

                        John Wilson
                        John Welch
                        William Marteny."

The double whiteoak mentioned stood near the site of the John D. Alderson law office, with the letter "N" marked on a square hewed on the side of the tree facing the road. John M. Hutchinson, who remembered seeing the tree, identified its location for the writer.

The Court immediately proceeded to appoint a building committee:

"Robert Kelly, Joseph McNutt, John Groves, Edward Rian and Samuel Neil, a majority of whom may act, are appointed by this Court as commissioners for the purpose of having public buildings erected necessary for the county, as required by law, on the land, as by the commissioners under act by the General Assembly have pointed out, which act is entitled an Act Establishing the County of Nicholas. The plan and cite of the said buildings to be certified to the next term of the Court by the said Robert Kelly, Joseph McNutt, John Groves, Edward Rian and Samuel Neil, commissioners aforesaid, at which time the said commissioners last mentioned are to contract for said public buildings."

No report of said commissioners is of record.

The Court fixed the rates of tavern keepers as follows:

"ORDINARY RATES:

Breakfast	25 cents
Dinner	25 cents
Supper	25 cents
Whiskey, one-half pint	12½ cents
Brandy, one-half pint	17 cents
New England rum, one-half pint	37½ cents
West India rum, one-half pint	50 cents
Cider, one quart	12½ cents
Madeira wine, one quart	$1.50
Common wine, one quart	$1.25
Hay to horse, 24 hours	21 cents
Corn or oats, one gallon	12½ cents
Pasturage, day and night	12½ cents
Lodging	12½ cents"

The September term was taken up mainly with road matters. Viewers were appointed to locate roads in every part of the county. Overseers named to open up and work on these roads. Usually they could only widen trails for pack horses at this time. The male citizens of proper age were alloted to the different overseers and ordered to work for a given number of days in road making.

The Building Committee named at the August Term submitted its plan for a jail:

"Agreeable to an order made at August Term last, the commissioners appointed have exhibited a plan for a jail which

Organization and Administration 55

the Court conceives will be sufficient; it is therefore ordered by the Court that the said Commissioners go on to make sale of the said jail to the lowest bidder, agreeable to the said plan."

The October Term was again given over to the pressing necessity for road building. A number of deeds were approved for record and Benjamin Hamrick, a Revolutionary soldier, was before the Court and examined as an applicant for a pension. His affidavit was filed and a copy certified to the War Department of the United States.

"On motion of Benjamin Lemasters, a Revolutionary soldier, his affidavit is ordered to be recorded and a copy transmitted to the Secretary of the War Department, agreeable to the act in such cases made and provided."

Later an order correcting the name of this soldier was entered as follows:

"On motion of Benjamin Lemasters, and it appearing to the satisfaction of the Court that his right as a pensioner of the United States was certified *Lamasters* in place of *Lemasters*. The Clerk is hereby authorized to alter said certificate and in place of *Lamasters* insert the name *Lemasters*."

The method of jury trial in the County Court is shown in the following order:

"*Commonwealth vs. Thomas Hughes*, on Indictment for Trespass, Assault and Battery. This day came as well the Attorney for the Commonwealth as Defendant by his Attorney; and the Defendant by plea saith that he is not guilty in manner and form as in the Indictment against him is alledged, and with this the Defendant puts himself on the Country and the Plaintiff doth likewise; and thereupon came a jury, to-wit: John Bailes, John Murphy, Robert Martin, Jacob Chapman, Joseph Pryor, Renick Brown, John McClung, Elijah Lightner, David Holliday, Benjamin Lemasters, Samuel Dobbins, and Isaac Collison, who after being duly elected, tried and sworn to try the issue between the Commonwealth, Plaintiff and Thomas

Hughes, Defendant, on their oaths say that the Defendant is guilty in manner and form as in the Indictment against him alledged, and do assess his amercement to one penny of damages beside the costs."

Thus in the quaint and solemn language of the common law of England, brought over by the Virginia colonists, did the County Court, in this its first criminal trial, begin the establishment of law and order in the new county.

The necessity for laying off the County into districts for local officers soon appeared. And the Court met the problem by including certain residences of citizens in a loose description as a district. The following order appointing constables and assigning their territory illustrates this proceeding:

"John Kincaid's district as constable shall be as high up Twenty Mile Creek as Daniel Holliday's and include the inhabitants of the lower part of the county; Thomas Legg's district shall include Peters Creek settlement and from Holliday's to the Court House and include the settlements south of Gauley; Robert Martin's district shall be from William Cottle's to the Court House to include the Mumble-the-Peg and McMillions Creek; Benjamin Duffield's district shall be from James Bragg's, including Duck and Otter Creeks, Elk and Birch Rivers; George Davis's district shall be from Bogg's up Elk to Jeremiah Carpenter's on Elk River; Joseph Brown's district shall include the balance of the County."

At the December Term the sheriff asked for the jail which had been recommended by the building committee at the August Term:

"John Duffield, Sheriff, enters his protest against the sufficiency of a place for the confinement of prisoners put into his custody as sheriff aforesaid; and the said sheriff having heretofore applied to this Court for a jail to make the proper confinement for the prisoners now in his custody; it is ordered that the commissioners heretofore appointed for the purpose of having the publick buildings erected for the county do proceed by advertisement at the next court to contract for said buildings or show cause why they have not performed the order of this Court."

There is nothing of record to show what action the commissioners took but an entry at the June Term, 1819, annuls a contract with Thomas Masterson for building the jail, and David Hanna, Joshua Stephenson and Nathan Hines are added to the Building Committee. In the meantime a temporary jail, built of logs and containing two small rooms had been erected by David Perkins and David Stuart at a cost of $200.00. At the November Term, 1819 John G. Stephenson was allowed the sum of $574.00 for a larger building. A "whipping post", stocks and pillory were erected on the public grounds before any jail was built:

"The commissioners appointed by the Court to superintend the public buildings for this county have examined and viewed the stocks and pillory and report that in their opinion the stocks and pillory aforesaid are not finished agreeable to contract and we the undersigned commissioners have hereunto set our hands,
> Samuel Neil
> John Campbell
> James Given
> Robert Kelly
> Joseph McNutt."

The action of the Court on this report is not of record, but "Whipping" post, stocks and pillory were kept on the grounds up to the Civil War.

Returning to history of our jail buildings, in 1824, Judge James Allen of the Superior Court received a report on the County jail which had been erected by John G. Stephenson. The report showed that the jail did not meet the requirements of the Virginia statute and Judge Allen issued a rule requiring the County Court to provide a jail in compliance with the law. Accordingly at the June Term, 1824, Samuel Neil, William Carnefix and John Groves were appointed commissioners to have a jail built as ordered by the Superior Court. Specifications for the new jail required it to be constructed of dressed stone, thirty-six feet by twenty-four feet, two stories in height and to provide rooms for the jailor's residence.

Alexander Spinks was employed to do the work and set about the construction at once. No contract for the work is of record, and the cost of the jail does not appear. The work was not completed until late in 1826. This building was in use about eighty years. In 1907 the building was condemned as unfit for use, and prisoners were committed to Webster and Braxton County jails.

On November 30, 1909 the County Court contracted with the B. F. Smith Fireproof Construction Company to build the jail now in use. The contract price was $23,093.00 and the work was to be completed in 1910. At the same time the Court employed the West Virginia Heating and Plumbing Company of Charleston to install a heating and lighting system for both the Court house and the new jail building at a contract price of $3,513.00. The work was completed and accepted January 27, 1911. David Dick, architect of Charleston superintended the work.

Organization and Administration

The commissioners appointed to procure the erection of public buildings had contracted with James Givens to build a court house, soon after the public grounds were laid off. No record of this contract exists. It appears that the building was sufficiently completed to allow the court to hold its first meeting therein on July 4, 1820. The contractor was slow to finish his work, and at its June Term, 1824, the Court entered the following order:

> "It is ordered that James Given, the undertaker of the court house of the county, be notified by the commissioners that unless he does by a certain day, to be specified by said commissioners, finish the court house according to his contract, that they shall be at liberty and are hereby authorized to proceed against the said James Given for non-performance of his said contract".

The record is silent as to the result of this notice, but the building was not painted until 1830, when James G. Neil was allowed $338.00 for this work.

This first court house was a frame building thirty feet by forty feet, two stories in height. The lower story was used as the main court room. The upper story was divided into three rooms for use of juries and witnesses. The timbers for the framing were hewn out, and the walls, floors and ceilings were of boards cut with whipsaws. John G. Stephenson and his brother, Joshua, furnished the lumber from their lands on Peters Creek. James Given was paid $800.00 for the carpenter work, but the record does not disclose the cost of the material furnished by the Stephensons. This building was in use until 1895.

At the June Term 1882 the County Court appointed a

committee to examine the Court House with the intention of repairing it.

This committee reported as follows:

"To the Honorable County Court of Nicholas County, West Virginia: We the undersigned committee appointed by your Honorable Court to examine and report upon the feasibility of repairing the present Court House would beg leave to submit the following report, that after being first duly sworn, we have examined the said building both above and under the roof, the floor of the second story, and other material parts of the building, and we are of the opinion that said building is unsafe to use and believe it will be labor lost and money uselessly expended and lost to remodel, repair and patch up the present building.

     (Signed) G. W. Pierson
           Wm. J. Fitzwater
           John Copenhaver
           A. B. Foster
           James Williams."

Notwithstanding the report of this committee the Court took no action. Sometime afterwards it became necessary to brace the leaning walls, and long timbers the size of telephone poles were set at an angle of about forty-five degrees against the eastern wall at the upper story, and for several years this makeshift kept the old building in use.

In the summer of 1894 an amusing incident unwittingly gave new impetus to the general demand for a decent court house.—A class in the Normal School in Civil Government called "a mass meeting to consider the building of a new court house". The meeting filled the Auditorium of the school building with many visitors and the question was vigorously debated *pro* and *con*. A resolution was passed condemning the old building and asking for a new court house. At the close of the convention, A. J. Horan, a prominent lawyer, made a short speech commending the students for their action and adding that the old house was not only unsafe but was used in violation of law as the statute required all court houses to be of brick or stone.

Alderson & Horan, attorneys for certain citizens and taxpayers, filed a petition in the circuit court praying for a mandamus to compel the erection of a proper building for a court house.

The County Court anticipating the result of this suit declared that it would make no defense but would attempt to provide a proper building for a court house as required by law.

At the September Term, 1895, James S. Craig, L. W. Herold and W. A. McClung were named as a building committee and directed to secure plans and bids for the proposed building. It was stipulated that the building was to cost not more than $22,000.00 payable in installments out of the annual levies of 1897, 1898, 1899 and 1900.

For several months plans were studied and on the 29th day of April, 1896, a contract was let to Fouse & Reich of Parkersburg, on their bid of $21,978.00 to erect the new building. It was completed in March 1898 and on the 13th day of April, 1898 was received and dedicated by program prepared by a committee appointed by the County Court. The proceedings at the dedication was held in the court room of the new court house, and are briefly recorded in Law Order Book 8 at page 324.

The new court house was at first heated by open grates

in each room and this method of heating was in use for about twenty years.

In addition to the contract price of $21,978.00 the metal furniture and fixtures in the offices cost $1,458.00, the wooden furniture $1,564.00 and the commissions paid the architects and some extra work by the contractors raised the total cost of the building to $26,000.00 in round numbers.

While the new building was in course of construction court was held for two terms in the Auditorium of the Normal School Building, and then for the remainder of the time in the Masonic Hall in the McQueen Building.

The Clerk's Office which stood on the northeast corner of the public lot just west of the location of the Morris Monument, was built by William Cunningham in 1825. It was of dressed stone twenty feet by twenty-four feet with two rooms. The north room was used by the county clerk, the south room by the circuit clerk. It was in use until 1898.

At the June Term, 1819, the County Court in an effort to protect the sheep of the settlers that were so badly needed to furnish clothing, entered an order offering a bounty for killing wolves:

> "Ordered by the Court that that there shall be allowed for the scalp of every old wolf killed in the bounds of the County of Nicholas by the inhabitants of said county, five dollars, which said wolves must be killed from this day henceforth to the first day of June, 1820, and half that sum for young wolves, and which said sum is to be paid out of the county levy of 1820."

The fierce gray wolves that infested the county had

Organization and Administration

preyed largely on deer before the settlement, but the deer were rapidly becoming scarce as the early settlers hunted them for their supply of venison, and the sheep offered an easy substitute to the hungry wolves. Sheep had to be kept under watch during the day and shut in pens at night, and with all this effort the wolves destroyed many of them. The bounty on wolves was paid annually up to as late as 1858, and prices were constantly advanced to encourage the killing of the cunning animals. A bounty of twelve dollars was finally paid for an old wolf's scalp.

At the August Term of Court entered the following order:

> "John Campbell and David Hanna being by this Court appointed as fit and proper persons in this county to celebrate the rites of matrimony in said county, whereupon they severally took the oath of allegiance to the Commonwealth and with security entered into and acknowledged a bond conditioned as the law required."

From time to time others were appointed to celebrate the rites of matrimony, as the few ministers of the early churches were not available at all times. The names of the persons so appointed appear in the early Records of Marriages. The court provided records for the purpose, but because of the negligence in reporting and recording our early records are far from complete.

The Court maintained order in all its proceedings and was respected by the citizens. The following order is illuminating:

> "Whereas, some persons are in the daily habit of amusing themselves with a game of ball called 'flies', by throwing a ball against the walls of the Court House, be it therefore

the rule and order of the Court that if any person or persons in the future shall presume to indulge themselves in the aforesaid practice of ball playing against the walls of said Court House, it shall be judged and construed as an indignity and contempt offered to the Court of this county and the person so offending shall be fined at the discretion of the court."

John M. Hutchinson in a letter published more than fifty years ago describes the punishment at the whipping post, in the Court House grounds, of a man charged with stealing, which he witnessed as a boy. Mr. Hutchinson says: "I call to mind a petty larceny case, but will call no names. A was charged with stealing a hog from B and was found guilty in a trial before the County Court. The President of the Court on stating the finding of the court and passing sentence said to the prisoner that it was a painful duty to punish him but that the law must be enforced. Under the sentence the sheriff was directed to take A, put him in the stocks and lay upon his back 39 lashes save one. The sheriff at once obeyed. The prisoner's shirt was taken off and his hands fastened in the stocks. The sheriff then asked the onlookers to count with him, and with a cowhide lash laid on 38 strokes. He set the man loose and gave him his shirt. The prisoner put it on with tears tracing down his cheeks and hurried away. He and his wife and five children moved out of the county at once."

Mr. Hutchinson adds that many years afterward a grandson of A, who was a prominent lawyer from the State of Kentucky, came to Nicholas County in a presidential campaign and in his speech at the Court House said: "I have always wanted to see Nicholas County, for the reason that my grandfather, A, had once lived

Organization and Administration 65

there but had moved away from the county with his family and had never given any history of his life there."

Perhaps this explains why the County Court in its wisdom omitted such cases from its record, out of sympathy for innocent relatives and to enable the offender to transmit his name without the blot of a criminal record.

The County Court licensed all millers and gave permits for constructing dams and locating mills. Under the law of eminent domain the court could condemn land for mill sites. Citizens depended upon mills for bread, and strict rules were enforced for their operation. The miller was excused from military service and from serving on juries. He must grind for each customer in turn as his "grist" was brought in. His "toll" for grinding was one-eighth of all grain ground into meal, and one-sixteenth of that ground for mash or hominy. Generally the miller used a "toll-box" holding one gallon dry measure. This was the toll for one bushel of eight gallons dry measure. The Virginia law was carried into our West Virginia Code after the Civil War.

The members of the County Court were representative men from the body of the county. They were as a rule religious, and were those who were in a better position to give the necessary time and attention to the work of the Court than many of their neighbors. None of them were trained in the learning of the day, but they had the rudiments of an English education of that time. They owned few books and had little time for study, but they did know the means at hand and how to use them. With only the Statutes of the State for a guide they operated and maintained an efficient local government.

With rare judgment they administered justice in the many phases of pioneer life to the satisfaction of the people. Without money, but with the willing labor of the citizens they opened roads. To the thoughtless reader their records may seem crude, but to a zealous student of the times and conditions under which the pioneers of Nicholas County labored, their faded pages of coarse paper, inscribed with a quill pen, etch an eloquent saga of rugged backwoodsmen whose strong hands and iron determination wrought the foundation of our government in the wilderness.

CHAPTER IV

Transportation, Post Office, Mails

TRANSPORTATION was the chief difficulty encountered by the first settlers of Nicholas County. On his way to Point Pleasant in 1774, General Andrew Lewis cut out the "Baggage Trail" that passed through Dogwood Gap, the present site of Ansted, over Gauley Mountain, down Rich Creek, down Gauley River to the mouth of Twenty Mile Creek and up Bell Creek and down Campbells Creek to the Kanawha River. Before this time the present area of the county was reached only over an Indian warpath or by game trails.

A few years later a rough wagon road had been opened from Fort Union by the way of Muddy Creek over Sewell Mountain to Bowyer's Ferry on New River and across the river by way of Vandalia and over Cotton Hill. This road was completed to the "Boat Yards" by 1790. Through Greenbrier it was known as the "Koontz Road" from the contractor.

In 1821 the construction of the James River and Kanawha Turnpike was commenced. This road followed about the present location of U. S. Route 60. It traversed Nicholas County from the Greenbrier line at Dogwood Gap to the Kanawha line at Gauley Bridge a distance of 20 miles. The right of way for the road was condemned by proceedings in the County Court of

Nicholas County through some farms owned by citizens of Nicholas County, A bridge was built at Kincaid's Ferry at the mouth of Gauley, costing $1800.00. On July 11, 1826 this bridge was destroyed by an incendiary fire charged to persons interested in the operation of the ferry. It was rebuilt in 1828 and was in use till condemned in 1849, and a new bridge erected in 1850. This third bridge was burned in 1861 in a raid by Confederate General Wise. The transportation of freight and mail to our settlements was very greatly improved by the opening of the James River and Kanawha Turnpike.

At the May Term 1818 William Simms, Joseph McNutt, Samuel Neil, Edward Rion and David Lilly were appointed "to view a way for a road from Spencer Hill's at the mouth of Twenty Mile Creek down Gauley River to the mouth of Scrabble Creek"; and on the same day Samuel Wiseman, James Scaggs, James Lykins and Samuel Masterson were appointed "to view the way for a road from Kincaid's Ferry to the Dogwood Knob". These were the first public roads established in the new county. They gave connection with the old "Wagon Road" and aided greatly in the matter of transportation. From this time on for several years the County Court gave much time and attention to the pressing necessity of opening up roads. In this work the Court adopted a very efficient system. Citizens asking for roads were required to file their petition to the Court. If the Court found the road could be established, a commission of "viewers" was named who under oath made a report on the proposed road. If approved and established, a "surveyor", (later termed "overseer"), was named by the

Court and took an oath as such officer and was authorized to open up and maintain the road, and to do this he was given a company of laborers by the Court who for a certain number of days fixed by the Court must work under the surveyor at his call. These laborers furnished their own tools, as directed by the surveyor, and also supplied their own food. Any one failing to work on call of the surveyor was subject to a fine for each day he lost. The surveyors were required to patrol the roads and keep them passable and could call on their men for special work. For their services the Court made the following order: "June 1, 1819, ordered that the overseers of the roads in the County of Nicholas be allowed for their services as such for every day they have served six and one-fourth cents."

No restriction was placed on the grade, but all roads were required to be opened twelve feet in width, and the "digging when necessary must be ten feet wide".

There was no road up Peters Creek from Drennen to Summersville, except a "bridle path" till after the organization of the county. The road from Summersville to Hughes Ferry a distance of four miles was opened in 1919 by ten men working seventeen days each.

The early roads usually followed the streams or game trails, were narrow, poorly graded and crossed the streams by fords or ferries. The first ferry in what is now Nicholas County was maintained by William McClung over Gauley River a short distance above the present bridge, and was authorized by the County Court of Greenbrier County. Later when McClung lost the ferry site in his famous law suit with Edward Hughes it became Hughes's Ferry. Daniel Brock, Sr., established the second ferry over Gauley at the mouth of Muddlety about 1820.

In 1848 the Gauley Bridge and Weston Turnpike, passing through the county on the same general route of State Route 39 and U. S. Route 19, was authorized as a State road. This road was completed in 1850 and its connection with the James River and Kanawha Turnpike gave Nicholas County systematic transportation of freight and mails from the eastern cities. Other roads were now opened connecting with the two State roads, and from mere bridle paths narrow wagon roads were gradually opened throughout the county, crossing the streams without bridges and often obstructed by fallen timber and sometimes impassable by reason of mud and flood waters. Even the Gauley Bridge and Weston Turnpike was at times impassable for lack of bridges over Twenty Mile and Peter's Creek, and freight and mails delayed on the main highway of the county. After the Gauley Bridge and Weston Turnpike came into use wagons began to be pretty generally employed on this highway, though sometimes it became necessary to employ four or even six horses to draw a loaded wagon over this road.

The opening of these two state highways marked an era of improvement in conditions generally in Nicholas County. The huge Conestoga wagons were soon bringing great quantities of freight westward and carrying back eastward the merchantable products of the new settlements.

In 1827 the first stage coaches began to operate be-

Transportation, Post Office, Mails 71

tween Lewisburg and Charleston. By 1831 the Post Office Department let mail contracts for mails over these lines. In 1832 the stages carried daily mails and the passenger traffic crowded all conveyances with emigrants to the Kanawha and Ohio valleys. The road also opened the way for driving cattle, sheep and hogs to the eastern markets. One of our historians states that in one year it was estimated that 60,000 hogs passed over this highway between the Kanawha Valley and Richmond. The immense traffic required many stations for the stages to change teams and numerous taverns and boarding houses were operated to accommodate the passengers and teamsters. The increased demand for grain to feed the live stock of the drivers and the teams of the stage drivers, and the call for farm and dairy products to supply the tables of the taverns created a ready cash market for the citizens far and wide along the highway. Although the James River and Kanawha Turnpike traversed only the short distance from Dogwood Gap to Gauley Bridge through Nicholas County the entire county realized the benefits of its traffic in the market for their live stock, and in the increased quantity and lower prices of merchandise now coming to them from the eastern cities.

It may be a matter of interest to note here that many famous persons used this busy highway. Among the prominent passengers Henry Clay was a great favorite along the route on his way to Washington as a United States senator. He often stopped at the tavern and stage station of Colonel George Alderson at Lookout. President Jackson in 1832, came by boat from Nashville to Charleston, spent the night there and took stage over the turnpike to Washington. Chief Justice John Marshall passed over the road while Hawks Nest was in Nicholas County, spent the night at McVey's tavern and measured the altitude of the famous cliff from New River. Maury's geographies gave it the name of Marshall's Pillar, but the old name prevailed. In 1843 Ex-President John Quincy Adams on his way to Cincinnati to lay the corner stone of the Cincinnati Astronomical Observatory traveled by stage over the James River and Kanawha Turnpike.

By 1843 travel on the turnpike began to fall off owing to the steamboats now in competition on the Kanawha and Ohio Rivers that diverted trade to Wheeling and Pittsburgh. By 1860 traffic had greatly diminished and the decline of the turnpike was completed by the ravages of the Civil War. Busy life along the road never returned, and traffic over this route only came back when the Chesapeake and Ohio Railroad was completed in 1873. This road and its branches brought an entirely new system of transportation to our county, and trade turned largely to the west, and Cincinnati, Wheeling and Pittsburgh began to supplant former trade with the eastern cities.

In the four years after the Civil War the roads were neglected and became almost impassable in many localities. Under the new State of West Virginia improvement of the roads came slowly. Under the Constitution of 1863 and the road laws thereunder the opening and maintenance of roads was dependent upon the labor of all able-bodied male citizens between the age of twenty-one and fifty. The townships were divided into road precincts and surveyors of the precincts appointed by the

Board of Supervisors for a two year term. The Board of Supervisors was authorized to lay a county road tax and citizens were permitted to pay this tax in labor at the rate of one dollar and twenty-five cents a day.

The Constitution of 1872 and laws that followed also adopted the old pioneer system of road building by the enforced labor of the citizens. A road tax was permitted and citizens could work out the tax as before. The restored County Court system had full authority over the roads. Roads now were required to be thirty feet in width and on a grade of not more than five degrees unless the court specifically allowed a greater grade.

The Gauley Bridge and Western Turnpike became the principal artery of transportation for the county, and was much used by the citizens of Braxton and Webster in hauling salt and other farm necessities from the Kanawha Valley. This road was macadamized but the soft sandstone used in the work soon disintegrated under the wheels of the heavy wagons and the surface became soft and muddy. To keep the road in repair resort was had to tolls. The road was turned over to the counties by the Legislature and a general rate of tolls authorized, but allowing these rates to be either increased or decreased by the County Courts. The following schedule of toll rates was fixed by statute:

"Single horse or mule with rider............ 5 cents,
Led horse or mule......................... 3 "
Two-wheeled carriage .... 7 "
Four-wheeled carriage drawn by one horse.. 10 "
Four-wheeled carriage drawn by two or more
    horses for each .... 3 "
Cart or wagon with tires over four inches... 7 "

And for each animal drawing such vehicle..	3	"
Cart or wagon with tire over six inches for each animal	2	"
For each sheep or hog	¼	"
For each head of cattle	½	"
For all vehicles and horses to and from funerals no charge		

County Courts were permitted by law to exempt persons and their horses and vehicles from paying toll to and from mills. Under this provision of the law the Court by its order exempted all vehicles, horses and persons who passed the gates in attending divine worship or funerals from paying toll. Later this exemption was extended to citizens going to and from grist mills with grain to be ground for family use. Families were allowed to contract for the payment of toll by the quarter, and the gate-keepers were authorized to make such contracts. Tolls collected were required to be settled quarterly with the clerk of the county court and collectors were allowed 12% of all collections for their services. Toll gates were established at the residence of James Williams near Summersville, at the residence of Nathan Van Bibber, near Gilboa, at the residence of M. B. Mason, top of Little Elk Mountain, at the residence of John Lloyd and at the residence of Miletus Simms.

By 1880 the Gauley Bridge and Weston Turnpike from Summersville to the Fayette County line had become the life-line of transportation in the county. Over this route merchants obtained the stock of goods and the bulk of the county's mail came this way for distribution over the various star routes from the county seat. Farmers transported their products over this road to the coal

Transportation, Post Office, Mails 75

mines and salt furnaces of the Kanawha Valley. For almost two decades the County Court wrestled with the problem of making the old turnpike fit for year-round traffic. In addition to a special road tax, the proceeds from the toll gates were also applied. The Court even tried the experiment of letting to private contract the upkeep of the road in sections. Agreement was later made with Fayette County to keep the road in repair from Twenty Mile to Gauley Bridge and share the expense of a bridge over Twenty Mile Creek. At the same time a bridge was built over Meadow River at Millers Ferry at joint expense of the counties. Cherry River was bridged at Holcomb about this time. The old structures still stand as exhibits of the crude concrete work at that time.

Citizens on the south side of Gauley River had for several years petitioned for bridges over Gauley River. In 1902 the bridge at Hughes Ferry was erected at a cost of $7200.00, and in 1904 the bridge at Brock's Ferry was built at a first cost of $9225.00, but the correction of a faulty pier on the west bank of the river raised the cost to something over $10,000.00.

The coming of the automobile about this time demanded better roads. The first step in the new order of road-making was the act of the Legislature of 1913 establishing the "Bureau of Roads", followed by the proclamation of the Governor appointing "Good Roads Day". Eager citizens gave time and labor in response and in 1921 the "State Road Commission" took over the public roads of the State. Progress at first was slow. Old roads must be surveyed, re-located and graded, machinery must be found to take the place of pick and shovel hand labor.

Slowly the improvement in road building reached Nicholas County. Twenty years after the State Road Commission took over the public roads U. S. Route 19 was opened from Belva through Summersville to the Braxton County line, and by 1946 the county had hard surface roads connecting Summersville with the county seats of adjoining counties.

The records of the State Road Commission for 1952 show 620 miles of public roads mapped for Nicholas County. The Primary Roads of the county include U. S. Route 19 extending from the Fayette County line at Nallen through Summersville to the Braxton County line, a distance of 36.98 miles; State Route 16 from the Fayette County line at Dixie to the Clay County line at Bentree, a distance of 2.6 miles; State Route 39 from the Fayette County line at Belva by way of Summersville, Nettie and Richwood to the Greenbrier County line on the North Fork of Cherry River, a distance of 21.31 miles; State Route 20 from the Webster County line near Camden-on-Gauley by way of Craigsville, Fenwick, Nettie and Carl to the Greenbrier line, a distance of 34.16 miles; State Route 41 from its junction with U. S. Route 19 two miles north of Summersville to Craigsville, a distance of 12.36 miles; State Route 43 from its junction with U. S. Route 19 at the Twin Churches on Muddlety to its junction with State Route 41 at the head of Persinger, a distance of 6.14 miles, aggregating a total of 138.76 miles of primary roads in the county.

The Secondary Roads are listed as 108.74 miles of "black-top" surface, 164.23 miles of "all-weather" graveled roads, and 108.20 miles of unimproved roads. These measurements exclude all overlaps, as where State Route 41 coincides with U. S. Route 19 from two miles north of Summersville to the Fayette County line at Nallen, and State Route 39 follows State Route 20 from Nettie to Fenwick.

If by a determined act of the imgination we of the present generation could blot out our postoffices and daily mails and realize our situation if we were deprived of this daily service that brings the world to our doors, we could then fully appreciate the isolated condition of our pioneer ancestors who were without even the beginnings of this intimate system of communication. No other government agency is so closely in touch with our every day life.

Greenbrier County was organized in 1777, yet its territory occupying about one-fifth of the present area of our state was without any mail service until the 4th day of October, 1794 when Greenbrier Court House was made a post office with Jacob Skiles postmaster. At that time the county had a population of something over 6000. The Morrises, Simmses, Youngs, and Johnsons, then living on Gauley and Peters Creek and the Cottles, Strawns Givenses and others in the Glades of Strouds Creek, had no communication with the outside world save from some one coming to them from the eastern settlements. We may be sure little or no mail reached them in their cabin homes from this post office seventy miles or more distant reached only by trails through a wilderness. Six years later on October 5, 1800, the new County of Kanawha cut off from Greenbrier, was given the post office of Kanawha Court House, with Edward Graham its first post master. From Lewisburg to Kanawha Court House mail was now carried on horseback once every two weeks, and a post office was now a few miles nearer to some of our settlers.

A letter written and mailed at that date would have been quite an undertaking. In appearance it would bear little resemblance to our present day missives. Written on one side of coarse unruled paper, the sheet was folded to conceal the writing, somewhat in the form of an envelope as we now have it, and fastened with tape or wax.

The address was placed on the letter and when received at the office of the addressee, the postmaster there calculated the postage, which usually amounted to from ten cents to twenty five cents, wrote this amount on the envelope and when this postage was paid delivered the letter. Stamps were not in use until July 1, 1847, and envelopes were unknown until ten years later.

The first post office in the new county of Nicholas was authorized as Nicholas Court House on January 7, 1820, and Robert Kelly was the first postmaster. Mail was carried by horseback once a week from Gauley Bridge, although this route was not established as a post road until 1827, and the carrier made complaint that the road was not twenty feet in width as the law required.

The next office in the county was authorized at the farm of Philip Metzker on the James River and Gauley Turnpike near the present village of Victor. Here Metzker had a stage station and operated a toll gate and a tavern. The post office was named Metzker and Henry

Metzker was the postmaster appointed on December 18, 1826. On May 5, 1827 the name of the office was changed to Mountain Cove. When this part of Nicholas County was included in the new county of Fayette in 1831, Clement Vaughan, who had purchased the Metzker property became postmaster at Mountain Cove.

Drennen post office on its present site was next established, and Jacob Drennen was appointed its first postmaster on April 25, 1831.

A road having been cut out by way of Strouds Glades to Pocahontas County, a post office named Strouds was located there, and on January 8, 1833, J. C. Warren was appointed postmaster.

Birch River post office was established June 4, 1840, and George W. Brown was the first postmaster.

John R. Vaughan, son of Clement Vaughan, and Fred Kessler came from Fayette County and opened a store in partnership near the home of John Hamilton where the county was organized. A post office was obtained and named for Kessler and the crossing of the roads there, Kesslers Cross Lanes. John R. Vaughan was appointed postmaster on April 19, 1854 and for nearly forty years kept the post office in his general store.

Hookersville post office, named for Levi J. Hooker, a large land owner in the vicinity, was established May 7, 1856, and John W. Powell was named the first postmaster.

After the Civil War when roads were opened up to most parts of the county and other post offices created, the mail service somewhat improved. A few letters, postal cards and weekly newspapers made up the meager contents of the mail bag that came in each week to the outlying offices, the weather permitting.

By 1880 daily mail service was begun between Gauley Bridge and Summersville. The mail was carried by horseback, and the schedule was arranged for the mail to leave Summersville one day go by way of Kesslers Cross Lanes, reach the turnpike at Drennen and continue to Gauley Bridge, and return by the turnpike to Summersville; the next day the process was reversed.

Some ten years later the volume of mail had increased to the extent that a buckboard and team was employed in the service. Gradually a limited passenger service was included in the carrying of the mail. The trip from Summersville to Gauley Bridge over the rough unpaved road required a full day, and two carriages were employed. One left Summersville in the morning, the other started from Gauley Bridge; they met at the "Half-way Place", now Lyonville, at noon for rest and refreshment, and then returned to their stations. This system continued till the advent of the automobile and the railroad that brought the mail to Belva. A combined mail and passenger service soon developed.

Rural Mail Delivery was authoirzed by act of Congress to be put into operation October 1, 1896. This was a radical change in delivering mail and was slowly developed. It was almost two decades before Nicholas County fully enjoyed rural delivery. Now the rural post roads are lined with mail boxes and the post office is at the front door of our homes.

The greatest extension of the mail service, however, came with the Parcel Post Act, in effect January 1, 1913.

Soon the great mail order houses were flooding the country homes with their illustrated catalogs, offering a market at their doors that hitherto only the urban citizens had enjoyed. Clothing, household and kitchen gadgets, groceries, medicines, and every imaginable product found in the city department stores were offered through this new method of purchasing. The parcel post law not only brought a revolution in our postal system but it brought a great change in the home life of our county.

Other features of the postal service as registration and insurance of letters and mailable articles, special delivery, money orders, postal savings etc. give the citizens of our county today, such manifold service as was not dreamed of a few years ago.

By railway, steamship and airplane mail may now be sent to all parts of the world from any post office in Nicholas County.

The telephone was invented in 1875. About fifteen years later C. P. Dorr and others had a line constructed between Webster Springs and Summersville. It was a single wire strung through the forests on trees and along the roadside on the highway between the stations. Service was uncertain because of the poor construction and maintenance. Later L. N. Alderson and others took over the line and it was extended to Gauley Bridge. The service was somewhat improved but still not dependable. At the December Term, 1905, the County Court had a telephone placed in the office of the Prosecuting Attorney by this line.

The Citizens Telephone Company, a co-operative organization formed in Fayette County, was extended to

Nicholas County about 1909. The line was constructed through Wilderness District to Summersville, extended to Kentucky District and from Summersville by way of Gad and Cross Lanes to Poe. A switchboard was maintained at Summersville. Each person joining the company paid for his telephone and aided in the construction of the line in his vicinity. This line provided connection with long distance lines and gave good local service. These local phones continued in use till the coming of the Chesapeake and Potomac Telephone Company in 1915.

Although the telegraph was in use since 1844 it was of little benefit to our citizens until telephone lines connected with telegraph stations. The only Western Union telegraph office in the county is at Richwood, but messages are readily transferred to other telegraph offices by telephone.

Nicholas County was long without railroads within its borders. The Baltimore and Ohio Railroad was extended from Clarksburg to Richwood in 1901. About the same time the Chesapeake and Ohio built branch lines from Gauley Bridge to Bentree on Bell Creek and to Vaughan on Twenty Mile. These lines were constructed for the coal mines but for a time gave passenger service. In 1906 the Kanawha and Michigan Railroad was extended from Gauley Bridge to Swiss and for several years carried passengers. The road now is a part of the New York Central system and has recently been extended up Peters Creek and Camp Fork as a coal bearing road. The Nicholas, Fayette and Greenbrier Railroad from Swiss up Gauley and Meadow Rivers to the Quinwood coal field has recently been extended into Nicholas County to coal mines on the headwaters of Hominy Creek. The Baltimore and Ohio in 1945 built a branch line from Allingdale by way of Tioga and down Muddlety Creek to within three miles of Summersville. The Baltimore and Ohio has also extended down Gauley to near the mouth of Persinger Creek.

The Reynolds Transportation Company that succeeded C. J. Bell's line, gives daily passenger service connecting all parts of the county with the railroads and the Greyhound Bus Lines. A "Highway Post Office" makes two trips daily between Charleston and Summersville distributing and receiving mail at post offices along the way.

Landing fields for airplanes are now provided in the county and private owned planes are to be seen flying over the hills where a generation ago were only trails and dirt roads, and travel was by foot or on horseback.

Radio and television brings to our homes current news and scenes day by day from all parts of the world.

Freight transportation by truck over State Route 39, and over U. S. Route 19 gives efficient service to the county from outside factories and wholesale dealers, and affords transportation for farm products to market.

What a world of change since the days of our pioneers who without roads or mails to give them touch with the outside world conquered the wilderness and made possible the comforts and privileges we now enjoy!

CHAPTER V

Local Government—Virginia and West Virginia

UNDER Virginia from 1818 to 1863, a period of forty five years, Nicholas County was governed locally by the County Court system as shown in the chapter on Organization and Administration.

At its organization Nicholas County was placed in the Eighteenth Circuit of the Superior Court of Law and Chancery with Randolph, Harrison, Lewis, Mason and Cabell Counties.

James Allen was our first judge and held the first term of court at the house of James Robinson, May 26, 1818. The record of his term which ended October 14, 1830, is well preserved in the office of the circuit court.

Edwin S. Duncan succeeded Judge Allen. His term was from May 25, 1831 to April 11, 1848. Judge Duncan was a native of Barbour County and a strong advocate of a system of free schools.

Allen Taylor, an exchange judge, held the April Term, 1832, and *Edward Johnson,* also an exchange judge, held the September Term, 1842, for Judge Duncan.

George H. Lee, succeeded Judge Duncan as regular judge of the circuit. His term began September 7, 1848 and ended September 11, 1849.

Nathan Dunbar succeeded Judge Lee and sat as judge from April 1, 1850 to September 1, 1853.

In 1850 Nicholas County was changed to the Fifteenth Judicial Circuit with Giles, Mason, Raleigh, Wyoming, Logan, Boone, Fayette and Clay Counties.

Edward B. Bailey succeeded Judge Dunbar and sat as judge from 1854 to 1859.

Evermont Ward, an exchange judge, held the September Term, 1860, the only term of court held that year.

David McComas, also an exchange judge, held the session of the court under Virginia, April 7-11, 1861.

Evermont Ward, who had held the September Term, 1860, held the last court under the Commonwealth of Virginia, beginning September 6, 1861 and closing September 9, 1861. On the first day he empaneled the following grand jury: John W. Hamilton, foreman, David Eagle, Michael Curran, Lewis M. Huff, Robert Whitman, John McCue, Jr., Rufus Bobbitt, Joseph H. Hutchinson, John Tyree, Samuel Rader, James B. Burroughs, Frank Duffy, Owen Duffy, Allen McClung, Peter Duffy, Andrew H. McCoy, Wm. O. Grose, James R. Wilson, and Wm. M. Odell. He then entered the following order:

> "The state of war now existing between the Confederate & United States of America and the Commonwealth being now invaded and the Public Enemy now in the adjoining county, it may be that the Records and Papers of the office may be endangered. To prevent such a consequence John A. Hamilton, Deputy Clerk of this Court, is hereby given special charge of all the Books, Papers, Records and Judicial Proceedings of this Court and is hereby authorized & directed on the approach of the Public Enemy to remove them or cause them to be removed to some place of security until the enemy

shall be driven from the County and they may be safely returned".

Court recessed until Monday the 9th, when the grand jury returned two indictments: James J. Bryant, Assault and Battery; Ellis Boggs and James A. Boggs; Treason. Court adjourned and the next day, September 10, 1861, the Battle of Carnefix was fought.

Robert Hamilton was clerk of the Court. He was appointed to this office by Judge Allen at his first session in 1818 and held the office till his death in 1863.

In order to understand the situation in Nicholas County at this time through the Civil war and even many years thereafter, it is necessary to look at the political situation in Virginia.

Governor John Letcher called the General Assembly of Virginia in special session January 7, 1861, to consider the question of secession from the Union. A bill was passed calling for a convention of the people of Virginia. The convention was to consist of 152 members, forty-six of whom were from the counties now comprising West Virginia. B. W. Byrne was the delegate chosen to represent Braxton and Nicholas Counties.

This convention met at Richmond on February 13, 1861. On the 17th the Ordinance of Secession was passed—88 yeas, 55 nays. The western delegates who had voted against secession hastened home. On May 13, 1861, an informal meeting was held at Wheeling, known as the "First Wheeling Convention". It recommended a convention of elected delegates to be held at Wheeling on June 11, 1861. On that day seventy-seven delegates from thirty-nine counties assembled in the "Second

Wheeling Convention". This convention proceeded to reorganize the Virginia government out of the loyal counties, vacating the offices and taking possession of the whole machinery of the old State, under the name of the government of Virginia. The convention elected Francis H. Pierpont Governor of Virginia, and he called the legislature under the reorganized government to meet in Wheeling on July 1, 1861. On July 9th this legislature proceeded to complete the organization of the restored government. Waitman T. Willey and John S. Carlile were chosen as senators replacing Senators Hunter and Mason who had vacated their seats as senators from Virginia when the state seceded. An election was held in October and delegates chosen to a convention to prepare a constitution for the proposed new state. This convention met in Wheeling on November 26, 1861. A constitution was written for the new State of West Virginia and on the 4th Thursday in April, 1862 was ratified by a popular vote of 18,062 to 514. On May 13, 1862 the General Assembly of the restored government of Virginia, by formal legislative action, gave consent to the formation of the new state, and on June 20, 1863 West Virginia became the 35th state of the American Union.

Under the Constitution of 1863 West Virginia rearranged all judicial circuits. Nicholas County was placed in the Fifth Judicial Circuit with Lewis, Upshur, Braxton, Webster and Clay Counties.

Robert Irvin was the first judge of the Fifth Circuit. His term extended from 1865 to 1869. He held his first court at Summersville in the old clerk's office on October

16, 1865. The first grand jury under the new state was empaneled: W. P. Rucker, foreman, Alexander Groves, Hiram Pierson, Alexander McClung, J. R. Ramsey, Andrew W. Dorsey, John F. Dorsey, Alexander Williams, Joseph McClung, Anthony McClung, John J. Craig, William Hill, John Rader, George W. Backhouse, Benjamin F. Backhouse, John Groves, Franklin Groves, John S. Malcom and Andrew Williams. The grand jury was in session for three days. Partisan feeling was intense. Numerous indictments against southern sympathizers and soldiers were found.

Homer A. Holt, Joseph A. Alderson, P. B. Wethered, J. J. Baxter, and A. C. Snyder were admitted to the practice of law. Kanawha County jail was adopted as the jail of the county was in bad repair. All County Court cases were removed to the Circuit Court and docketed for hearing. The record of Judge Irvin's term shows most of the litigation arose from the animosities growing out of the Civil War.

Nathaniel Harrison succeeded Judge Irvin. Nicholas was now placed in the 7th Judicial Circuit, composed of Pocahontas, Greenbrier, Nicholas and Monroe Counties. Judge Harrison was bitterly partisan and dictatorial on the bench. In 1870 a petition was filed with the Legislature asking for his impeachment on the ground of official misconduct and neglect of duty. He resigned his office before the date set for his trial.

J. M. McWhorter succeeded Harrison in 1870 and served until 1873. His term was shortened by the rearrangement of the judicial circuits. Nicholas now was in the 8th Judicial Circuit with Braxton, Clay, Fayette, Greenbrier, Monroe, Pocahontas, and Summers.

Henry L. Gillespie, exchange judge from the 13th Judicial Circuit, held the May Term 1871, for Judge McWhorter.

Homer A. Holt followed Judge McWhorter, in the newly established 8th Judicial Circuit. His term was from 1873 to 1881. In 1890 he was appointed to the Supreme Court of West Virginia and served on that court six years.

Henry Brannon, whose term was from 1881 to 1889, was judge of the 11th Judicial Circuit composed of the counties of Upshur, Lewis, Nicholas, Webster and Braxton. Judge Brannon was elected to the Supreme Court of West Virginia and served from 1889 to 1905. He is considered one of the ablest jurists to occupy the bench of that tribunal.

William G. Bennett succeeded Judge Brannon and served two terms from 1889 to 1905. He has the distinction of never being reversed by the Supreme Court in any of his decisions in Nicholas County.

J. C. McWhorter was the successor of Judge Bennett in the 12th Judicial Circuit, in which Nicholas had been placed with Webster, Upshur and Braxton Counties. His term was from 1905 to 1913.

Jake Fisher succeeded Judge McWhorter for the term from 1913 to 1921. In 1920 the 12th Judicial Circuit was formed of Fayette and Nicholas Counties, and Judge Fisher was transferred to the 14th Judicial Circuit composed of Braxton, Webster, Clay and Gilmer Counties. He remained judge of this circuit until his death in 1951.

J. W. Eary succeeded Judge Fisher for two terms in the 12th Judicial Circuit, from 1921 to 1937.

H. E. Dillon followed Judge Eary on the bench of the 12th Judicial Circuit for the term from 1937 to 1945.

R. J. Thrift succeeded Judge Dillon for the term from 1945 to 1953.

Charles L. Garvin was elected to succeed R. J. Thrift and began his term January 1, 1953.

The Constitution of 1863 changed the style of the legislative body from "The General Assembly" to "The Legislature". The judicial system of a Supreme Court, Circuit Courts and Justices was retained, but the County Court was abolished. In its stead was "The Board of Supervisors". The districts into which the county was divided were designated "townships". Each township elected a supervisor, clerk, surveyor of roads, overseer of the poor, one or more justices and one or more constables. The county officers were a sheriff, prosecuting attorney, assessor and recorder. The Board of Supervisors was composed of the several district supervisors and the Recorder performed the duties of the clerk of that body. The state was divided into three congressional districts, ten senatorial districts and five delegate districts. Nicholas was placed in the Third Congressional District, the Fifth Senatorial District and the Third Delegate District.

The First Legislature met at Wheeling on June 20, 1863. Dr. Anthony Rader was the delegate from Nicholas. At this session the state seal was adopted, the State motto: *"Montani semper liberi"* was also adopted. The Auditor's office reported Nicholas County and several other border counties had no sheriffs for the year 1863, "because of the dangers incident thereto".

The Second Legislature met at Wheeling January 10, 1864. Dr. Anthony Rader represented the Third Delegate District composed of Nicholas, Braxton and Clay Counties.

The Third Legislature met at Wheeling January 17, 1865. Benjamin L. Stephenson of Clay was the delegate from the Third Delegate District.

The Fourth Legislature met at Wheeling on January 16, 1866. Dr. Anthony Rader again was the delegate from the Third District.

The Fifth Legislature met at Wheeling January 15, 1867 and James Grose of Clay County represented the Third Delegate District.

The Sixth Legislature met at Wheeling January 21, 1868, and William Waggy of Braxton County was the delegate from the Third District.

The Seventh Legislature met at Wheeling on January 19, 1869. Thomas G. Putnam of Nicholas County was the delegate from the Third District.

The Eighth Legislature met at Wheeling January 18, 1870. Thomas G. Putnam came as a delegate from the Third Delegate District, till he was unseated by Dr. Anthony Rader in a contest of the election.

The Ninth Legislature met at Charleston on January 17, 1871. The delegate districts had been abolished but Nicholas County had no delegate in this session. On the 23d day of February, 1871, the Legislature passed a resolution submitting to the voters of the state the question of calling a Constitutional Convention. An election was held on the 4th Tuesday in August, 1871 and resulted in a favor of calling the convention. Delegates to the convention equal in number to the members of the Legislature were elected and met as the Second Constitutional Convention in the old South Methodist Church in Charleston on January 16, 1872. Nicholas County was not represented in this convention.

The Tenth Legislature met at Charleston on January 16, 1872—the same day of the meeting of the Constitutional Convention—Dr. Anthony Rader was the delegate from Nicholas County. This was the last session under the first Constitution.

The Constitutional Convention was in session eighty-four days. The new constitution, like its predecessor of 1863, exhibits the marks of partisanship of the period.

Among the principal changes in the organic law were the terms of state officers, voting by ballot, biennial meetings of the legislature, return to "districts" for "townships", and to the County Court in place of The Board of Supervisors.

The Eleventh Legislature—first under the new constitution—convened at Charleston November 16, 1872. Nicholas County was not represented in the House of Delegates. Winston Shelton of Nicholas County was in the Senate. John D. Alderson of Nicholas County was Sergeant at Arms in the Senate. This legislature was in session from November 16, 1872 to April 7, 1873, and in special session from October 20, 1873 to December 22, 1873, a total of 205 days. Many acts under the Constitution of 1863 were repealed and new laws enacted.

The Twelfth Legislature convened at Charleston on

the second Wednesday in January, 1875, the date fixed by statute for its meeting, and continued in session till December 23, 1875. Nicholas County had no senator, D. D. Dix of Nicholas County was the delegate, and John D. Alderson continued as Sergeant at Arms in the Senate.

The Thirteenth Legislature met at Wheeling on the statutory date, 1877. Nicholas County had no senator. Henry Samples of Clay County was the delegate from the 5th Delegate District formed from Nicholas, Webster and Clay Counties. John D. Alderson was continued as Sergeant at Arms in the Senate.

The Fourteenth Legislature met at Wheeling on the statutory date 1879. Nicholas County had no senator. Winston Shelton of Nicholas County was the delegate from the 5th Senatorial District, and John D. Alderson Sergeant at Arms in the Senate.

The Fifteenth Legislature met at Wheeling on the statutory date, 1881. Nicholas County had no senator; Charles M. Dodrill of Webster County was the delegate from the 5th Delegate District and John D. Alderson Sergeant at Arms in the Senate.

The Sixteenth Legislature met at Wheeling on the lawful date, 1883. Nicholas County had no senator, David McQueen was the delegate, and John D. Alderson was Clerk of the Senate.

The Seventeenth Legislature met at Wheeling on the statutory date 1885. Nicholas had no senator. H. C. Callison was the delegate from Nicholas County, and John D. Alderson was Clerk of the Senate.

The Eighteenth Legislature met at Charleston on the

statutory date 1887. Nicholas County had no senator. John E. Peck was the delegate from Nicholas County. The permanent location of the capital had been settled by popular vote. Wheeling was the capital from 1863 to 1870; Charleston from 1870 to 1875; Wheeling again from 1875 to 1885.

The Nineteenth Legislature met on the statutory date, 1889. Nicholas County had no senator. John E. Peck was the delegate from Nicholas County.

The Twentieth Legislature met on the statutory date, 1891. Nicholas County had no senator. Thomas C. Brown was the delegate from Nicholas County.

The Twenty-first Legislature met on the statutory date 1893. John E. Peck of Nicholas County was the senator from the 9th Senatorial District and F. L. McGee was the delegate from Nicholas County.

The Twenty-second Legislature met on the statutory date 1895. John E. Peck was in the senate and John D. Groves was the delegate from Nicholas County.

The Twenty-third Legislature met on the statutory date 1897. Nicholas County had no senator. John D. Groves was again the delegate from Nicholas County.

The Twenty-fourth Legislature met on the statutory date 1899. Nicholas County had no senator. R. L. Walker was the delegate from Nicholas County.

The Twenty-fifth Legislature met on the statutory date 1901. A. J. Horan of Nicholas County was senator from the 9th Senatorial District and John D. Alderson was the delegate from Nicholas County.

The Twenty-sixth Legislature met on the statutory

date, 1903. Nicholas County had no senator; I. A. Dix was the delegate from Nicholas County.

The Twenty-seventh Legislature met on the statutory date, 1905. Nicholas County had no senator. W. D. Huff was the delegate from Nicholas County.

The Twenty-eighth Legislature met on the statutory date, 1907. Nicholas County had no senator. L. C. Williams was the delegate from Nicholas County.

The Twenty-ninth Legislature met on the statutory date, 1909. Nicholas County had no senator. Philip Hinkle was the delegate from Nicholas County, after ousting L. C. Williams in an election contest.

The Thirtieth Legislature met on the statutory date, 1911. Nicholas County had no senator. F. N. Alderson was the delegate from Nicholas County. Mr. Alderson introduced the bill establishing Nicholas County High School at this session.

The Thirty-first Legislature met on the statutory date, 1913. Dr. James McClung of Nicholas County was in the senate from the 9th Senatorial District. G. G. Duff was the delegate from Nicholas County.

The Thirty-second Legislature met on the statutory date, 1915. S. C. Dotson was the delegate from Nicholas County and Dr. James McClung was in the senate.

The Thirty-third Legislature met on the statutory date, 1917. H. G. Vencill of Nicholas County was in the senate from the 9th Senatorial District, and W. G. Graves was the delegate from Nicholas County.

The Thirty-fourth Legislature met on the statutory date, 1919. H. G. Vencill was in the senate and Jettes Mollohan was the delegate from Nicholas County.

The Thirty-fifth Legislature met on the statutory date, 1921. E. F. Ramsey was the delegate from Nicholas County. Nicholas had no senator.

The Thirty-sixth Legislature met on the statutory date, 1923. Nicholas County had no senator. S. R. King was the delegate from Nicholas County.

The Thirty-seventh Legislature met on the statutory date, 1925. E. P. Alderson was in the senate and S. R. King was the delegate from Nicholas County.

The Thirty-eighth Legislature met on the statutory date, 1927. E. P. Alderson was in the senate and E. D. Dorsey was the delegate from Nicholas County.

The Thirty-ninth Legislature met on the statutory date, 1929. P. N. Wiseman of Nicholas County was in the senate from the 9th Senatorial District and J. E. Brown was the delegate from Nicholas County.

The Fortieth Legislature met on the statutory date, 1931. P. N. Wiseman was in the senate and E. S. Frame was the delegate from Nicholas County.

The Forty-first Legislature met on the statutory date, 1933. P. N. Wiseman was in the senate and J. A. Neal was the delegate from Nicholas County. Mr. Wiseman introduced the bill creating Carnefix Battlefield a State Park.

The Forty-second Legislature met on the statutory date, 1935. P. N. Wiseman was in the senate and J. A. Neal was the delegate from Nicholas County.

The Forty-third Legislature met on the statutory date, 1937. Nicholas had no senator. J. A. Neal was the delegate from Nicholas County. This legislature took Nicholas County from the 9th Senatorial District in

Local Government—Virginia and West Virginia 97

which it had been since 1872 and placed it in the 13th Senatorial District with Braxton, Webster, Pocahontas, Randolph and Pendleton Counties.

The Forty-fourth Legislature met on the statutory date, 1939. Nicholas County had no senator. J. A. Neal was the delegate from the county.

The Forty-fifth Legislature met on the statutory date, 1941. Nicholas County had no senator. G. G. Duff was the delegate from Nicholas County.

The Forty-sixth Legislature met on the statutory date, 1943. Nicholas County had no senator. Wendell H. Holt was the delegate from Nicholas County.

The Forty-seventh Legislature met on the statutory date, 1945. Nicholas County had no senator. O. J. Carroll was the delegate from Nicholas County.

The Forty-eighth Legislature met on the statutory date, 1947. Nicholas County had no senator. O. J. Carroll was the delegate from the County.

The Forty-ninth Legislature met on the statutory date, 1949. Nicholas County had no senator. O. J. Carroll was the delegate from Nicholas County.

The Fiftieth Legislature met on the statutory date, 1951. Nicholas County had no senator. O. J. Carroll was the delegate from Nicholas County.

The Fifty-first Legislature met on the statutory date, 1953. Nicholas County had no senator. J. A. Neal was the delegate from Nicholas County.

Nicholas County has been in the Third Congressional District from the birth of the State. Changes have been made from time to time in the counties composing the district. At present the Third District comprises Braxton,

Calhoun, Clay, Doddridge, Fayette, Gilmer, Harrison, Lewis, Nicholas, Ritchie and Upshur Counties.

John D. Alderson of Summersville represented Nicholas County from the Third District in the Fifty-first, Fifty-second and Fifty-third sessions of Congress for the years 1889 to 1895.

John M. Wolverton of Richwood represented the Third District from Nicholas County in the Sixty-ninth Congress for the years 1925-1927.

The records of Nicholas County are wanting in many instances. No systematic method of recording births, deaths and marriages was employed until recent years. No records of our schools were preserved. No election records kept; and until some time after the Civil War the recordation of deeds, wills and settlements of estates were negligently omitted. The entire record of the Board of Supervisors, that replaced the County Court system during the ten years of the State under the Constitution of 1863, has disappeared from the files of the County Clerk's Office without any explanation. A complete list of County officials cannot be compiled from our records.

A list of County superintendents of free schools, made from the reports of State Superintendents, appears in the Chapter on Education. A list of our judges from the organization of the County has been worked out from the Court records. The names of the clerks of the circuit and county courts are obtained by page by page study of the order books of these courts, and the names of our sheriffs in the same manner. A complete list of our other county officers for the period of the State's history cannot be had from the records in the county offices.

Clerks of the Circuit Court: James S. Craig, 1865-1871, A. F. Rader, 1871-1891, Joseph A. Alderson, 1891-1903, William Crookshanks, 1903-1909, Jennings J. Summers, 1909-1921, J. O. Dodrill, 1921-1933, Frank Stone, 1933-1934, Bennett Bell, 1934-1939, H. V. Summers, 1939-1945, Guy Dunn, 1945-.....

Clerks of the County Court: J. S. Craig (Recorder), 1865-1871, A. F. Rader (Recorder), 1871-1873, J. A. Hamilton, 1873-1903, J. A. Alderson, 1903-1909, P. N. Wiseman, 1909-1921, C. E. Stephenson, 1921-1933, Ira E. Hill, 1933-.......

Sheriffs: John D. Groves, 1865 (Resigned), J. G. Malcom, 1866-1869, Henry Hendrickson, 1869-1873, J. J. Halstead, 1873-1877, J. G. Malcom, 1877-1881, Henry McQueen, 1881-1885, John Koontz, 1885-1887 (Resigned), W. G. Graves, 1887-1889, H. W. Herold, 1889-1893, W. G. Graves, 1893-1897, A. W. Bobbitt, 1897-1901, H. W. Herold, 1901-1905, A. W. Bobbitt, 1905-1909, David McQueen, 1909-1913, Jettes Mollohan, 1913-1917, W. E. Morton, 1917-1921, A. L. Hinkle, 1921-1925, G. W. Shawver, 1925-1929, W. E. Morton, January 11, 1929-March 18, 1929, Ray Lambert, March 18, 1929-1933, W. E. Morton, 1933-1937, F. C. Perkins, 1937-1941, T. N. Hicks, 1941-1945, T. C. Odell, 1945-1949, John C. Bell, 1949-1953, L. W. Boley, 1953-.....

Prosecuting Attorneys: Thomas G. Putnam, 1866-1873, John D. Alderson, 1873-1889, Robert A. Kincaid, 1889-1893, T. B. Horan, 1893-1897, W. A. McClung, 1897-1901, T. B. Horan, 1901-1905, W. G. Brown, 1905-

1909, S. R. King, 1909-1913, J. M. Wolverton, 1913-1917, G. G. Duff, 1917-1921, J. M. Wolverton, 1921-1925, G. G. Duff, 1925-1929, R. E. Horan, 1929-1933, G. D. Herold, 1933-1941, Brooks B. Callaghan, 1941-1945, G. D. Herold, 1945-1949, Claude H. Vencill, 1949-1953, Ralph Dunn, 1953-.......

CHAPTER VI

Nicholas County in the Wars

THE *Revolutionary War* ended twenty-five years before Nicholas County was organized.

How many soldiers of the Revolution came to the county is uncertain. The following names are of record: *Jacob Chapman*, enlisted in Greenbrier County, served fifteen months as a guard in the border settlements; *Martin Delaney*, no record of his service; *John Dobbins*, no record of service; *Abraham Duffield*, enlisted in Greenbrier County, no record of service; *Jonathan Dunbar*, enlisted in Pennsylvania, fought at Guilford C. H., Hotwater and Jamestown; *William Foster*, enlisted in Greenbrier County, fought at Stony Point, was taken prisoner at the Capture of Charleston, South Carolina; *Charles B. Fulham*, no record of his service; *Benjamin Hamrick*, no record of his service; *William Johnson*, no record of service; *Benjamin Lemasters*, enlisted in Berkeley County, fought at Monmouth, Princeton, Germantown, and Brandywine, was with Washington at Valley Forge; *William Lilly*, enlisted in Frederick County; *Jeremiah Odell*, enlisted in Virginia, served as border guard; *Isaac Rose*, no record of service; *James Simms*, enlisted in Culpepper County, no record of service.

These fourteen soldiers filed applications in Nicholas County Court Clerk's office for pensions. Their affidavits, showed their enlistment, services, and gave a list of property owned at time of applications for pension. The law required the Clerk of the Court to record their affidavits, and forward the original to the War Department of the United States in Washington, where they are still carefully preserved. In only a few cases did the clerk of the County Court comply with the law in recording these affidavits.

The War of 1812 called a number of the citizens of Nicholas County into the army by draft. No record of this service is to be found in our County. Colonel Edward Campbell in his letters makes the following statement: "I will now give the names of the parties who were drafted and served a six months term in the Army of the North under General Harrison, during the War of 1812: Isaac C. Fitzwater, George Fitzwater, Joshua Stephenson, James Nicholls, David Given, William Lilly, Moses Ewing, John Bailes, John Hamrick, James Wilson. John Henry was captain and Edward Rian lieutenant, of the Company which was in Kanawha Regiment of the Virginia militia. They marched to Gallipolis, and were placed under General Harrison. While in winter quarters in Ohio many were taken sick. In the Spring only seven of the men named marched to Fort Meigs. These men: Isaac Fitzwater, George Fitzwater, David Given, Jilson Hamrick, James Wilson, John Hamrick and John Miller, served their time and returned home. The drafted soldiers who were sent to Norfolk were Conway Foster, Jonathan Pierson, Solomon Bailes, George Hardway, Elijah Lilly, Andrew Hutchinson, David McCue, Elijah Odell, George Rader, Ezekiel Alderman, Presley

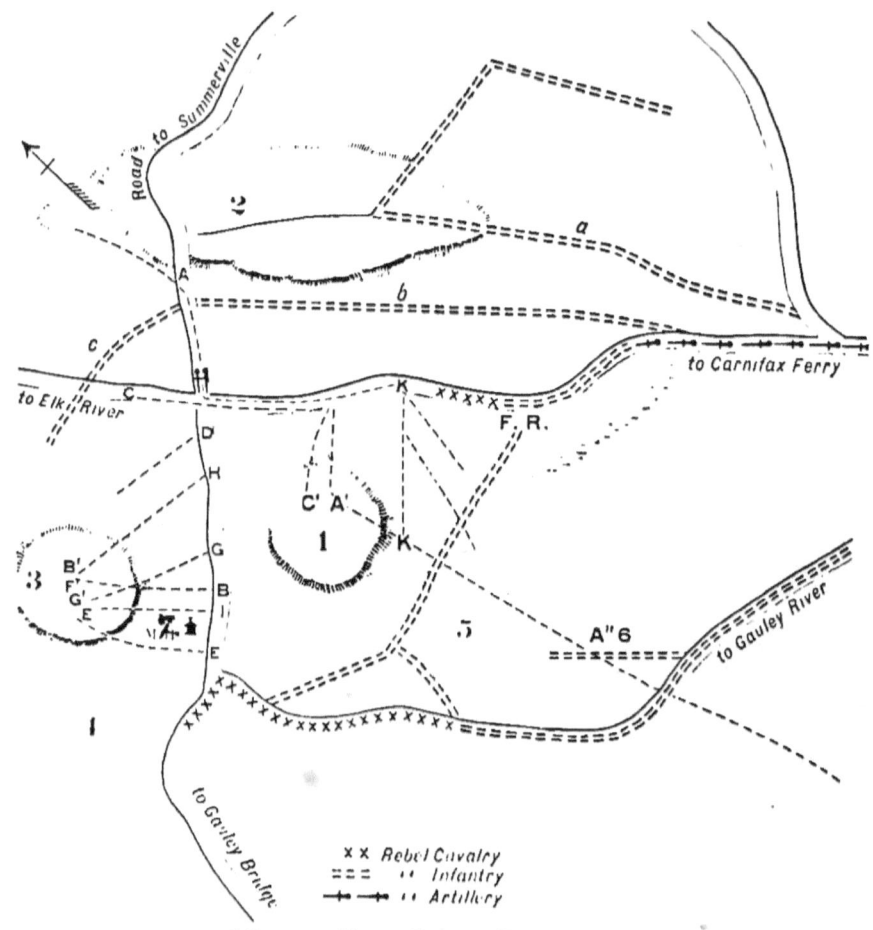

MAP OF CROSS LANES BATTLEFIELD

The map of the battlefield of Cross Lanes was drawn by Lieut. T. T. Sweeney. The following explanation will assist in reading the map:

F. R.—Ferry road on which the firing first commenced and on which Companies A, C, and K rallied, eventually taking position on hill 1.

M. H.—Meeting-House—Colonel Tyler's headquarters, and pathway nearly opposite on which and in the woods 5 the firing next commenced on our extreme left.

2—Our former camp-ground and hill on which the enemy next appeared in overwhelming force at "A," formed in line of battle at "b," and subsequently worked their way around to "c."

3—Hill on which the companies in the road attempted to rally, but were driven off to the woods 4 by the rebel artillery, which had come up the Ferry road (F. R.) and formed at the crossing of the roads.

4—Woods through which Chaplain Brown, Colonel Tyler, and Lieut.-Col. Creighton escaped, and where Major Casement collected the scattered forces, and carried them in safety across the country.

6—Rebel company which Company A cut to pieces, taking their standard bearer prisoner and capturing his flag.

The position of the different companies in the roads previous to the fight are marked by the company letters A, B, C, etc. Their positions after retiring and rallying are shown by the letters and figures A 1, B 1, C 1, etc.

Foster, Israel Brown, John D. Sutton, and John G. Stephenson who was ensign. Of these Solomon Bailes, Elijah Lilly, Andrew Hutchinson, and Ezekiel Alderman died in Camp."

The Mexican War was fought by volunteers enlisted in the regular army, and no recorded list identifies the volunteers by counties. On the great monument, erected by the State of Texas on the battlefield of San Jacinto, are inscribed the names of the soldiers by states who fought under General Houston on that field, and many Virginians with names common to our ancestors are there given.

The Civil War, of all our wars, was most destructive of life and property as its ravages came to the homes of Nicholas County. In the contest for the territory now in West Virginia two battles were fought by the regular armies.

The Battle of Cross Lanes, fought Monday August 26, 1861, between the Federals under Colonel E. B. Tyler in command of the 7th Regiment of Ohio Volunteer Infantry, and Brigadier General John B. Floyd in command of the Confederates, consisting of an estimated force of at least three regiments of infantry, a company of cavalry and three pieces of artillery. The Confederates attacked about 5 o'clock in the morning while the Federals were preparing breakfast. The battle lasted about one hour and the forces of Colonel Tyler were completely routed. The Federal loss was 15 killed 20 wounded and 38 taken prisoners. The Confederate loss was 5 killed and 6 wounded.

Captain Dyer of Company D was mortally wounded

while heading his company. He fell in the Hamilton Meadow opposite the Vaughan residence, and was taken by Major Thornburg to the porch of Vaughan's house where he died. The Confederate officer and Captain Dyer had served together in the Mexican War. Captain Shurtleff was taken prisoner. Colonel Tyler and about 200 men escaped to Gauley Bridge, and Major Casement with 404 men returned through the mountains to Elk River and thence to Charleston and Gauley Bridge. Several other stragglers retreated through the forest to Gauley Bridge.

The dead were buried by General Floyd's troops, and the wounded cared for, and in his report to General Robert E. Lee he said: "Tyler's command is said to be of their best troops. They were certainly brave men".

The Battle of Carnefix Ferry was fought Tuesday, September 10, 1861, on the Henry Patterson farm, two and a half miles from Cross Lanes, and one and a half miles from Carnefix Ferry.

The Federal army consisted of six and one half Ohio regiments under General W. S. Rosecrans, and the Confederate force of 1800 Virginia and Kanawha volunteers was commanded by General John B. Floyd.

General Rosecrans had marched from Clarksburg over the Gauley Bridge and Weston Turnpike and had encamped the night before the battle on the Anderson Herold farm on Muddlety. On the day of the battle he had dispersed a small Confederate force at Summersville, and going over Samons creek and McKees creek road, encountered Confederate pickets at Cross Lanes. The Confederates were massed behind a log barricade across

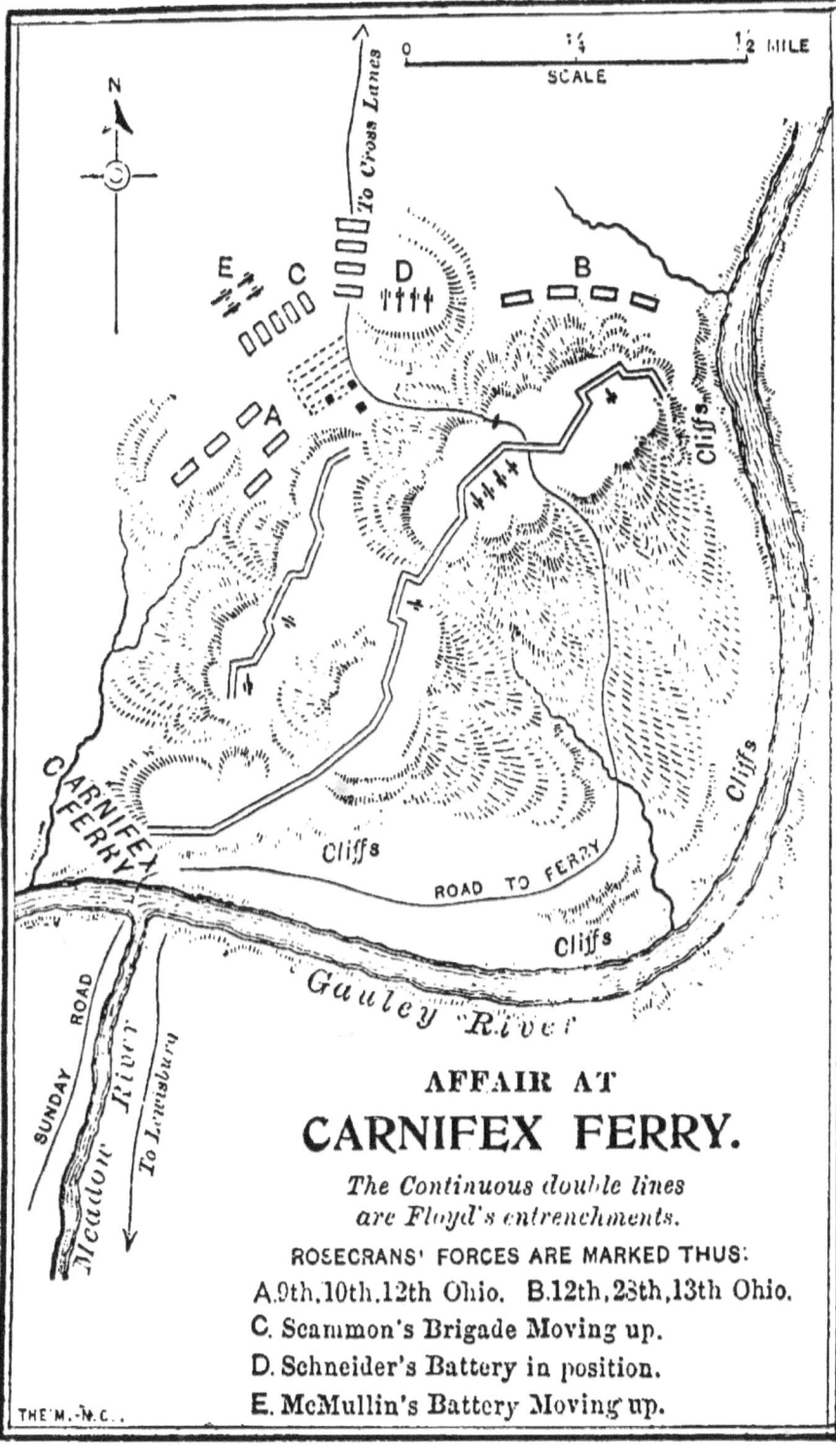

AFFAIR AT CARNIFEX FERRY.

The Continuous double lines are Floyd's entrenchments.

ROSECRANS' FORCES ARE MARKED THUS:
A. 9th, 10th, 12th Ohio. B. 12th, 23th, 13th Ohio.
C. Scammon's Brigade Moving up.
D. Schneider's Battery in position.
E. McMullin's Battery Moving up.

the road leading to Gauley River. Ignorant of the entrenched position of the Confederates, the Federal troops in irregular formation came in contact with the Confederates about three o'clock in the afternoon. Fighting in dense woods they could not see the enemy, and their disorganized attacks were repulsed. By the time General Rosecrans had organized a storming party night brought an end to the fighting.

During the night General Floyd abandoned his fortifications, crossed the river and retreated over the Sunday Road to Sewell Mountain. Pursuit by General Rosencrans was prevented by Floyd's destruction of his temporary bridge and all boats and by a flood in the river. Ten days after the battle the Federal army joined the forces of General Jacob D. Cox at Gauley Bridge.

The Federal army had seventeen killed and one hundred forty-one wounded, Colonel J. W. Lowe of the 12th Ohio regiment was killed and Colonel W. H. Lytle wounded. The Confederates reported none killed and twenty wounded. General Floyd had a slight wound in his right forearm.

Two future presidents of the United States, Rutherford B. Hayes and William McKinley were privates in 23rd Ohio regiment in this battle. Others, who became notable in our history, were Stanley Mathews, who became a justice of the Supreme Court; Whitelaw Reid became a vice-president of the United States, and six colonels: Robert L. McCook, W. H. Lytle, W. S. Smith, Jacob Scammon, Augustus Moore and Hugh Ewing became generals in the Civil War. General Floyd, the Confederate commander, had been a governor of Virginia and served as Secretary of War in the cabinet of President Buchanan.

The Battle of Carnefix Ferry was of the longest duration, closest combat and heaviest firing of any battle in this part of the State. It is generally regarded by historians as the most important battle of the Civil War in the State. It virtually decided the separate statehood of West Virginia.

The Carnefix Ferry Battlefield Commission was created by a bill introduced in the State Senate by Senator P. N. Wiseman, and became effective March 14, 1931. The first members of the Commission appointed by Governor Conley were P. D. Koontz, C. A. Goddard and W. G. Brown. Under the authority of the act establishing the Commission a tract of 275 acres was purchased, including the battlefield, as a State park. On September 12th of that year, a large assembly of citizens from Nicholas and surrounding counties, met on the battlefield in celebration of the 70th anniversary of the battle. No appropriations were made for improving the grounds until the administration of Governor Okey L. Patteson. In his term the park has been given a resident care-taker, the old Patterson house restored and picnic grounds and other facilities for visitors arranged.

Count Louis Phillippe (Comte de Paris), was an observer for the French Government in the Civil War. He was present at the Battle of Carnefix and the following account is taken from his "History of the Civil War in America—Battle of Carnifix Ferry", Volume 1, Page 374:

"We have followed the movements of the Confederate General Wise who had gone into the Valley of the Great

Kanawha for the purpose of raising troops to defend the cause of Seccession. He found himself in difficulties when McClellan conquered Garrett in the north, and he was soon compelled to fall back before the forces of Federal General Cox. After the cavalry affray at Cissonville, Wise evacuated Charleston, burning the Elk River Bridge behind him. On the same day Cox, with the aid of a light draught steamer abandoned by Wise, entered and established headquarters in Charleston and dispatched a few troops in pursuit of Wise. Wise had hastily crossed Gauley River and burned the bridge situated near its confluence with New River to withdraw to Lewisburg. Thus at the end of July, 1861, the Confederates found themselves driven back everywhere into the mountain region. They resolved to make a desperate effort to get out of it. General Floyd who had been Mr. Buchanan's Secretary of War, was sent from Richmond with a few troops to reinforce Wise and assume command in the Valley of the Kanawha. Unfortunately for their cause, Floyd and Wise were two characters not very well calculated to harmonize. Floyd, proud of the service he had rendered to the pro-slavery faction by disorganizing the Federal army during his administration of the War Department, made Wise feel the weight of his authority, while Wise, believing he was better acquainted with the country and its inhabitants, and mode of making war there, resisted Floyd's attempts to dominate. Remnants of Pegram's and Garnett's forces had been placed under General Lee. He had no intention of disputing Northern West Virginia with his adversaries, and fell back toward the south leaving only a few detachments around Romney. Lee's small army in Greenbrier Valley was about 16,000 in August.

The Federals had the independent brigade of Cox, 2 or 3,000 facing Floyd and Wise. Cox, following the retreat of Wise had occupied the whole Kanawha Valley as far as the summits of Sewell Mountain, while more to the north forces commanded by McClellan until July were now under Rosecrans. He had been dilatory at Rich Mountain, but was a distinguished soldier beloved by his men, and he knew what he could exact from them. The greater part of his forces had been brought by Baltimore Railroad to Clarksburg, and he now had 10,000 men under General Benham, and Colonels McCook and Scammon. Both parties passed the first half of August 1861 in quiet. At last Floyd resolved to take the offensive and re-enter Kanawha Valley. Cox was too weak to oppose him and Floyd took the Sewell Mountain Road and compelled Cox to fall back to the southwest on New River. Leaving Wise to watch Cox, Floyd proceeded in a northwesternly direction toward Gauley River in order to cross that stream at Carnifix Ferry near its confluence with Meadow River, and thus cut off any reinforcements Rosecrans might send Cox. In the region between Gauley and Elk River there was but a single Federal Regiment under Colonel Tyler who had formerly traveled that region dealing in furs. His present mission was to pursue gangs of confederate guerillas.

On Floyd's arrival at Carnifix Ferry Tyler fell back toward Gauley Bridge, not being strong enough to dispute the passage of the confederate troops. But upon hearing of an accident which befell Floyd he retraced his steps. At Carnifix Ferry the Confederates had but one barge and one ferry boat with which to cross the river. It was not fordable and in the midst of the long and tedious crossing the boat capsized and was battered to pieces on the rocks. Floyd found himself on the right side of Gauley with his infantry and two guns, the cavalry on the other side. Tyler took advantage of this perilous situation and tried to attack but was not quick enough. In 24 hours a new boat was built and on August 25th Floyd had all his forces reunited on the right side of Gauley. He immediately marched with the view of forestalling Tyler who had halted at Cross Lanes a short distance away, and on the summit of the gorge of Gauley River. The Federals had failed to adopt even the simplest precautions customary under such circumstances; had sent out no scouts and were bivouaced as though no enemy was near to fear. This culpable neglect cost them dear. On the morning of the 26th Floyd fell upon them suddenly, killing a few and capturing fifty before they had time to recover The remainder were dispersed in the wood, where many lost their way and fell into the hands of the enemy.

After this success Floyd took up a strong position at Carnifix Ferry on the right side of the river and waited for Wise to join him in order to penetrate further into that region occupied by Federals. He surrounded with entrenchments a steep hill which a turn of the river enveloped on two sides. This hill was separated from neighboring heights by deep wooded ravines to northeast and northwest. Confederate artillery commanded all approaches, especially the Summersville Road which passed through the center of the position. These skirmishes were only the prelude. Rosecrans and Lee were preparing for a new campaign and it was expected they would soon clash. Rosecrans was quickest. September 3rd he left Clarksburg with three brigades and proceeded toward Weston. Reaching there he proceeded toward Suttonville instead of turning eastward on the Beverly Road to attack Lee as expected. He crossed Elk River into the scarped passes of Gauley Mountain, which separates Elk and Gauley Rivers. Roads were difficult and gorges narrow. Finding no place to camp, the troops crossed the dangerous passes in the night and reached Summersville. As soon as the exhausted soldiers had some rest Rosecrans set out to descend the course of Gauley River in search of Floyd whose exact position he had not been able to ascertain so great was the difficulty of obtaining information in a region so little inhabited(?) ! !

On the evening of September 9th, he encamped at the foot of Gauley Mountain, sixteen kilometers from Summersville and 28 kilometers from Carnifix Ferry after driving back Floyd's scouts sent to watch the Suttonville Road. Floyd ignorant of Rosecrans Army was preparing to make a forward movement. On the 10th of September the whole Federal Army started before daylight, reached Summersville during the morning and without halting continued to follow the course of Gauley River. The soldiers were mostly conscription, without war experience, but they bore the fatigues of the long march well and at 3 o'clock reached the point where the road which leads to Carnifix Ferry leaves the main road to Gauley Bridge.

Informed at last of Floyd's position, Rosecrans decided to use the last of daylight making reconnaissance, notwithstanding the weariness of his men and the density of the forest which did not allow him to see the disposition of the Confederates or direct a concerted movement. The redoubts with which Floyd had surrounded the heights were mounted with a dozen guns, and connected by strong breastworks of logs. He had with him 1800 men. As soon as his pickets reported approach of Federals, he sent for Wise who had remained in the vicinity of New River.

Benham's Brigade composed of the 10th, 11th, and 13th Ohio Regiments commanded by Colonels Lytle, Smith and Lowe was at the head of the Federal column. Lytle is the first to descend into the wooded ravine which extends to the foot of the enemy's position. He is hardly in sight when he is received by well sustained fire. After a few shots he emerges from the wood, and climbs the opposite acclivities to reach entrenchments on the heights. But he fails to reach them. He is severely wounded and his men fall back to the skirt of the wood behind which they shelter themselves to continue the fight. Field pieces soon come to their assistance. In the meantime Benham's Brigade was deployed as well as the nature of the ground permitted. Smith, deceived by report of musketry had first moved to right, now to left and he engaged the extreme right of the Confederate line near the river. He might have carried that position which was more accessible than the others had he been supported but his small band, sent on a simple reconnaissance was not sufficiently strong to attack it alone.

In the meantime the Generals being prevented by the thick forest from seeing all the movements, the troops renewed the fight of their own accord, and the reconnaissance assumed the proportions of a regular battle. The 12th Ohio became separated in the wood and the largest portion of that regiment took position on the right of the 13th. Lowe led it to the assault a little to the left of the road but was killed at the first fire and his command driven back in disorder. Although it was getting dark Rosecrans decided to make one last effort and part of McCook's brigade deployed to the right of the road to attack the entrenchments on that side. Four guns were sent to the center and two of McCook's regiments were ordered to join Smith who gathered around him his own regiment and part of the 12th, forming a new column of attack. But at the moment McCook appeared in front of the Confederate entrenchment, a counter order stopped his movement and darkness overtook Smith's column before it could deploy on the other side of the ravine, which it had already entered. Smith convinced of the impossibility of progressing further brought back his column but not without confusion. During the movement his soldiers unused to night fighting, shot at each other adding thirty wounded to the day's losses. The Federals had fought bravely and many officers had fallen, but they had been badly handled; their movements had been disconnected, and scarcely two thousand soldiers with six pieces of artillery had engaged in the conflict in which 150 men were lost. They prepared to renew the conflict the following day with all their forces, but Floyd himself wounded, gave them no chance. Wise had formally refused to respond to his summons, and Floyd's little army although it had lost only 15 to 20 men, was too much shaken to sustain another shock. He evacuated his camp during the night, leaving behind the Federal wounded he had captured a few days before from Tyler, and he crossed the Gauley to fall back on Sewell's Mountain justly accusing Wise of having abandoned him at the decisive moment in a position which timely reinforcements would have enabled him to defend."

Ex-Governor, Henry A. Wise was a leader in the secession movement in Virginia. He bitterly resented the action of the western counties opposed to secession. He was commissioned a brigadier general and at his request undertook to counteract this movement. With headquarters at Lewisburg he enlisted a force of volunteers from the border counties including Nicholas. He was a fiery partisan and in recruiting his army he and his agents violently denounced all opposed to secession as "damned yankees", whose soldiers were reported to be invading Virginia as savages, seizing and destroying property and killing even women and children. This propaganda had its effect and was the beginning of the hatred that devastated Nicholas county during the war and embittered its people for years afterward. An incident that occurred while Wise was at Lewisburg is in point. It was reported to General Wise that John R. McCutcheon, John Groves and Dr. William Brown in Nicholas County were active in opposing secession and favored a new state.

They were arrested and Dr. William Brown's wife, who belonged to a prominent Greenbrier family, insisted on going with the prisoners. With the help of Samuel Price and others, whom she knew, she was allowed to be present when the accused were brought before General Wise. After harshly upbraiding them as traitors to their state he asked McCutcheon to give his church affiliation. "I am a Baptist" was the reply. "Not so bad" said Wise. To the same question Groves said, "I am a Methodist". "A damned bad sign", snapped the General. Turning to Brown he said "What are you?"—With an oath came the answer:—"From the way you cuss I must belong to your church".

Finally Samuel Price, who had been lieutenant governor of Virginia and had practiced law in Nicholas many years, was allowed to speak in behalf of the prisoners. He said he knew each of the men personally, that they were well known, law abiding citizens, and he vouched for their future conduct. Reluctantly they were released and warned against further activity.

Apparently moved by the rumors of the brutality of the Federal troops, Judge Evermont Ward as the army of Rosecrans approached, directed that the records of his office be taken to a place of safety because of the advance of the *public enemy*.

The day before the Battle of Carnefix Ferry a group of frightened men, led by a man named Young, armed themselves with their rifles and shot guns and on the summit of Powells Mountain, secreted themselves in the woods by the road to repel the ruthless enemy they had been informed was coming to attack them. The scouts thrown out by General Rosecrans to protect from ambush suddenly came upon the men found behind logs and trees with guns, and in routing them Young was killed and buried where he fell. Years afterward a marker was placed at his grave with the inscription that seems to present him as a heroic defender of his country.

At the camp of the Federal Army on Muddlety the night before the battle, soldiers appropriated the hay and burnt the fence rails on the farm of Anderson Herold. After the battle Mr. Herold was agreeably surprised when an officer sent by General Rosecrans, came and made settlement and paid for the damages to his property.

T. C. Brown related that as a half-grown boy on his father's farm, now owned by J. D. Hamilton, he saw soldiers come from the camp at Cross Lanes and purchase supplies from his mother. They were friendly and courteous and paid in cash for their supplies. That on one occasion a soldier came and insisted on taking corn which was not for sale and left without paying. This was reported and the soldier severely punished.

A story was current at the time that John Groves, who lived near the camp of General Rosecrans, on a visit to the general, remarked that his wife, Catharine, was not only a *rebel* but a *Catholic*. Rosecrans laughingly replied, "I, too, am a Catholic", and presenting a large bag of green coffee, said, "Take this to your wife with my compliments."

In the same spirit General John B. Floyd in his campaign in the County respected the rights of non-combatant citizens, and treated his prisoners humanely, but this conduct of the war was not left behind when the regular armies moved out.

Four days after the Battle of Carnefix Ferry, Nicholas Ramsey, a son of James Riley Ramsey, was shot from ambush and killed, almost in sight of his home. Today there stands a tombstone on the road leading from Carnefix Ferry to Mount Lookout, about two miles from Gauley River, with the inscription: *"Nicholas H. Ramsey, born January, 1839, murdered Sept. 14, 1861".*

The only reason ever given for the killing was that the father, James Riley Ramsey and the father-in-law, Alexander McClung and their families were openly for the Union cause. James Remley who was suspected as leader of the assassins fled the country, and while others doubtless were accomplices no evidence was found against them.

The pitiful story of how Ramsey's body lay three days where he fell while his young wife and baby daily watched for his return has been told and re-told in the years since the tragedy.

In the winter of 1861-2 Federal troops occupied a training camp in Summersville. Colonel Wm. H. Lytle was in command. Mr. James S. Craig who knew Colonel Lytle informed the writer that it was while Colonel Lytle was stationed here, that the poem: "Antony and Cleopatra" was composed by this officer. At the first celebration held on the Carnefix Battlefield, State Senator Clyde B. Johnson gave a sketch of Lytle and recited the poem.

While the Federal troops were in camp at Summersville, a young woman, Nancy Hart, was arrested charged with spying for the Confederates.

She was permitted to go about the grounds around the jail and a careless guard allowed her to handle his gun. Without any warning she shot him dead with his own weapon and ran away. She was aided in her escape by sympathizers, who probably suggested her deed. No evidence is of record that she was a spy.

After the war she married a squatter by the name of Josh Douglas, and spent her life with him in a backwoods cabin in the mountains of Greenbrier County.

After the Federal troops had been withdrawn in 1862, a local guerrilla warfare followed that continued till 1865.

John J. Halstead was enlisted in the Confederate 22nd Virginia Infantry early in the war. This regiment was commanded by Colonel George S. Patton, grandfather of the famous George S. Patton of World War II.

John Amick had organized a company of volunteers in Nicholas County, and this company chose Halstead as their Captain. William H. McClung, generally known as Dr. Bill McClung, was detailed from the Confederate Army as "drill master" for Halstead's Company and was made first lieutenant. In this way Captain Halstead came on the scene in the local war that raged in Nicholas County.

To meet the local conflict in the border counties the New State of West Virginia authorized a system of "Home Guards".

In Nicholas County James Riley Ramsey enlisted a

company late in 1863 which was maintained in service till discharged on June 30, 1865.

In April 1864 Isaac Brown was commissioned Captain of a second company of "Home Guards" that was in service for one year.

The State furnished arms and equipment for this service and the volunteers were sworn into the service for one year. In addition to their duties as home guards they could be called into service as scouts and guards in the regular service. A company was limited to a membership of not less than twenty-five nor more than fifty.

With the organization of the home guards the conflict in the county increased in bitterness and involved all non-combatants who manifested any sympathy for either side.

Soon after Captain Ramsey was commissioned an attack was made on his home where a few of his company had assembled. James Clark Ramsey in his history of the Ramsey Family, tells of this incident and describes how bullets from the attacking force entered the kitchen and struck the legs of the dining table. He states the attack was made by the company of John Amick. John Amick, known as "Big John", was later killed when pursued by some of Captain Ramsey's men.

Under date of December 12, 1825, Captain Halstead in a letter to J. C. Ramsey tells of a second attack on Captain Ramsey's home, that they termed the "shop fight". Captain Ramsey and the six men with him at the time escaped. In this letter he also tells of his capture by Captain Ramsey in October 1863. Halstead states that after his capture, Dan McCoy one of Ramsey's men insisted on shooting him, but Captain Ramsey protected him and sent him under guard to Charleston where he was imprisoned about two weeks. Halstead and two other prisoners escaped and returned to Nicholas. At the close of this letter Captain Halstead added: "Captain Ramsey was as cunning as a red fox for I tried to pen him seven or eight times but he would slip out and always got most of his men out with him".

Captain Ramsey had erected a "fort" on the hill now used as the Zoar Cemetery at Cross Lanes.

In August 1864, Colonel V. A. Witcher, with a large force guided by Captain Halstead, captured and burned the fort. Of the 18 men captured at the time and sent to Andersonville prison in North Carolina 9 died in prison, 1 was shot by guards and 2 died on the way home. Those who returned at the close of the war were, Hiram Pierson, Wesley Chapman, John F. Dorsey, Addison Ramsey, Lewis Halfpenny and Middleton Brown.

The intensity of the local conflict can hardly be appraised by these sketches.

From the 9th day of September, 1861, when Judge Evermont Ward signed the last court order under the Commonwealth of Virginia until October 16, 1865 when Judge Robert Irvin signed the first court order under the State of West Virginia, Nicholas County was in a condition of anarchy—During this time of more than four years, there were no public offiicals to control crime, enforce legal rights, or keep records. For this *interregnum* Nicholas County still has no land book records or reports on vital statistics.

The maxim that war unleashes the worst in human nature was fully demonstrated in this period. When one side captured prisoners and seized property a retaliatory raid would follow from the other side. Non-combatant citizens were constantly involved no matter how carefully they tried to carry on peacefully. Neither side hesitated to carry off the property of any person that might be even in the slightest way suspected of sympathizing with the other party. Horse stealing was continually carried on by a lawless element that had no interest in the principles involved in the war. For this class it was an opportunity to steal and plunder. Farmers would try to save their horses and cattle by secreting them in out-of-the-way places but with little success. As a result farms were deserted or scantily cultivated. Hundreds of people abandoned their homes. Union sympathizers took refuge in Ohio, Confederates fled to Greenbrier, Monroe and other parts of Virginia. Rebecca Harding Davis graphically pictures, in *"David Gaunt"*, her story of the war, the condition in the border counties, and in no county was this description more pertinent than in Nicholas. She says: "I write from the border of the battlefield, and I find no theme for shallow argument or flimsy rhymes. The shadow of death has fallen on us; it chills the very heaven. No child laughs in my face as I pass the home. Men have forgotten to hope, forgotten to pray; only in the bitterness of endurance they say in the morning, 'Would God it were evening!'; and in the evening, 'Would God it were morning!'"

The close of the war ended the reign of lawlessness, and refugees slowly returned to their devastated homes to begin the slow, hard work of returning to peaceful living. In 1860 the population was 4,627, in 1870, after five years of peace, only 4,458. The old animosities had to be overcome. The war had divided families, estranged friends, and left hatreds that for more than a generation was to dominate politics, and even affect the churches and schools.

The Spanish-American War, which lasted only 113 days was lightly felt in Nicholas County. No soldiers were drafted and none from the county was engaged in the fighting.

World War I touched every family in Nicholas County. The Selective Draft Law, passed May 19, 1917 was for the first time applied in selecting soldiers under our government. Major George S. Wallace was appointed Director of the Department of Military Census and Enrollment and at once selected as the Draft Board for Nicholas County, the following names: H. W. Herold, L. D. McCutchen and Dr. H. H. Veon. As the Clerk of the County Court P. N. Wiseman became Secretary of the Board. The law provided certain exemptions of draftees from service, as in case of physical disability, sole support of family, employment in production of war essentials, etc. In order to aid the board in passing on applications for exemption, W. G. Brown was commissioned by Governor Cornwell to represent the draftees.

The Legislature was called in special session, Congress authorized the President to control business as he might deem it necessary to aid in mobilizing the nation for the war. Then came *"Liberty Loan Drives," "Food and*

Fuel Conservation," and *"Four Minute Men,"* to appeal to the patriotism of the people. Even the school children were organized by their teachers to assist in the appeals for buying government bonds, and saving food and fuel. We had *"meatless days," "heatless days,"* and *"Children's gardens."* For one and a half years, the citizens were also "drafted" in the War. Nicholas County responded to these demands and there was little complaint. It seemed a slight sacrifice compared to that of the young men drafted and hurried into the training camp. The greater number from Nicholas County were sent to Camp Lee in Virginia or Camp Meade in Maryland. Early in 1918 they were in France engaged in the fierce fighting at St. Mihiel and in the Meuse-Argonne Drive. Farmer boys from the hills of Nicholas County fought, bled and died in the bloody struggle that broke the "Hindenburg Line" and ended the War.

The Casualties of that campaign were heavy—from Nicholas County, Clay L. Brown, Andy S. Brown, James E. Crabtree, Paul B. Dupuy, Ira S. Keith, William O. Lambert, Benjamin Martin, Andy L. Persinger, Henry J. Pittsenberger, and Edward P. Smallridge were killed in battle. Ezra E. Craze, Elliott A. Donelson, Bert H. Hickman, Marvin R. Rutledge, James Tucker, Andrew J. Chapman, Gussie D. Patton and Ray M. Stutler died of wounds; James G. Curry, George Douglas, Joe Hamilton, Roy L. Hypes, Wilson McKinney, Raymond E. O'Connor, Henry R. Sleeth, and Roy O. Young died of disease in Camp.

The record of the enlistment and discharge of the soldiers from Nicholas County in World War I is preserved in the office of the Clerk of the County Court, and is a record of which their friends and relatives should be proud.

After the war the American Legion was organized by the ex-soldiers and has been an influential factor in keeping alive the "American Way" of life. In Nicholas County the organization maintains posts at Richwood and Summersville.

Other organizations growing out of the war, are "Veterans of Foreign Wars" and "Disabled American Veterans."

World War II was declared December 8, 1941, just 22 years and 27 days after the end of World War I. It continued until the treaty of peace was signed by the Japanese, September 2, 1945.

The Selective Service Draft Law of September 16, 1940, which provided for "State Headquarters for Selective Service" was in effect, and General Carleton C. Pierce was Director of our State headquarters.

The Nicholas County Draft Board was composed of T. R. Richards, Howard B. Campbell and Homer Ransberger. Mr. Ransberger died and was replaced by Lundy Champ. Hobart Hypes was Secretary, A. N. Breckinridge Appeal Agent, Wiley Mason Re-employment Committeeman, and Flavius H. Brown, Eugene S. Brown and John E. Echolls were Examining physicians.

Casualties were greatly in excess of World War I. Following is the list for the army for Nicholas County:

Woodrow Wilson Bell, Cecil R. Bess, Casper Breckinridge, Claude Bryant, David E. Casto, Chancey R. Chapman, Guy R. Dillon, James C. Dobson, Luther C. Faith,

James A. Foster, Charles O. Frame, Morris J. Gray, Heber E. Harlow, Roscoe C. Hoover, Carl O. Hosey, John O. Huffman, Jesse C. Hughart, Harley L. Johnson, Warren S. Johnson, Theodore N. Lee, Ross E. Marks, Clyde McClung, Tommy C. McLaughlin, Harley C. Neff, Hazel G. Nicholas, Arthur B. Norman, Ernest Sloan, John G. Stephenson, Samuel J. Swartz, Thomas D. Williams, Donald H. Wilson, Destil Phillips, Wyatt R. Pritt, Sammy T. Rowan, James W. Wilson, and Nathan H. Young killed in battle.

Allen W. Bailes, Joe Hughes, Victor H. Humphreys and Robert D. Odell, died of wounds.

Samuel O. Burkholder, Orville E. Dorsey, David B. Foster, Robert W. Hughes, Russell L. Keenan, Troy L. Legg, Virginia L. Link, John M. Legg, Glen D. Marsh, Gilbert W. Milam, Bert J. Moyer, Harry E. Sturgill, Johnnie M. Ward, Wade H. Williams, died of disease or injuries.

Clifton E. Dennis, Willard E. Nicholason, James D. Radcliff and Arthur R. Underwood "finding of death".

Korean War. In June 1950, after less than five years of peace, the United States became involved again in foreign war. In the beginning styled "a police action", and without a declaration of War by Congress, it was considered as an action of the United Nations to stop Communist aggression in Korea. However only a few of the allied nations contributed to the war, and for almost three years our country bore the burden; and contributed billions of dollars and our army suffered thousands of casualties. The indefinite and uneasy truce of

1953, continues with opposing armies facing each other ready to renew the struggle.

No official report of the costs and casualties on our part in the war has been given out.

From many homes in Nicholas County our young men have been called to Korea to serve in this costly and bloody conflict still pending and whose inglorious history remains to be written.

CHAPTER VII

Home Life, 1818-1861

IN the twenty-five years from the first settlements up to the organization of the county, progress had been made in living conditions. While many of the poorer people still lived in their log cabins with dirt or rough puncheon floors and "cat and clay" chimneys, the more able and progressive citizens were building hewed log houses with shingle roofs, stone chimneys and small glass windows. Men with substantial means had been coming in from the older settlements bringing their families, household furniture and live stock.

John Hamilton in 1805 came to Cross Lanes to a good house and outbuildings he had built before moving in. Benjamin LeMasters and George Rader located on Hutchinsons Creek some years before, and both had cleared out good farms, and Rader had set up a blacksmith shop. Edward Ryan a millwright, had built the first good grist mill on lower Peters Creek. C. W. Cottle was operating a large stock farm in Cottle Glades, and Samuel Neil had purchased the farm of Conrad Young and was improving it and beginning his trade as wagon-maker. Jacob Koontz and his brother John, had purchased the tan-yard on Line Creek started by John Bird, and developed a business in tanning leather and making shoes. Samuel Grose, an expert saddler, and his

Home Life, 1818-1861 127

sons, settled near the Koontz Tannery and were making saddles for the county. Robert Kelly opened the first store at Cross Lanes in 1816; and James Boggs about 1812 was operating the first grist mill on Muddlety where later stood the Jones Mill. Many other ambitious men came to the county and became well known as tradesmen, teachers, and religious leaders before the county was organized. These leaders had made much advancement in clearing farms, growing better crops, erecting better buildings and organizing schools and churches, but were greatly handicapped in their local government, since they must go to Charleston to record their wills and deeds and to attend other legal business, and even to mail their letters and to cast their votes. How they finally succeeded in establishing the new County has already been shown in preceding pages.

In the census of 1820, the new county was shown to have a population of 1853, about one person to the square mile at its organization.

To understand the many problems of our forefathers, and to know how they solved them in laying the foundations of the society that is ours today, let us go back to their homes and their daily tasks.

The first settlers had to wring their subsistence mainly from the forest. A brush camp or rough log cabin, a small clearing for a "patch" of Indian corn, surrounded by a brush fence, and food and clothing from the wild animals and the wild fruits in the woods.

The times had changed. Increased population with trained workers, experienced farmers, and better equipment was improving living conditions. Farmers enlarged the cleared lands, planted rye, oats and wheat, in addition to larger fields of corn, raised cattle, hogs, sheep and poultry, began to cultivate pastures and meadows, plant orchards of apples and peaches and, above all, to open roads.

In all these steps in advanced living these was *a system*. Grain fields and meadows were fenced to *keep out* depredatory animals not to *keep in* the live stock of the owner. From the "brush" fence, and the "buck" fence, (two rails held in place one above the other at each joining by four cross sticks), to the "worm" rail fence that was required to be "pig-tight", "horse-high" and "bull-strong", even our fences might be called historical monuments, as the wire fences of today show the decrease of wood and the increase of mineral supplies. The methodical construction of the worm fence is worthy of mention. By a rule of unknown origin, the rails for the fence were eleven feet in length, and with about twelve inches of lap at the corners, forming an angle of about forty-five degree. A double panel of the fence was a rod. This gave a basis for calculating the area of the field. The rails were five or six inches in diameter and seven rails of the proper size made a legal fence. An old writer of the time said, "I judge of the progress of a settlement by observing the fences".

As the danger from bears and wolves decreased the cattle, sheep and hogs were allowed to range the woods and subsist on the herbage and nuts of the woodland. Wild grasses, pea vine and many other plants in the summer and chestnuts, acorns and beech nuts in the fall and winter furnished an abundance of food for these animals. They ranged at will and the property of the neighbors mingled, but a system of marking the animals was in universal use. In many of the colonies these ear marks were required to be recorded along with other property titles. This was not required in Nicholas County, but these individual marks of ownership were rigidly observed. To illustrate the markings: the tip of the ear cut squarely off was a "crop", a split of the ear was a "split-fork" and if the split was enlarged by cutting out and widening it this mark was a "swallow fork", a notch cut under the ear was an "under bit" and if cut on the upper part was an "upper bit".

Food was a prime necessity to our pioneers, and they must take it from the land. Indian corn was the one essential food the backwoodsman must have. Without it he could hardly have conquered the savages and the Wilderness. The irony of American history is depicted in the many ways the Indians taught the white man the secrets of living in the new world and thus aided in their conquest. In 1608 Powhatan, influenced by Pocahontas, taught Captain John Smith how to grow Indian corn and thus saved the Jamestown Colonists from starvation. In 1621, Quanto, the friendly Indian, taught the same lesson to Governor Bradford and his Puritans, in the Plymouth Colony.

Indian corn is a native of America. The first explorers in the new world saw the tall Indian corn waving its green blades, and graceful tassels in fields along the river bottoms from the what is now the Carolinas to New England. It was a staple food of the red men. When our pioneers in Nicholas County planted their corn, they followed the method their forefathers had learned from the Indians. There was the same planting in hills, the same number of stalks to the hill, with pumpkin and squash vines running among the hills and beans climbing the stalks.

The Indians taught the colonists much more than planting and raising corn. They showed how to grind and prepare the corn and cook it many palatable ways. The various foods we use today made from Indian corn are cooked as the Indians cooked them and taught the Colonists. We call them by the Indian names: hominy, pone, sup-pawn, samp and succotash. To make meal the Indians pounded the grain in a mortar or hollowed stone with a stone pestle. Samp was meal boiled as the pioneers made "hasty-pudding" or mush. Pones were the Indian's "appones". "Succotash" is the Indian word we still use for corn cooked with beans. The "Johnny cake" of the pioneers, baked on a "cakeboard" covered with live coals and ashes, was made as the Indians made hasty bread by baking it on smooth flat stones. They often made a delicious food by mixing dried huckle berries in preparing this bread. The Indians used the "roasting ears"; parched and popped the corn as is still done. Our pioneers in Nicholas County had this knowledge of the use of corn and the further advantage of mills to grind it and better implements for preparing it for food. A volume could be written on the use of Indian corn and its contribution to the nation's welfare.

There were many other good foods found on the tables of the early citizens. Pumpkins and squashes were grown in abundance. Potatoes, beans, peas, parsnips, turnips and melons were grown in the gardens, "truck patches" and cornfields. Huckleberries, blackberries, strawberries and wild grapes abounded. Apples and peaches were grown around the homes, and were in general production in the early years of the county. Both apple and peach trees were produced as seedlings until after the Civil War. Two popular varieties, the "Milam" or "VanBibber" and the "John Young", named from the settlers that propagated them, were widely grafted and the "VanBibber" is still found occasionally in the county.

The art of canning vegetables and fruits was then unknown and they were dried for winter use. Pumpkins were peeled and cut in circles and dried on small poles in the Indian fashion. Apples were dried after being peeled and cut in quarters, by stringing them on linen threads and hanging on the attic rafters or on the walls near the fire. Sometimes apples, peaches and berries were dried in the sunshine. Apple butter was made with the pared apples boiled down in cider. Apple pies were made through the whole year and when fresh apples were not to be had dried apples were used.

The preparation of apples for drying and apple butter was the occasion in many homes for an "apple peeling". The neighboring young folks with sharp knives and skilful hands soon filled the tubs with the prepared apples for the owner's use. Then followed a "frolic" of games and sometimes a round dance. Days were spent in making apple butter and cider for winter use.

Wheat was successfully grown at this time and the grist mills were producing flour, that at first was unbolted and was run through a sieve as corn meal was treated; later the mills installed crude bolting apparatus that produced bran, "shorts" and flour.

Meat was supplied from the forest that still contained deer, bear, wild turkeys and smaller game. Squirrels and rabbits were so numerous that they were pests. The streams were filled with fish. Beef, pork and mutton was available in almost every home. Fresh meat could not be kept as there was no refrigeration then. Meats were pickled or cured. November was a busy month as that was "killing time". Beeves and hogs were slaughtered and the meat pickled or "salted down" for curing. Sausages were made and tallow and lard carefully kept for special purposes. The "smoke-house" was common in which beef and bacon were cured by "smoking", usually with hickory wood or corn cobs.

Milk, butter and cheese were common foods. The beverages were teas, from spice-wood, sassafras and dittany, cider and metheglin. Sweetening was procured from maple sugar and honey. Bees were slowly introduced but "wild honey" could be obtained from "bee trees" in the forest. Little coffee was used in the first half of this period but was coming into use before the Civil War.

The first coffee brought into the county was the green coffee berries, usually in 100 pound bags. The people were slow in learning the art of properly roasting the berries. Substitutes for coffee were made from roasted rye grains and chestnut kernels. In brief the farms and the forests furnished the foods of this period. A farmer writing to eastern friends boasted: "My farm is giving me and my whole family a good living. Nothing to eat, drink or wear has been bought this year, as my farm produced all".

Only few families moving in from the older communities brought well made furniture for household and kitchen. Tables, chairs, cabinets, chests, desks and bed steads that had been carried over the mountains from Virginia were rarely seen. Boards laid on trestles somewhat like a carpenter's saw-horse, served for tables in the crowded one or two room houses. Long benches were used for seating at the tables and stools for chairs.

The table-ware of the ordinary home was limited to few dishes, plates, and drinking vessels, usually of pewter or tin. Gourds were grown plentifully and used as drinking vessels and containers for salt, maple sugar and other foods. The general use of knives and forks, cups and saucers came a quarter of a century after the county was formed.

It was the custom in the early days for the children to stand at meals. They were served by the father and mother and the rule was for them to eat in silence. If company was entertained the children had their food after others had eaten. This custom was general even after the Civil War.

Clothing was home-made. Even after 1818, buck skin leggings, and moccasins were in use. Tradition has it that John G. Stephenson walked to Richmond from Nicholas County to serve as a delegate in the General Assembly, dressed in a pioneer hunting shirt, wearing moccasins and carrying his rifle.

John M. Hutchinson relates, in writing of early customs, that when a young man, he saw the justices of the county sitting as the County Court. They wore the customary hunting shirt with fringes and knee-breeches, some of them of buckskin. A few of them wore moccasins and wigs. All wore home-made hats or caps. The hats were made by the women from plaited bulrush, wheat or oats straw, with low crowns and narrow brims. The caps were made of fox or coonskins. This was the dress of leading men as seen in 1829.

Thomas Jefferson was the first president to wear full length breeches or "pantaloons". He brought the style from France and it was readily adopted by the upper class citizens. John Hamilton's appraisement of personal property in 1818 lists three pairs of "pantaloons". But "pantaloons" came into general use slowly in the County.

Sheep had been producing wool in the early colonies long before the Revolution. Flax and hemp also were cultivated and used. West of the mountains and especially in the early years of Nicholas County, sheep raising and the production of wool was hazardous because of the wolves and foxes that were numerous and preyed upon the sheep. Flax was grown and manufactured into the first cloth product of the County. It was used as the "chain" in weaving after the yarn from wool could be had. The "linsey-woolsey" which furnished clothing for both men and women takes its name from the linen "chain" into which the "filling" of woolen yarns was woven.

The story of the industry and skill of the pioneers, in constructing their looms, spinning wheels, counting-reels, flax-brakes, hackles, swingling or scutching knives and blocks, and the artistic weaving and dyeing of their lin-

Home Life, 1818-1861 135

ens, linsey-woolsey and jeans, would involve a vocabulary now unspoken and almost wanting in our dictionaries.

Sheep were raised in small flocks in the county as early as 1800, but had to be guarded close the home and securely penned at night because of the wolves. Some woolen clothing and woolen yarn for weaving had been brought across the mountains by the early settlers.

The manufacture of woolen clothing required additional implements, greater labor and and skill, than was employed in making linen. The wool must be cleaned and carded before spinning and the yarn or cloth dyed. The large spinning wheel now came into use, and the coloring of woolen cloth was an art attained by the pioneer women, now lost and forgotten. At first dyes were made from native trees and plants. The bark of red-oak and hickory made pretty shades of brown and yellow. Sassafras bark was used for dyeing orange. Soon madder, indigo, logwood, copperas and cochineal were imported and came into general use. Madder, cochineal and logwood combined made a bright red. Flowers of the goldenrod boiled with indigo and alum gave a deep green; and juice of pokeberry boiled with alum a crimson dye. Blue, in many shades, was a favorite color, and was made with indigo. Many other colors and shades were made from combinations familiar to the weavers.

The manufacture of woollen cloth led to other industries. The hand wool-cards by which the wool was made into "rolls" for spinning, were in great demand all over the nation. An inventor by the name of Amos Whittemore, constructed a complicated machine for manufacturing these wool-cards. John Randolph said this machine "had everything but an immortal soul".

Our great-grandmothers wove linen for bed-sheets, table-cloths, towels, grain-bags and many articles of dress. They prepared, carded, spun, dyed, wove and made linsey-woolsey clothing for themselves and daughters, and shirts for the men and boys. Jeans for the men's clothing was heavier than the linsey-woolsey, woven with cotton chain and yarn filling, sometimes twice spun to give weight and strength. The jeans was usually colored brown or gray. Jeans made from the wool of black sheep mixed with that from white sheep made a pleasing gray.

Two homely sayings: *"All wool and a yard wide"* and *"Dyed in the wool,"* are still found in the language of today though the source is forgotten.

Knitting kept pace with weaving. Before they were large enough to spin, girls were taught to knit. A pioneer mother boasted that her four year old daughter could knit her own stockings. Boys had to knit their own suspenders. Stockings, mittens, scarfs, and "comforters" were common products. Special forms of knitting were beadbags, purses and reticules. Much fine knitting was done in making these articles. "Knitting needles" were slender steel rods about ten inches in length as usually employed. Crocheting, another form of knitting, sometimes called "pegging'" was done with a single, hooked needle. Mittens, scarfs and hoods were often "pegged".

A dozen years before the county was established the Koontz brothers were operating a tannery on Line Creek and making shoes, but the majority of the settlers tanned their own leather and the father usually made shoes for the family. One pair a year was sufficient. Some times the leather was tanned at the settler's home, more often some one in the neighborhood prepared to do the work for his neighbors and would tan a hide for half—or one "side"—as it was termed.

The family shoe-maker made "lasts" out of soft poplar wood, after taking necessary measurements, then with a sharp knife, a "sewing-awl", a "pegging-awl", and light hammer he did his work.

Bed-steads were at first made with posts shaped roughly from poplar, maple or walnut, and rails with augur holes through which ropes called "bedcords" were drawn and stretched both sidewise and lengthwise to form a net work to hold the mattress or "bed-ticks". Usually two "bed-ticks"—one filled with straw or chaff and the other laid over it filled with feathers, made the mattress. The covers, blankets, quilts and counterpanes—all "home-made", completed a comfortable bed. Later "cabinet-makers" with "turning-laths", made bedsteads with tall, fancy posts.

Often only one bed could be placed in the crowded one-room home. Under this bed was placed a low bed-stead, called a "trundle-bed", that could be drawn out to accommodate as many as four little ones if necessary. The houses were built one and a half stories in height, and in the attic or "loft", as it was termed, beds were kept for the older children. The loft was reached usually by a ladder—sometimes from the outside to an open window. Only the better homes had two-story residences with stairways.

Heating was from an open fire-place, often five or six feet wide, where the fuel made of big "back-logs" and "fore-logs" that often had to be drawn in by hand sleds were placed, and then filled with smaller sticks and cuttings. Whittier in his "Snow-Bound" pictures such a winter fire:

> "We piled with care our nightly stock
> Of wood against the chimney back—
> The oaken back-log, green and thick,
> And on its top the stout back-stick;
> The knotty fore-stick laid apart,
> And filled between with curious art
> The ragged brush; then hovering near,
> We watched the first red blaze appear."

Andirons—"dog-irons"—our forefathers called them—held the fire in place.

Lighting by tallow candles was in general use for the household in early Nicholas—though pine knots and "betty-lamps" were often found in the poorer homes. The house-wife, with the "candle-moulds" and a supply of tallow and beeswax, could soon provide a supply of candles. "Candlesticks" were the holders for the candles, and "snuffers" were kept for trimming the wicks. Candles were used in the lanterns. The first lanterns were made of tin-cases punctured with many holes to emit the light of the candle. The early churches were lighted by candles held by rude chandeliers called "candle-beams".

Church services for the night were announced to begin at "early candle-lighting".

When by ill-fortune the fire went out a small boy often was sent to a neighbors to bring back on a shovel, or perhaps a broad strip of green bark coals for relighting the fire. But most families kept a tinder-box, with flint and steel with which to strike a spark to be caught on some combustible matter as tow or "punk", and then blown into flame. Another way of starting fire was by flashing the powder in the pan of a flint-lock gun, in which a little twist of tow had been placed.

The ingenuity and skill of our forefathers in taking from the woods, not only their buildings, their food and their clothing, but the many implements and household articles that were necessary, has long since been forgotten.

The house-wife was supplied with a "hickory broom", "cake-board", loom, spinning wheel; counting reel, flax-brake, scutching-knife, churn, buckets, kegs, tubs, trays, and various other articles.

The men, in this wooden age made and used wooden plows, harrows, pitch-forks, shovels, ox-yokes, troughs, flails, sleds, ax-handles, cane-mills, barrels, mauls, lasts, shoe-pegs, and so on *ad infinitum*. They knew just what trees furnished the best material for a given purpose and how to cut and season it.

The freaks of nature in the forest furnished "crooked sticks" more useful than straight ones. Hames for his harness, runners for his sled, snath for his scythe, could with little work be whittled or dressed with a "draw-shave" into proper form. In this age, when the axe was the prime implement, some men had a knack that was "almost genius" in shaping the "axe-helves" or handles. The handle was carefully selected hickory, split and whittled into shape with a curve that let the heavy stroke jar the hand as little as possible. Then scraped as smooth as ivory with broken glass, it was the triumph of the woodsman's skill. Our factories today cannot approach its perfection.

Boys with their "Barlow" knives made elder pop-guns with their hickory rods, bows and arrows of willow and hemlock, whistles of chestnut, papaw or willow, cornstalk fiddles, wind-mills, water-wheels and other toys.

The forests were the unfailing source from which came the pioneers substance. It is amazing to us how he could wring from the woods all this wealth of necessities with the tools at hand. The ax, broad-ax, draw-shave, auger, foot-adze, jack-knife, and rarely a few other simple tools, and the skilful use of them was the magic that brought results.

Barlow knives had a great popularity for more than a hundred years. Few persons now living owned a Barlow. The Smithsonian Institution cherishes some of them. Daniel Webster said: "Jack-knives were the direct forerunners of the cotton-gin and thousands of noble American inventions. The pioneer boy's whittling was his alphabet of mechanics".

Rev. John Pierpont pays tribute in rhyme to the whittlers:

> "His pocket knife to the whittler brings
> A growing knowledge of material things,
> Projectiles, music and the sculptor's art.
> His chestnut whistle, and his sour-wood dart,
> His elder pop-gun with its hickory rod,
> Its sharp explosion and rebounding wad,
> His corn-stalk fiddle, and the deeper tone
> That murmurs from his leaf trom-bone
> By his genius and his jack-knife driven
> Will solve ere long any problem given."

The early farm implements of wood had gradually given way to iron and at the organization of the county iron plow points, shovel-plows, mattocks, hoes, fittings for harness, and wagons and other farm implements were being made by local blacksmiths. Wrought iron in bars and sheets was brought in from the eastern factories and supplied by the local stores that had been established. The firm of Beirne Duffy and Company, located at Summersville, carried such material, along with general supplies for the farmers, and for most of the period before the Civil War, did an extensive business in the county.

Notwithstanding the daily toil of the men in clearing their land and building their homes, they found time for public and social duties.

The Virginia law provided that each county should organize and train a regiment of militia composed of the able-bodied citizens between the ages of sixteen and sixty, except certain classes exempt from military duty. There were usually from eight to ten companies, the number of men in each ranging fifty to seventy-five. Every Captain must call his company together for drill four or five times a year and at least once a year the regiment came together for a general muster. "Muster Day" was a general holiday for the citizens of the County and was held at the County seat.

The Nicholas County militia was known as the 126th Regiment of Virginia Militia, and the officers were selected at the first meeting of the County Court, in 1818.

At the musters there was usually public speaking and the question of government and public interest discussed.

Roads were opened up by labor of all able-bodied citizens directed by overseers who directed the work under supervision of the County Court.

The first generation of our citizens in Nicholas County had little voice in selecting their local officers. The governor of Virginia appointed the justices, sheriffs and all officers of the militia. Only freeholders had the right of suffrage.

The Virginia Constitution of 1850 made several revolutionary changes that favored the western section. Now, in Nicholas County, every white male over twenty-one two years resident in the State and twelve months in the district where he votes, was given the right of suffrage. Voting was still *viva voce*. Justices, sheriffs and other local officers were now elected by the people, and jurors paid for their service. Previously they had been chosen at the pleasure of the sheriff and served without compensation.

Elections had been held at Sutton as the one voting place where only a few freeholders could vote. Now the County Court was given the power to establish voting places at convenient places in the County.

The county acting upon this authority appointed the following voting places for 1852: Jeremiah Neals, Twenty Mile; John R. Masons, Panther Mountain; James C. McClungs, Meadow River; John C. Curran's in the Wilderness; William Prices, at Strouds Glades; Mary Arthurs, near Fork Lick; and John Browns on Birch River.

As the suffrage acts of 1852 required voters to be residents of *districts* in which they could vote, the County Court appointed a Commission to divide the County into districts. The nine members of the Commission: E. C.

Home Life, 1818-1861 143

Trent, Benjamin C. Morris, John W. Jones, William King, John Groves, Sr., Kyle Bright, John Given, James McLaughlin and Henry Jones, laid off the County into three districts, whose boundaries are not now of record.

It should be noted that the County at this time had been reduced greatly in area by the creation of Fayette County in 1831, and Braxton in 1836.

The population of the County by the census of 1830 was 3,346. In 1840, after the loss of area to Fayette and Braxton the population was 2,515.

In 1850 the population had risen to 3,963, but the erection of Clay into a new County, in 1858, took more than 300 square miles of territory from Nicholas and reduced the population to about 2,500. With the final slicing off of another large section to form Webster County in 1861, Nicholas was reduced to its present area, about one-third of its original territory, and the population which was 4,627, by the census of 1860, was only 4,458 in 1870.

The men and women that settled Nicholas County were distinctly different in character from the first white men that reached the frontiers. This class of adventurers, made up of traders, bringing the Indians fire-arms and "fire-water"; hunters, looking only for game and adventure; surveyors, spying out and selecting the best lands for Eastern speculators; and lastly the refugees, escaping from their crimes and the bonds of civilization, had bypassed Nicholas County.

Another factor was the geographical location. Many of the early settlers of Western Virginia followed up the Potomac and its branches to the headwaters of the Monongahela and its branches, and then down to the Ohio

River. Others occupied the valley of the Greenbrier, followed New River and the Kanawha to the Ohio, and from both sources the Ohio Valley was occupied. The advantages of water transportation had led to these settlements that encircled a great island of mountain forests lying west of the high ranges and bounded by Gauley and Elk Rivers and the headwaters of the Little Kanawha. The lure of easy transportation and the rich river bottom lands, had preserved this mountain region for the home-builders that came later. The future Nicholas County lay entirely within this area and its settlement began and continued when the *Scotch-Irish*—the Morrises, McClungs, Hugheses, Hamiltons, Campbells, Craigs, Dunbars, Fosters, Keenans, Browns, Bells, Neals, Odells, and more of that hardy race came with their families; when the *Germans*—the Amicks, Backuses, Cottles, Cutlips, Copenhavers, Dotsons, Drennens, Hardways, Herolds, Huffmans, Nutters, Raders, Seberts, Skaggses, and Vaughans and others of that sturdy blood, came with their families: when *English* of the best blood in the Old Dominion:—The Aldersons, Brocks, Bobbitts, Hills, Masons, Simmses, Stephensons, Wisemans, Walkers, made their homes beside the Scotch-Irish and the Germans; when a few of *French* descent—the Bennetts, Burdetts, Dorseys, LeMasters, and Rippetoes, and the *Dutch*, Halsteads, Summerses and Van Bibbers, were added, and all lived together as neighbors and friends, to become fellow citizens and Americans, the *future character of the county was determined.*

How quickly these Scotch-Irish Covenanters, German Mennonites, and English Episcopalians became Baptists and Methodists; how soon they adopted the same dress and modes of living; and how quickly they forgot race and language, because of common danger, common hardships and common ambition to create a new way of life in this new world!

Historians have continually marveled at this amalgamation of race, language and religion that has produced the American citizen.

Dr. Callaghan speaking of this epoch in our history says: "The story of the settlement and development of this trans-Appalachian region constitutes one of the most fascinating chapters of American History".

Pressed with the tremendous tasks of subduing the wilderness and establishing their government, our ancestors found time for schools and churches.

They were not illiterate. How they established their schools and trained their children is shown in another chapter. That their labors were not in vain appears from the census of 1850, when out of an adult population of 1,083 only 53 could neither read nor write.

Their ancestors had forsaken home and country in the Old World to find religious freedom in the New World, had trained them in morals and religion. In their first cabin homes they gave welcome to the Baptists and Methodists whose Missionaries and "circuit riders" brought religious instruction before churches were built. A place of meeting for religious worship was at first appointed at some cabin fitted by its size and location for the meeting. This became known as the "meeting house", and the name was given to the early church buildings. Bethel church on Laurel Creek was the first

Methodist church erected in the county. It was built about 1810 as near as the date can now be ascertained. Gilboa church on Peters Creek and Anthony's Chapel on Muddlety were later in building. Zoar church at Kesslers Cross Lanes was the first Baptist church in Nicholas County. The census of 1850 gives 1 Baptist church and 7 Methodist churches in the county. Two or three early Baptist churches in Nicholas County had been included in Fayette County in 1831.

The Methodists had a "Camp-Meeting" ground on Laurel Creek, just below the present Bethel church. The deed for this five-acre tract, dated June 10, 1842, from John Dunbar and Ruhama, his wife, to William Kincaid, David R. Hamilton, John Grose, John Dunbar, Hiram Walker, Andrew Keenan, James Grose, John R. Mason and Samuel Neil, Trustees, granted the land to said trustees as "a place of worship for the Methodist Episcopal Church"—This deed is of record in the County Clerk's Office in Deed Book No. 5, p. 223.

There was little money in circulation in the early days of the county. Trade at first was largely by barter. Ginseng abounded in the black loam of the mountains and was current as an export to China. J. M. Hutchinson stated in an article on early history of the county that James Robinson sold enough gingseng to buy a negro woman and child. Furs of beaver, fox and raccoon were in demand in the eastern colonies. Bear and deer skins, and cured venison hams, wool, feathers and some grain could be traded at the local stores for the wrought iron bars then in demand and for cotton yarn for the looms; and for coffee, calicoes and imported dyes, and other articles now coming into use. In the middle 1820's cattle and hogs were in demand by dealers for shipment to eastern markets over the new James River and Kanawha Turnpike. This was the first source of actual money. By 1830 the salt furnaces of the Ruffners on Kanawha and some newly developed coal mines in the Kanawha valley were new sources for turning farm products into cash.

There were no newspapers in the County. Short-lived journals first appeared in Kanawha as the nearest news papers. The Kanawha County Gazette in 1826, followed by the Kanawha Banner in 1831, and then the Kanawha Republican in 1841, had a few readers in Nicholas County.

The Wheeling Intelligencer, established in 1852, is the only newspaper of the period read in Nicholas County, that still survives. The newspapers of that day still found in a few files, differ widely in appearance from today's dailies. The editorial page was prominent. Only scant items of local news appeared. General news of the national and state governments was printed; some advertisements with little display appeared, very little space was given to crimes, scandals and local gossip—and no comics. Letters on some public matter and occasionally a short story was printed. Foreign happenings, months after occurrence, was news, as it came by sailing vessel and stage coach. No telegraph lines nor telephones is the explanation.

The darkest side of life in our early history was the want of skilful medical treatment and surgery. The "doctors" of the time were self-appointed, passed no tests for professional training, and required no license. In many minor ailments and injuries they doubtless were helpful, but in the serious diseases prevalent then, as fever, rheumatism, tuberculosis, flux, small-pox and many others, they could give no effective treatment. Measles and scarlet fever were often fatal and diphtheria and croup were seldom relieved in the children. Administration of purgatives, blood-letting and "cupping" were the general methods of medical treatment. Calomel was considered the indispensable drug, and rhubarb and ipecac were usually combined with it. The flowers, roots and barks of many plants were employed as medicines. One of the most dreaded diseases—dysentery, generally called "flux"—was usually treated by the internal use of "oak-ooze". May-apple root, walnut bark and slippery elm bark teas were also used in treatment of this disease. Surgery and dentistry were painfully endured as chloroform had not come into use.

Even these primitive doctors were scarce and each family made its collection of native flora—boneset, sarsaparilla, blood-root, snakeroot, lobelia, mullen leaves and scores of other leaves, flowers, barks and roots, in preparation for their use as remedies. Such was the medical practice sustained by our forefathers.

Prior to the Civil War little improvement was made in agricultural implements. Wooden mould-board plows were being slowly replaced with iron parts by the more progressive farmers. Corn was still dropped by hand and covered with hoes in planting. Plows, harrows, mattocks, hoes, rakes and all other farm tools, except turning plows, were made by the local blacksmiths. The sickle, scythe and cradle were generally used for cutting grain and grass. Wheat, rye and oats were threshed with a flail or trodden out by horses and cleaned of chaff by a "fanning mill" operated by hand. Corn was the principal product. Wheat was grown principally on new ground following a crop of corn, and supplied abundant flour for local use. No commercial grains or flour came into the county before the Civil War. Both Colonel Edward Campbell and John M. Hutchinson, insist, in their articles on this period, that more corn, wheat and oats was produced, and more cattle, sheep and hogs raised in Nicholas County annually than has been produced in any year since. The people supported themselves from their farms. Cattle and sheep ranged the woodlands. Hogs fattened on "mast"—chestnuts, acorns and beech-nuts, that carpeted the ground in the fall and winter. Fruits and vegetables were grown with little injury from insects and blight, and required no control by dusting and spraying.

Whip-saws, cross-cut saws, and the crude "sash"-saws operated by water power produced rough lumber for floors, ceilings, doors, window-frames and cabinet work, but was not used in building houses before the 1840's.

Much fine timber was necessarily cut and destroyed in clearing fields. The census of 1850 gave 19,335 acres of improved farm land. In clearing this land, fine walnut and yellow poplar trees growing on the best soils, were made into fence rails or burnt.

In everything the early citizens were bound together in community interests. Far removed from the laws and conventions of the older colonies, they became united by the need of cooperation and their neighborly ties that developed local customs which for three generations had the force of unwritten law.

Cooperation in work was a universal custom in "house-raisings", "log-rollings", "corn-husking" and similar labor of the men; and in the "quiltings", "apple-peelings", "flax-scutchings" and similar work of the women. *Community* service in the care of the sick and helpless and the burial of the dead, were customs faithfully observed before the coming of hospitals and "funeral homes". Custom required the proper marking of live-stock; the correct marking and preservation of the line and corner trees, bounding every tract of land; in the construction of fences, and even the seating of the men and women in church, and the order of grinding at the mill.

For three generations there was much confusion and litigation in land titles in Nicholas County. This grew out of the defective land laws in Virginia.

In 1792 Virginia by statute offered western lands at the price of two cents an acre. This offer, in the next twenty years, resulted in speculators acquiring title to the greater part of the lands, in what was later Nicholas County. These grants to non-resident land grabbers were in large tracts. Even before the law was enacted fixing this low price for the lands, the surveyors were busy marking off the most desirable lands.

Jeremiah Warder, in 1787, patented 12000 acres on the waters of Gauley and Beaver Creek; Wilson Cary Nicholas, in 1795, patented 32045 acres on Birch River; Andrew Moore, in 1795, patented three tracts, one of 43417 acres, one of 11300 acres and one of 5867 acres on Hominy Creek and Gauley; Henry Banks, in 1795,

Home Life, 1818-1861

patented 32300 acres on Williams River and Cranberry, and Jacob Skile patented 32097 acres on Gauley and Little Elk, later known as the Maury land; James Welch, in 1799, patented 52000 acres, and Thomas Williams, 20000 acres on Gauley River.

Andrew Moore, a member of congress from Virginia, Alexander Welch, a surveyor and William McClung, a pioneer settler in Greenbrier, were partners in a land-grabbing scheme—McClung looked up the land desired, Welch surveyed and Moore secured the grants, and in a period of several years they secured grants for a greater part of the territory south of Gauley River in what is now Wilderness and Kentucky Districts.

Henry Crammond had a survey made for 24630 acres on Birch River and tributaries, Wilson Cary Nicholas and Hudson Martin purchased the survey from Crammond, then assigned it to Robert Morris, who received his grant for it in 1795. William Wilson, in 1796, patented 93000 acres in the western part of the county, and later W. H. Edwards patented 90000 acres adjoining Wilson.

In laying of these grants Virginia allowed every buyer to fix his own boundaries. This led to over-laps in the grants. These speculators held their lands and did nothing to encourage settlements, and often did not even enter their lands for assessments.

The early settlers came in and took junior grants, or "squatted", on small tracts, disregarding the large grants of the non-resident speculators.

Finally Virginia, in order to protect the pioneers who were braving the dangers and facing the inconveniences of the frontier, in 1831-8, passed laws that protected the junior grantees and "tomahawk rights" of the settlers by allowing them to perfect title by adverse possession and by forfeiture of title for non-payment of taxes.

However it was not till 1840, that Nicholas County began to take advantage of the Delinquent Land Laws. John G. Stephenson was in that year appointed Commissioner of Forfeited and Delinquent Lands for Nicholas County.

His reports are of record in the Office of the Clerk of the Circuit Court in a book marked *"Order Book C"*. These reports were made to the Superior Court of Law and Chancery and by that Court's orders the delinquent tracts of land were ordered sold. The large tracts were surveyed and divided into "convenient lots", and sold to the highest bidder.

"Order Book C" shows the lots by plats and boundaries, costs of survey etc., the purchaser and purchase price.

Only a few sales were made by Commissioner Stephenson before he was succeeded by Alexander Brown and John Brown, as commissioners. After a few sales by the Browns as joint Commissioners, John Brown was made sole commissioner. He seems to have done the surveying from first to last.

From 1842 to 1858, Deed Books No. 5, No. 6, and No. 7, in the County Clerk's Office, are almost taken up with the deeds of John Brown, Commissioner of Forfeited and Delinquent Lands, to the purchasers.

As a surveyor, Commissioner Brown was poorly trained and equipped for this work. His surveys, hurriedly made, with an old fashioned compass and chain, were far from accurate.

Home Life, 1818-1861 153

In tracing the lines of the grants his surveys did not often coincide with the original calls, and later caused much confusion in locating boundaries. This was particularly the case in the large tracts of the Moore-Welch-McClung lands in Wilderness and Kentucky Districts.

In fact the surveys of the original grants were not accurate; they were made hurriedly with poor instruments, and closing lines often protracted. A famous example of this work caused the long continued law suit between William McClung and Edward Hughes over the location of the western line of the 43417 acres patented in the name of Andrew Moore. This line was not surveyed but protracted from a point on Dogwood Ridge, now in Fayette County, to a point on Gauley River near Hughes's Ferry. The line when surveyed crossed Gauley River several times. The Supreme Court of Virginia held that as *the crossing of the river was not mentioned in describing the line, it must be located south of Gauley river*. Accordingly Hughes won after thirteen years of litigation and "McClung's Ferry" became "Hughes's Ferry".

In 1892 the suit of Maury Heirs, against Benjamin Fitzwater and others, in Ejectment, in the U. S. Court for the District of West Virginia, was ended. This suit was brought many years before against all the citizens who had settled on land by junior grants or other instruments conveying color of title. Most of the tillable land on lower Twenty Mile, Little Elk, Lower Peters Creek and Line Creek, lying within the original tract of 32907 acres to Jacob Skiles, was involved. The object of the Maury Heirs in this action was to define the boundaries of the tracts of the various settlers, and save for themselves the unoccupied wild lands in their grant. No question arose as to the title of the defendants to lands actually held in adverse possession; *but how far did this possession extend to surrounding uncultivated lands?* On Twenty Mile it was agreed that the possession of defendants should extend a distance of *ninety poles* measured from the Creek up the mountains on either side; which explains the *"90 pole line"*, so often mentioned in conveyances in that area. In other cases compromise decrees fixed definite boundaries to lands of the defendants.

Finally after much litigation land titles in the County are now fairly well settled.

The full story of the community life of this time cannot now be given. The dress, the tools, the daily food, the methods of farm work, the roads traveled, the country stores, the methods of transportation, the social gatherings, the work of the schools, and the forms of church services, all have been forgotten. Many of the prominent men and women of the period sleep today in unmarked graves. Their names and deeds soon will be entirely forgotten unless their descendants gather up the fragmentary records left us and rescue this early history from oblivion.

What school boy today can sit at his desk and describe the cabin in which his great grandfather lived, the dress he wore, the food he ate and how he procured it?

What school girl today can draw a word picture of her great grandmother's home, her dress, her household duties and her daily occupation?

CHAPTER VIII

Home Life After the Civil War

1. Under the First Constitution—1863-1872

NICHOLAS County had little part in the Secession of Virginia and the organization of the Restored Government of Virginia. Joseph A. Alderson was a senator in the General Assembly from Nicholas County and voted against Secession. B. W. Byrne represented the delegate district of Braxton and Nicholas in the Virginia Convention that voted the Ordinance of Secession. The population of the county, which by the census of 1860 was 4,627, gave a majority vote in ratification of the ordinance of secession.

The second Wheeling Convention included Nicholas County in the new state proposed to be cut off from Virginia, and provided for the selection of delegates to a Constitutional Convention to be held in the City of Wheeling on the 26th day of November, 1861. John R. McCutcheon of Kesslers Cross Lanes was chosen as the delegate from Nicholas County to this convention. The convention met on the appointed date, completed its work on February 18, 1862, and on the third Tuesday in April, 1862, the constitution was adopted by a vote of 18,862 in its favor and 514 against it. The admission of the State of West Virginia into the Union on June 20, 1863, gave the constitution legal effect. However the occasional raids by Confederate forces and local disorder in the border counties prevented the organization of local government in the border counties until the close of the war in 1865. Several counties along the southern boundary of the new state were partially under the control of the Confederacy until the close of the war, and "were forced to pay heavy taxes to the Richmond Government and to furnish soldiers for the Confederate army". In Nicholas County there was no sheriff or other collector of taxes, "because of the danger incident thereto", until the Spring of 1865. The first court since 1861 was then held and local officers installed.

The Constitution of the New State differed materially from that of the mother State, though retaining many similarities in fact.

The state officers were given terms of two years; the name of "General Assembly" for the law-making body, was changed to the "Legislature"; Senators were elected for two years and members of the House of Delegates for one year. The Judiciary followed the Virginia system. The greatest change was in local government. The districts of the county were designated "townships" after the New England style. A "Board of Supervisors" took the place of the County Court, and the clerk of this board was styled "Recorder".

The enduring provision of the Constitution was the excellent system of Free schools.

The Wheeling conventions had adopted the name "Kanawha" for the state, but the Constitutional convention, substituted "West Virginia".

Virgil A. Lewis commenting on the change said: "Thus

was the name changed, and it seems that while the members were determined to sever political connection with the "Old Dominion", they were not willing to abandon the name of "Virginia".

The first Legislature adopted the State Seal and our motto: *"Montani semper liberi"*, both of which the people have proudly accepted.

The act providing for the forfeiture of property belonging to enemies of the State, passed at this session, was never enforced.

No radical partisan legislation was enacted until the Legislature of 1865 passed the "test-oath" law requiring from all voters an oath that they had neither voluntarily bore arms against the United States, nor aided those so engaged. It seems that the action of small numbers of ex-Confederates who were denying the authority of the new State and advocating the return to Virginia had provoked this legislation and this act was opposed by the conservative citizens as unjust to the great majority of the southern soldiers who had accepted the results of the war and the new state, and by 1870 this opinion had prevailed and the proscriptive laws had been repealed.

Before the war the political parties in the county were nearly equally divided as Whigs and Democrats. After 1865 when the county was organized under the first constitution a new political alignment soon followed. In the election of 1866 few of the southern soldiers attempted to vote. By 1868 strict registration of voters under the test oath was now enforced by the new county officials and this led many Union men to join with the southern soldiers and sympathizers in protesting such partisan government. Two outside men, William P. Rucker and Thomas G. Putnam, were largely responsible for keeping alive bitter partisan spirit. The result was the citizens became divided into "Radicals" and "Conservatives". The aggressive Radicals carried on their political policy by publishing the first newspaper in Nicholas County. On September 5, 1868 the first number appeared, styled *"The Bastinado"*. It was a small four-page sheet. The anonymous owners and editors were announced as, *"Asmodeus Jr. & Co., Editors and Proprietors"*. The motto, a quotation from Shakespeare, was: *"Law on MacDuff and Damned be he who first cries, Hold, Enough."* The initial editorial announced: *"This day we fling our* banner to the breeze. On that banner is the word RADICALISM. Our paper is *Radical out and out"*. The local tickets for the coming election were published as follows:

RADICAL TICKET: House of Delegates, Capt. T. G. Putnam; Prosecuting Attorney, Capt. T. G. Putnam; Recorder, J. S. Craig; Assessor, John H. Rader; Surveyor, J. Haymond Robinson.

CONSERVATIVE TICKET: House of Delegates, M. L. Rader, Prosecuting Attorney, Dr. W. P. Rucker; Recorder, W. Y. Callaghan; Surveyor, S. B. Koontz.

The Radicals won the election on November 4, 1868, and *The Bastinado*, in its issue after the election, gloated over their victory as follows:

"MOURNING IN SUMMERSVILLE, MELANCHOLY DEATH"

"The Town of Summersville was thrown into considerable excitement a few days ago in con-

Home Life After the Civil War

sequence of the suicide of a well known citizen. Mr. Conservative Party cut his throat and expired. The funeral was large and imposing. The pallbearers were Hon. (?) Joseph A. Alderson, ex-senator of the defunct rebel senate, Austin Groves, John Groves, senior, Dr. Rucker, Isaac Hart, M. L. Rader, Dr. Hereford, David R. Groves, and Dr. Bill Brown. The funeral oration was delivered by Rev. Joseph McClintock, a well known minister of New Jerusalem Church." After sundry personal gibes, the final statement was made: "We have routed the enemy. We had a powerful combination opposed to us. The Conservatives and rebels joined forces." Among the leading conservatives named and lambasted in the campaign were the following prominent Unionists: John Groves, Austin Groves, David R. Groves, Dr. William Brown, William Bryant, William Grose, James G. Malcolm, M. L. Rader and John D. Simms. In the election of 1870 Dr. Anthony Rader was the only Conservative to win, over Thomas G. Putnam for the House of Delegates. Before the election of 1872, both Rucker and Putnam had left the county, the sentiment was against the radical element, and in that election the Conservatives won in the county and state, and the Constitutional Convention of 1872 followed.

In Nicholas County the situation was entirely different from the decade before the Civil War. The results of more than four years of anarchy on the land and the people was evident. Farms had been neglected, the fields were overgrown with brush and weeds, and live stock had almost disappeared. Many buildings had been destroyed or were dilapidated, the roads were out of repair and the stores and shops without business. The citizens who had been neighbors and friends were suspicious and antagonistic of each other. There had been three hundred and fifty citizens enrolled in the Union forces and at least double that number in the Confederate armies. These men from the two forces returned from camps and prisons to their desolated homes, tired of war and anxious to return to former living conditions. Many of them were broken in health and all without money to finance the return to civil life. The condition of Nicholas County in the year 1865 presents the darkest picture in its history. Slowly our people began the work of reconstructing their lives. Refugees came back home and started the task of repairing and restoring their property. The men who had fought and suffered in the war were the first to forget and forgive. The lawless element that had plundered their neighbors and kept up the strife at home continued their partisan activities. In many respects greater hardships were endured in rebuilding community life after the war, than the early settlers had undergone in establishing their homes. There was that lack of friendly cooperation of neighbors formerly prevailing. The churches had been divided and disorganized and a few political partisans kept the old animosities stirred up.

In the first three or four years under the new state many gave up in discouragement, abandoned their homes and returned to Ohio and Virginia. Those remaining, bravely turned once more to pioneer methods of wresting a livelihood from their neglected farms. Slowly they cleared the overgrown fields and meadows, acquired a few sheep and hogs, a team of horses or a yoke of oxen and returned to growing flax and wool and spinning and weaving material for clothing.

The woods were thronged with wild life that had accumulated during the war. The cornfields had to be guarded to protect the planting from the crows and squirrels that would often take up a whole planting. In the autumn the earing corn was attacked by the same enemies, and fortunate was the farmer who did not lose heavily from the depredations of these enemies. It was the task of the half-grown children to protect the corn crop. Boys set "deadfalls" with "figure 4 triggers" to catch the ground and gray squirrels and with their dogs kept continual watch over the crop. Chickens and geese, so necessary for the home life at this time, had also to be constantly protected from the numerous hawks, foxes, opossums, skunks and weasels that abounded and preyed on the farm-yards. The present generation can have no conception of these daily difficulties no longer existent. Money was scarce, almost non-existent in the average family. Farm products were bartered for the few necessities to be had from the local stores. James Miller at Gauley Bridge, Thomas Drennen at Drennen, John R. Vaughan at Kesslers Cross Lanes, Armstrong & Frame at Summersville and two or three other stores there, were the principal local stores. They bought the products of the farms, chickens, eggs, butter, feathers, wool, pork, beef, grain of all kinds, ginseng, furs, etc. etc. They in turn bartered these products. Some of the products were marketed to local purchasers and generally the food products were sent by their wagons to the Kanawha Valley where the coal mines and salt furnaces were now being opened up and their employees were ready purchasers of the country products. Prices current at that time seem unbelievably low to us now. The maximum price for corn was fifty cents a bushel; fifteen cents a pound for butter was the average price; wool was sold for as low as twenty cents a pound, goose-feathers was usually thirty cents a pound, frying-size chickens were usually one dollar a dozen, and beef and pork was available at prices from three to five cents a pound. Ginseng was in demand and the children and women found time to do some "senging".

Many farmers after planting their spring crops worked for some neighbors who had lived through the war and had some grain or other products to exchange for extra help. The usual prices for such work was a bushel of corn for a day's work, one bushel of wheat for two days' work, ten pounds of bacon for a day's work, and a dollar's worth of farm produce for making and laying up one hundred fence rails.

Others found employment in the years 1869-72 working on the Chesapeake & Ohio Railroad then building. The road was constructed mainly by manual labor. In addition to the colored laborers brought in from Virginia, many native people along the line were employed. The steel rails were brought over the mountains in wagons and the ties were cut from timber along the line by natives using whip-saws. Men from Nicholas County earned money for their taxes and other necessities by furnishing cross-ties and timbers for other use in constructing the road. The last spike was driven on the New River Bridge at Hawk's Nest on January 29, 1873.

At this time primitive methods in farming were necessarily employed. While there had been advancement in methods of farming, and farm machinery had been invented and put to use in the more favored parts of the state, the people in Nicholas County had no money to buy up to date farm implements. Corn was still planted by dropping by hand and covering with hoes. Wheat and oats were sown broadcast and the grain cut with sickle or cradle and threshed by flails.

Little attention was given to fruit growing. A few seedling apples and peach trees were found around the home. Two seedling apples were favorites. They were the "John Young" and "VanBibber" or "Milam", named from the pioneers who first grew them. It is of interest to recall how fruit growing in the county was first encouraged. Just before the Civil War, Henry Backus, a grandson of pioneer Joseph Backus, adventured into Ohio and found employment with a man named Hubbell, who owned a large commercial apple and peach orchard in Meigs County, Ohio. For a year or so young Backus worked in the Hubbell orchard and learned the methods of the orchardist step by step from the nursery to the gathering and sale of the fruit. He returned home, married and located on a farm on Backus Branch. His ambition was to have an orchard. He began by starting a nursery of seedlings. At the close of the war he went back to the Hubbell orchard and procured cuttings for grafting from all the favorite varieties of apples and at once started his orchard. In a few years he had two acres in fine young apple trees, bearing fruit from early summer to late autumn, in great variety. Among his early apples were the later well known "Early Harvest" and "Golden Sweet"; mid-season varieties were "Maiden Blush," "Lady Finger", "Rambeau" and "Golden Pippin"; late fall and winter apples were "Rome Beauty", "Roxbury Russet", "Baldwin" and "Rhode Island Greening"; a very late winter apple he called, "Grindstone Russet". His orchard was soon of much interest to neighbors and he was called upon to assist them in starting to grow improved fruit. He grafted their seedlings and gave instruction in cultivating and pruning their orchards. At the same time he introduced the Concord grape and grew fine grapes in quantity. His fine apples and grapes were exhibited at the country stores and at the terms of court in Summersville, and soon the question of growing improved fruit was of importance throughout the county. In a few years the "Early Harvest", "Golden Sweet" and "Rome Beauty" had become favorites and were largely grown. The Concord grape was soon seen in all parts of the county. No spraying was needed at this time and it was easy to have fruit without much care.

Henry Backus was not only the pioneer grower of improved fruit in the county, but was a pioneer in other branches of farming. He was a subscriber and reader of the "American Agriculturist". He attended the Centennial Exposition in 1876 at Philadelphia and came home with many new ideas in the care of his orchard and his other farm products. He had apples all the year round. He cultivated and fertilized his trees each year. With

BETHEL METHODIST CHURCH
Oldest Church in Nicholas County

leaves and stable manure he made his fertilizer for his orchard. In the winter he banked snow around his trees to hold back the bloom to save from frost killing. He demonstrated the fine possibilities of fruit growing in Nicholas County.

The great solvent that finally ended the discordant community life of this period was the devoted work of the churches. Two evangelistic denominations, the Methodists and the Baptists, had predominated in the county from the earliest settlements.

In 1784 the Methodist Episcopal Church was organized in America at the City of Baltimore, with Francis Asbury the first bishop. In 1785 Edward Keenan donated four acres of land near the present Town of Union for the site of a Methodist Church. The building of unhewed logs was dedicated by Bishop Asbury in 1788. The church was named Rehoboth and is still standing and preserved by Monroe County. Soon Bishop Asbury and his "saddlebags" circuit riders were carrying the gospel message into the backwoods settlements of the Trans-Alleghany wilderness. It is not of record who the preachers were but meetings were first held at the homes of Alexander Brown and Elverton P. Walker on Laurel Creek. About the year 1810 a substantial hewed log building was erected, on a lot donated by Alexander Brown where Thomas Hughes had once located his hunting camp. The church was named Bethel and was in use till after the Civil War. Alexander Brown and Elverton P. Walker and their families, the Johnsons, Simmses, Smiths and Backuses from Gauley and Twenty Mile were regular attendants. The writer has an old class-book dated in 1821 in which John Johnson, Joel Hamrick and David Nutter are named as class leaders. Members enrolled that year include John Dorsey, Cornelius Dorsey, Nancy Dorsey, Arie Dorsey, Elizabeth Linager and black Jude and black Fanny, slaves of the Simms family.

The history of the Baptist Church in the county goes back to John Alderson, a young Englishman who had left his native land on account of religious persecution. He came to Linville in Rockingham County, Virginia, in the early 1770's and was the pastor of a Baptist Church there. In 1777 he located on Greenbrier River at the site of the present Town of Alderson named for him. In 1781 he organized the "Old Greenbrier Church", the first Baptist organization west of the Alleghanies. The church building was erected on a lot donated by William Morris, brother-in-law of Rev. Alderson. The building, completed in 1784, was of logs and was only 17 feet by 25 feet. The first members numbered twelve: Rev. John Alderson, Mary Alderson, Thomas Alderson, John Skaggs, Joseph Skaggs, Katherine Skaggs, Lucy Skaggs, Bailey Wood, Ann Wood, James Wood, John Kippers and John Sheppard.

From the oldest records now extant, in the keeping of Miss Gladys Vaughan, the first Baptist church organized in the county was at the home of John Morris on Peters Creek in March 1824. Joseph Skaggs, who had been a charter member of the Old Greenbrier Church was moderator of the Hopewell Baptist church that released the membership of fourteen members to form the organization in Nicholas County. James Ellison who had served as pastor of the Greenbrier church was the first pastor in Nicholas County. For a time meetings were held at the homes of members. John Morris, James Rippetoe, John Campbell, David Lilly, Joseph Backus, and Edward Rian are named as entertaining meetings in their home. In 1840 it was determined to erect a church building, and meetings at this time were held in the Kessler school house at Cross Lanes. The first church, built of logs, was twenty-six feet by forty feet and located on the lot where the present church stands. It was completed in 1841 and named Zoar. John Foster, John R. McCutcheon and Fred Kessler were the trustees. Edward Rian was a charter member and John Campbell a deacon. The building was in use until 1861, when its occupation by Colonel Tyler as headquarters and later as hospital rendered it unfit to serve as a church. A new building was erected after the Civil War.

The Catholic church was organized in the early history of the county at Summersville, by the Duffys and other Irish emigrants. About 1825-6 they erected a small log church which was later replaced by a neat brick building.

During the Civil War this Catholic Church was occupied by Federal soliders and used as a fort. Traces of the earthworks on the hill around it are still visible. Port holes were opened in the walls and in the end the church building was ruined.

The members of Bethel and Zoar, mother churches of their respective denominations, came from all parts of Nicholas and from the borders of adjoining counties, often traveling twenty-five or thirty miles. Their attendance was regular as required by their rules and discipline. They came, not in buggies and automobiles, but on horseback or on foot in many instances. Distance and weather were not hindrances that kept our pioneers from attending their "meeting houses" as they called their church buildings, erected at a sacrifice by them. Their services were largely by the laymen, as their pastors could only meet with them at long intervals. They had regular services, in the way of prayer meetings, protracted revival services and Sunday Schools. To them it was joyous and willing service and a vital part in living.

Continuing the later history of the churches, Old Bethel, the first Methodist church in the County was replaced by a new building in 1867. Rev. L. H. Jordan, a young minister from New England was the pastor and was active in building the new place of worship. He planned the building and when he had time from his services labored on its erection. The building was thirty by fifty feet; the frame work was hewed out and the weather-boarding, floor and ceilings, all cut by whip-saws from fine yellow poplar. It was the first church painted in the county and was often referred to as the "white meeting house". It is still in good condition.

Zoar, the first Baptist church erected in the county, had also been replaced by a second building in 1875. In 1888 this building was destroyed by fire, and was replaced by the present building in 1891. This third building occupies the same commanding site as its predecessors and back of it lies one of the most beautiful and well-kept cemeteries in Nicholas County.

ZOAR BAPTIST CHURCH, Third Building
First Building, 1824

Old Alderson Baptist Church at Craigsville
James F. Brown, founding pastor

These mother churches of the two leading religious denominations in the county had much in common.

They were in the same community, and the members were friends and neighbors. The same pioneer customs and conditions prevailed. The churches were at first lighted with candles. The night meetings began at "early candle lighting". The congregations were seated with the women on the right and the men on the left as the church was entered. There was no organ or piano with a choir to lead the music. No hymn books were for distribution to the worshippers. The great gospel hymns of the reformation were "lined" and sung to a few well known tunes; and in the annual revival meetings whether at Zoar or Bethel the congregations were largely the same people.

For a generation Rev. A. N. Rippetoe was pastor at Zoar and other churches, and at Bethel Rev. L. H. Jordan, George C. Wilding, N. C. Beckley, and F. H. J. King were the successive itinerant pastors during the ministery of Rev. Rippetoe. While in the early days of the churches the difference in doctrinal beliefs were often stressed, this did not interfere with the fraternal relations of the pastors and leaders of these two pioneer churches. The Baptists of Zoar and the Methodists of Bethel could join in singing the gospel hymns of Cowper, Watts and Wesley.

A generation later, James F. Brown and L. J. Huffman were two successful ministers of the Baptist Church, and A. T. Morrison and A. S. Arnett able leaders of the Methodists. Both denominations soon had congregations in every community.

The benign influence that flowed from these early churches cannot be measured in words.

From Zoar church John L. McCutcheon went out to become president of Broaddus College, and later an eminent minister in Virginia; Robert Crookshanks became a well trained and successful preacher in Virginia and U. S. Knox whose family was affiliated with Zoar made a fine record as pastor of Falls Church, Virginia. Wyatte Rippetoe was a teacher of vocal music in Nicholas and adjoining counties. Many teachers and successful business men came from Zoar.

Miss Gladys Vaughan, grand daughter of Rev. A. N. Rippetoe in writing of Zoar says: "From the records it appears that more than 1000 members have belonged at Zoar. Her membership includes from the Revolutionary War to World War II."

From Bethel came George R. Grose, a popular minister, president of Du Paw University and later a Methodist bishop; L. S. Grose, son of a leader in Bethel Church was a well known minister and district Superintendent; R. G. Backus whose father was also a member of that church was an eloquent preacher and a district superintendent; Lowell Hypes went out from Bethel as a teacher to become dean of the University of Connecticut. Many teachers and leaders in public life were inspired by the society there. As at Zoar its members included Revolutionary soldiers and men who served in all our wars.

The old Camp Meeting Ground of the Methodist church, heretofore mentioned was not used after the Civil War, and the site is now owned by Walter Gray.

In 1876 the last Methodist Camp-meeting in Nicholas County was located on Laurel Creek just above the present residence of John Bennett.

About one-acre of land was cleared of all undergrowth and a group of small log-cabins built in a semi-circle around the edge of the clearing next to the creek. In the center of this arc of cabins a two-story cabin was built for the preachers and leaders of the meeting. A porch built in front of the upper story was used as the speakers' rostrum. On the ground were seats made of small split chestnut logs arranged in tiers with aisles. The area was shaded by many trees left standing when the ground was cleared. A unique system of lighting was provided. Upon posts set firmly in the ground about eight feet in height a platform about three feet square was covered with clay and on this blazing pineknots made a brilliant light. A dozen or more of these lights illuminated the camp ground at the night services which often lasted until midnight.

Hundreds of people from adjoining counties attended, and were entertained in the cabins and the homes of nearby residents. The presiding elder of the Methodist church usually directed the meetings and pastors of all denominations were speakers. Among notables from a distance were Rev. Edward W. Ryan and Rev. Wellington Young who had begun their ministry in Nicholas County.

The meetings continued for nearly two weeks in the month of August and was largely attended from all parts of the county till the last service.

The writer, then twelve years old, attended with his

parents as the home was in easy walking distance. The great crowd attentive to the sermons and lectures, the singing of the old gospel hymns from memory by hundreds of voices led by some one on the rostrum, the prayers and shouting in the testimonial services held each day, and withal the good behavior and friendly intercourse in the great congregation, was never to be forgotten.

One notable occasion was Rev. Ryan's singing of the *"Ninety* and *Nine"* just composed and sung by Moody and Sankey in their revivals. His fine strong voice carried the beautiful words to the bounds of the encampment. The audience scarcely breathed till the song closed with the rapturous words: "Rejoice, Rejoice, I have found my sheep", when with one accord all stood up in applause, with shouts of joy and praise. At the request of the congregation Rev. Ryan repeated the song each meeting till all could join in the singing.

Substantial church buildings by this time had been erected in many communities and "meeting houses", school houses and camp meeting grounds were no longer needed. Religious services, and Sunday Schools were held in all the principal communities and the Sabbath was strictly observed.

From the earliest settlements, the predominant sentiment was for orderly government and moral conduct by the citizens.—Though alcoholic beverages were sold with little legal restriction, drunkenness was not prevalent. "The Sons of Temperance" the earliest temperance movement in the United States, had a society in the County soon after its formation.

The organization included many of the leading citizens and county officials, and a "Temperance Hall" was erected at Cross Lanes.

This building was on a lot adjoining the land of John R. Vaughan and was well constructed of hewed logs, two stories in height with rooms 36 feet by 48 feet, in which the meetings of the members were held regularly till the Civil War. About 1876 the Patrons of Husbandry, usually known as "Grangers" organized a lodge in the county and secured the "Temperance Hall" for its use as a Cooperative Store and a Council Hall. In a few years the Grangers gave up their venture and sold the store to Thomas Fitzwater, a son of Captain George Fitzwater, who soon gave up the business. In 1890 W. G. Brown secured the building and had it remodeled into a school house which was used till his school was removed to Summersville.

Nicholas County was one of the three counties that voted in favor of the Prohibition Amendment in 1888; and again in 1912, gave a large majority vote for the Amendment in the successful campaign.

In all these years Gray's lines from the Elegy could well apply:

> "Far from the madding crowd's ignoble strife,
>   Their sober wishes never learned to stray;
> Along the cool sequestered vale of life,
>   They held the noiseless tenor of their way."

2. *Under the Second Constitution of 1872*

The second Constitutional Convention met in Charleston January 6, 1872. The session continued eighty-four days and its work was ratified by popular vote on the 4th

Tuesday in August, 1872. Nicholas County had no delegate in the convention.

Numerous changes were made in returning mainly to the Virginia form of state government. The terms of State officers were changed from two to four years and the Secretary of State was changed from an elective to an appointive office; and the State Superintendent of Schools from appointive to elective office. Annual sessions of the Legislature were changed to biennial and terms of delegates from one to two years, and that of senators from two to four years. County government was returned to the Virginia system. "Townships" were again designated "districts" and the "Board of Supervisors" was replaced by the "County Court". The new constitution like the first, exhibited the marks of partisanship.

In Nicholas County slow progress had been made in community life. While the census of 1870 showed the population 169 less than in 1860, property valuation had increased and the citizens were beginning to enjoy better home comforts. By 1870 coal in parts of the county was coming into use as fuel. School houses and churches were being furnished with stoves. "Coal oil", as kerosene was first called, and the small glass lamps first using it, appeared in some homes and could be purchased in the local stores.

Although Deere and Oliver steel plows were being produced in the 1830's and McCormick had invented the mowing machine, they had not yet appeared in Nicholas County. The devastated condition of the county at the end of the war and the panic of 1873 had placed the county almost a generation behind the most prosperous parts of the State. The greater number of the people were too poor to possess the latest in home appliances and to purchase improved agricultural machinery.

The use of improved tools and methods came slow in the first decade after the Civil war. From 1872 to 1882, there was more progress. The hand corn planter relieved the drudgery of dropping by hand and covering with hoes, the cast iron cane-mill took the place of the old wooden mill; cooking stoves began to appear but many house wives still held to the open fire cooking even in the late 1880's; wheat and oats were sowed by hand. J. C. Ramsey states in his family history that he brought the first wheat drill to the county in 1883. The "chaff-piler" threshing machine operated by horse power was used to some extent soon after the civil war. The sewing machine patented by Howe in 1846 was twenty-five years in coming into use in Nicholas County. By 1880 steam was being used for motor power in many ways. Saw mills, gristmills and threshing machines were operated by steam engines. By 1900, the farmer was equipped with mowing machine, corn planter, wheat drill, and cast iron cane-mills all operated by horse power. Steam driven saw mills and grist mills were in service. In the home the cooking stove, sewing machine and kerosene lamps appeared.

The country stores were now supplying many groceries. Flour had been a home product but now could be purchased by the barrel. Clothing, table-ware and many home appliances could now be had in the local stores.

Many farmers still living in one room log cabins, had

no horses or oxen with which to cultivate their crops, and small clearings were planted and cultivated with mattocks and hoes only. The women and children worked in the fields; and the daily fare was scanty. In the memory of the writer children of the poorer people had no shoes in winter. Nevertheless from these homes of poverty came some of our best citizens.

At the close of the Civil War the cleared lands on the farms were surrounded by woodlands in which scarcely any of the great, virgin trees had been destroyed. Giant yellow poplars grew on the north side of the hills and in the rich coves and on the benches. Immense chestnut trees stood thick on the south slopes and level stretches. Oak trees hundreds of years old could yet be found in the forest. Besides the larger wild animals still numerous, the woods were alive with smaller animals. Squirrels and rabbits especially were numerous. The streams were full of the native fish. A small boy with hook, line and willow rod, could in an hour bring home a larger catch than our modern angler with costly equipment can now show on his most fortunate day from any of our streams and ponds.

One of the most amazing sights of those days was the great flock of passenger pigeons to be seen in the early fall days. Only those who have read the accounts given by the great naturalists, Audubon and Wilson, can imagine the vast flights of these birds once to be seen in Nicholas County. Wilson states that in the year 1808 he observed a flock of pigeons estimated to contain 2,220,-272,000 birds, and he calculated they would devour in a day 17,424,000 bushels of beech nuts. This seems incredible, but a flock is of record as roosting in Michigan, as late as 1876, that occupied a stretch of forest 28 miles long and 3 miles wide. The writer can readily believe these statements as he vividly recalls witnessing the flight of pigeons near Pool in the Wilderness District in the autumn of 1876. On several days about an hour before sunset the sky was completely covered by a vast multitude of the pigeons pouring into the roost in the Wilderness, with a roar of wings like a heavy windstorm. Trees were broken down at the roost by the weight of the birds, and foxes and other wild animals feasted on the wounded birds falling to the ground. The land where this roost was located was enriched by the droppings of the birds. Doubtless today people in that community remember the story of this pigeon roost handed down from their ancestors. Though there is no record of destruction of grain by the birds of this county, a writer describing the passenger pigeons, states that in 1875, pigeons in Minnesota and Wisconsin would alight in immense flocks in fields of wheat just coming up and "scratch up and destroy the sprouting wheat under the very muzzle of the farmer's shot gun".

Soon after the great flight of passenger pigeons in 1880, their autumnal appearances ceased, and by 1880 the birds were practically extinct in the United States. Naturalists have not been able to explain the mystery of this sudden disappearance.

The squirrels were present in countless numbers many years longer than the pigeons. The wide-spread forests covered the ground with mast that fed and fattened them the year round. The common gray squirrel is migratory, and in those early days a general migration of squirrels occurred about every five years. The writer was teaching at Dixie in the fall of 1884, when a migration of squirrels occurred. Boys coming home from school killed squirrels with rocks as they crossed the road or swam across Twenty Mile and Bell Creek. All along Gauley River from Swiss to Gauley Bridge, men killed the squirrels with clubs or caught them as they were swimming the river. This migration continued about two weeks. The last migration witnessed by the writer was ten years later in the fall of 1894.

The destruction of the forests and the mass killing with repeating shot guns is rapidly bringing about the extinction of the squirrels.

The greatest change in the natural features of Nicholas County was the passing of the original forest. At the close of the Civil War only the clearings on the farms had taken toll of the fine timber in the primeval woods. The fine yellow poplars, white-oaks, walnuts and chestnuts had little commercial value. The trees were enemies of the early farmers, and had to be destroyed to make room for grain fields and meadows. This was the attitude of the people of the county trying to restore their homes by hard labor and little capital when the panic of 1873 struck. Many land owners who were barely subsisting could not pay their taxes or find local employment to help in clothing and feeding their families. Several hundred land holders in the five years the panic prevailed gave up their homes and sought for employment in other parts of the state or drifted to Ohio and other western states. Their lands were returned delinquent, and sold by the Commissioner of Delinquent and Forfeited Lands. This continued through the 1870's. Timbered lands underlaid with coal were sold at the Court House door at prices as low as one cent to ten cents an acre. Local and foreign speculators grabbed these bargains. The records in the County Clerk's Office reveal the extent of this sacrifice of delinquent real estate. In the 1880's the fine timber in the Appalachian region began to have market value. The Baltimore and Ohio and the Chesapeake and Ohio railroads were now available to transport lumber to eastern cities and for export to Europe. Some local dealers began to purchase poplar timber along Gauley River and made an attempt to float the logs out in high water. One operation was started in the Panther Mountain community to cut the poplars on the mountain and run the logs down a sluice-way and dump them into the river. The loss of logs from falling and splintering on the rocks and the loss from drifting down the river to the Kanawha was so great that the project was given up. For eight or ten years the wasteful method of floating timber out of Gauley River persisted. Uncounted thousands of feet of the finest timber lodged in drifts along the river and was burnt by fishermen or rotted on the banks of the river. Perhaps fifty per cent of the logs reaching the boom in the Falls Basin was damaged by wear and tear of the passage against the boulders in the river.

As the demand for lumber increased outside dealers began to look for undeveloped timber lands. In the middle 1880's the firm of Fay, Crozer and Miller began systematically to buy timber and mineral lands in Wilderness and Kentucky Districts.

Our citizens not informed of the changed conditions in the lumber business and of the real value of their timber were easy victims of the speculators. From their plausible representatives many citizens were led to believe that fifty cents to one dollar an acre was a fair price for "mineral that would never be of any possible use to them". Five dollars an acre for their "wild" land seemed a bargain for the timber and all in fee. The purchases of this firm were soon transferred to the Gauley Coal & Land Company, and the acquisition of the "wild" lands of this part of the county under the continual pressure of its agents soon gave this concern a monopoly of the timber and coal south of Gauley River. In the same period the Pardee & Curtin Lumber Company had through its agents bought timber land and trees in the same territory. Fine poplar trees that would produce a thousand to fifteen hundred feet and more of merchantable lumber were bought for the pitiful sum of fifty cents a tree, never more than one dollar a tree, and with the additional right to stand for five or more years. Similar proceedings were in progress throughout the County thus passing the ownership of the best timber to the speculators.

In the period from 1880 to 1900 much fine whiteoak timber was made into staves in the county. Some years before the advent of the railroads, Rippetoe Brothers established a "stave-yard" at the mouth of Twenty Mile Creek where the staves were collected and shipped by bateau to Gauley Bridge. Select timber for the staves was purchased from local owners, manufactured on the ground and hauled by wagon or "drifted" to the stave-yard. Along Twenty-Mile Creek thousands of staves were manufactured in the early 1880's and in flood water "drifted" down stream to the stave-yard.

With the coming of the railroads the stave trade increased; and the use of stave-saws were employed. Much good timber was wasted in the making of staves. Only the finest timber, free of knots, worm holes and other defects could be made into staves and the residue of the fallen trees was left to rot in the woods. The stave business was conducted by local dealers but it culled a large amount of fine oak timber out of our forests.

About the same time much fine walnut timber was being taken out of the county by agents buying for furniture manufacturers. The following episode illustrates the general attitude of the owners in respect to their timber lands: A great walnut tree stood on the farm of Thomas Bennett on Laurel Creek. About 1878-9 an agent of a furniture company bought the tree for a small sum, as Bennett said he was anxious to get rid of the tree so he could clear the land and could think of no way to remove it. The diameter of the tree was more than seven feet, and about sixteen feet from the ground it branched into three great limbs. In felling it the immense boll was notched around so a saw could be used. The trunk was cut off just below the branches and squared by hewing off great juggles; then with a team of four yoke of oxen it was hauled to Drennen. There it lay for months where the team had stalled in the creek, and was finally split into parts and hauled away. Fifty years later a government buyer paid the new owner of the Bennett farm a large sum for the stump of the giant tree to be used in making gun-stocks for the army. From limbs of the tree shingles were made to cover Bethel Church, but about one-third of this fine figured walnut lumber was burned in clearing the land. In the same neighborhood fine walnut trees were made into fence rails or burnt in the clearings.

By the early 1900's outside capital controlled the major part of the timber and coal lands of Nicholas County. The "Big Mill" at Camden-on-Gauley, The Pardee & Curtin Lumber Company, The Cherry River Boom & Lumber Company, The Tioga Coal & Lumber Company, The Birch Valley Lumber Company, The West Virginia Timber Company, The Flynn Lumber Company, The Wilderness Lumber Company, The Laurel Manufacturing Company, The Fenwick Lumber Company and numerous smaller concerns were beginning the onslaught that in the next twenty-five years swept away our forests.

The lion's share of the spoils went to the Pardee & Curtin Lumber Company with its big band mills at the mouth of Cherry River and on Hominy. Great yellow poplars producing fifteen hundred to two thousand feet of lumber and that had cost from fifty cents to a dollar a tree, were cut into export boards two inches thick and twenty-four to thirty-six inches wide, and sold in the export trade for as much as $80.00 to $100.00 a thousand feet.

By 1925 the mass lumbering operations were well over. The wealth of the woodlands had flowed out of the county; the greater part of it out of the State. Little of value was left to the original owners.

While the lumbering operations were in full progress money was more plentiful than in any previous period in our history. The young men and even many farmers had left the farm for the lumber camps and sawmills, attracted by good wages in cash. Farmers could use their teams in logging jobs that brought more money and quicker returns than could be realized in the drudgery of farm work. Farm products were also increased in value and had a market at hand in supplying the population of the lumber camps. This prosperity was short lived, and vanished with the end of the big lumbering operations. Farm work now seemed rather dull and profitless to many who had made good wages in lumbering, and consequently farm products were much reduced. The population of the county which had increased from 11,403 in 1910 to 20,217 in 1920, numbered only 20,686 in 1930.

With the extension of the Chesapeake & Ohio Railroad from Gauley Bridge into Nicholas County, coal mines were first opened on Bell Creek and Twenty Mile. Bentree near the Clay County line was a thriving mining town for a time, and Vaughan became a mining center on Twenty Mile. In less than a dozen years mining in this territory was abandoned, though only a small percentage of the merchantable coal had been removed.

Returning to our early local papers after *The Bastinado* another short lived paper, *The Nicholas County Local*, made its appearance, with John Huff editor and proprietor. The first issue of this diminutive paper, printed in two columns on four pages 6½ by 9½ inches, is dated September 13, 1876. The subscription price was fifty cents a year, and the proprietor announced that "marketable produce, a load of firewood and a few bushels of coal would be accepted in payment of subscription". A few items from a faded copy of *The Nicholas County Local*, dated October 4, 1876, will give an interesting glimpse of the period:

PROGRAM OF NICHOLAS COUNTY TEACHERS' INSTITUTE,

To Be Held at the Court House,
December 28th, 29th and 30th, 1876.

Opening Oration,—F. H. King
Drill on Orthography,—L. W. Herold
Debate,—Ought Emulation in schools be encouraged?
    Affirm: R. E. Robinson and A. T. Groves,
    Deny: S. P. Schindell and A. A. Hamilton.
Drill on Arithmetic,—William Y. Callaghan,
Art of Teaching,—John E. Kern,
Essays: Laura Cox, Mary A. Stanard, A. T. Groves, B. C. McNutt, E. P. White, and J. H. H. Duffy,
Reading in School,—George Grose.
Queries,—By the Institute,
Debate,—A bad Education is worse than no Education.
    Affirm:—J. Haymond Robinson and George A. Herlod,
    Deny:—C. R. Hanna and I. N. Cox.
Miscellaneous Questions to be Answered on the Exercises and Lectures.

MARRIAGE NOTICE.

Married on Tuesday the 12th day of September, 1876, at the residence of the bride's father, Dr. M. R. Hereford, by Rev. A. N. Rippetoe, Mr. Edmund Suthern and Miss Martha Hereford.

ADVERTISEMENT

James S. Craig, Real Estate Agent and Broker,
Nicholas C. H. W. Va.

Farming, Timber and Coal Lands for Sale, in Nicholas, Clay and Webster Counties, in large or small tracts on easy terms.

DEMOCRATIC PRIMARY ELECTION

Candidates:
    For Prosecuting Attorney, John D. Alderson.
    For County Surveyor of Lands, John M. Hutchinson.
    For President County Court, James R. Miller.
    For Sheriff, Lanty W. Herold.
    For Assessor, Samuel Bell.

After the two transient papers mentioned Nicholas County had no local paper until 1880. In August of that year Howard Templeton began the publication of *The Nicholas Chronicle*. He was a successful publisher and in 1891 had the paper well established. He sold to John A. Grose and David O. Grose that year. David O. Grose continued as editor until his death in 1898. John A. Grose was then editor and publisher until 1905 when he sold to J. T. Williams. In 1907 Williams sold to P. N. Wiseman and L. J. Groves. For one year the paper was managed by W. R. Howlette and Robert A. Kincaid. In 1908 J. L. Stewart purchased and published the paper until 1911, when he was succeeded by his brother A. Lee Stewart who was owner and publisher until January 1921. He sold to Ruskin J. Wiseman who was editor and publisher for the next seven years. In 1928 J. T. Williams again became the owner and publisher for two years. In 1930 Ruskin J. Wiseman, the present owner, again took over the paper. *The Nicholas Chronicle* for more than seventy years has been the leading local paper in the county.

The Nicholas Republican was established in 1903 at

Summersville, by W. G. Brown, S. C. Dotson and Logan S. Dotson, partners. It was first printed on the press of *The Nicholas Chronicle* by John A. Grose, a silent partner. The office of *The Republican* was in a small two-room building owned by W. G. Brown, located on the lot now occupied by the residence of Porter Herold. In a short time a full printing outfit was purchased and for the paper, and A. Powie Smith was employed as office manager and printer. Powie took great interest in his work and did much to give the new venture a large circulation. W. G. Brown served as the principal editor the first year and until his election as prosecuting attorney. Soon under the pressure of the work in his office he resigned as editor and sold his interest to S. C. Dotson, in 1905. Mr. Dotson then controlled and edited the paper for about two years. After his election as County Superintendent of Schools he sold the paper to Dr. James McClung who removed the publication to Richwood, and in a short time sold to James J. Dotson. Mr. Dotson who had started a paper he called *The Gauley Record*, discontinued this paper and published The Nicholas Republican under the caption of "The Nicholas News Company". The paper which had a general circulation when moved to Richwood, soon lost its general circulation to a large extent, but was liberally supported in Richwood and adjacent territory. At the death of Mr. Dotson the paper in time passed to W. S. Dodrill, and by him was transferred to Don Crislip the present owner.

The *News Leader*, established at Richwood in 1946 was an innovation in local newspaperdom. The publishers, Jim Comstock and Brownson McClung, at first styled their adventure "*News Letter*", but under a government directive the name was changed to *News Leader*.

The illustrated news items and reproduction of old scenes and stories from actual photographs was one of the novel features of the paper that caught the interest of the public.

The attractive makeup of the *News Leader*, and the originality of the publishers has won for it a substantial circulation.

In the early days of Richwood, "The Yew Pine Independent", "The Advance", "The Gauley Record", and C. Donee Cook's "Hoot Owl", were evanescent ventures, and had little circulation out of the town.

In the past few years the local papers have greatly changed in form and contents. The first publications were without illustrations and were actively political. Today the papers are profusely illustrated and touch rather lightly on political questions.

3. *Under the Change of Conditions Following World War II*

After the brief Spanish American War an era of peace and goodwill followed. Our leaders in church and state believed that the time was almost at hand when "swords would be beaten into plowshares and spears into pruning hooks". The poet Tennyson saw:

> "Earth at last a warless world, a single race,
>   a single tongue;
> Every tiger madness muzzled, every serpent
>   poison killed,
> Every blazing desert tilled."

The shock of World War I dispelled the dreams of peace. Words cannot picture the abysm of suffering and sacrifice that resulted. Millions of our best young men, from the peaceful homes of Nicholas County, and from all the homes of the nation, were suddenly drafted from farm, workshop, office and school, and thrown into the demoralizing evils of war. Thousands died on the battlefield, thousands came out shell-shocked, soul-scarred, mentally and morally unbalanced, too stunned by their terrible experience to take up their normal life.

Before the wounds of this conflict had time to heal, veterans with their sons were thrown into a still greater carnage. And then came Korea as an echo of the passions and hatreds of the evil forces war had unleashed. The cumulated evils of a generation of war has wrought a complete metamorphosis in the social, business and moral life of Nicholas County. Let the records speak. The disruption in social life is reflected in our homes, our schools and even in our churches. The home life that existed before the era of war has almost faded out. Our homes are more like filling stations for the family that spends more time in the automobile than in friendly intercourse around the fireside. Too many mothers have abdicated the noblest function in life—*Motherhood* and have delegated their duties to the schools, the churches, and "*baby-sitters*". Our schools were established to train our boys and girls in morals and manners, and in the language of our first constitution "to furnish the State exemplary citizens". This fundamental reason for a free school system was kept in mind and parents and teachers co-operated in enforcing discipline and obedience to authority. But there arose a new philosophy, grounded in materialism and disregarding the universal verdict of history, which was promulgated chiefly by a certain school of atheists. They presented their theories so plausibly it seemed to offer a "royal road" to learning and to widen the "narrow road" of the Christian way of living. Many parents and teachers in the confused life of the war period gradually gave consent to the doctrine of John Dewey and his disciples that *"children should not be disciplined but allowed to follow their natural impulses."* We are now reaping the harvest of this sowing in widespread "juvenile delinquency" and spiritual barrenness in our churches. This spurious philosophy has poisoned every stream of our social life. Witness the return of the liquor traffic; the surge of divorces; dishonesty in business; and corruption and "spendmania" in government. In 1952, the latest statistics, it is reported officially that $242,714.30 was spent for liquor at the State Liquor Store in Richwood. The Liquor Dealers Association in a recent bulletin classes Nicholas County among the "wettest", declares it profitable territory for their business. The chancery docket of Nicholas Circuit court for 1953 lists 88 divorce suits, as compared to only 8 such suits in the year 1917. The headlines of our dailies continually display great embezzlements by prominent bankers and numerous frauds in large sums discovered by the collectors of Internal Revenue. Glance at your daily paper to read of ghastly murders and other crimes by "teen-agers". It is no longer startling to read that a young boy or girl has shot, knifed or poisoned father or mother for some immaterial reason. These deplorable conditions are the direct consequences of the brutalizing effects of war. Every war in history has been followed by social and moral disintegration. As the long duration of the world wars and the immeasurable excess of its atrocities rise above that of all wars in history, just in such proportion has been the fearful impact of these world wars upon our civilization. The effect of war has wrought a greater change upon the character and outlook on life of the people of Nicholas County than have the destruction of our soil and forests and the pollution of our water course changed the natural features of the land. Only the few men and women now living, who remember the conditions before the first world war, can appreciate the abrupt change that has swept us so far away from the settled social and moral principles that characterized preceding generations in our county.

In Grecian mythology beautiful Pandora was sent by the gods to avenge the theft of fire from Heaven by Prometheus. To execute her mission of vengeance she was given a box filled with all evils of which humanity was heir. Then she opened the fateful box and all human virtues save Hope was destroyed from the earth. Like in the Greek myth War has opened a Pandora's Box upon our world; and the demons of inhuman hate and cruelty born in the inferno of war have been let loose upon our world. Yet again, as in the myth, Hope has survived. It springs eternal in the human heart.

With the optimism Christian faith inspires our hope is bright that the rising generation will turn back the wave of materialism and false theories of life, and battle to restore our lost virtues. In the veins of the young generation descended from the heroic pioneers that gave us this goodly land still flows the red blood of their ancestors. May we not trust that weary of the reckless and dissolute way of life, with its false promise of peace and security, that now prevails, they will undertake the noble task of restoring our lost virtues; *justice, moderation, temperance, frugality and morality and build a new life on these fundamental principles.*

A striking change in the natural features of the county has taken place in the past generation. Our mountains and hills remain as of old. The forests that once crowned them have lost their virgin beauty. Beginning with the era of lumbering the original forests have disappeared. Nature ever trying to replace them has been hindered by the ruthless cuttings of the young growth, leaving brush scattered through the timber, to add fuel to the fires that sweep the woods each spring and autumn.

The chestnut was a favorite tree of the early settlers prized for its valuable nuts and its use for making fence rails and shingles. In the clearing of their fields and later in selling their "wild" lands they had kept "chestnut orchards" near their homes and reserved chestnut timber for farm use. Toward the close of the lumbering era in the county, a fine stand of young chestnut trees was growing up in the "cut-over" lands. Suddenly in 1926 the mysterious "chestnut blight" attacked the eastern fringe of the chestnut forests in the Blue Ridge region. In less than five years its deadly touch had crept across the entire *habitat* of the chestnut forests and the beautiful trees and their luscious nuts were no more. For a few years the dead trees loomed like ghosts in the verdant foliage of the woods, then suddenly dropped from sight. Little remains in the woodlands of Nicholas County today to show the great loss to man and wild life of the chestnut trees. To the boys and girls of the past generation, the pleasure of gathering the annual crop of rich, brown chestnuts that covered the ground under the trees on frosty mornings, is but a fading memory.

The sugar maple grew abundantly and furnished maple sugar and sirup for three generations. Groves of the trees were preserved for the purpose, but for several years the making of this fine product has been almost abandoned.

The channels of the streams maintain their course, but no longer brim with the clear pure water that sustained fish life and gave charm to the landscape. Beginning with the lumbering period the streams were choked with saw dust, brush and refuse from the camps, and fish destroyed by dynamite and wholesale seining. Gauley and its tributaries especially, Twenty Mile, Peters Creek and Muddlety, were teeming with native fish. Meadow River and Birch River were alive with fish less than forty years ago. Last summer the author inspected Twenty Mile Creek from Belva to Vaughan, where he once saw this beautiful stream alive with fish. Not one fish was found in the six mile stretch. Bell Creek and Twenty Mile had become convenient garbage dumps, filled with tin cans, old auto tires, discarded crates, and trash of all descriptions. The beauty of these streams and the purity of the water is gone. The same inspection was made of Meadow River from Anglins Creek a distance of at least a mile up stream and though the water was clear

Home Life After the Civil War

not a single fish could be seen, where once they flashed through the water in schools. Peters Creek has become a sewer, black with washings from a coal mine, that destroyed it as a bass stream. To a greater or less degree this has happened to our once fine water courses.

Development of the county's mineral resources began some time after the lumbering industry had slowed down. Prospecting for oil and gas in the county began in the early 1900's. In 1911 the Enon Oil & Gas Company was organized by local citizens, with Allen Rader president. Two wells were drilled in the Bucks Garden territory that produced gas in sufficient quantity for export but no line was available and only a limited amount of gas was used locally.

In 1924 the Hamilton Oil and Gas Company drilled a number of producing wells on the waters of Brushy Fork and tributaries of Muddlety Creek. This production is sold to the Hope Natural Gas Company and transported by their pipe line to market. Richwood is supplied with gas from this operation.

Producing wells in Jefferson and Grant Districts owned by Columbia Carbon Company and Southeastern Gas Company are supplying gas to market through a recently constructed pipe line.

Only a narrow strip along the northwest boundary of Nicholas, in Jefferson, Grant, Summersville and Hamilton Districts, lies in the proved oil and gas belts of the State. Outside of this strip a few scattered wells have been drilled, but most have proved to be barren.

In Beaver, Kentucky and Wilderness Districts, lying

south of Gauley a few tests have been made, but only slight traces of oil and gas have been found.

In only one well has oil been found in sufficient quantity to be classed as a producer. In several other wells oil has been found in small showings.

Recently good producing wells have been drilled in the proved territory mentioned, especially on the waters of Twenty Mile Creek and Birch River. Much of this territory is under lease principally to the Columbia Carbon Company, Hamilton Gas Corporation and Hope Natural Gas Company.

Many leases outside the western strip mentioned have been cancelled, and rentals on leases that once rated as high as one dollar an acre are now reduced to twenty five cents an acre.

Leases for coal, oil and gas in Nicholas County on record since 1909, fill 19 large volumes in the office of the County Court.

After the coming of hard roads and some further extension of railroads into the County, mining of coal was resumed.

In 1941 only 268,471 tons of coal were reported shipped from the county. Shipments rapidly increased during the next ten years and in 1951 the shipments reached a total of 4,234,597 tons. For that year the State Department of mines reports 26 companies and 30 operations in the county, employing 2,928 men. Mines are in operation in all the districts of the county; and extensions of the Baltimore & Ohio Railroad, the Chesapeake & Ohio Railroad and the New York Central Railroad are now carrying coal shipments on the branch lines recently extended to the coal fields. Trucks are also extensively employed in the shipment of coal, especially from the numerous small operations.

Beside the men reported as employed in the mines of Nicholas County, a number of miners who live in the county find employment in the mines of adjoining counties and reach their work daily by automobile.

The prospect is promising for continued and increasing development of the coal industry, as the estimated reserve of commercial coals in Nicholas County is in excess of six billion tons.

Farming and farm life in Nicholas County is no longer the hard struggle with the soil endured by our pioneers. Modern farm machinery, development of better species of the staple grains as corn and wheat; improved varieties of fruits and vegetables, thorough-bred live stock, scientific methods of soil conservation and fertilization, directed by trained specialists in the use of these discoveries and appliances, all combine to make country life more attractive and remunerative. One trained farmer with his tractors and other motorized equipment can without drudgery accomplish more in a day, than could a dozen men in former days, with their primitive tools and backbreaking labor.

In the field of education we are spending thousands of dollars in contrast to hundreds twenty years ago. Our consolidated schools are housed in modern buildings that are palaces in comparison to the small one-room houses of the past generation. Our system of transportation carries the pupils in comfortable buses to and from school in all weather. Sanitary conditions are provided and maintained on the school grounds. Free text books, hot lunches and health preservation are stressed. Teachers are well paid, have a system of pensions, and reach their work by automobile to find a well kept school room awaiting.

In the past decade much advancement appears in the building of more up-to-date churches. In the towns and many populous neighborhoods the buildings are constructed in durable cinder-block, brick or stone instead of the wooden frame structure. The furnishing of pews, heating and lighting, musical instruments, organ, or piano, choir seating, with hymn books, bibles and Sunday School literature are now required in the modern church building. Pastors regularly minister to the congregation and direct the activities of the membership by organized groups for old and young. Attendance is rendered easy even in the country districts by automobiles and good roads.

In general it must be said that our complex modern life with its many innovations, freedom from manual labor and swift and easy transportation, cannot here be pictured in detail. We have clothing and food without the long and tedious production from harvest field to kitchen; and the toilsome process of growing wool and flax, weaving and spinning into cloth, and tanning the leather and making our shoes, that fed and clothed our forefathers and their families not so long ago. Homes are now heated, lighted, and supplied with water by setting a thermostat, throwing a switch or turning a spigot. Our daily mails bring to our doorsteps our letters, daily papers, books, magazines, and merchandise. Our automobiles transport us over smooth hardtop roads and our airplanes lift us above the clouds in a speed that outstrips the eagle.

Sitting in our homes the world comes to us by radio and television. With shortened hours of labor we take the time for amusement in the movies, in athletic games and sports, in summer camps, vacation tours, and the other multifarious diversions offered on all sides.

In preceding pages of this history of Nicholas County the epic story has been meagerly though truly presented. Until the paralizing shock of world war and its reactions the record portrays a busy, industrious and moral people, content to give their best energies to home life; interested in their schools; devoted to their churches and active in their attention to questions of government. The common ideal was the creation of a better life for their children. They remembered the *past*, and in their *present* looked forward to a brighter *future*. To this end children were *disciplined* in their behavior, and *obedience* to authority enforced. It is needless to say this generation has almost lost sight of these ideals. It is too obvious in our every day life. Parental laxity in the home training is so gross that small boys and girls pay little attention to the authority of their parents; and even to a great extent dominate the situation. This break-down of home government has extended into our schools and our churches. In the school room and our school buses good order and proper discipline can scarcely be demanded. At long last we are learning that *"juvenile delinquency"* is the direct result of *"parental delinquency"* ... J. Edgar Hoover, distinguished head of the Federal Bureau of Investigation, has repeatedly pointed this out, and is pleading with parents to recover their parental duties in home government. In some of our best governed cities the courts are bringing parents into cases of juvenile offenses and holding them responsible as parties to violations of law. The end results of anarchy in home government is seen in disrespect for law, disregard of property rights, roadsides and parks littered with rubbish, beautiful water courses polluted, forest fires, hourly accidents from reckless driving, and insane desire for "thrilling amusements."

The verdict of history places the responsibility of the present deplorable condition of our society upon the generation following world war. We can understand the loss of the former ideals of life when we stop to reflect upon the convulsion that suddenly took millions of our best young men and women from their homes and disrupted all their plans and ambitions and destroyed the peace and hopes of their parents. They were trained in camps to hate and kill, and thrown into the hell of war. They came home in such confusion and bewilderment that blinded them morally and socially. The results that followed fall upon their children today. Much is now said of youthful delinquency and irresponsibility. *The children are more sinned against than sinning.* The mother in the home moulds the character of her children and that shapes the destiny of the nation.

There are hopeful signs that present day young people are being led into an age of responsibility. In many homes the real values of life survived, and earnest leaders, in the field of education and in the churches are fanning into a new life the lost social and moral principles that had almost faded away. The Four H Clubs, Future Farmers, Boys and Girls Scouts, and like movements are steps in that direction. A growing sentiment to give the right to vote to our youth at 18, is noteworthy. Why should our rulers, often selfish and sometimes stupid, be allowed to send our youth into all parts of the world to give up useful lives to become mere tools for carrying on war. Surely the young should have a voice in determining the right to be so called into such service. This opportunity to share in the government of our land will inspire and encourage to better things in our political life. All through history young men and women have led in reforming life. Luther, Calvin and the Wesleys were young men when they started the Reformation in religion. Wilson Cary Nicholas was 18 when he became the captain of Washington's bodyguard in the Revolution.

Our foundations are already laid in Nicholas County for return to a more healthful social, and moral life. Modern churches, school houses and recreation centers offer inducements to our young folks and invite them to healthy recreations and useful work.

Carnefix Battlefield Park has for years been a popular meeting place for our citizens, and its splendid programs present able speakers, and delightful reunions of friends and neighbors. The basket dinners, songs, and playgrounds for the children, are enjoyed annually. Throughout the summer the park is used by picnic parties and is thronged with visitors having a day's vacation, or perhaps a Sunday School meets for an outing. The park has been lately improved and can be made one of the most beautiful in the State.

Nicholas County Memorial Park, on U. S. Route 19, three miles north of Summersville, was established in 1946 and dedicated to Veterans of World Wars. It has an area of 140 acres, with a residence occupied by the Coach of Nicholas County High School. A large barn and three small buildings have been made over to be used as display rooms for the County Fair. A dining room is to be added to the large kitchen now used by 4-H Clubs and other gatherings of the youth organizations. A grand-stand is provided for public speaking, square dances, wrestling matches, etc., and a small golf course is in course of construction, to be followed by other attractions as required. The cost of this park was met by voluntary contributions of citizens, aided by annual additions from the County Court, the County Board of Education, and funds raised by the various youth clubs of the county. The Board of Directors in control consists of a member of the County Court, a member of the Board of Education and an attorney chosen by them. The present members are, Arley M. Johnson, Russell Sebert, and Ben. F. Brown. The park is for the county at large and is open to private picnic parties and re-unions.

An important contribution to our religious life has been quietly underway for the past ten years. In 1944 "the Church of the Nazarene", directed by Dr. Edward C. Oney, Superintendent, bought 37 acres of land on State Route 41, near the intersection with U. S. Route 19, on which Camp Meeting Grounds have been constructed. Funds were provided by the church, and work began by setting up a sawmill and planer, using timber taken from the tract, and by purchasing the Old Paper Mill building at Richwood and those of the CCC Camp at Marlinton. There is now on the ground an Auditorium 120 feet by 82 feet, with seating capacity for 1500; a three-story cinder-block dormitory that accommodates 500 with sleeping quarters, a basement with baths and toilets, a dining room seating 200, and a lunch stand. There are 28 cottages, owned by individuals, and by churches for their pastors. A fine cottage is provided for the District Superintendent, and a residence for the caretaker. The grounds are lighted by electricity; and four driven wells with electric pumps supply a water system.

The first meeting was held in July, 1946, and annual meetings are held beginning the first of July, and continuing till September.

The meetings open with a 3-day session of *"The Assembly of West Virginia District"*, at which the *General Superintendent presides*. A 10 days "Camp Meeting" follows, this is succeeded by the "Boys Camp" admitting boys from age 6 to 14; a "Girls Camp" admitting girls of the same age; and lastly the session of the "Nazarene Young People" whose members are limited in ages 18 to 40.

Hundreds of people from all parts of the country attend these inspiring meetings. Everybody finds a welcome.

The problems of our social life have been amply presented elsewhere. There are hopeful signs that people are once again beginning to crave something more than sensual enjoyment and material progress. The responsibility of our preachers, teachers, writers and leaders of the many social organizations now presents itself to awaken individual responsibility and to lead to a search for the abiding values of life. The closed pages of national history can be reopened and the vision of our "Founding Fathers" brought to view. In the wisdom of the "old Book" we are admonished: "Where there is no vision the people perish". The men who gave us our Constitution, which Gladstone declared was the "greatest political document ever struck from the brain of man", warned us that "eternal vigilance was the price of liberty". When the Constitution was ratified Franklin said: "We have given you a republic if you can keep it." Jefferson answered that the common people must be trained to maintain self-government. He gave the best of his life to that end, and the "Statute of Religious Freedom", and the plan for our free school system and local government was his contribution. Washington insisted that "We shall preserve our liberty only by the religious education of our youth". In 1872, the Constitutional Convention in our State, wrote Section 20 as the climax to our Bill of Rights: "Free government and the blessings of liberty can be preserved to any people only by a firm adherence to justice, moderation, temperance, frugality and virtue, and by a frequent recurrence to fundamental principles." President Woodrow Wilson, who had presided over Princeton University and was a student of educational methods in the nation, said to those who were then neglecting the fundamental goal of education: "You know with all this teaching you train nobody; with all your instruction you educate no one."

The coming generation must meet many problems laid upon it by the apathy and ignorance of its predecessors. Public opinion is already vocal. Centralization and totalitarian administration of State government instituted by a series of arbitrary laws beginning in 1933, has revolutionized our society. The right of self-government, emphasized by Thomas Jefferson as a necessity in maintaining the Republic, has been taken from our counties and districts. Our County Courts have been stripped of their chief functions. The common schools so fundamentally belonging to the people are now manipulated by a State Board of Education appointed by the Governor and with the only qualification that members be politicians—trained schoolmen being *persona non grata*. The State is now A Liquor Dealer; and the traffic in liquor is now forced upon the people by a statute that defines alcohol in beer "*non-intoxicating*"—A law that Judge Jake Fisher, one of our able and fearless jurists, declared in a public opinion is "*a legislative lie.*" Our county is flooded with "beer-joints", and has a flourishing liquor store, bound upon it by this same statute that denies voters the right of local option. Our State government under these arbitrary and totalitarian statutes has permitted its officials to prostitute their departments as opportunities for personal gain or as political assets. This is most apparent in the management of the Road Commission and the State Liquor Commission. These conditions can be righted by the electorate now awake, and even a new constitution may be adopted. The coming generation must solve the problems.

About 1876, Sir Edwin Arnold, the English poet, in an

address to the students of Harvard College said: "Young men; your pioneer ancestors conquered the savages; their sons conquered the wilderness; the next generation conquered slavery; your fathers are now conquering the drudgery of human toil with the machine. A greater conquest awaits your action. *When will you conquer yourselves?*"

CHAPTER IX

Municipalities and Villages

RICHWOOD, situated in the extreme eastern part is the only city in the County. Its elevation is about 2200 feet above sea level. The name comes from "rich woods", the name given by early settlers to the fine forest lying around the junction of the north and south forks of Cherry River.

The history of Richwood begins with the development of timber lands of the Cherry River Boom & Lumber Company about 1900. This company had acquired a large tract of timber in the Counties of Nicholas, Greenbrier, Webster and Pocahontas, and located its plant on the site where the settlement began. At the time the region was sparsely settled. The Spencers, Mullenses and Hinkles were residents and a post office named "Richwood" had been established. In 1900 the post office was moved to the new development and the name followed.

The Town of Richwood was incorporated November 3, 1901, and E. E. Deitz became the first mayor.

From the beginning the citizens of the new town were interested in churches and schools. The Presbyterian church was erected in 1901, the Catholics, Methodists and Baptists soon followed with their Church buildings.

In 1903 the Independent School District of Richwood, after a spirited legal action, was laid off and a system providing for the grades and a high school was adopted, as mentioned in the Chapter on Education.

In 1902 the Citizens Banking & Trust Company opened for business, soon followed by Cherry River National Bank. Later the Citizens Bank was organized.

The Baltimore & Ohio R. R. had been completed to Richwood in the Spring of 1901, and the town was thus connected with the business world. The first store which had been established by Cam Griggs, in anticipation of the development was opened in 1899.

Soon the Cherry River Boom & Lumber Company opened a large department store under the name of The Richwood Store Company and a number of stores covering all classes of merchandise were soon in business. The first hotel was the Aylor House, later styled the Yew Pine Inn.

Richwood owes its existence to the large lumber plant of Cherry River Boom & Lumber Company, the largest lumbering operation in the county and one of the largest in the State. Its forest lands cover an area of 310 square miles—almost half the size of Nicholas County. In its operation the company built and operates a broad gauge railroad, to convey the timber to the mill and in connection with its saw mill operates a lath mill, planing mill and a large well equipped machine shop. Although the Cherry River Boom & Lumber Company has been in operation more than half a century, it is still Richwood's chief industry. Beginning its history under the management of J. W. Oakford, the company has co-operated with the local citizens in the making of the town. In encouragement of development valuable building lots were laid off from the Company's property, and no attempt made to monopolize business.

Soon the advantages offered by the supply of material from the lumbering operation, the efficient means of transportation by the B. & O. Railroad, and attractive labor conditions, brought Wm. Mosser Tanning Company, The Cherry River Paper Company, The Steele Wallace Corporation and other industries to the town. Tan bark and pulp wood from the logging operations, were to be had in abundance at a low cost. Other factories manufactured clothes-pins, broom-handles, hubs, wooden dishes, chair rounds, and even kindling wood was shipped in large quantities, from by-products of the Lumber Company.

In twenty-five years the little backwoods community of twenty or thirty natives had grown to a city with a population of 7000 and boasted a presidential post office, and busy industries.

The panic of 1929 hit Richwood hard. In a few years most of the subsidiary factories had closed down; the population dropped to about 5000; and the Richwood Banking & Trust Company and Citizens Bank had closed their doors. The William F. Mosser Company, The Cherry River Paper Company, The Steele Wallace Company and other factories moved out, but The Cherry River Boom & Lumber Company survived and saved the day. Gradually with the recovery of business the city took on new life. The development of coal mining in the vicinity, the extension of the B. & O. R. R. down Gauley River and the construction of hard surfaced roads, connecting the city with the State Road system have been the chief factors in restoring its prosperity and assuring the future progress of the city.

From its early days Richwood has had two hospitals that have been of great service to Nicholas and adjoining Counties. The McClung Hospital founded by Dr. James McClung, has maintained an excellent corps of physicians and surgeons. The Sacred Heart Hospital, established by the Catholic Church, has likewise served the county, and has recently erected a fine new building on the site of the old Tannery Plant.

The Cherry River National Bank survived the panic and is now in business as The First National Bank of Richwood.

Richwood is now a third class city with a population of 5,321, according to the census of 1950. The city has paved streets, concrete walks, both electricity and gas, an up to date water system, a motorized volunteer fire department, a public library, two newspapers—The Nicholas Republican and The News Leader—an attractive post office building and a large three story brick municipal building.

The city has an excellent school system. Buildings for the grades are modern and well equipped, the high school occupies a good building and has a gymnasium and athletic field. The city also has commodious and attractive church edifices. Two churches are Methodist, each with a resident minister. The Baptists have recently erected a fine new building, occupied by a large and representative congregation. The Catholics have a large membership, and conduct a parochial school in connection with their church, and the Presbyterians are well

Municipalities and Villages 209

represented and occupy the building erected soon after the establishment of the city. The Church of the Nazarene and other of smaller denominations are represented.

For several years the new town was greatly handicapped by lack of roads connecting with outlying territory. The adoption of the State Road System and generous bond issues of the municipality and district brought hard-surfaced roads. State Route 39 extending from U. S. Route 60 at Gauley Bridge by way of Summersville and Nettie to Richwood crosses the mountains to Marlinton; State Route 20 from Camden-on-Gauley by way of Craigsville to Richwood, continues from Fenwick by way of Nettie and Quinwood to its intersection with U. S. Route 60 at Charmco; and State Routes 41 and 43 connect U. S. Route 19 with State Route 20 at Craigsville. This system of good roads furnishes the city ideal communication with all adjoining counties and the outside world. Thus situated Richwood becomes a natural trade center for the surrounding territory. Its well-stocked stores, shops, hospitals, law offices, newspapers, schools, churches, movie theaters, and banks offer many of the advantages of larger cities to Nicholas and adjoining counties.

SUMMERSVILLE, is situated at the head of Peters Creek south of the center of the county. The elevation above sea level is 1894 feet at the front door of the Court House. The name was given in honor of Judge Lewis Summers.

The town was established by act of the General Assembly of Virginia, January 19, 1820, as follows:

"Be it enacted by the General Assembly, That thirty acres of land the property of the heirs and legatees of John Hamilton, deceased, as the same hath already been laid off, be established as a town by the name of Summersville: and that Robert Hamilton, Robert Kelly, William Hamilton, John Groves, Samuel Hutchinson, John G. Stephenson, James Robinson, John Campbell and Edward Rian, be and they are hereby appointed trustees thereof."

"The trustees of said town or a majority of them are empowered to make such rules and orders for the regular building of houses therein, as to them shall seem best; to settle and determine all disputes concerning the bounds of the lots; and to make such by-laws, rules and regulations, not contrary to the laws and constitution of this State, or of the United States, as they may deem necessary for the good order and the government of said town."

"So soon as the purchaser of any lot in said town shall have built a dwelling house thereon equal to twelve square feet, with a brick or stone chimney, such purchaser shall enjoy the same privileges which the free holders and inhabitants of other towns, not incorporated, shall enjoy".

Forty years later Summersville was "incorporated" under the new system in Virginia. The act so incorporating the town is found in the Acts of the General Assembly of Virginia of 1859-60 at page 337.

The town was governed by the Virginia charter until the formation of the new State of West Virginia, but no town government was in force during the Civil War; and the town was not incorporated under West Virginia law, till 1897 when it was incorporated by general statute, in the Circuit Court.

At the establishment of the town in 1820, it was laid off in lots with streets running east and west, and was so maintained until the Civil War. During the war many buildings were destroyed and when building began in a rather desultory way no attention was paid to the original plans. Main Street of today is the only street that occupies the original location.

The boundaries of the incorporation as fixed by the Circuit Court included an irregular area, as it was laid off to exclude certain citizens opposing the incorporation and only including the main business places and the citizens sponsoring the measure. No orderly municipal organization was set up and no record was kept of proceedings, until 1916, when S. R. King as mayor opened a record, now to be seen in the Mayor's office. There was no street lighting until Henry Campbell constructed a small electric generating plant at his mill on Muddlety Creek. On May 17, 1927, the Campbell Electric Company was given a franchise by the town, for a period of fifty years to furnish electricity to Summersville and vicinity. This service was continued until 1930 when the plant was purchased by the Monongahela Power Company. This company continues to furnish electricity to the town and a greater part of the county.

Prior to Acts of the Legislature of 1923, fixing the terms of office for mayors and councilmen for a term of two years, and a minimum council at five members, the mayor of the town had been elected annually, and usually only three councilmen were elected.

In 1930 the population of the town was 536. A water and sewage system was installed in 1934, under the supervision of J. E. Settle, engineer. The work was a federal project and the work was done by the Pittsburgh-Des Moines Steel Company at a cost of $26,842.87.

Beginning with the mayoralty of W. G. Brown, in 1935, the town was first laid off into wards. A careful survey was made by C. H. Craig, engineer, the town divided into five wards, and a plat showing the boundaries of each ward filed in the Mayor's Office. From this time a proper record of all municipal proceedings has been kept.

In 1937 Dr. Eugene S. Brown was elected mayor and continued in the office for twelve years. In 1938 a motorized fire truck was purchased at a cost of $3,000.00. A poorly equipped voluntary fire company was succeeded by a competent organization. The population reported by the census of 1940 was 643.

Jettes Mollohan was chosen mayor in 1943 and re-elected in 1945. During his term the Municipal Building located on Church Street was erected at a cost of $5,000.00. Funds for the building were provided by a bond issue. Guy Vaughan, Recorder, served as acting mayor after Mr. Mollohan's death, completing the term in 1947.

A petition, dated July 19, 1945, was filed in the circuit court, asking for the enlargement of the corporate limits. A survey was made by A. B. Rader. Although this petition and survey flouted the law, in that it was made to include an amount of territory *disproportionate to the number of residents and did not show the amount of the area contained therein*, and was followed by continued

Municipalities and Villages 213

litigation, the court finally approved the enlargement of the town limits. A map showing the present boundaries of the corporation is on file in the Recorder's Office.

In 1946 parking meters were installed and are in use on Main Street.

In 1947 Wiley Mason became mayor. The chief event in his administration was the bond issue for a new water and sewage system. The system in use had proved entirely unsatisfactory, and bonds were voted to the amount of $252,000.00 for the new system, which in addition to water from the wells, draws water from a pool in Muddlety Creek located just above the mouth of Arbuckle Branch. The water storage tank is situated at a good elevation on the mountain side west of the town. It gives good pressure for the residential section, and for water supply for fighting fires. Insurance rates have been reduced because of this efficient water system.

The population as given by the census of 1950 is 1628. The town has been almost completely rebuilt in the last decade. The old home of Dr. Hereford, the John A. Hamilton residence, the John H. H. Duffy house, the Southern Methodist Church and a few other small buildings still exist from the pre-war period. Many new residences and public buildings of brick and stone have taken the place of the old frame, wooden structures. The Court House, Jail, the High School building, and the two bank buildings are of native sand stone; other public buildings of brick and cinder blocks have modernized the town. Hard surfaced roads connect Summersville with all adjoining counties and U. S. Route 60. U. S. Route

19 passed through the town; and daily bus service is maintained over these highways.

The post office is located in a new building well-equipped, and in addition to the several mail routes, a "Highway Post Office" makes two daily trips from Charleston to Summersville.

Two banks, two movie theaters, up-to-date stores, laundry, offices of doctors and lawyers, automobile sales rooms and repair shops, and other business offices, bring business from all parts of the county.

The office of the County Superintendent of Schools and Board of Education, the High School, with its beautiful grounds, the modern graded school, and the Court House with its offices for the county officials and for various welfare organizations, offer additional attractions for prospective citizens.

The churches are well represented. Methodists, Presbyterians, Baptists, and Catholics have large congregations and modern buildings. The Church of the Nazarene occupies the old Southern Methodist Church and lesser denominations are represented. Summersville has a beautiful and healthful location, with Lone Tree Mountain rising to nearly 2600 feet above sea level as its western background.

The following unincorporated villages are important community centers.

BELVA: named for Belva Lockwood, candidate for vice-president at the time the station was established, is located at the junction of the Chesapeake & Ohio and the New York Central railroads, and of State Routes

Municipalities and Villages 215

39 and 16. It has a post office, but is no longer an important railroad station since the advent of good roads.

DIXIE: located on State Route 16 and a branch of the Chesapeake & Ohio Railroad, has a post office, graded school, stores, restaurants, a lumber plant and nearby coal operations. Bell Creek Baptist Church is in the vicinity. The village has electricity, telephones and gas for domestic use.

VAUGHAN: located on Twenty Mile Creek and Secondary Road 20, connecting with State Route 16, is named for A. L. Vaughan, a former merchant, and was at one time a busy mining center. It has a church and graded school. The surrounding country is in coal and gas territory.

SWISS: located on Gauley River and State Route 39 at the junction of the New York Central and Nicholas-Fayette-Greenbrier railroads, takes its name from the Swiss Colony that settled there about 1880. It has a post-office, stores, restaurant, express and freight office, ramps for loading coal, charcoal ovens, and is in gas and coal territory. There is a graded school, a Methodist and a Baptist church. The village had its origin when the Flynn Lumber Company set up its lumbering operations there.

LOCKWOOD: on State Route 39 shares with Belva the name of Belva Lockwood, the famous Kansas politician. The name was given by H. C. Hill who was postmaster and first merchant. This community is of historic interest on account of the Morris Massacre which occurred just east of the village. A marker commemorates the tragedy, and is located on the highway in view of the grave of the Morris children. The village has a Baptist Church, a post office, modern store and a graded school in the vicinity.

DRENNEN: is on State Route 39 at the intersection of Secondary Road 11 leading to Cross Lanes and Carnefix Battlefield Park. A marker points the way to the park. The name is in honor of Jacob Drennen the first postmaster appointed in 1831. A general store is operated in connection with the postoffice. Tipton Methodist Church, and Salem Baptist church are within the distribution of the office, as well as a one room school and the Parsonage of Bethel Methodist Circuit.

TIPTON: Named for "Tip" Legg a former resident who operated a grist mill there, was a post office for more than fifty years, but recently discontinued. The village is on Secondary Road 11 at the intersection of Secondary Road 22, which passes through the Panther Mountain neighborhood by way of Bucklick to intersect State Route 39 at the mouth of Otter Creek. There is a store, graded school, Methodist Church and local sawmill nearby.

POE: A postoffice, on Secondary Road 11 at the intersection of an improved road, designated 11 leading from Laurel Creek by way of Backus Branch to Secondary Road 22, has two stores, a one room school and Bethel Methodist Church, the oldest in the county. The surrounding territory on Laurel Creek was the scene of early pioneer settlements. Thomas Hughes built a hunting camp on his land a short distance east of Bethel Church, where the first church building stood. The hunting camp was located there before the Morris Mas-

Municipalities and Villages 217

sacre. The site is still marked by the neglected burial ground of the pioneers of the community.

KESSLERS CROSS LANES: This is the site of a postoffice dating from 1854. Fred Kessler and John R. Vaughan opened a store there in that year and the name comes from Kessler and the intersection of the roads. The village is at the intersection of Secondary Road 11 with secondary Roads 9 and 23. Carnefix Battlefield Park lies about two miles south. A battle of the Civil War occurred here, and the county was organized here in 1818 at the house of John Hamilton which stands on the hill just west of the post office. Zoar Church, the oldest Baptist Church in the county is located here, and a one room school serves the community. Captain George Fitzwater and Edward McClung were living here at the time of the Morris Massacre; their cabin was plundered by the Indians at that time. The beautiful natural meadows found here were long known as "McClung's Meadows".

ZELA: The postoffice here bears the name of a daughter of George H. Alderson and is located on the New York Central Railroad and State Route 39 at the intersection of Secondary Road 9 leading to Cross Lanes. Zela has a general store, a modern graded school, and Pierson Chapel, a Methodist Church is located on Whitewater Creek in the near vicinity.

GILBOA: The village is located on State Route 39 and the New York Central Railroad at the mouth of Bucks Garden Creek. The name comes from Gilboa Church, one of the pioneer churches of the county. It has stores, a lumber working plant, and a modern restaurant. There are two churches: Gilboa Methodist Church and Church of God; and a one room school serves the residents. The post office takes its name from the Methodist church, one of the oldest in the county. The valley of Bucks Garden nearby is a fine farming area and was one of earliest settled localities on Peters Creek.

HOOKERSVILLE: located in the Muddlety Valley on U. S. Route 19 and the Baltimore & Ohio Railroad, is named for Levi J. Hooker, a pioneer landowner and the first postmaster. The Baltimore & Ohio Railroad has a freight station and a coal loading ramp here. There is a graded school and the Methodist and Baptist Churches, located at the intersection of State Route 43 with U. S. Route 19, standing side by side, are known as "the Twin Churches".

CRAIGSVILLE: Here is a prosperous village on State Route 41 at its intersection with State Route 20. The post office was named for James S. Craig, former owner of the site. The bus line from Summersville to Buckhannon has a transfer station here on the line to Richwood. The village is in the plateau region with a fine location and attractive homes. There are two Methodist Churches, a modern graded school building, stores, filling stations, shops and restaurants. Alderson Baptist Church on Secondary Road 5, near the former post office of Beaver Mills, is one of the pioneer churches of the denomination.

FENWICK: The village is located on State Routes 39 and 20, and the Baltimore & Ohio Railroad, and lies on either side of Cherry River in Beaver and Kentucky Districts. It has been a center of the lumber industry for

Municipalities and Villages 219

more than fifty years and still has a large lumber plant. There are stores, graded school and church. A branch of the Baltimore & Ohio Railroad extends up Big Laurel Creek to the coal mines at Saxman.

DAIN: This village with its post office, La Frank, is on State Route 39 and 20 just west of Richwood.

CANVAS: a postoffice on State Route 39 at its junction with Secondary Road 34, is in the plateau region and has good farming lands in its vicinity. There are two Methodist Churches, Jordan Chapel and Salem Church. The Parsonage of Earl Methodist Circuit is located at Jordan Chapel. There are two general stores, and a modern graded school. The Groves Dairy Farm is located nearby.

NETTIE: this post office, named for Nettie Bailes, located at the intersection of State Routes 39 and 20, is a busy community center. There are two general stores, a graded school and three churches, Olive Branch Baptist Church, and Mt. Zion and Downtain Chapel Methodist Churches. A quarry of good building sand is operated in the vicinity, and a "drive-in" movie theater is located on State Route 39 nearby.

LEIVASY: this postoffice has its name from its first postmaster, Valentine Leivasy. It is situated on State Route 41 at its intersection with Secondary Road 13 leading to Hominy Falls. It has a graded school, a store, and three churches in the community, Baptist, Methodist and Church of the Nazarene. A branch railroad extending from Quinwood serves the mining of coal in the recent development east of Leivasy.

HOMINY FALLS: is the postoffice for this pioneer

community. It is located on Secondary Road 13, connecting with U. S. Route 19 at Mount Nebo. It has a store, one room school, and a Methodist Church and Church of the Nazarene in the neighborhood.

MOUNT NEBO: is situated on U. S. Route 19 at its intersection with Secondary Road 13. It has a general store, graded school, Fowlers Knob Baptist Church and Glad Tidings Methodist Church. "The Tabernacle", a commodious auditorium erected by contributions of the citizens, is located here. Annual camp meetings are held here and are largely attended.

NALLEN: located on U. S. Route 19, and State Route 41, is a station on the Nicholas Fayette and Greenbrier Railroad. It takes its name from J. I. Nallen, a superintendent of the Wilderness Lumber Company, whose operation there created the village. Nallen lies partly in Nicholas and partly in Fayette, and the post office is in Fayette County. Its one room school is known as the Bays School.

MOUNT LOOKOUT: situated on Secondary Road 24, that connects with U. S. Route 19 and State Route 41 near Pool, is the pioneer community center of Wilderness District. There is a general store, Baptist church and a one room school known as the New Milton school. This part of Wilderness District lies in the central plateau region of the State, and its soil is well adapted to fruit growing, and potatoes grown here are equal in quality to the much vaunted Maine and Idaho products. It is especially noted for its cherries, that have grown there from the earliest settlement.

TIOGA: located on the Baltimore & Ohio Railroad

Municipalities and Villages 221

and Secondary Road 3, connecting with State Route 39, on Little Beaver Creek and near the Webster County line, takes its name from the town in Pennsylvania where the promoters of the Tioga Lumber Company lived. This company started development of its large timber holdings in the early 1900's, then sold to the Birch Valley Lumber Company that for many years operated an extensive lumber business there. Extensive coal operations are now carried on and gas is also being produced in this area. The village has a graded school and churches in the vicinity.

BIRCH RIVER: This is a pioneer settlement and had a post office at an early date, named from the River. The village is a thriving community center located on U. S. Route 39, at the intersection of Secondary Road 1, The town has general stores, graded school, restaurants, shops, and a modern Baptist Church. It is in coal and gas territory, and gas wells are now in production.

Other villages and postoffices in the county are located as follows: BAYS situated on U. S. Route 19 near Braxton County line; BENTREE on State Route 16 near Clay County line; BRUCE on Secondary Road 26, leading from Mount Nebo to Hominy Falls; CALVIN on State Route 41 at junction of Secondary Road 4; CARL on State Route 20 near Greenbrier County line; COTTLE on State Route 20 near Cottle Knob; GAD on Secondary Road 9 at its intersection with Secondary Road 23; HOLCOMB on State Route 41 and Baltimore & Ohio Railroad; JETTSVILLE on improved public road on Big Laurel Creek near Greenbrier County line; MARYBILL on Baltimore & Ohio Railroad on Gauley

River, connected with State Route 39 by paved road from Lowland; MORRIS on Secondary Road 1 near the head of Strange Creek; PERSINGER on State Route 41 at the intersection of Secondary Road 5; RUNA on Secondary Road 4 connecting with U. S. Route 19 and State Route 41 near Pool; SPARKS on Secondary Road 9 at its intersection with an improved public road leading to Carnefix Battlefield Park.

The thirty-eight post offices in the county are well distributed and located mainly on improved roads to give efficient mail service to all the people of Nicholas County. Churches and schools are in easy reach of the school houses, or reached by school bus. Mail boxes on all mail routes make delivery regular and with little inconvenience. From any office a letter may go to our soldier boys in any part of the civilized world.

The day of the weary mail carrier on horseback astride leather mail-pouch, containing a few letters and postal cards, and perhaps a weekly newspaper, reaching the post office weekly, if weather permitted, has forever past. Each post office is in direct contact with the rest of the civilized world.

CHAPTER X

Education, Schools, Teachers, Textbooks

LIFE with our pioneers was a struggle for subsistence. Parents and children worked together clearing the land, building their crude houses and makeshift furniture, planting and cultivating the stump-dotted clearings, protecting growing crops and live stock from wild animals, hunting game and preparing food and clothing in the most primitive manner. All of these essential duties left little time for books and study.

However, the hard conditions under which they lived did not destroy the strong desire for schools and learning. Many of the pioneers had enjoyed educational advantages before they came to the wilderness and they of course gave instruction to their families in so far as time and means allowed.

The "Parish Schools" and the famous "Old Field Schools" that flourished east of the Blue Ridge were practically unknown to the early settlers in Nicholas County.

When a few families became established in a community they sought a teacher for their children. Perhaps someone living in the settlement could give instruction, and the school was kept in some cabin home.

Usually though a log cabin school house was built by voluntary labor, and for a few weeks in winter school was "kept". These first schoolhouses were built of round logs, usually twelve by eighteen feet. The roof was made of bark or rough clapboards, held in place by weight poles; the floor was laid of rough puncheons, or sometimes only the packed earth served. Split logs held up by legs driven into auger holes formed the benches. At one end of the building was the fireplace of field stones so wide it could take logs six or eight feet long. The chimney with a rough stone base was topped with sticks laid in mortar,—"cat and clay" work. There was one door made with shutter of heavy slabs and hung either with wooden hinges or deerhide straps. The greater part of a log was cut away in one sidewall to give light, and this opening was usually covered with greased paper. That was the only window provided. A smooth slab was placed just below this window in a slanting position against the wall, and supported by pegs driven into the wall. This was the writing desk, and seated on a bench in front of it the pupils practiced their penmanship from copies furnished by the teacher. Each pupil had his "copybook", usually made of coarse unruled white paper about the size of our legal cap, and composed of a quire or more of sheets stitched together and covered with strong brown paper. Later ruled white paper known as fool's cap was used. Each pupil furnished his own copy book, quills and ink for his work.

The teachers were of varied and uncertain attainments. No certificate or diploma was required. If he could read, shape a pen from the quill of a goose or turkey, write a "legible hand" and "cipher to the rule of three", he qualified. Of course he must possess a strong arm and be skillful in wielding the rod.

His employment was consummated by the parent signing his "article" or subscription list, which stipulated the tuition for each pupil, the length of the term and the subjects to be taught. The teacher "boarded around" with his pupils and looked after the school house, usually assisted by the larger boys in getting firewood and keeping up the fires.

Pupils were not graded, only classed in spelling and sometimes in reading. Individual instruction in arithmetic and writing was the custom. Yet with a quill pen, ink made from oak galls, poke berry juice or some similar concoction, the boys and girls learned to write, as is evidenced by the old records of the county, in handwriting thus learned. From Pike's Arithmetic they mastered the fundamentals of addition, subtraction, multiplication and division, and sometimes conquered "vulgar fractions" and even "ciphered through the single rule of three". They learned to read by using Webster's Elementary Speller, the New Testament, Franklin's "Poor Richard's Almanac", and they thought about what they were reading. Indeed they learned and practiced more of the practical side of life in business and civil government than is taught is some of our boasted schools of today. From this primitive training in their work-a-day lives came the men and women who made Nicholas County. They laid the foundation on which is built the liberties and institutions we now enjoy.

John M. Hutchinson, in a newspaper article written half a century ago, tells of the pioneer school he attended:

"The boys and girls came with Dilworth's Spelling Book, Pike's Arithmetic, and the New Testament for a reader. The teacher, sitting on a chair, would rise and speak politely to all that came, and they to him. The first that came would recite their lessons first, and be permitted to go out first in the evening, each one nicely bidding the teacher "Good evening". Any one failing to do so was called back. Good manners and politeness were always taught. A boy or girl not polite to old folks was not respected by any one. The test of the teacher in my school days was his success in teaching politeness and good demeanor."

Pupils walked long distances, often three to five miles to school and though there were home chores, both morning and evening in the way of tending live stock, preparing firewood, etc., school usually began at eight o'clock in the morning and continued until four in the afternoon.

When "books" took up in the morning the teacher usually called the spelling class. The "head" and "foot" method was applied. When a word was misspelled it was passed to the "next"; and on till correctly spelt, and the winner passed up to the place of the one who had "missed". At the close of the lesson the pupil who had maintained position at the "head" of the class was given a "head mark" and retired to the "foot", to contend again for the "mark" by "turning down" poor spellers.

A recess of ten or fifteen minutes was usually given between ten and eleven o'clock, and a "noon recess" from twelve to one o'clock; an afternoon recess was also given between two and three o'clock.

The first part of the "noon hour" was taken up with the basket and bucket lunches which each family group had brought from home. After eating the time was given over to vigorous play.

Favorite games of the boys were "townball", "Bullpen ball" or "shoot the buck", "Prisoner's Base", and "Fox and Hounds". The girls usually played "Ring-around the Rosy" or "Drop the Handkerchief". Some of the older girls might range the hillside for wintergreen, and boys not engaged in the games might be chasing a ground squirrel or ground hog, or "twisting" a rabbit or opossum out of a nearby hollow tree.

Nevertheless from these primitive schools came many pupils, who with a few terms of three or four months each, were able to complete courses in college or enter the professions, and make names for themselves in our early history.

Until the year 1810, Virginia had no public school law. By Act of Assembly that year the "Literary Fund" was established. Its primary purpose was to provide means of education for the poor white children of the State. By this law a "Board of Commissioners" was set up for each county consisting of not less than five nor more than seven persons, whose duties were to determine the number of poor children in the county for which they could provide schooling, from the amount of the Literary Fund apportioned to their County, and to send them to school to be taught reading, writing and arithmetic. The first board for Nicholas County was appointed August 5, 1818 and was composed of David Frame, Robert Kelly, Robert Duffield, Samuel Hutchinson and Samuel Neil.

This act did not take the place of the subscription

schools, that had existed from the earliest days but only attempted to provide schooling for the poor who could not otherwise go to school.

In 1830 Nicholas County had seven Commissioners and they reported 18 schools attended by poor children. Of the 150 poor children enumerated, 99 attended school; the average attendance by each child was 52 days; average sum paid for each child was $1.82, and the total expenditure that year for the county was $179.80.

In 1846 the school law was amended providing that each county should be divided into precincts, each containing as many school districts as were necessary for the schools; each precinct was to elect a commissioner annually and the several commissioners so chosen, formed the County School Board. This board appointed three trustees to each school district, who chose the site of the school house, and had charge of the building and grounds. Teachers were hired by the County School Board, and the schools were financed from the Literary Fund supplemented by taxes collected from the county as other taxes were laid.

However this law did not take effect unless ratified by a two-thirds vote of the County. It was not adopted by Nicholas County. Only Ohio, Kanawha and Jefferson Counties adopted the school system of 1846.

The census of 1850, showed 17 public schools with teachers, 189 pupils, and a total income of $230.00 from the Literary Fund. This system for schooling the poor was not popular, and was denounced; "as *calculated to create and keep up distinctions in society, and so abhorrent to the feelings of the poorer class of people that the children of the poor man dread to come within the pale of its provisions".*

Subscription schools, however, flourished and did effective work as shown by census of 1850, there being only 52 persons in the county who could neither read nor write.

While Nicholas County did not adopt the Free School Act of 1846, its provisions for school districts, sub-districts, school commissioners, County Superintendents, trustees, locations and erections of buildings, and employment of teachers, became the basis for the free school system inaugurated by the new state, when West Virginia adopted her first constitution in 1863.

Leaders from the birth of the Republic saw the necessity of trained citizenship. In 1841 a Convention met at Clarksburg to consider the problem of free schools. Judge Edwin S. Duncan, Judge of the Circuit Court of Nicholas County said in his address to the convention: "The Literary Fund intended for all is applied without any system and without practical benefit". Alexander Campbell pleaded for moral training. The Convention issued an "Address" headed "THE PEOPLE MUST BE EDUCATED". The Free School Act of 1846 followed, and in 1859, The Kanawha Valley Star declared, "the past ten years has brought a great change in our schools. The first young men in talent and education are now turning their attention to teaching."

Chapter 45 of the Code of 1868, contains the school law that gave West Virginia her free school system:

A State Superintendent of free schools was chosen, by the Senate and House of Delegates in joint session, for a term of two years. He had general supervision of the schools of the State. The County superintendents were elected at the general election, on the 4th Tuesday in October for a term of two years, beginning January 1st of the succeeding year. Their duties were to examine and certify teachers, visit the schools, aid and advise teachers and report annually to the State Superintendent; counties were divided into townships, and each township elected three commissioners who constituted the Board of Education. This board elected one of its members president and appointed a secretary. The Board of Education divided the townships into school districts, and appointed three trustees for each district. These trustees employed the teachers, had custody of the buildings and made reports to the Board of Education. Teachers must be of good moral character and were required to file a certificate showing qualification to teach orthography, reading, writing, arithmetic, English grammar, and geography. The county superintendent examined the teachers. His examinations were given individually and usually the questions were given and answered orally. Five grades of certificates were given: "Number One *a very good teacher*", "Number Two *a good teacher*" "Number three *Medium*", "Number Four *Below Medium*"; "Number Five: *Indifferent*". Number Five was only issued once to the same applicant and Number Four twice.

All certified teachers were required to take the oath prescribed for State officers.

The school term began September first and the school

month consisted of twenty days. School was not in session on Saturdays.

The teacher kept a daily and also a term register of pupils on forms furnished by the State Superintendent, reported monthly to the Secretary of the Board of Education, took an enumeration of all pupils in his district and filed his term register with the secretary of the Board of Education, and the secretary in turn made a general report of his township to the county superintendent.

The general duties and requirements of teachers and school officers were specifically set out in our first school law in West Virginia: "All teachers employed in the public schools shall read or cause to be read one chapter from the Bible, in a language understood by the scholars, every day at the opening of school; inculcate the duties of piety, morality, and respect for the laws and government of their country; and all teachers, boards of education and all other school officers are hereby charged with the duty of providing that moral training for the youth of this State which will contribute to securing good behavior, and to furnish the State with exemplary citizens".

Schools were supported by interest of an invested school fund, net proceeds of all forfeitures, confiscations and fines, and by general personal and property taxes.

The text books prescribed under the new law were, McGuffey's readers, Ray's arithmetics, Pinneo's grammar, Mitchell's geographies and Goodrich's U. S. history. McGuffey's readers had been used in the County prior to the Civil War.

Unfortunately the school law made no provision for permanent record of school work. Teachers reports to the secretary of the Board of Education were not preserved; the secretary's report to county superintendents was not recorded and saved, and the County Superintendent left no record of his office. All that exists today in the way of official records is found in the reports of the several State Superintendents.

The first State Superintendent, Rev. W. R. White, was not elected until February 16, 1864, and then for the unexpired term ending March 3, 1865. He was twice re-elected for two year terms, and ended his service March 3, 1869, to become principal of Fairmont Normal School.

Dr. Callahan in his History of West Virginia, says, "It was a great good fortune to this State that the direction of her education interests was at the very first committed to so wise a leader as Dr. William Ryland White". He was a student and co-laborer with Horace Mann, our great educational statesman. During his service from 1864 to 1869 he did much to lay the foundation of our free school system. Under his advice the Legislature established the State University at Morgantown, and the Normal School at Marshall College, with a branch school at Fairmont. He called the "State Teacher's Association in 1866; the name was changed in 1874 to "The State Educational Association", and in 1909 to "The West Virginia Education Association," now familiarly styled the "W. Va. E. A.".

During the Civil War educational activities practically ceased in Nicholas County. After the adoption of the

Education, Schools, Teachers, Textbooks

free school system by the new state it developed slowly in this county. This was due to the unsettled condition after the war, the sparse settlement of the county and the straitened financial condition of our people.

Dr. Wm. P. Rucker was the first county superintendent of Nicholas County. His first report to State Superintendent White is dated September 9, 1866, and appears in the Third Annual Report of the Superintendent. He names the six townships: Kentucky, Mumble-the Peg, Wilderness, Grant, Summersville and Jefferson, and complains of the "rebels'" opposition to the free school system. He was a violent partisan and provoked much of this opposition.

In 1867 W. H. Baldwin succeeded Rucker. He made one brief report that appears in the Fifth Annual Report of Superintendent White. He states that the County then had but 16 schools and only 2 school houses built of logs. He too complains of indifference and opposition.

In 1868 Wm. Y. Callahan, who succeeded Baldwin, reports 26 schools and 10 log houses and 1678 pupils of school age.

In 1869, Mr. Callahan, who was our first superintendent to actually work at his job, reports 23 schools, 22 log school houses, 1750 pupils of school age and lists the following 22 teachers examined by him: Patrick D. Horan, No. 1; A. T. Groves and Adaline Gray each No. 2, Thomas Maston No. 3; Col. John Brown, Archibald McQueen, Mary Price, Franklin Atwood, Thos. B. Callison, George Grose, George W. McMillion, Andrew C. McClung, Henry McCutcheon, and Francis G. Morriston, No. 4: Maria A. Rader, Jacob Young, Sallie Morris,

Mary J. Martin, Sarah Thomas, Isaac Hart, Andrew C. Chapman and Henry Beirne No. 5. This appears in the sixth report of H. A. Ziegler, State Superintendent, successor to W. R. White.

In 1870, J. H. Robinson, County Superintendent, reported to A. D. Williams, State Superintendent, 39 school districts, 31 schools in operation, 27 school houses, 8 of the buildings were now frame, and lists the teachers with their grades.

In 1871, Mr. Robinson's second report made to C. S. Lewis, State Superintendent, shows school taught in all 39 districts. Many well known names first appear as teachers in the two reports: T. C. Brown, L. W. Herold, I. A. Dix, Van Pelt Neil and Walter Stanard, holding No. 3 certificate, James S. Hill, Miss Virginia Marrs, Bernard N. McCutcheon, Renick Hanna, Holly C. Perkins and T. B. Stephenson, No. 4 certificates, Peter H. Craig and Francis M. Odell, No. 5 certificates. Mr. Robinson's reports are found in the 7th Annual report of Superintendent A. D. Williams and in the 8th Annual report of C. S. Lewis.

In 1873 W. K. Pendleton was appointed to fill the unexpired term of C. S. Lewis who had resigned. This term, ending March 3, 1873, marked the end of the first school law. The report of County Superintendent John E. Kern to Superintendent Pendleton, last under the old law, shows only 25 schools in operation. This lapse resulted from the confusion caused by the changes in the law.

Much progress had been made in our county in the eight years under the first school law. The log cabins were replaced by hewed log houses with glass windows, heated with stoves; and the split-log benches exchanged for desks made of neatly dressed poplar boards and graduated to accommodate the age of the pupils. Slates and the adopted text-books were in use, and even black-boards began to appear. Instead of quills the steel pen was used, and better teachers were in charge; but best of all the free school had come into favor. Superintendent Pendleton declared that "There was not a person in the new state who would dare to raise his hand against the free schools."

Up to this time, however, the greatest drawback was the lack of competent teachers. The normal schools were remote and our people were too poor to attend them. They had no aids in the way of school journals and books on pedagogy. They had no organization in the way of teachers' meetings, and could only apply the methods learned in the short terms of the schools they had attended. Teachers' Institutes, text-books on the art of teaching and reading circles were still in the future.

Notwithstanding the meager requirements to pass the examinations, only one teacher, P. D. Horan, held a first grade certificate under our first school system.

Under the second Constitution, in effect September 30, 1872, a new school law was enacted. This law substituted the "district" for "township", and the school districts of the townships were designated "sub-districts". The State Superintendent of schools was elected by popular vote for a term of four years, at the general election, and was given the same powers and duties as under the old law. County superintendents and school officers were chosen for a term of two years at a special election held on the first Tuesday in August and the school year began on September first next following. In 1881 the election of County superintendents and school officers was changed from the third Tuesday in August to the third Tuesday in May. In 1893 the terms of county superintendents were changed to four years, and they were chosen at the general election in November. Boards of Education elected for each district first consisted of a president and four commissioners. The boards at first appointed but one trustee for each sub-district and also hired the teachers; later the commissioners of the boards were reduced to three members, and three trustees were appointed who employed the teachers.

Teachers were required to pass written examinations, on orthography, reading, arithmetic, writing, English grammar, geography and U. S. History, before a Board of Examiners, consisting of the County Superintendent, and two teachers selected by the presidents of the several boards of education.

Two examinations were held each year and three grades of certificates were given. Number 1, requiring a grade of 87% to 100%; Number 2, 77% to 87% and Number 3, 67% to 77%—Graduates of the State Normal schools were given the right to teach on the qualifications of a first grade certificate.

The school month was extended to 22 days exclusive of Saturdays.

Reports were required of teachers, boards of education, County Superintendents and State Superintendents as under the old law, except the State Superintendent's report was made biennially.

Teacher's Institutes were provided to be held within the months of July and August, in each county for a term of five days, conducted by an instructor appointed by the State Superintendent.

In 1873, John E. Kern who was the last superintendent under the old law and the first to report under the new law, in his report to B. W. Byrne, first State Superintendent, under the new law, gives 41 schools in operation, lists 40 teachers examined that year, and reports holding the *first County Institute for teachers*.

The new law for examination of teachers was applied. First grade certificates were issued to Wm. Y. Callaghan, J. A. Cassidy, George Grose and J. Haymond Robinson; second grades to A. T. Groves, A. A. Hamilton, C. R. Hanna, J. M. Koontz, S. P. Schindell and E. P. White.

In 1874, the report of H. C. Tinsley, County Superintendent, appears in the Biennial Report of B. W. Byrne, State Superintendent, which gives 49 schools in operation, and lists 45 teachers examined. First grades were given Lanty W. Herold, H. W. Herold, Wm. Y. Callaghan, Margaret A. Thornton, John E. Kern, N. C. Hendrick, S. P. Schindel, Alpheus Shepard, P. D. Shepard and P. D. Horan; I. N. Cox, Kyle B. McCue and David McQueen, first appear as teachers with second grade certificates.

In 1875 and 1876, J. Haymond Robinson, County Superintendent, made report each year, to State Superintendent Byrne.

In 1876, he gives 52 sub-districts and 50 school houses,

10 of which are frame buildings, the others are of logs. He lists all teachers examined showing 12 first grade certificates issued. B. C. McNutt, W. S. Henderson, Joseph A. Alderson, Joseph L. Smith, George A. Groves, H. B. Davis and T. B. Horan, are listed as teachers.

In 1877-8, the last report of J. Haymond Robinson, appears in the Biennial Report of State Superintendent, W. K. Pendleton, giving 54 schools in operation and lists 54 teachers. New names of teachers listed are Jeremiah Murphy, A. W. Bobbitt, H. P. Hardway, H. C. Hill and R. V. Dorsey.

In 1878-80, Joseph L. Smith, County Superintendent, made a written report found in the second Biennial Report of State Superintendent Pendleton. In this report he lists J. C. Ramsey, W. W. King, A. M. Stephenson, Hansford Pierson, M. A. Keenan, J. T. Grose, J. E. Grose, C. A. McClung, W. W. Backus, E. G. Simms, S. C. Cavendish, Jas. A. White, C. N. Walker, Lelola J. Crites, S. W. Hypes and E. C. Bennett, beginning their work as teachers. In the first Biennial Report of State Superintendent, Bernard L. Butcher, Smith is listed as making no report for Nicholas County.

In 1881-5, Jos. A. Alderson was County Superintendent. In the second Biennial Report of State Superintendent Butcher, Mr. Alderson reported 62 schools and 65 teachers, but teachers and their grades were not listed. In his written report, found in the First Biennial Report of State Superintendent, B. S. Morgan, he lists 72 schools in operation, and reports as teachers new to the profession, L. C. Groves, Prudence Fitzwater, J. H. Groves, J. L. Dotson, C. H. Dunbar, N. M. Dorsey, W. M.

Education, Schools, Teachers, Textbooks

Crookshanks, W. G. Brown, W. C. Dodrill, Edgar Halstead, W. R. Bennett, Margaret E. Groves, Mary Huffman and Bettie Cox.

In 1886-7, T. C. Brown's report as County Superintendent is found in the second Biennial Report of B. S. Morgan, State Superintendent. For the year 1887, he listed 79 schools and names as teachers, H. P. Rippetoe, P. N. Wiseman, L. V. Koontz, Samuel Collins, John Bell and Geneva Amick.

In 1887-9 W. S. Henderson, County Superintendent, has no reports of record in the Biennial Reports.

In 1889-93 H. B. Davis in his two terms as county superintendent, gave no statistics in his reports, but submitted a few generalities, as appears in the Biennial Reports.

In 1893-5 J. A. White, last county superintendent to serve a two year term, made one report of record showing 102 schools and 95 school houses.

In 1895-1903 W. S. Henderson, serving two four year terms as superintendent, has full reports of record to Superintendent Trotter and Superintendent Miller. His last report gave 108 schools and listed teachers examined.

In 1903-07 S. C. Dotson has two reports of record in the Biennial Report of Superintendent Miller. He lists 123 schools and dwells on the proceedings of his Teachers Institutes.

In 1907-15 Harrison Groves, superintendent for two years, gives 156 schools and 4641 pupils enrolled. His reports appear in the Biennial Reports of Superintendent Shawkey.

In 1916 E. W. Skaggs, made one report to Superintendent Shawkey, giving 168 schools and 6701 pupils enrolled. In 1918 Superintendent Skaggs resigned, and L. O. Bobbitt was elected by the several presidents of the Boards of Education to succeed him.

In 1918-24 L. O. Bobbitt was county superintendent. He had been elected for a four year term in 1920. His report to Superintendent George M. Ford was briefly summarized and gives 160 schools in operation in 1922.

Beginning with this period the reports of the county superintendents are given little space in the Biennial Reports. The State Superintendent assuming the right to note only what in his opinion was pertinent.

In 1924-28 I. Ray McCutcheon succeeded L. O. Bobbitt as County Superintendent. His two brief reports to State Superintendent George M. Ford gives 139 school buildings in the county, and makes no mention of his activities as county superintendent.

In 1928-30 Milroy F. Brown, County Superintendent, reported to State Superintendent Ford 149 schools in the county, and gives the total cost of the schools for 1930 as $267,211.58. The last County Institute for Teachers was held in 1930.

In 1932 Shirley Morton was elected County Superintendent, but served only to July 1, 1933 under the old law. However he was continued as superintendent under the "County School Unit Act" until July 1, 1934. He reported to State Superintendent W. C. Cook 144 schools in 1932 and gives the total cost of the schools in the county for that year at $245,334.28. He was succeeded by L. O. Bobbitt, who was the first superintendent elected by the new "County School Board of Education", recently appointed by State Superintendent W. W. Trent. Mr. Bobbitt took office July 1, 1935.

The "County School Unit Act" passed May 22, 1933, effective from passage, abolished the 398 school districts of the State and established in their place 55 "County Districts". The several district boards of education retained their legal status under this act until July 1, 1933.

This was the most revolutionary enactment in the history of the State in the administration of the free school system.

Beginning with the term of Morris P. Shawkey, who had been trained in his native state of Pennsylvania in the theories of the McMurrays, an entirely new theory of education was gradually introduced into our school laws. Commenting on this trend away from the policies of our leading educators, Dr. Ambler in his history of education says: "Through the teachings of Thorndike, Giddings, Butler, Dewey, Kilpatrick and the McMurrays they embraced the new philosophy with the eagerness and confidence of slaves newly emancipated from bondage. Flaunting the lessons of experience, many of them were convinced that they had found a royal road to learning."

Teachers

The early teachers in the pioneer subscription schools were of very indifferent attainments, but served their period in keeping alive the flickering flame of learning.

Even under our first school law, in the new State of West Virginia, teachers in Nicholas County were poorly qualified to give instructions in the fundamental branches required to be taught. But they were generally men and women of the best families in the county and they did much to lay the foundation of free schools.

After the school law of 1873 requiring written examinations and higher standards, and the County teacher's Institute was established, steady progress was made in the methods of teaching.

The teacher was chosen by the patrons through the agency of their boards of education and trustees, and had the cooperation of the parents in the conduct of the school. The teacher was on intimate terms with pupils and parents, often visited in the homes, and morality, obedience to authority, and respect for persons and property were inculcated.

From the Teachers' County Institute, where the latest methods in teaching were presented by competent instructors, school problems discussed by teachers and school officers, and by the supervision and personal instruction given by the County Superintendent, a body of efficient teachers gradually resulted. Reading Circles and the use of school journals, insisted upon by the County Superintendent, gave instruction in pedagogy. As a result Nicholas County teachers soon had a reputation for efficiency that extended to neighboring counties.

The tedium of study was often relaxed on Friday afternoons, by the teachers. "Spelling matches", readings and recitations were given by the pupils. Parents and trustees usually attended these exercises.

In the long winter evenings, "debates" and "exhibitions" were given, in which two or more schools often united. Great interest was taken in these programs by both pupils and parents. A proud father and mother saw

Education, Schools, Teachers, Textbooks 243

a daughter "spell down" the whole school, or listened to their boy declaim the speech of Patrick Henry, memorized from his McGuffey's Reader, or their small girl recite, "Twinkle, Twinkle Little Star".

Teachers were usually good readers, and taught oral reading well; all pupils were trained in the Spencerian method of writing, and much attention was given to arithmetic.

In the fifty years preceding the transition to the new theories of education, the "Three R's" were taught and mastered as never before nor since.

Teachers' Institutes

Teachers' Institutes were held annually in the county from the year 1873 to 1931. Programs were prepared by the State Superintendent, and supplied to County Superintendents, Instructors appointed by State Superintendents assisted the County Superintendent. Teachers were required to attend and pay an enrolment fee. School officers and parents attended and the meetings were usually enlivened by night sessions, in which lectures were given by prominent educators, varied with round table discussion, musical entertainments, etc.

The prescribed course of study set out in the State Superintendent's Manual was presented, methods of teaching the various branches were demonstrated, the object of the schools to train the children in morality and the social duties of good citizenship was upheld and emphasized.

Such outstanding educators as Superintendent George S. Laidley, Prof. Waitman T. Barbe, Dr. J. N. Deahl, T. E. Hodges, L. J. Corbly and R. A. Armstrong, and special lecturers as Dr. A. E. Winship, Dr. R. G. Boone, Dr. H. R. Sanford and Susan F. Chase brought to our teachers the latest and best methods in teaching.

The proceedings of the Institute covered all features of the free school system. A committee on resolutions usually reported at the close of the session. The report submitted to the members, was discussed and adopted as the sense of the body. Teachers' salaries and duties, school buildings, length of the school term, compulsory attendance, text books, consolidation of schools, the unit of taxation, many other matters pertaining to education were passed upon and reported to the State Superintendent's office. This expression of the teachers had a great effect upon school legislation, and marked *practical* and not a *theoretical* advance in educational work.

The Teachers' Institute was stressed in the local papers; the names of instructors and teachers, given and the daily proceedings furnished by the secretaries of the institute and especially the resolutions adopted by teachers and school officials were published. Institute week was a *red letter* occasion for the citizens.

State Superintendents Morgan, Lewis, Trotter and Miller stressed the value of the County institute in their reports and took much interest in the preparation of programs for the institute.

In a biennial report, Superintendent Miller lists as follows, the benefits of the institute:

1. The profession of teachers is elevated.
2. Their professional spirit is quickened and energized.
3. Organization, management and instruction of schools are improved.

4. The school children realize a new life by the impartation of the improved power and spirit of the teacher for "As the teacher so is the school."
5. Teachers and school officers are brought into more intimate relations in their common work.
6. Teachers and patrons are brought together in sympathy and co-operation.
7. Teachers and patrons learn the relative qualifications of the teachers of the County.
8. Teachers have the opportunity of comparing their attainments in the science and art of teaching.
9. Finally an educational spirit is awakened. The importance of education is better understood, and the work of the genuine teacher is felt and appreciated. The people realize the true mission of the teacher and the teacher feels his force as a factor with the people.

During the last 12 years the County Institutes have done a great work for West Virginia, and the results are beginning to be seen.

In short the Teachers' Institute existed on the assumption that the *schools belonged to the people*. The abolishment of this institution marked one of the first steps in taking the schools away from the people.

Text Books

In our schools under Virginia no text books were provided. Teachers accepted any book the pupil could bring to school, Dilworth's Spelling Book, The United States Reader, Pikes Arithmetic, the New Testament and even Pilgrims Progress and Fox's Book of Martyrs, were made use of in reading.

The school law of 1863, adopted McGuffey's Readers and Speller, Ray's Arithmetic, Mitchell's Geographies, Pinneo's Grammar, and Goodrich's U. S. History. Kidd's "Elocution and Vocal Culture", and Gow's "Good Morals and Gentle Manners", were extensively used by the teachers.

The law of 1873, under the new constitution, prescribed as text books, McGuffey's New Revised Readers, McGuffey's New Electic Spelling Book, Kidd's Elocution and Vocal Culture, Ray's arithmetic and algebras, Harvey's Grammar, Mitchell's New Revised Geographies, Knote's Geography of West Virginia, Goodrich's common School History, Holmes' History of the United States, Cutter's Anatomy and Physiology and Webster's Dictionaries.

Text books continued to be prescribed by statute until the County School Book Act of 1897. This law provided for a county board, composed of the County Superintendent and "eight reputable citizens and tax payers of the county". At least four members must be freeholders and not teachers; at least three members must be teachers holding first grade certificates and actively engaged in teaching, and not more than five members should belong to the same political party. The members holding office for a term of four years, were appointed by the County Court.

The board appointed for Nicholas County on the 12th day of June, 1897, consisted of the following members: V. C. Legg, A. T. Groves, W. R. Grose, T. C. Brown,

J. H. Robinson, L. W. Herold, P. N. Wiseman and T. G. Shackelford. Although this law proved unsatisfactory it remained in effect until 1909.

The Legislature of 1909, created a State School Book Commission, consisting of the State Superintendent of Schools and eight citizens of the state, at least five of whom should be experienced educators of known character and ability and who at the time of their appointment were in actual educational work. Not more than five of the members should belong to the same political party. The term beginning April 1, 1912, was for a period of five years. *The State Superintendent* was empowered to contract for the continued use of the books selected by the several County boards for the period from June 30, 1911, to July 1, 1912.

In 1919, the Legislature created a State Board of Education consisting of seven members, of whom the State Superintendent of schools was a member *ex officio;* the other six members were appointed by the governor by and with the consent of the senate. The only qualification of the member required that he be a citizen of the state and member of one of the two dominant political parties, and not more than four of the members from the same political party. The Act abolished all other state boards connected with the schools of the State and gave full authority for the general control and management of the schools and educational affairs of the state.

Textbooks for the first time were now selected by political appointees.

An advisory board, consisting of the State supervisor of colored schools, and two negro citizens were appointed in the same manner and received the same salary as the principal board.

In 1933, a State Board of Education was provided for in "The County School Unit Act".

The board consisted of the State Superintendent of Schools and six members, serving for six years, with the only qualification that they be citizens of the state chosen from the two dominant political parties. The board is a corporation known as "The West Virginia Board of Education".

In 1947, after the constitutional amendment based on the "Strayer Report", and proposing to make the State Superintendent an appointive officer, was defeated by popular vote, the Governor and Legislature, disregarding the repudiation of their plans by the people, demoted the State Superintendent from an active member of the board to a *non-voting member*, and thus by legislative enactment carried out the provisions of the defeated amendment so far as possible. The West Virginia Board of Education was now composed of nine appointive members.

A history of Nicholas County schools that omitted notice of the textbooks of McGuffey, Ray, Mitchell and Harvey would be incomplete. These textbooks for two generations did much in moulding the characters of our people.

McGuffey's Readers. These texts beginning with the First Reader and Speller were first published in 1836 by Winthrop B. Smith & Company, succeeded by Wilson Hinkle & Company and then by The American Book Company which continues to produce these readers to meet the demand for them by "McGuffey Clubs" all over the nation. In 1930 Henry Ford had the 1879 edition of the Sixth Reader reprinted and bound just as it first appeared, and he maintained a school in his "Greenwich Village" at Detroit in which the McGuffey texts along with other textbooks of his day were used.

The First Reader unlocked the gates of learning through the daily surroundings of the child. Of the sixty-three lessons, fifty have to do with horses, dogs, cats, birds and other animals that especially appealed to the child mind.

The Second Reader led the children a step higher into the enchanted world around them.

The Third Reader was alive with unforgettable lessons in manners and morals.

The Fourth Reader began to introduce the Classics and the Fifth and Sixth Readers continued the choicest collections from all languages. For four generations these readers moulded the character of the nation. For many "self-educated" men they were his only Alma Mater, they taught industry, thrift, temperance, kindness, patriotism and morality in the most effective way.

Ray's Arithmetics. These texts comprising four books —Primary, Intellectual, Practical and Higher—succeeded Pike's Arithmetic in 1863, and gave a thorough course in arithmetic. In the four month school terms, the goal was the mastery of Ray's Practical Arithmetic. The Higher was really a college text and required some knowledge of elementary algebra and plane geometry but many teachers studied this advanced text.

Mitchell's Geographies. These texts were prefaced by

General O. M. Mitchell the celebrated geographer and astronomer and gave thorough treatment to local and general geography.

Harvey's Grammar. This text replaced Pinneo's Grammar in 1873 and was in use about twenty-five years. The examples in parsing and analysis were taken from classic literature, and teachers and students were led to a clear knowledge of our language. These texts were not compositions of publishers, but were the work of our ablest educators who knew their subjects and were great teachers.

William Holmes McGuffey was one of our very greatest teachers. His genius as a teacher and textbook writer was recognized throughout the nation and in 1845 he was called to the University of Virginia where he spent the last one-third of his life, dying in 1873. He and his wife lie buried in the University Cemetery.

Dr. Joseph Ray, a native of Ohio, was a great mathematician and noted teacher.

General O. M. Mitchell was our first noted astronomer and geographer. He was the founder of the Cincinnati Observatory and brought the first large telescope to America. He spent his life in the study of geography and astronomy. Mt. Mitchell, North Carolina bears his name. It was from this height he fell to his death.

Thomas Harvey was a fine English scholar and his grammar grew out of his experience in teaching.

Summer Normals

In the late 1880's, new branches added to the common school curriculum and higher standards of teaching being demanded, the "Summer normal" came into existence.

Education, Schools, Teachers, Textbooks 251

Nicholas County was remote from the state normal schools, and few could attend them. Teachers who had some normal school training, and others who by special effort and experience had qualified as successful teachers, found ready work as instructors in these schools. A leading educator said of the "summer normals", "they served a useful purpose in the transitional period between the academy and high school; and many of the teachers in these schools knew their business and did their work effectively from the academic and experience angles and from the self-taught professional angles as well". Prominent among teachers in the "Summer Normals" of Nicholas County mention should be made of George Grose, W. S. Henderson, H. B. Davis, J. C. Ramsey, T. C. Brown, W. R. Grose, W. C. Dodrill, P. N. Wiseman, W. S. McCutcheon and J. J. Dotson.

The Summersville Normal School began its existence at Cross Lanes in the spring of 1889, when W. G. Brown taught a "Summer Normal" in the public building. In 1890 the school was taught in the old "Temperance Hall" which had been fitted up for the purpose. In this two room building the principal assisted by H. R. Groves, H. C. Robertson and wife, and Luther Gibson maintained the school till it was removed to Summersville in 1892.

A joint stock company comprising more than forty of the influential business and professional men of the county had been organized and had erected a commodious building on the town hill just east of the Court House. The school was incorporated October 12, 1893, with a Board of Directors as follows: James S. Craig, President; James A. Mearns, Vice-president; W. G. Brown, W. G.

Graves, James A. White, Allen Rader, H. W. Herold, Geo. H. Alderson and Daniel Brock, Directors; A. J. Horan, Treasurer and B. H. White, Secretary.

W. G. Brown was employed as principal for a term of six years; B. H. White was associate principal; and during the term of Mr. Brown's employment, H. C. Robertson, James A. White, R. M. Cavendish, A. L. Craig, Miss Lily McAdams, Miss Kate Ogden, Miss Lizzie Horn and Miss Etta Sexton were among the prominent teachers employed.

The courses of study were: *Preparatory, Business, Teachers Music* and *Collegiate*. Diplomas, authorized by charter, were granted to graduates in the Teachers, Business and Collegiate courses:—Catalogs outlining the course of study, giving methods in teaching, listing students, etc., were published each year; and a monthly school paper, "THE SEARCHLIGHT" was issued.

The school was well attended. The first year two hundred and fifty-one students were enrolled, representing eight counties, the highest enrollment in one year reached 339, representing eleven counties.

At the close of Mr. Brown's term in December 1898, his connection with the school ceased.

In the spring of 1899, Thomas L. Bryan of Tennessee succeeded as principal, with Claude N. Feamster of Lewisburg as his assistant. In the fall of 1900 J. L. Stewart and Pat H. Murphy leased the building and conducted the school. In 1902 they were succeeded by E. W. Skaggs, who continued as principal till 1914, when the Nicholas County High School replaced the old Normal School.—Some of the prominent teachers working with Mr. Skaggs, were H. D. Groves, E. L. Lively, Henry Dorsey, J. Ben Robinson and J. S. Lilly.

Of the work of the Summersville Normal School under W. G. Brown, Dr. C. H. Ambler makes the following statement in his History of Education in West Virginia:

> "The Summersville Normal was the most important of all the private or select schools of its kind in West Virginia. Located in an agricultural area and far removed from a state-maintained school, it functioned the year round. The resulting alumni and patron loyalties were such that this school might have evolved into another state normal but for a prohibitionary provision of the state constitution. It was first established in 1889 at Cross Lanes, Nicholas County, by Wm. G. Brown. In one year it had outgrown its quarters and was moved into the nearby "Temperance Hall", a two-story frame structure near Vaughan's store. Here the school again outgrew its quarters and after three years was moved to Summersville, the county seat, where adequate quarters had been provided by a joint stock company composed of about twenty residents of Nicholas County. Thus housed, the school grew rapidly. In 1894-95 the enrolment passed the 300 mark. The following year "Professor" Brown, the principal, edited and published The Searchlight, a monthly journal "devoted to the interests of Parents, Teachers and Students".
>
> "The Normal" was then offering five courses: The preparatory, covering the common school branches, except bookkeeping, civil government, and general history; the teachers, "designed to give a liberal pedagogical training"; the business, offering instruction in bookkeeping, shorthand, etc. The music, for beginners in that subject; and the collegiate, designed to prepare for college entrance and to lay the foundation of a liberal education.
>
> In 1898 "Professor" Brown severed his relations with the Summersville Normal and, as director of teacher training, associated himself with H. C. Robertson, Principal of Fayetteville Academy, Fayette County, which Robertson had estab-

lished a few years previously. After one year this relationship was terminated and Professor Brown sojourned for a brief period in Oklahoma, where he was a superintendent of schools. Meanwhile the Summersville Normal continued active under a joint principalship arrangement into 1902, when "Professor" E. W. Skaggs was selected to the principalship. He continued to function in that capacity to 1914, when the Normal was forced to give way to a newly established county high school".

In the Teacher's Course in the Summersville Normal School stress was laid on written work.

For a generation the school slate alone was used in written work—mainly in solving problems in arithmetic, class blackboards and note books had not come into use.

The slate was cumbersome and the manner of its use was unsanitary. Erasures were usually made by the pupil spitting on the slate and using his hand or coat-sleeve as an eraser. Soiled hands and clothing resulted. From the beginning slates were banned in the normal school work, and class blackboards and writing tablets were employed. At first it was necessary for a stock of pencil tablets and note books to be kept for supplying students. Problems in arithmetic and exercises in other studies were explained by the students on class black boards and written work on note books taken up by the teacher for correction.

Summersville Normal School should be given credit for banning school slates and introducing class black boards, and written work in the schools of Nicholas County.

These innovations were up for discussion at the county Teacher's Institute in 1890. The Instructor, Superintendent George S. Laidley of the Charleston schools, strongly advocated class black boards and written work. He had ruled out the slate in his schools.

A prominent old teacher said: "I'm against this 'Norman' method. How can a boy *figger* without a slate"? The question of blackboards and written work was discussed in district institutes, and Boards of Education were soon supplying blackboards.

In less than five years the slate had disappeared from the school rooms of the county.

NICHOLAS COUNTY HIGH SCHOOL

On February 22, 1911, a bill introduced by F. N. Alderson, was enacted by the Legislature, establishing a county high school for Nicholas County. A Board of Directors consisted of three members of the County Court, the County Superintendent, and an elected member to be chosen at the next general election for a term of four years commencing July 1, 1911; the four *ex-officio* members were to constitute the board until the elective member was chosen and qualified. This board was made a body corporate, with full authority to locate the school on a site near the town of Summersville, and to manage and control the school. The act further provided for a levy not exceeding 12 cents on the $100.00 valuation of County property for the years 1911 and 1912 for securing grounds and erecting and equipping suitable buildings for the school, and not to exceed 2 cents on such valuation in succeeding years; and for maintaining the school a levy of 5 cents annually was allowed.

But before the act should take effect it was to be submitted to the voters at a special election.

Pursuant to this requirement the Board of Directors

met on June 8, 1911, and called a special election to be held on the 4th day of August, 1911, and directed a registration of voters for same.

Opposition to the proposed high school was at once organized and the question fully presented in the local papers and by public addresses for and against the proposition.

Advocates of the school urged the necessity for higher educations than the free schools give and insisted the cost to tax payers would be light.

Opponents argued that the tax burden was too great and that only the citizens of Summersville and vicinity would be benefited.

The election was duly held on the 4th day of August, 1911, with the following results:

Beaver District cast 356 votes for and 233 against;
Grant District cast 70 votes for and 114 against;
Hamilton District cast 151 votes for and 155 against;
Jefferson District cast 219 votes for and 57 against;
Kentucky District cast 85 votes for and 148 against;
Summersville District cast 232 votes for and 76 against;
Wilderness District cast 158 votes for and 112 against.

On August 10, 1911, the County Court convened as a Board of Canvassers declared as a result of the election, 1,271 votes were cast *"For County High School"* and 895 votes were cast *"Against County High School"*.

On the same day, August 10, 1911, that the result of the election was declared, C. D. Backus, W. S. Henderson and Granville Odell, members of the County Court and *ex-officio* members of the Directors of Nicholas County High School, and Harrison Groves, County

Superintendent, and *ex-officio* president of said Board of Directors, met and by resolution duly entered of record, organized as such board. On motion of W. S. Henderson seconded by Granville Odell, W. G. Brown was elected Secretary of the Board.

The Board then proceeded to make up an estimate of the levy necessary for securing grounds and erecting buildings for the high school, for the year 1911.

The secretary was directed to correspond with architects and construction companies, with a view to have plans and estimates submitted for the Board's consideration.

Pursuant to adjournment the Board of Directors of Nicholas County High School met on August 22, 1911, and in due form ordered a levy of 10 cents for the year 1911, on the valuation of the County's taxable property.

On November 8, 1911, Price, Smith, Spillman & Clay, and Squire Halstead, attorneys for H. W. Herold and thirty-eight others, presented their bill of complaint before Judge J. C. McWhorter and obtained an injunction against David McQueen, and the Board of Directors of Nicholas County High School, prohibiting the collection of the levy for the high school.

The bill was promptly answered by W. G. Brown, A. B. Koontz and F. N. Alderson, attorneys for the defendants, and on November 27, 1911, the injunction was dissolved. Plaintiffs appealed to the Supreme Court of West Virginia and on the 25th day of April, 1912, that Court affirmed the actions of Judge McWhorter, and Nicholas County High School was established by legislative action and judicial decision. The opinion of the Court is found in 71 W. Va. at page 43.

The Board of Directors now proceeded to obtain a site for the school. At a mass meeting of the citizens, a committee was appointed, consisting of P. N. Wiseman, O. C. Lewis and W. G. Brown to decide upon a site. Six locations were offered. Finally the Committee, with the advice of H. Rus Warne, the architect, already employed, adopted the 15 acres of the old "Alderson Homestead", which was purchased from O. K. Sutton, Trustee for the sum of $1,500.00, contributed by citizens of Summersville, and donated to the Board of Education.

After considering a number of bids and consultation with the architect Warne, a contract was given to P. Q. Schrake & Son, on his bid of $33,000.00, dated February 25, 1913, and work on the building was started.

On July 4, 1913, the cornerstone of the building was laid in the presence of a large assembly of citizens from all parts of the County. The Masonic Lodge of Summersville at the request of the Board of Directors, was in charge of the exercises, and Judge Charles W. Lynch of the Supreme Court and State Grand Master, at their invitation, delivered the formal address.

Preliminary to laying the cornerstone a picnic dinner was given by the citizens of Summersville on the Court House grounds. Afterwards the Masons under the direction of O. C. Lewis and John G. Malcolm, formed in their regalia and followed by a throng of school children and citizens marched to the site of the building.

Harrison Groves, President of the Board of Directors called the meeting to order and made the opening address. Following short speeches were made by Assistant State Superintendent Hubbs, and W. G. Brown, pointing out the scope and benefits to be expected from the schools.

O. C. Lewis then presented Judge Lynch whose able address was the special occasion of the day. The cornerstone which had been quarried nearby and inscribed by the contractor, was then formally placed by the Masons under the direction of their grand master, and the memorable day was over.

The erection of the building progressed slowly and was not completed till late in 1917.

After much delay occasioned by disagreement with contractors, the lower story and part of the basement was made ready and the school opened September 14, 1914.

Delay and unsatisfactory work on the part of the contractor continued and upon the advice of the Architect, the Board of Directors effected a settlement with him and employed M. H. Brock to superintend the completion of the work. The auditorium was not completed in time for commencement exercises of 1915, and the meeting was held in the Baptist Church.

The building is constructed of native sandstone quarried in the vicinity, and cost something over $40,-000.00.

In 1924, the Board of Directors, adopted a plan for a gymnasium, prepared by Herbert Kyle, Architect, and employed J. H. Love, contractor to erect the building at a cost of $17,000.00.

The feeling engendered over the establishment of the

school soon passed, and those who opposed the high school became its patrons. Almost every community in the county is represented in the school.

During the thirty-six years since the first commencement, much improvement has been made. The bare hill of 1915 is now crowned with fine trees and shrubs. An athletic field, lighted for night games, has been provided, and a modern annex to the original building erected.

The middle-aged men and women that attended in the early years of the school, can scarcely recognize their Alma Mater in their sometime visits.

RICHWOOD INDEPENDENT DISTRICT

On February 21, 1903, an act of the Legislature established the Independent District of Richwood, subject to approval by a majority of the voters of Beaver District. The Board of Education of Beaver District pursuant to this act called an election, and appointed election officers only for Precincts No. 1 and No. 2, but refused to appoint officers for the new voting precinct that the County Court had recently established in Richwood, on the ground that said precinct had not been legally fixed. The citizens in Richwood met and appointed officers and held their election. At the election held on the 22nd day of March, 1903, 317 votes were cast against and 1 vote for the independent district outside Richwood. And in Richwood, 416 votes were cast for and 15 against the independent district. The Board of Education refused to count the votes cast in Richwood and declared the vote against the proposed independent district.

Litigation followed. J. E. Rader, B. G. Smith and R.

M. Dyer representing the Independent District petitioned the Circuit Court for a *mandamus* to compel the board to count all the votes. The case was not tried until April 16, 1904, when Judge W. G. Bennett issued an order to compel the counting of the Richwood votes. The Board asked for an appeal which the State Supreme Court refused and on January 23, 1906, the Independent District was legally established.

The act provided for a Board of Education comprised of five members, to have exclusive control of all schools in the district, to prescribe textbooks and appoint a superintendent of schools, who with two assistants appointed by the board should examine all applicants for positions as teachers in the schools of the district. Teachers' Certificates were authorized in grades of one to three; "*Number one shall denote a very good teacher.*" "*Number two a good teacher*" and "*Number three medium.*" A teachers' fund was provided for by a levy not to exceed 60 cents on each one hundred dollars assessment made for State and County taxation, in addition to the moneys received from the state for free school purposes. The "Building Fund" was limited to 40 cents on the one hundred dollar valuation. The Board was also given the power to establish a high school and prescribe its course of study.

"In 1925 the act establishing the Independent District of Richwood was amended enlarging and defining the powers and duties of its Board of Education. The board no longer was permitted to examine teachers. The act provided that "The qualifications of superintendent, principal and teachers shall be the same as prescribed by general law for teachers in the public schools of the state".

The secretary of the board was required to keep a full record of its proceedings and report to the county superintendent of schools as was required of the other school districts of the County. Unfortunately this provision of the law was never enforced and much of the school history in Nicholas County is lost.

The Richwood High School was maintained by the independent district which was released by statute from the county levy for Nicholas County High School.

From the first the State has retained the control of the free schools by general law, but leaving the administration of the laws to the local authorities in the counties and districts. This system of maintaining our free schools persisted for about fifty years.

However, beginning with the term of State Superintendent Morris P. Shawkey in 1909, a new theory began to develop in our school system. The selection of textbooks, heretofore controlled largely by the recommendation of teachers and school officials, was now given over to political appointees, beginning with the *"School Book Commission"*, and culminating in the *"West Virginia Board of Education,"* created in 1947, which controls the educational policies of the State, excepting the State University and Potomac State School.

During the three terms of Superintendent Shawkey, the school laws were amended, and the course of study for the schools altered to meet the theories of the "New Education". The leaders in the movement were disciples of Nicholas Murray Butler and John Dewey. Text books were changed, teachers and educational leaders had less and less to do in shaping policies, the "Teachers Institute" was abolished, and under the slogan "Remove the school from politics", the contrary has resulted, and our schools are now *a political asset.*

"The Old Education"

The old school educators insisted upon making learning "difficult enough to develop character through the mastery of worthwhile problems." They accepted the theory of Thomas Jefferson that the mastery of the "Three R's" is necessary to intelligent citizenship. They insisted on moral and spiritual values in the training of future citizens. They demanded that the schools teach obedience to authority, respect for persons and property and the duties of citizenship as the aim and end of our free schools. Stress was laid on the teacher's mastery of his subject and the co-operation of parents.

Superintendent Joseph Rosier writing in the School Journal says: "There is no power that awakes, inspires and directs a pupil so well as an *absolute and thorough mastery of the subject by the teacher* and no amount of *theory and observation of mental operations,* can be substituted for broad and comprehensive knowledge".

The New Education

The philosophy of the new school educators was in opposition to the "puritanical" methods of the old school in teaching morals and circumspect manners. Textbooks in reading must not "preach" and teachers must not be bound by "puritanical habits" as a requisite of moral character. This philosophy of the new school educators, says Dr. Ambler in his History of Education, "affected their private lives for some of them went so far as to accept a contention to the effect that children should be allowed to follow their natural impulses even when they led to such unconventional acts as throwing biscuits at each other over the dining table".

At the inception of the new philosophy the law enacted in 1889, requiring the teaching of the effect of alcoholics and narcotics on the human system and which had produced a strong moral effect upon the succeeding generation, was dropped from the school law. In 1927 as "a sop to the good people" an act requiring the teaching of the effect of alcoholics and narcotics upon the human system was again passed but the text books in use slight the matter, and the law in effect is a dead letter.

The present course of study for our elementary schools carries out the theory of the new education.

The teaching of the fundamentals of mathematics is slighted in not requiring mastery of the basic operations of addition, subtraction, multiplcation and division and in practically omitting training in common fractions, decimals, percentage, square and cube root; civics, history and geography are combined as one subject. Grammar is almost ignored, and language reading and literature are combined. This jumbling of subjects in the text books leaves much to the teacher's skill in clearly presenting subjects.

Progress Under the "Old Education"

The foundation of the free school system of West Virginia was laid in 1863 by the report of the House Committee on Education, drafted by Prof. A. F. Ross of Bethany College. Based on the theory of Thomas Jefferson that "each county should be divided into townships with a free school established therein, forming a little republic, which being under the eye of its people, they would better manage the larger republic", our free school system was inaugurated.

The system accordingly made the district the unit under control of *"trustees"* elected by the voters; the township had a "board of education" also elected with supervision over the district; the county had a superintendent, elected for a term of two years, who certified teachers and supervised the teachers of his county and made annual reports to the State Superintendent. By this system the schools were "of the people, by the people and for the people".

A brief synopsis of the progress made in Nicholas County under this system, beginning in 1863 with a few log cabins for school houses and a little group of incompetent teachers, through the seventy years until the County School Unit Act of 1933, speaks for itself.

Beginning with the term of William Y. Callaghan, the law was actually put to work. He prepared himself as a teacher by study of the subjects then taught, and by studying works on teaching. He tested teachers in his examinations and in his visits to their schools. He was a good reader, a fine penman and proficient in arithmetic, and the mastery of the "Three R's" was his goal.

His successors, H. G. Tinsley, J. H. Robinson, who served two terms, and John E. Kern, gave much attention to providing school buildings and increasing attendance. Many prominent names in the history of our county appear on the lists of teachers certified by them.

J. E. Kern, who continued as Superintendent under the school law of 1873, held the first County teachers institute and the first written examination; two advanced steps in the progress of our schools.

Joseph L. Smith who succeeded Mr. Robinson, was well grounded in the branches taught and raised the standard in the examination of teachers. During his term a large number of efficient teachers came into the work.

In the two terms of Joseph A. Alderson, State Superintendent Butcher issued the first manual and course of study for the schools. The course embraced, orthography, reading, penmanship, arithmetic, English grammar, physiology, general United States and State History, general and state geography, single entry bookkeeping and civil government. Teachers were now examined on theory and art of teaching.

In the term of T. C. Brown, who followed Mr. Alderson, the manual was slowly introduced, and better schools and equipment came into use.

In 1887, W. S. Henderson, who had been a successful teacher for several years, became one of our most progressive superintendents. Mr. Henderson was a reader of the Illinois School Journal, that was then applying the theories of Comenius, Pestalozzi and Froebel. He insisted on two of their cardinal principles; "Learn to do by Doing" and "From the Known to the Related Unknown"—He had a County Reading Circle, and listed as "must" books for his teachers; "White's Pedegogy" and "Baldwin's School Management". He visited the schools, demonstrated methods in the school room, and in his examinations gave 50% of the grade on theory and art to the teacher's work as he observed it.

H. B. Davis, who had the advantage of training in Glenville Normal School succeeded Mr. Henderson. The law requiring the teaching of the effects of alcoholics and narcotics was put in force during his term, and he stressed the "State Manual and Course of Study".

Under the administration of J. A. White, the State Superintendent, was required by statute to prepare a program for the teachers institute and to include a two year course of instructions for the institute. Mr. White was enthusiastic in support of the institute, conducted district institutes and gave carefully prepared examinations for teachers.

In W. S. Henderson's two four year terms he did excellent work in improving methods of teaching along the lines of his former term. He especially stressed the teaching of reading by the "word method" for beginners. The County School Board, compulsory attendance, and state certificates for teachers in the primary schools, were provided for in the amendments to the law in this period.

During the term of S. C. Dotson, the school law was amended to provide for truant officers, the county system of examining teachers was abolished, and the uniform examination of teachers under regulation of the State Superintendent was substituted, and the provision for free text books enacted.

In the two terms of Harrison Groves, significant changes began to appear in the school laws. In 1909 the State School Book Commission was created. In 1911 the Nicholas County High School was established by popular vote. In 1913 the "cigarette law" was passed forbidding any one to smoke or use cigarettes in a school building or on school grounds. The county superintendent was made financial secretary *ex-officio*, and given an office in the court house.

In 1915 many changes were made in certification of teachers and the State School Book Commission replaced the State Board of Examiners, and prepared the course of study for the common schools. Boards of Education were authorized to consolidate schools.

In 1917, in the short term of Superintendent Skaggs, the amended law required teachers under penalty to attend the County institute, District institutes and round tables were provided with certificates of merit given for completion of the course of study prescribed by the State Superintendent, in Reading Circles.

Under the superintendency of L. O. Bobbit, 1918-1923, the theories of the old and new were in conflict; less attention was given to moral and ethical training and stress was laid on consolidation of schools and emphasis placed on physical and vocational education. In 1923, the law required display of the flag on school buildings, oath of allegiance by teachers and the giving of regular course of instruction on the constitutions of the State and Nation, "for the purpose of teaching, fostering and perpetuating the ideals, principles and spirit of Americanism".

In 1925, during the term of I. Ray McCutcheon, the law was amended authorizing a normal training department in the county high school for the "better training of the teachers in the elementary schools of the county".

Education, Schools, Teachers, Textbooks 269

In 1927 boards of education were given further authority in consolidation of schools and transportation of pupils.

An act of the legislature again required the teaching of the nature of alcoholic drinks and narcotics upon the human system. The law however, was given but "lip service", as Dr. Ambler puts it, "because of the strangle hold of the new educators", the law was blissfully ignored by teachers and school officers, they themselves became addicts to the "cigarette evil"; and "while attacking the uncensored movies", in a short time were frequenting "the movies even on Sunday *for their educational value.*"

The last Teacher's County Institute, was held in the term of Superintendent Milroy F. Brown, as the Legislature had abolished it under pressure of the theorists.

In the term of Shirley Morton, last county superintendent elected by popular vote, the new school educators, having thrown overboard the practical lessons of experience in the past seventy years, in their zeal "for change and reform", shaped their course in conformity with the socialistic philosophers and experts, and brought forth "The County School Unit Law of 1933."

Superintendent Morton gives 144 schools in operation in 1932, and the total cost of the schools in the county for that year, $245,384.28.

As a basis of comparison of the results and trends of the two theories of education a brief synopsis of progress of the new education from 1933 to 1951, should be studied.

The regular session and the first extraordinary session of the Legislature of 1933 set up The County Unit School

System. The second extraordinary session of that Legislature which met November 21, 1933, and continued to March 24, 1934, worked out a "general school fund" to meet the financial requirements of the new system. This general fund is gathered from the following sources: (1) Proceeds from the capitations; (2) Income of present school funds; (3) Fines and forfeitures; (4) All moneys arising from forfeited and delinquent lands and other sources named in art. 12, sec. 4 of the constitution; (5) Interest on public moneys received from State depositories, (6) State license tax on marriages; (7) State tax on forfeitures; (8) State tax on certain State licenses; (9) All funds paid into the treasury for school purpose and not otherwise appropriated.

The Legislature of 1935, enlarged the authority of the county boards of education, and especially provided for insurance against the negligence of drivers of school busses, and directed that at least one year be given to instruction in the history of West Virginia, prior to the eighth grade.

The Legislature of 1937, amended the law in two important particulars: County Boards of Education are required to publish financial statements annually of all receipts and disbursements; and qualifications and authority of county superintendents enlarged and specifically set out.

The Legislature of 1939, made several important amendments to the school law; the compulsory school law was amplified; free text books provided for pupils whose parents are unable to furnish them; teacher's contracts and tenure, teacher's retirement system and basic salary were all elaborated in this legislation.

The Legislature of 1941 gave boards of education authority to employ county directors of instrumental music and an agricultural club agent for the organization of boys and girls agricultural clubs. The course of study was amended to include courses of study in history, civics, constitutions, alcoholic drinks, and narcotics. Teacher's certificates were now issued solely on the completion of a certain number of semester hours in some approved institution, and the various grades and classes of certificates specifically listed. The free text book law was amended and extended to students in private schools whose parents could not provide the text books.

The teachers' retirement act of 1939 was re-written, as the "State Teachers' Retirement System". A "Teachers' Retirement Board", consisting of the governor, state superintendent of schools, the state treasurer, the state insurance commissioner, and three teachers appointed by the governor, was given authority to manage and administer the retirement system. The attorney general is made legal adviser of the board. Membership of teachers is voluntary and four per cent of the "earnable compensation" must be contributed by each member. Basic salaries and advanced salaries were again prescribed.

The Legislature of 1945 amended the school law by increasing salaries and revising the retirement system. An "Interim Committee", consisting of the president of the senate and four senators appointed by him, the speaker of the house and four delegates selected by him, and fifteen citizens appointed by the governor, was authorized to study and recommend in a report to the governor and legislature "a financial, administrative and functional *plan* for the educational system of the State."

The extraordinary session of the Legislature in 1946, acting on the report of the interim committee, embodied in the "Strayer Report", submitted the "Education Amendment".

The Legislature of 1949 amended the school law in almost every feature. The course of study "amended" by repeating in the same terms the various former statutes requiring instruction in history, civics, the constitutions of the State and Nation, and including instruction on the subject of scientific temperance showing the nature and effect of alcoholic drinks and narcotics. Salaries of county superintendents and librarians, the retirement system and teachers' contracts were all retouched by amendment.

A bid for Federal Aid was indicated by the authorization of the State Board of Education to accept federal aid for vocational education, for use of the state colleges and other state institutions, *or for any other educational purposes*, "subject to the provisions and conditions of applicable federal laws". The "School Bond Amendment" was submitted, and a joint resolution of the Legislature submitted to the vote of the school children the selection of a "state bird" and a "state tree". Later the announcement was made that the *cardinal grosbeak* was chosen as the state bird, and the *sugar maple* as the state tree.

The Legislature continued the amendment of the school laws, in the session of 1951, in the following important particulars: The State Board of Education was required to make biennial reports to the governor, as had formerly been required of the State Superintendent; the authority of the district boards of education was enlarged and more specifically set out; basic salaries of teachers were increased on a graduated scale based on the kind of certificate held, ranging from the sum of $165.00 a month for teachers holding five year certificates awarded on examination, to the highest salary of $290.00 per month paid to teachers holding a doctor's degree; advances on salary to be given for experience and other conditions to be determined by regulations. The compulsory attendance law was re-written, with new restrictions and exceptions.

This torrent of legislation has brought a revolution in the schools of our state and county. Greater sources of revenue have been found for the support of schools, consolidation of schools, transportation of pupils, new and better buildings, a new system of certifying and placing teachers, more attention to health and hygiene, greater stress on athletics, an enlarged curriculum, and a complex administration are the prominent characteristics of the legislation.

The report for the school year 1949-50 gives 119 schools in Nicholas County, 192 teachers, an enrollment of 5,627 pupils and the total costs of the schools of the County, $1,052,373.99.

"The County School Unit Law" is a misnomer. For more than a generation educational leaders favored the County as the unit for the school taxes, as an equalizing measure in school finance. The new law did equalize taxes in producing revenue for the schools, as one item only, but under a misleading caption it took the schools from control of local communities and gave us a totalitarian State control. The act of 1933 and all succeeding enactments have perfected the system.

When the measure came up in the special session of 1933, the public began to see the drift to State control. Petitions signed by some ten thousand persons were presented to the Legislature. Many protests appeared in the public press. However the politicians had a stranglehold, and while they allowed the same concessions to both the old system and the new, they definitely took over the schools and created The West Virginia Board of Education, an appointive body, with full power to "determine the Educational policies of the State". This board is a political organization of the political party in power.

Dr. C. H. Ambler, reviewing the sixteen years this State system has been building up says:

> Regardless of this course of events, progress in public free school education continued to be retarded by a more or less veiled political control centering in the state capital, which at opportune times made it diffiicult to get legislative approval of educational measures and appropriations without a green light from 'the powers that be'. They had a part, sometimes a determining one, in selecting members of the state board of education and of the legislature. Generally, they could depend upon a considerable bloc of delegates and senators who, because of their inexperience and their conservative backgrounds, were easily led. Because of the demands of their profession and of custom, teachers were generally eliminated from leadership, for one of the surest ways to nullify one's influence in education, except in small spheres, was to become 'an educator'.

Moreover, beginning about 1935, conflicting personalities and ambitions among the leaders divided 'the educators' themselves into semi-hostile factions. As a consequence the State Education Association tended to pursue a somewhat independent course to the common goals, and ten years later the state board of education named one of its appointed members president instead of the state superintendent who had been the presiding officer since the board was constituted. At the same time the board undertook a teacher training program and named its secretary as the director. Politicians and selfish interests took advantage of the resulting situation to alter, minimize, and defeat school programs regardless of their sponsorship. What better cooperation could have done is of course only a matter of conjecture. Whether for weal or for woe, it might have arrested evident disintegrating tendencies.

"The Educational Tree is known by its fruit". Thoughtful parents are not willing to surrender their unalienable rights and duties to the State in the training of their children. This grave responsibility cannot be delegated. Many parents and teachers, like Thomas Jefferson, can find no substitution for *"highly energized local interest in public education."* The sentiment of our people was expressed in their voting down the "School amendment". It was voiced by the editor of *Morgantown Post*, March 3, 1946, when he said: "As long as we remit our school problems to Charleston the results are going to be unsatisfactory. We can really get down to the business of running our schools on something better than a crisis program only when the principal responsibility rests with the local communities as a constant work-a-day obligation."

The results of the materialistic spirit that pervades the "new education", that has come to us from the pragmatic and socialistic philosophy of John Dewey and his disciples, may be seen all around us.

Dr. Cook of the educational department of our University, believes that the failure of so large a percentage of people to go to the polls and vote is due to the failure of our schools to teach the principles of our government and the duties of citizenship. The failure of the schools to train pupils thoroughly in the fundamental branches and to stress moral and spiritual values is becoming of great concern to earnest citizens. Our State Superintendent is voicing concern for lack of these values.

The "new education" has brought many *material* improvements to Nicholas county: better buildings, better equipment, better pay for teachers, better transportation, etc. *This is but the framework of an educational system.* The vital factors are, *teachers*, *parents* and *pupils*. The vice of the new system is the *dissolution* of this natural partnership. All past experience proves that the *home* and the *school* mould the character of a people. The character and learning of the teacher are paramount qualifications.

The school officials and teachers of Nicholas County are not chargeable with the present condition. It comes down from *State control*. Our local school officials and teachers are regimented and indoctrinated by the theorists and politicians through their machine, The West Virginia Board of Education. As long as our governors and legislatures import "Brain Trusters" and "Experts" to tell us how to train our children and manage our schools so long will we fail to educate "exemplary citizens", but the trend will continue to its climax in a socialistic and dictatorial government, when our schools shall have been made to produce *subjects* instead of *citizens*. Our *Free* school system is fast becoming the *State Compulsory System*.

COLONEL EDWARD CAMPBELL

Edward Campbell was born August 22, 1800, in a pioneer's cabin on the headwaters of Whitewater, in Kanawha County, Virginia. He was the son of John Campbell, Scotch-Irish emigrant, who had met and married Nancy Hughes, at the block house at the mouth of Hughes Creek, in 1795. Her father was Edward Hughes, one of the early pioneers of the region from whom the creek and the present town of Hugheston take their names.

His father, John Campbell, at the age of twelve, had sailed from Ireland with his parents to find a home in America. The parents both died on the long voyage and found a grave in the North Atlantic. The kindly captain, obtained a home for the orphan boy at the end of the voyage in New York City, and later he made his way in the westward movement to the valley of the Great Kanawha, to become one of its pioneer settlers and one of the first group of officials in the organization of Nicholas County.

In these primitive surroundings Edward Campbell grew to manhood. Taught chiefly by his parents, he acquired a practical education for that day. He taught school for a number of years and in his letters published in 1883 gives us a picture of the schools of his time.

Later in his life he was commissioned a justice of the peace and became what was known as a "traveling justice". This work took him over the large territory then comprised in Nicholas County. He tells us that there

Colonel Edward Campbell

were no roads "to speak of" at that time and he made his way from place to place by "woodcraft or scout signs" he had learned from his father. After the formation of Fayette County in 1831, he was for a time judge of the County Court of that County.

Edward Campbell was not only interested in the educational and civic affairs of his community but was also deeply interested in religion and the upbuilding of his church. He was a Baptist, and in early life assisted in the organization of congregations who met in the homes of the settlers for want of church buildings. As early as 1824 he was connected with the organization of Zoar Baptist Church. His practical interest is shown by his donation of the original land for Zoar Church and cemetery. In a long, busy life he always found time for the duties of church membership. In the little church at Alloy, Fayette County, may be seen the portrait of Annie Lloyd, after whom the Sunday School first organized there was named, and Edward Campbell, the subject of this sketch was first superintendent of that school.

The first wife of Edward Campbell was Margaret Masterson, who died September 29, 1849. His children of this marriage were William, Mary Jane, Sidney Masterson, Elizabeth Nancy, Robert Spotts, John Franklin, Nathaniel Redmon, Luther Rice and Lycurgus.

His second wife was Miss Susan Dunkle of Bridgewater, Virginia. No children were born of this marriage. She died in 1883.

In the Civil War, he and three of these sons enlisted in the Confederate Army. Sidney M., the other son, joined the Federal Army. His sons, Robert and Redmon, gave their lives for the Southern cause, and the father, after the hardships of camp and field and imprisonment at Camp Chase, Ohio, returned home as Colonel Edward Campbell.

After the close of the war, Colonel Campbell returned to Kesslers Cross Lanes, and spent most of his remaining years, with his youngest son, the late Lycurgus Campbell.

In 1883, he wrote a series of twelve letters in which, in clear and concise language he narrates *"Some of the hardships endured by the pioneers, and other interesting matters concerning our county, from its first settlement up to the time of its formation in 1818."* These letters were first published in the Nicholas Chronicle in 1883, and in 1892 were reprinted; Edited and published in the Nicholas Chronicle in 1933 by W. G. Brown at the request of Lycurgus Campbell.

Colonel Edward Campbell died January 29, 1886, and lies buried at Zoar Cemetery in the soil of the county he loved and had helped to carve out of the Wilderness.

CHAPTER XI

Pioneer Families

A brief sketch of the biography and genealogy of Nicholas County families from the earliest settlement to the Civil War.

BIOGRAPHY is the nucleus of history, and the history of the county is best shown in the record of the acts of its people. Space forbids more than a brief outline of our pioneer families.

A family name is the preface to the life of each of its members; for by the laws of heredity and environment a *family character* develops. And a family that bequeaths a good name bestows more than a material possession. The "Wise Man" thousands of years ago declared that: *"A good name is rather to be chosen than great riches"*, and *"is better than precious ointment"*. The good name of Nicholas County is built on the good name of its founders.

"A country without memories is without history; a country without history is without traditions; a country without traditions is without ideals and aspirations; a country without these is without sentiment; and a country without sentiment is without capacity for achieving noble purposes, developing right manhood, or taking any truly great place in the history of the world." *John Sharp Williams.*

The rising generation of Nicholas County can take pride in the epic achievements of its pioneer families.

The 120 families here recorded lived within the present bounds of Nicholas County. A number of the first settlers mentioned in the early history are not included as they were not permanent residents. Families resident in the territory now belonging to Fayette, Braxton, Clay and Webster are not included as founders of Nicholas County, though active in its early history. The families here listed were the very bone and sinew of the community. They cleared the land, and gave the grain fields, orchards and meadows; they organized schools and churches, opened roads and bridged the streams, intent on making a better life for their children, and their children's children. They set up courts of justice in the wilderness, and unconscious of their greatness they lived and died in the making of Nicholas County.

The author, in his work as teacher and in his profession of law, has been privileged to know members of all these families. As a boy he listened to the saga of settlement told by many of the great-great grandfathers of the present generation, and associated with their grandfathers and fathers. As a member of one of the pioneer families, it has been a work of love to recall their labors and record their achievements.

ALDERSON, *English*. The Nicholas County Aldersons trace their relationship to Rev. John Alderson who was born in England. He came as a young man to Virginia before the Revolution, and in 1777 located at the site of the present town of Alderson. In 1781 he organized the first Baptist Church west of the Alleghanies on a lot donated by his brother-in-law William Morris. The Alderson Hotel is now located where that church stood.

Sons of the Rev. John Alderson were George, Joseph and John. George moved to the Kanawha Valley and built his home on Georges Creek, named for him. There was born his son George, known as Colonel George Alderson. He kept a tavern and stage coach station on the James River and Kanawha Turnpike near Lookout in Fayette County. He was twice married and the father of 28 children. One of his sons, Joseph A. Alderson, came to Nicholas County about 1855. He was a lawyer and as a member of the Virginia Senate, voted against secession. Two of his sons became prominent in public life—John Duffy Alderson as an eminent lawyer and politician, served in the state in different capacities, and was three times elected to Congress; Joseph A. Alderson was a teacher, county superintendent of schools, clerk of the county court and later clerk of the circuit court. His family is well known in the county. Fleming N. Alderson, son of John D., is a lawyer, and as a member of the State Legislature, introduced the bill creating Nicholas County High School. George Henry Alderson, a half brother of Joseph A. Alderson, Sr., came later to the county and operated a farm and store at Enon. He later established the "Big Hardware" store at Summersville.

For almost a century the Alderson family has been active in the political and social life of Nicholas County.

AMICK, *German*. The Amick family probably came to America in the German Mennonite emigration from the Palatinate. The family tradition has it that three brothers, Henry, Jacob and John came together and settled in Pennsylvania. Later one of the brothers came to Pendleton County, and there in 1780 his son, John, was born. About 1826 this John Amick came with his family to Nicholas County. He bought a farm from Jeremiah Odell near the Wilderness Road and built a grist mill, and reared a family of fourteen children. He taught school along with his farming and mill activities. Six of his sons joined the Confederate army, and three of them lost their lives in the Civil War. His son Arnold remained neutral and married Nancy McCutcheon and was the father of twelve children. Byron Amick and Perry Amick, sons of Arnold, settled in the home community and were well known and respected citizens. Their sister, Geneva Amick Dyer, was a prominent teacher and later in life published a sketch of her family, giving many glimpses of the pioneer life of that day, and items of human interest of her family.

The Amicks of Fayette County are closely related. Their ancestor, Jacob Amick was a brother of Nicholas County Pioneer John Amick. Many descendants and relatives of the family still live in the community, and are well known and useful citizens.

Mrs. Dyer says of her family: "My people were among the pioneer settlers of West Virginia—a strong, brave religious people."

BACKUS, *German*. (Bachaus, meaning Bakehouse). The name was written "Backhouse" on the records until after the Civil War.

Joseph Backhouse came from Pennsylvania in 1800 and located on Hutchinsons Creek for a short time. He then moved to Twenty Mile and acquired several tracts of land there. His sons, Joseph, John, Pascal and James acquired land and settled near the present town of Vaughan. Later Joseph Backus married Sallie Brown, daughter of Alexander Brown, and moved to the Backus Branch where his entire life was spent. He was expert with the broad-ax, and an old building still in existence, shows his handiwork, smooth and even without an ax mark. His sons, Franklin, Henry, Isaac and Alexander all settled in the county and raised families. Rufus G. Backus, son of Franklin, was an eloquent preacher, and served as Presiding Elder of the Methodist Church. Arthur H. Backus, a grandson of Franklin, is a merchant in Summersville, and his son, A. G. Backus, is a minister of the Methodist Church. Weldon W. Backus, son of Henry was a teacher and farmer, and his son, E. C. Backus, lives on the home place. George W. Backus, son of Pascal Backus, was well known as a successful farmer, and spent his life on Twenty Mile in the house erected by his father. His son, Cornelius D. Backus, succeeded to the home place and was a successful farmer and stockman. He was highly respected by his neighbors and was a member of the County Court. His extensive real estate was divided among his children. George A. Backus, his oldest son, owns the ancestral home, which is in good condition although built more than a century and a quarter ago. Landon L. Backus, son of Cornelius D. Backus, lives on his farm adjoining the home place. Many other descendants of pioneer Joseph Backus, his great grandchildren and their children, are respected citizens of this and adjoining counties.

BAILES, *German*. The name appears on the records of Nicholas County as *Bale, Baile, Bailes* and *Bayless*.

Thomas Bailes came from Montgomery County, Virginia, and settled on Peters Creek near Gilboa Church in 1800. He had four sons and several daughters. The sons were John, Solomon, Jabez L. and George, named in his will of record in Will Book No. 1 at page 31. His son John Bailes settled on McKees Creek about 1807, where John J. Halstead afterward lived.

John A. Bailes, son of John Bailes, located on McKees Creek and operated a store and postoffice at Gad for several years. He sold out and moved to Ohio. George W. Bailes, another son of John Bailes, was a farmer and highly respected citizen. His son, J. Elmer Bailes, was a successful teacher, and now operates a farm near Summersville. He is prominent in church work as a local minister of the Methodist Church. His well known family are great-great-grandchildren of Thomas Bailes.

Another branch of the pioneer's family located south of Gauley River in Wilderness and Kentucky Districts, and are well known citizens.

Soon after Thomas Bailes came to Peters Creek, another Thomas Bailes settled on Birch River. His descendants still living in this community spell the name "Baile". Thomas Bailes of Birch River names as sons, Hiram, Thomas and Robert in his will, which is of record in Will Book No. 1 at page 36.

From the similarity of family names it appears that the two families may be distantly related.

BAKER, *English*. Michael Baker came from England, settled on Tates Run in 1806, on what was afterward known as the John B. Dorsey farm. He was a teacher and conducted a school in 1807 in a log cabin on Laurel Creek near the present Bethel Church. He was an excellent instructor and taught in the neighborhood for several years. His daughter married Elverton P. Walker. Later he sold his farm to Samuel Neil and moved away.

In 1820 Bakers came to the Elk Valley, then to Nicholas County, and later moved to Twenty Mile. Similarity of name suggests the relationship to pioneer Michael Baker. In 1872 Peter L. Baker was conveyed a tract of 100 acres of land on Twenty Mile Creek, described as "adjoining the land on which Michael Baker now lives." The record does not show the source of this Michael Baker land, nor when he came to the county. Dempsey Baker, who married a daughter of Joseph Backhouse, stated that the family came from Botetourt County, Virginia, and were all related. Robert S. Baker, a brother of Dempsey, was a soldier in the Confederate army, owned land near Beaver Mills and was residing there at the time of his death.

James Baker and Joseph Baker, who came from England and settled on Persinger about 1900, were not related to the other Bakers in the County.

BAUGHMAN, *German.* The Baughmans came from Germany in the Mennonite migration from the Palatinate. Christopher Baughman, first of record on our Land Books, settled on Birch River, above the "Salt Works" sometime before the organization of the county. His wife was Sarah Gregory. In 1823 Robert Duffield conveyed his 200 acres of land on Birch River near William Dodrill's place, to Christopher Baughman. The record shows Samuel Baughman and John Baughman, sons of Christopher. Emmett Baughman, Henry Baughman, Lorenzo and Cornelius were sons of John Baughman. Emmett Baughman was a successful farmer on Little Beaver. He married Florence Hanna. Rebecca Fitzwater, Belle Given and Delilah Murphy were daughters of John Baughman. Ira Baughman and Guy are sons of Emmett Baughman. Guy Baughman married Rita Grose, daughter of Dixon Grose, and is a prosperous farmer at Calvin. Their family of two sons, Walter and Sherman, and two daughters Mary and Rachel, live in the county. Both sons have been called into military service. Sherman is in the Air Service and Walter is now employed as an automobile mechanic. Their two daughters are both employed as stenographers in Summersville.

The children of Guy Baughman are great-great-grandchildren of Christopher Baughman.

BELL, *Scotch-Irish*. Samuel Bell came from Bath County, Virginia in 1809, and purchased a farm on Camp Fork near the VanBibbers. He married Dorothy Rader, oldest daughter of George Rader. His sons, George, John, William and Alex, Samuel and Addison Mc., all settled in the county except Samuel who went west in early life. Samuel Bell, grandson of the pioneer, was the son of William Bell. He married Maria Shelton and lived on Peters Creek near the Stephensons. Mrs. Annie Bell Young, a daughter, is a great-granddaughter of pioneer Samuel Bell. Flem Bell and Ben Bell are sons of Alexander Bell. Billy Bell, the shoe-maker, was a grandson of the pioneer Samuel, and foster father of C. W. Bell, the teacher and local historian.

John Bell, who lived and died in Summersville, was a justice of the peace for many years, and a mail contractor, carrying the mail from Gauley Bridge to Summersville. His son, Robert G. Bell, later operated a mail and passenger service over the same line. His son, Robert, is a printer, employed in the office of the Nicholas Chronicle.

Claude J. Bell, youngest son of John Bell, was prominent in business and politics in the county. He succeeded his brother Robert in the mail and passenger service. With the advent of automobiles, he first employed Ford Cars in this work when the mud roads would permit, but he retained his teams and used wagons and hacks when necessary. When, in 1921, the new law required permits for common carriers to be issued by the State Road Commission, C. J. Bell, because of service was given license as a common carrier on the line from Belva to Summersville, and from Summersville to Richwood, and maintained an efficient passenger and mail service until he sold the services to the Reynolds Transportation Company in 1947. Bennett Bell, son of C. J. Bell, was clerk of Nicholas Circuit Court, and his brother John Bell was Sheriff of Nicholas County for the term ending in 1953. They are great-grandsons of the first Samuel Bell.

BENNETT, *French.* John Bennett, ancestor of the Bennetts of this County and Fayette, was born in Allegheny County, Virginia in 1801. He came to Nicholas in 1853, and bought 1000 acres of land near Pool in Wilderness District. His brother, Henry Bennett, settled near the site of the present town of Richwood. His son, Jacob Bennett, was the father of Dr. E. C. Bennett, a well known physician and politician of Richwood.

Thomas Bennett, a relative of John Bennett, who had located in what is now Fayette County, near Leander, moved to Laurel Creek in this county about 1870. His wife was Mollie Ryan, sister of the celebrated E. W. Ryan, a Methodist minister. The sons of Thomas were Edward, Howard, William R., Jacob and George. Edward was a teacher and the first superintendent of the State Teacher's School at Montgomery. Howard was also a teacher, moved to Fayette County and was superintendent of schools there. William R., after teaching a short time, took up law, and was a Judge of the Circuit Court of Fayette County. Jacob, who studied for the ministry, died in youth. George remained in the community and spent his life on the farm, and was a respected and useful citizen. His sons, Howard and Dan, who left home to engage in business outside of the State, now own homes in their native county near Cross Lanes.

Garrett M. Bennett and Luther Bennett, brothers and close relatives of the Thomas Bennett family, married and settled in Nicholas County. John Bennett, son of Garrett M. Bennett, is a farmer near Poe, and a great-grandson of the John Bennett who lived in Fayette County.

BOLEY, *German*. Presley Boley, first of the name on our records, bought a tract of 500 acres of land on Hominy Creek from William Johnson in 1848. He never located on this land.

Blueford Boley, ancestor of the family in the county, lived and died in Virginia. His son, William Boley was

BOBBITT, *English*. The Bobbitts were early settlers in Greenbrier County. Rufus Bobbitt, first of the family on our records, bought a number of tracts of land of George Gibson and others and settled on McMillions Creek about 1848. His sons were John W. Bobbitt, Alexander Winfield Bobbitt, Elijah Bobbitt, Lee Hill Bobbitt and Newman Bobbitt; his daughters Lydia Ann. Nannie, Victoria and Hulda. A. W. Bobbitt whose home was on McMillions Creek, served two terms as sheriff of the county. Elijah Bobbitt was a farmer on Muddlety and the father of L. O. Bobbitt, O. H. Bobbitt, Samuel Bobbitt and Sterling Bobbitt. His daughters were Lola, and Jennie. L. O. Bobbitt has had a prominent part in school work in the county, as a successful teacher, County Superintendent of Schools and Principal of Nicholas County High School. Dr. O. H. Bobbitt is one of the leading physicians of Charleston, and Sterling Bobbitt is a teacher and Assistant Superintendent of Schools in Mercer County. Lee Hill Bobbitt is a farmer in Webster County.

Elijah Bobbitt married Rouena Robinson, a daughter of James Robinson, junior. The children of Elijah Bobbitt have as their maternal great-great-great-grandfather David Robinson, the pioneer ancestor of the Robinsons in Nicholas County, who came from Virginia, and was a son of John Robinson, presiding officer of the House of Burgesses in 1753.

James Robinson, son of David, married Elizabeth LeMasters, and the children of Elijah Bobbitt are also great-great-great-grandchildren of Benjamin LeMasters.

with the Confederate Army at the Battle of Carnefix Ferry. In 1873 he bought a tract of 575 acres of land from William Caraway on the waters of Meadow River, where he built his home and was an influential citizen. A. N. Boley, another son of Blueford, married a daughter of Joseph Huffman, and located on a farm near Mt. Nebo. His son, Lance W. Boley, now owns the home farm and has converted it into a modern uptodate place. He was elected Sheriff of Nicholas County in 1952. H. O. Boley, another son of A. N. Boley, located in Fayette County, and was active in the business and political life of that county. He was elected as a senator to the State from Fayette County, representing the Ninth Senatorial District. Verna Boley Odell, a daughter of A. N. Boley, was for many years a popular teacher in Nicholas County.

Henry N. Boley, son of Silas O. Boley, is a prominent minister in the Methodist Church. He has served with success in all of his appointments, and was for a time pastor of Bethel Circuit in the county.

Descendants of Blueford Boley live in this and adjoining counties and are well known citizens.

BROCK, *English*. Daniel Brock by deed of record purchased 200 acres of land from William D. Cottle on Gauley River at the Mouth of Muddlety Creek in 1831, his sons were Daniel, Samuel and Thomas M. Brock. His son Daniel for many years operated a grist mill and ferry over Gauley River at the mouth of Muddlety Creek. Later he moved to Summersville and carried on the business of manufacturing and finishing lumber. He also maintained a shop in which he manufactured fine splitbottom chairs that are still to be found in many homes in the county. Daniel Brock was a prominent member of the Masonic Lodge of Summersville and the father of a large family. Samuel Brock, a son, owns and resides in the fine old residence built by his father. Calvin Brock, another son, now lives in Florida.

Samuel Brock in 1851 purchased a tract of 519 acres of land from Fielding McClung on the north side of Gauley River adjoining the Daniel Brock land. Here he spent his life as a farmer and the home passed to his son, John W. Brock, who was a well known farmer and stockman. He was active in church work and much interested in the education of his daughters, all of whom became teachers. Miss Lucy Brock, for several years a teacher in the Charleston city schools now lives in that city. Her sister, Annie M. Brock, married Rev. O. M. Pullen, one of the active leaders in temperance work in the State. She resides in Charleston and after her husband's death has devoted her life to the education of her four sons, Oden, Joseph, George and Paul. Oden and Paul are ministers of the Methodist Church, and her daughter Mary is engaged in special work as a teacher.

BROWN, *Scotch-Irish*. The Browns in Scotland, and later many of them in Ireland, were of the Mc-Brayne Sept in the McMillian Clan. Three different branches of this family were pioneer settlers in the county.

William Brown, about 1740, came from County Ulster in Ireland to Prince William County, Virginia, and soon continued west to Augusta county. He lived but a short time, and his widow, Mary Brown, came to the new settlements in Greenbrier Valley bringing her family with her. Her sons, Samuel and William, patented large tracts of land in what later became Greenbrier and Monroe Counties. Samuel never married, and at his death in 1793, left his home to his aged mother, and divided his large holdings among his brothers Alexander and John, his brother-in-law James Nelson and his nephew John Brown, son of William. His will is of record in Greenbrier County and in it he gives his profession as "weaver". His brother, William Brown, died in what is now Monroe County in 1806, and his will is recorded at Union in that county.

Alexander Brown, son of William, and his sister Jane came to Laurel Creek, then in Kanawha County around the year 1803-04. Alexander purchased land from Captain George Fitzwater, Edward Hughes and others, and patented several tracts in what is now Nicholas, Clay and Kanawha Counties. Jane married John Morris in 1807. Alexander married Polly Foster, and their family of 14 children consisted of the eight boys, John, William, Henry, Edgar, Andrew, Isaac, Alexander and George, and six girls. Mary, the eldest, married David Pierson; Betty married William Hamrick; Sallie married Joseph Backhouse, Virginia married Pascal Backhouse, and Rosa married John Dunbar. Peggy, the youngest girl married Jerry Neal. Numerous descendants of this family now live in Nicholas, Clay, Webster and Kanawha Counties. Dr. William Brown, son of Alexander, married Frances Dunbar, who was a daughter of the Revolutionary soldier, Jonathan Dunbar.

William H. Brown, son of Dr. Brown, was the writer's father. His sons are W. G. Brown, Augustus L. Brown, J. Mat Brown, Jennings E. Brown and Elmer E. Brown.

Paul E. Brown, son of Jennings E. Brown, is Judge of the Sixteenth Judicial Circuit of Virginia. He resides at Fairfax, and is a great-great-great-great-grandson of the emigrant, William Brown.

Israel Brown, who came from Pendleton County to Powells Creek in Nicholas about 1816, was the father of John Brown, a pioneer surveyor of the county, whose name adorns many pages of county records. With old fashioned compass and chain, he traversed hundreds of miles of tangled woodlands in surveying early boundary lines. In a land case in court he was once asked how he made a certain survey. "I did it by God and by guess," he replied. His son, James F. Brown, was a much beloved Baptist minister, and served his people many years in the county. His sons, Richard J., Homer and Flavius all became doctors. Dr. Eugene S. Brown, son of Flavius, is a prominent physician in Summersville. Rev. James F. Brown's daughters, Ella, Agnes, Rose, Mollie and Zela, were successful teachers. His son, Pat A. Brown, is principal of the Craigsville graded school. David Brown, son of Pat, is a promising young physician at Craigsville. He and James Creasy, a county superintendent of schools are great-great-grandsons of Israel Brown.

Hunter Brown, a son of Thomas Brown of Greenbrier County, related to emigrant William Brown, came to Nicholas about 1857 and purchased a farm of Robert Campbell on Meadow Creek near Cross Lanes. His sons, Thomas C. Brown, William Webster Brown and James Brown married and located in the community. Thomas C. Brown was one of our most successful teachers. He later held office as county superintendent of schools, member of the legislature, member of the county court and justice of the peace. He had a large family, none of whom now live in the county. Herbert Brown, a grandson, lives in Charleston.

Since the Civil War other Brown families have come to Nicholas and taken their places as useful and prominent citizens in community life.

BRYANT, *Irish*. Family tradition gives William Bryant as the first known ancestor of the Bryants in Nicholas County. He came from Massachusetts to Rockbridge County, Virginia, at an uncertain date, with his wife and children. The family was broken up when his wife drowned in James River. Two sons, William H. Bryant and James Bryant wandered west into what is now West Virginia, and William found employment in Kanawha County with his uncle Fielding Bryant who was a tanner. The record shows that he married Jane Groves, daughter of John Groves, and in 1835 he purchased Lot No. 5 in the Town of Summersville and built his home there. In 1868 the heirs of John Groves conveyed him a tract of 179 acres of land on Donnallys Branch, now known as Camp Fork. His sons by his first wife were Harrison and John. Harrison lost his life as a Union soldier. Austin Bryant, well known farmer of Enon, who recently died, was a son of John Bryant. William H. Bryant's second wife was Ruth McClung. She was the mother of Lizzie Copenhaver, Letitia Graves and Cassie Alderson, daughters, and Richard M. Bryant and E. M. Bryant, sons. S. W. Bryant, son of Richard, is a lawyer in Clay County.

James Bryant located in Kentucky District, and his

sons, Joseph M., John K., Austin, George and Fielding, all acquired farms in the neighborhood. Edward M. was the son of Joseph M. Bryant, and Aaron is a son of Austin. Hayes, Dexter, Harrison and Irving are sons of George Bryant. Burt and Dayton are sons of Fielding, and Walter and C. W. are the sons of John K. Bryant. His daughter, Mary Elizabeth, married John A. Stowers who owned a prosperous farm near Summersville. C. W. Bryant became a teacher and later operated a store at Canvas. His son, C. Z. Bryant is a teacher in Nicholas County High School. He, and Arthur E. Stowers, a merchant in Summersville and Charleston, are great-great grandsons of their pioneer ancestor William Bryant.

BURDETT, *French.* (Burdit) The Burdetts settled in Monroe County shortly after the Revolution. William Burdett built his home on Flat Top Mountain about the year 1800, and Giles Burdett in 1824 is charged on the Land Books of Nicholas County with 100 acres of land on "Peters Creek Road". Other members of the family acquired land in the county.

Shortly before the Civil War, John Burdett together with his wife and family came to Nicholas County and located on Laurel Creek. A son, William A. Burdett, married Susan Dunbar and lived for a time in that community. Upon the death of his wife Susan, he married Martha Brown, daughter of Dr. William Brown and later lived on the old home place of his father-in-law. He had a family of four sons, William T., Rufus, Lemon and James, and four daughters, Elizabeth, Sallie, Luella and Quindora by his second wife Martha. He was the father of two girls, Alice and Frances by his first wife.

Quinnie, who lives at Boomer in Fayette County, is the only survivor of the family. William T. Burdett was a teacher and business man. He married Lulu Koontz and died without children. Elizabeth married A. J. Legg and was the mother of a large family, most of whom are successful teachers well known in the county.

Many other descendants of this family of Burdetts from Monroe County live in Nicholas and adjoining counties.

CALLAGHAN, *Irish.*

Thomas Callaghan of Allegheny County, Virginia, first of the name of record in Nicholas County, purchased 500 acres of land on Muddlety Creek from Henry Depew in 1819. He married Elizabeth Campbell, daughter of pioneer John Campbell, and later moved to Missouri.

John Callaghan came from Allegheny County, Virginia, and purchased two large tracts of land on Big Beaver Creek in 1846. The will of his widow, Maria Callaghan, recorded in Nicholas County Will Book No. 1, page 117, names as sons, John, Thomas D., William Y., Edwin B., and Robert D. Callaghan. William Y. Callaghan was a teacher and the third superintendent of schools, 1868-69. He was well educated for his day, was a fine penman and did much to organize our school system. Thomas D. Callaghan was a farmer, and his son, Dennis M., and daughter Ada, were teachers. Edwin B. Callaghan's sons were C. Dewitt, David T., Luther, Romeo, Black and Hansford Callaghan. Adlai E., Eulai B., Teslai T., Brooks B., and C. D. Jr., are sons of C. Dewitt Callaghan. D. E. Callaghan, Glenn S., and Zela Callaghan Brown are children of David T. Callaghan.

William Yates Callaghan had one son, Dr. Walter F. Callaghan.

Brooks B. Callaghan is a prominent member of Nicholas County Bar.

CAMPBELL, *Scotch-Irish*. John Campbell, pioneer ancestor of this family, was born in Ulster, North Ireland. Both parents died on the voyage to America, leaving the twelve year old boy an orphan. The captain of his ship found him a home in New York City. After a time he made his way to the settlements on the Kanawha River in Virginia. In 1792 the records show he purchased land of Edward McClung at the head of Whitewater, near Cross Lanes. In 1795 he married Nancy Hughes in her father's fort at the mouth of Hughes's Creek, and located his cabin home on his land in what is now Nicholas County. His children were: Elizabeth, married Thomas Callahan; Miram, married James Walkub; Abram J., John Davidson, Edward, Mary and Robert. Abram J. Campbell's sons were, Columbus C., Paley L., John Seneca and Andrew N. Campbell. John Davidson Campbell, married Mary Kessler and settled in what is now Fayette County, where many of his descendants now live. Jason W. Campbell, a well known teacher and writer is a grandson of John Davidson Campbell. Edward Campbell, most distinguished son of the pioneer, was father of John Franklin, Charles William, Mary Jane, Sidney Masterson, Elizabeth Nancy, Robert Spotts, Nathaniel Redmon, Luther Rice and Lycurgus. Three of these sons, Robert Spotts, Nathaniel Redmon and Luther Rice, were in the Confederate army with their father, and were killed in battle. Sydney Masterson was

Pioneer Families 299

in the army. He was a fine scholar, graduate of Ohio State University, studied law, but gave his life to teaching. Charles William Campbell was a farmer in the Kanawha valley. His son the late Sterling P. Campbell was a business man in Fayette County.

Lycurgus the youngest son was a well-known citizen and lived and died on the home place of his father. John Andy and Charles Paley were sons of Columbus C. Campbell. Lydia Ann Morrison was a daughter of Albert Campbell a son of John Seneca Campbell. Virginia D. Campbell (Jennie), lived on her father's place, and Mary Alice VanBibber of Redland California are daughters of Paley L. Campbell.

Andrew N. Campbell, youngest son of Abram T. Campbell, was twice married—two daughters, Vina and Nora by his marriage were teachers—none of his children by the second marriage live in the County.

Many of the leading families of the County are related to this distinguished pioneer family.

The family of Lycurgus Campbell still own and occupy the old home place of Col. Edward Campbell.

CARNEFIX, *German.* William Carnefix came to Kanawha County before the oganization of Nicholas County, and settled in what is now Fayette County. He owned several tracts of land in what is now Fayette County, and on his land at the mouth of Meadow River he built a mill and established the ferry across Gauley River which still bears his name, and gives name to the battlefield of the Civil War nearby. In 1820 he was appointed deputy for Samuel Hutchinson surveyor of lands for Nicholas County. He was overseer of a road from the James River & Kanawha Turnpike to his ferry and superintended its construction.

In 1818 he purchased land from William McClung on Anglins Creek, but the records do not show what disposition was made of this land.

In 1849 he conveyed 100 acres of land on south side of Gauley in Wilderness District to Mary H. Carnefix, and in 1853 she made a conveyance of same to John Pittsenbarger. The record does not show her relation to William Carnefix.

Mary Ann McVey, grand daughter of William Carnefix married Henry Patterson, and they settled on the site of what is now Carnefix Battlefield State Park, and this land was given her by William Carnefix.

Some descendants of William Carnefix still live in Nicholas and Fayette Counties.

CAVENDISH, *Scotch-Irish*. The Cavendish family, originally from Scotland, also had a branch of that name in England. Cavendishes settled in Greenbrier County. In 1822 William McClung sold to Andrew Cavendish, then living in Greenbrier, a large tract of land in Nicholas County. In 1853, Alexander Cavendish came from Greenbrier and purchased a tract of land from Jane Dorsey in the Panther Mountain community. His wife was Sarah Dorsey. His sons, Robert, Benjamin B., Samuel H., John M., Socrates Clark and Joseph F. all married and located in the county.

Homer D. Cavendish and Joseph A. Cavendish are sons of Samuel H. Cavendish. Kenna Cavendish, son of John M. Cavendish married Amata Cutlip, and lived for a time in the county then moved to Kanawha County.

Joseph Cavendish married Ermina J. Legg, and spent his life on his farm in the Panther Mountain Community. He had a large family, who are well known in the County and State. His sons, Theodore and Otis are successful business men in Cabell County. Vina Cavendish, daughter of Joseph F. made a fine record as teacher in the schools of Cincinnati. Oliver, another son, lives in Fayette County. Orbin Cavendish, youngest son of Joseph F. Cavendish, is a successful farmer, near Drennen in this County.

CHAPMAN, *Scotch-Irish*. Jacob Chapman, ancestor of the Nicholas County family of that name, settled on Little Mountain about the year 1813. He patented several tracts of land in the county. His sons were Jacob C. Chapman and Andrew L. Chapman. They too, were large land holders. Jacob C. Chapman had a son, Jacob Chapman, who was the father of Rev. Scott Chapman, who married Annie Groves, daughter of John W. Groves. He joined the Methodist Conference and rose to prominence as a minister. Andrew L. Chapman settled in Kentucky District. He was the father of William J. Chapman, John A. Chapman and George D. Chapman.

John Wesley Chapman and Andrew J. Chapman were prominent members of this family. Benton Chapman and Leonard Chapman were sons of John Wesley Chapman. Malinda Chapman, a daughter of John Wesley Chapman, married Gordon G. Duff. Blaine Chapman, son of Leonard, is a prominent business man in Summersville. H. W. Chapman, son of Andrew L. Chapman, was a well known farmer of Kentucky District, but moved to Summersville and spent his life there

COPENHAVER, *German.* Jacob Copenhaver, pioneer of the family in Nicholas County, patented three tracts of land in the early days of the settlement: 112 acres on McKees Creek in 1833, 65 acres adjoining in 1836 and 25 acres on Gauley River in 1850. He also purchased several adjoining tracts.

His sons John and Joseph located on farms given them by their father. David H. Copenhaver and William D. Copenhaver, two other sons, were also given farms, but they soon moved to Kanawha County. John and Joseph lived and prospered on their farms. John Copenhaver's sons were, John Alexander, Joseph H. and Stewart H. John Alexander and Joseph H. were farmers. Stewart H. was a teacher. Joseph's son was James Allen Copenhaver: his five daughters, Mrs. Nannie Skaggs, Mrs. Julia Ramsey, Fanny Hughes, Mrs. Abbie Hughes and Mrs. Ed Dorsey.

Joseph Copenhaver, Sr., was a leader in organizing Dotson Chapel, and also furnished the first Southern Methodist parsonage,—a log cabin that stood where James Skaggs afterwards lived. Ed Copenhaver and his son Russell are the only descendants of pioneer Jacob Copenhaver, living on the Copenhaver lands.

Mayor John T. Copenhaver of Charleston is a lineal descendant of Jacob Copenhaver, the pioneer.

CORRON-CURRAN-KERN, *Irish.* In 1821, John G. Corron came from Greenbrier and bought a tract of 300 acres on Cogin Knob from William H. McClung. In 1832 his widow, Lucy conveyed this tract to James P. Corron.

In 1850 Levi J. Hooker conveyed a tract of land on

Muddlety to James M. Corron. His relation to John G. Corron does not appear. James M. Corron's sons were George W. Corron, Luther Haymond Corron and Henry Sheridan Corron; his daughters Martha Bruffy, Eliza Spencer, Alice Holcomb and Rebecca Butcher. James M. Corron was twice married. His first wife was Lydia Ann McCoy and his second wife Susan Taylor.

Henry S. Corran's first wife, Maggie Spinks, his second wife was a daughter of Francis Odell. Luther Haymond Corron married Susan Herold and lived on his father's home place and cared for his parents during their life. In 1919 he located in Summersville and resides with his son, Pearl Corron, since the death of his wife. Pearl has for some years made a business of growing vegetable plants for sale to gardeners. He is also a sign painter. In Haymond Corron's family Bible is the record of Joseph Corron's birth in 1788 and that of his wife born in 1795— his grand parents.

The Curran family is not related to the Corrons.

John E. Kern was for a time a resident of Summersville and was a teacher and land surveyor.

COTTLE, *German*. Charles William Cottle is the ancestor of the Nicholas County Cottles. He came from Greenbrier to Nicholas, then Kanawha County, about 1810. He purchased a tract of 800 acres of land in the glades, still known as Cottle Glades. He soon had about 200 acres in meadow and engaged in raising cattle. He is said to have sometimes wintered as many as 200 head of cattle. He was an influential citizen and was sheriff of Kanawha County before the organization of Nicholas County. He took an active part in the organization of

Nicholas County. His name appears often in the early records of the County.

Two of his sons, Uriah and William D. Cottle are named. The latter was one of the justices named at the organization of the County.

The late William D. Cottle and John R. Cottle were grandsons of Charles William Cottle. Some of their children and grandchildren live in the County.

Cottle postoffice and Cottle Knob are monuments to this pioneer family.

CRAIG, *Scotch-Irish*. William Craig, a covenanter, came with his family from Ulster, Ireland to Pennsylvania in 1721. He moved to Augusta County, Virginia, and died in 1759. His will is of record in Staunton, in which he names two sons, John and Robert; and two daughters, Ann and Rebecca. He settled in Greenbrier County above Spring Creek. His children were Nancy, Margaret, Sarah, Elizabeth, Rebecca and Robert. His will is of record in Lewisburg. Robert Craig, third of the name came to Nicholas in 1837 and located on what is now the Fielding Herold farm. In 1844 he purchased 500 acres from Thomas Callaghan. His son, John James Craig, born in Greenbrier in 1817, married Frances Hawver in 1839. Their family was James S. Craig, Peter H. Craig, John H. Craig, George W. Craig and Cynthia Frances Odell. James S. Craig was a Federal soldier, Clerk of the Circuit and County courts after the Civil War, and served two terms as postmaster at Summersville. He had a wide acquaintance with business and professional man of his day and acquired extensive real estate holdings. His children were Sterling M. Craig, Arden

L. Craig, C. H. Craig, Lillie P. Craig, Dainty E. Craig and Camilla V. Craig. Sterling M. Craig resides in Summersville and is a well-known businessman. Arden L. Craig (Bruddy) was a prominent lawyer and real estate dealer. Eugene Craig, his only child, lives in Columbia, South Carolina. Peter H. Craig served in the army under General Custer. Arthur Craig and Murray Craig are sons, and Phern Craig a daughter of Peter H. Craig. Phern is a teacher and lives on the home place of her father. John H. Craig was a farmer and had a family of twelve children, all well-known citizens. George W. Craig, also a farmer, reared a large family. He took an active interest in politics and public life. His son, Dr. J. Sherman Craig, is a physician, and as such held the rank of colonel in World War II. He was with General MacArthur in the Philippines and was a captive of the Japanese for several months. His health was lost by this imprisonment, and he is now in retirement in Florida.

CROOKSHANKS (CRUIKSHANKS), *English*. Robert Crookshanks, first of the name on our Land Books, came from Greenbrier in 1847, purchased from Elijah Hall and others a tract of 50 acres of land adjoining the farm of John Groves not far from Cross Lanes. He settled there and later purchased other lands from Johnson Reynolds in the same community. A son, Franklin Crookshanks, located on his father's farm and reared a large family. William M., son of Franklin, was a teacher, merchant and justice of the peace. He was elected Clerk of the Circuit Court of Nicholas County in 1902. Another son, Robert, studied for the ministry, and became a prominent Baptist preacher in Virginia.

Leonard Crookshanks, another son of Robert Sr., was a farmer and resided on a portion of his father's home place.

Two other sons of Robert Sr., Charles A. and John Crookshanks, were well known farmers on Whitewater Creek.

Few of Robert Crookshanks' descendants remain in Nicholas County.

CUTLIP, *German*. The Cutlips came to America from the Palatinate in Germany in the great Mennonite emigration, and some of them found their way to what is now Nicholas County. They came from Pennsylvania and up the South Branch of the Potomac, across the mountains and down Gauley River to the Glades along that river in what is now Nicholas and Webster Counties. This appears from tradition and the records of the refugees that fled to Donnally's Fort at the time of the Strouds massacre some years after the killing of the Morris children. George Cutlip was the first of the name on the Land Books of the county. He purchased land on Muddlety Creek in 1816. He was the first class leader of the Methodist Church there. At his death his farm passed to his son Nathan Cutlip. Nathan Cutlip's sons were Haymond, Chauncy, Homer, Calvin, and Edward. His daughters were Margaret Herold, Virginia Groves, Ann Huff, Sarah Dyer, Georgia Boso, Julia Summers and Emma Dotson. Haymond Cutlip's children A. L. Cutlip, Purdum Cutlip, Alvin Cutlip, Nevie Cutlip, Amata Cutlip Cavendish and Evie Cutlip Brown all lived in the county except Rev. Nevie Cutlip, who became a Methodist minister and served his church in New Jersey and New York. His family still live in these states. Homer Cutlip's son

Pioneer Families 307

Ira, lives on the home place near Summersville. Chauncy Cutlip and his brother Calvin located in Richwood. Edward lives in Morgantown.

Henry Cutlip who settled on Elk River and D. H. Cutlip who was a farmer near Craigsville, and perhaps others of the name, are doubtless descendants of this pioneer family, but the relationship is not definitely known. Many of the name live in Braxton, and Webster Counties and are prominent in public life in their communities.

DAVIS, *Scotch Irish*. Silas Davis was granted three tracts of land in Nicholas County on Hominy Creek, in 1848.

James Davis, his son, in his will in 1868, names as sons, Bernard C. Davis, and Henry B. Davis.

Bernard C. Davis was a minister of the Southern Methodist Church.

Henry B. Davis was a leading teacher of Nicholas County. He was a graduate of Glenville Normal School, and served one term as county superintendent. Later he was a Director of Nicholas County High School.

His son, Ira B. Davis, is a resident of Kanawha County. Relatives of this family still reside in the County.

DEITZ, *German*. William Deitz came from Botetourt County, Virginia, to Greenbrier at an early date. He purchased land in what is now Nicholas County. In 1831, William McClung conveyed to Catherine Williams, Elizabeth Deitz, Nathaniel Deitz, Polly Deitz, Joseph Deitz, John Deitz, Robert Deitz, Phebe Deitz, Rebecca Deitz and James Deitz, heirs at law of William Deitz, deceased, of Greenbrier County, a tract of 50 acres, in

Nicholas, described as adjoining the land of William Deitz, Jr., recorded in Deed Book 2, page 367.

The marriage record shows that James W. Deitz married Nancy Hendrickson of Botetourt County, Virginia, in 1857. It appears from the record that James W. Deitz and J. D. Deitz were sons of William Deitz, Sr.

In 1898, J. D. Deitz and Virginia, his wife, conveyed to their sons, J. W. Deitz and E. E. Deitz a tract of 120 acres of land in Nicholas County.

J. W. Deitz and E. E. Deitz, twin brothers, were well known in the public life of the county. E. E. Deitz was the first mayor and postmaster of Richwood. His sons are prominent in the business life of that city. Oakford Deitz is assistant superintendent of Nicholas County schools.

In 1884, the heirs of A. S. Skaggs, deceased, conveyed 160 acres of land in Wilderness District to George W. Deitz. Nathan Deitz and Wallace Deitz are named as citizens of Mt. Lookout community. William Henry Deitz in business in Summersville, is a son of Fraza Leonidas Deitz and a grandson of Wilson Deitz.

The relation of the Deitz family of Richwood to the family of that name in Wilderness District does not appear from the record.

DODRILL-DODDRIDGE, *English*. William E. Dodrill (English Bill) married Rebecca Dougherty in Greenbrier County in 1784. He is the ancestor of the Nicholas County Dodrills. After living a short time on Peters Creek, about 1799 he moved to Birch River. He had eight children: James, John, George, William, Mary, Martha, Nancy and Rebecca. His oldest son John was the father of six sons: Isaac, George, William, Robert, Charles, Joseph. Charles who lived in Webster County was a unique character. He held important local offices, was a natural orator and famed for his Fourth of July orations. John the second son of "English Bill", was the father of William, James Walton, Franklin, Martin, Arthur and Addison. James Walton Dodrill was the father of Martin V. Dodrill, John N. Dodrill, known as "Big John," W. C. Dodrill often styled "Rattlesnake Bill", Addison Dodrill and Rush Dodrill. "Big John" Dodrill was the father of J. O. Dodrill who served a term as Circuit Clerk of Nicholas County, and now a well known businessman of Clay County. "Rattlesnake Bill" was a successful teacher, a gifted speaker and writer and the author of "Moccasin Tracks and Other Imprints", an interesting sketch book of events in the early history of the county. Martin V. Dodrill was the father of "Big Sam" Dodrill, W. H. Dodrill, John F. Doddrill and James Dodrill. Dr. Bernard Dodrill, formerly of Nicholas County now resides in Webster County. W. S. Dodrill, editor of The Clay Messenger, and his brother Carl Dodrill belong to the Nicholas County Dodrill family.

Space forbids further listing of prominent members of the hardy pioneer family, whose original was Doddridge, but seems to have been first written "Dodrill" by pioneer William E. Dodrill about the time of his marriage in Greenbrier County, and the name has been so accepted by his numerous descendants.

DORSEY, D'ORSAY, *Norman-French*. The D'Orsey's came to England with William the Conqueror in 1066, and were given estates in Lincolnshire. Descendants of the family are of record in the earliest history of Maryland and Virginia, under the Anglicized names Darcy, Dorcey and Dorsey. It is uncertain just when the first Dorseys came over the mountains to Nicholas County. John Dorsey, who was one of the first settlers on Twenty Mile Creek, is the first of the name on our Land Books. A son, Benjamin B. Dorsey, married Jane Neil, daughter of Samuel Neil, and settled on a part of the Neil estate. His sons were Jackson, Cornelius and John B. Dorsey. Maria Dorsey, daughter of Cornelius, married George W. Backus. John B. Dorsey lived on Tates Run. His son, Lorenzo Dorsey, was the father of Rev. Manning Dorsey, a prominent Baptist minister.

Andrew M. Dorsey, son of John and Airy Dorsey, came from Virginia in the early history of the county. He had four sons and eight daughters. His son, Aaron Milise Dorsey, was the father of Adam Dorsey, whose son, Henry Dorsey, is a distinguished educator. John F. Dorsey was the father of William Dorsey and the grandfather of Ervin, John and Rufus Dorsey. Marshall Dorsey, a Union soldier, lost his life in the Civil War. Andrew M. Dorsey, Jr., youngest son of Andrew M., Sr., was the father of thirteen children, all well known citizens. His son, E. Dalton Dorsey, represented the county as a Delegate in the Legislature of 1927. Samuel, Cornelius, Addison, Wellington, David and Jacob, brothers of Andrew M. Dorsey, Sr., have many descendants in the county.

The Dorseys are related to many of the old families in the county, and the family is respected for its intelligent citizenship. The Dorsey family has produced prominent ministers and teachers. E. Dalton Dorsey in a sketch of the family has this to say: "The Dorseys are a home-loving, God-fearing family". All who know them will agree that this statement truly describes the character of his people.

DOTSON, *German*. Jacob Dotson and his brother Richard came to Nicholas soon after the County was organized. Richard Dotson purchased Lot No. 30 in the Town of Summersville, from Addison McLaughlin, and then disappears from the record. Jacob Dotson bought 118 acres of land on Peters Creek from Edward Rion in 1830. His sons, Andrew J., Jacob L., Jackson and Isaac F., are mentioned in his Will of record in Will Book No. 1, at page 196. His daughters were Sarah A. Wiseman, Eliza Bays, and Virginia Halstead.

Jacob L. Dotson had seven sons, Lightburn, Logan, Alexander, John, Daniel, James and Edward. Lightburn Dotson taught school and later became a minister of the Methodist Church. Logan S. Dotson was one of the founders of the Nicholas Republican and was assessor of Nicholas County, and active in politics. James J. Dotson was a well-known teacher and for many years owner and editor of the Nicholas Republican. Edward Dotson is a justice of the peace living in Summersville.

Richard, William, Addison Mac, and Peter K. were sons of Isaac Dotson.

William E. Dotson, son of William, is a farmer and owns the home place of his father.

Samuel C. Dotson, son of Addison Mac Dotson, was a teacher, County Superintendent of Schools, and represented the County in the House of Delegates. Later he entered the ministry of the Methodist Church and now retired from the pastorate, lives near Wheeling.

Newton Dotson, Gordon Dotson and Frank Dotson are sons of Peter K. Dotson.

Dexter N. Dotson, grandson of Addison Mac Dotson, is a teacher in Nicholas County High School.

DRENNEN, *German.* Jacob Drennen came to Nicholas County in its earliest days and bought land from Samuel Neil. He was appointed postmaster of Drennen post office April 25, 1831. After several years he was succeeded by his son, Thomas Drennen, who operated a successful general store in connection with the post office. Thomas Drennen was twice married, and by his first wife, Catherine Walker, there were two daughters, Annie who married Wm. R. Bennett, and Annie who married Thomas Ryan of Roane County. His second wife, Lenona Renick, was the mother of Eugene Drennen and Fred Drennen.

Charles Drennen, son of Jacob, lived just above Drennen post office, where for many years he kept a "tavern". He took much pride in a fine chalybeate spring near the residence and loved to extol its health giving properties. His sons were Gaines and Austin, and his daughter, Silvena, who married Ira W. Groves.

John Drennen, the other son of Jacob, lived adjoining his brother Charles. His sons were T. C., Joseph R., William J., Samuel J., and John Floyd Drennen. Camden and John Floyd were song-leaders and music teachers. He had one daughter, Mary Drennen Bell.

Many of the children and great-grandchildren of Jacob Drennen live in the county.

DUFFY, *Irish*. The Duffy family came directly to Summersville in Nicholas, as emigrants from County Monaghan, Ireland. The first group, Michael, Peter and John, came in 1821, and about ten years later Owen, Francis, Philip, and their sister, Catherine, cousins of the first group, arrived. The Duffys soon acquired land and settled in and around Summersville. They were Catholics and without delay joined in organizing a Catholic Church.

John Duffy's will of record in Nicholas County Will Book No. 1, page 143, names a son, John H. H. Duffy and three daughters, Mary, wife of Joseph A. Alderson, Sarah who married Felix J. Baxter, and Teresa who became the wife of John F. Campbell.

Francis Duffy's will of record in Will Book 1, page 200, Nicholas County, names no children, but mentions a niece, wife of Samuel Pettigrew; nephews Michael C. and James B. Duffy, and sister, Alice Thornton.

Owen Duffy was the father of John Duffy, Jr., who lived on Brushy Fork. He was the father of Robert Duffy and John Duffy and seven daughters. Celia Duffy, daughter of Robert, is a teacher.

Michael Duffy was the father of Pat Duffy, an auditor of the State who lived in Webster County, Terrence Duffy, a priest, James B. Duffy and Michael C. Duffy, farmers.

John Duffy and *Philip Duffy*, in partnership with Patrick Beirne in the firm of Beirne, Duffy and Company, operated the largest store in the county for many years.

John H. H. Duffy was a lawyer. His children, John Kane, Cora Reddy and Annie Duffy Groves were citizens of Summersville. The Duffy family is connected by marriage with many of the early families.

DUNBAR, *Scotch-Irish*. Jonathan Dunbar, whose family had moved to Monroe County, Virginia, from Pennsylvania in 1790, came to Nicholas County in 1806, and bought James Foster's place on Backus Branch, and a tract of land from Mathias Young on Laurel Creek near Bethel Church. He had enlisted as a soldier of the Revolution while living in Pennsylvania. His sons John and Jonathan settled on land given by their father. His daughter, Frances, married Dr. William Brown and his daughter, Elizabeth, married John Odell, son of Sylvanus Odell.

John Dunbar divided his land among his three sons, John C. Dunbar, Jonathan, Jr., and Jabez L. Jonathan, Jr., married Leah Legg. Their family consisted of one son, Washington Dunbar and seven daughters: Jane Walker, Esteline Miller, Susan Burdette, Matilda Legg, Mary Grose, Elizabeth Johnson and Agatha Cavendish. Many descendants of Jonathan Dunbar still live in Nicholas County, but none bearing the Dunbar name.

John M. Dunbar, a close relative of pioneer Jonathan, came from Monroe County and purchased land on Peters Creek. His sons, Alexander, George W. and Abner T. were well known citizens. Alexander Dunbar married Mary Jane Groves. Two sons, Bedford and Edwin, died in early life. Laura, his only daughter, married Russell Kitchen, her only son, Lon Kitchen, married Mertie Bennett. Their family is well known. Dr. James C. Dunbar, a successful physician, who married Rufina Dorsey, was the son of George W. Dunbar. His widow,

Mrs. Rufina Dunbar, reared a fine family who are well known. She was chosen Mother of the Year in 1950.

James H. Dunbar and David W. Dunbar, sons of Abner T. Dunbar, were lawyers.

EVANS, *Irish*. Elkanah Evans came from Greenbrier County in 1836 and located at Mount Lookout. His wife was Mary Bear. They were married in Greenbrier in 1833. Alexander Evans married Edna Skaggs and moved to Mount Lookout in 1854. William A. Evans married Sallie Skaggs and established a home at Mount Lookout in 1848. Obadiah Evans was also an early resident of the same community. The relationship of these settlers does not appear from the records now available.

C. L. Evans, long a resident and office holder in the county, came from Kanawha County. His first wife was Lily Legg, a daughter of John Legg. His second wife was Ollie Walker, daughter of Levi Walker.

John L. Evans, who was deputy county clerk under Joseph A. Alderson, and an active and well known citizen of Summersville, was a son of Winfield Scott Evans, whose wife was Caroline Hutchinson, sister of John M. Hutchinson.

These three families were not related so far as the records show.

EWING, *Scotch-Irish*. Moses Ewing was in Nicholas County several years before its organization. His marriage to Peggy Brown in 1811 is of record in Kanawha County. In 1828 he purchased 50 acres of land from Samuel Jones on Sugar Branch of Gauley River, and soon acquired several other tracts in that vicinity. In 1823 he patented 50 acres on Gauley River and 220 acres on

Glade Creek and in 1832 190 acres on waters of Peters Creek. Allen Ewing, his son, married Rachel Johnson in 1832 and in 1835 located on Smiths Creek, now called "Whitewater." In 1841 he patented 250 acres on Peters Creek. He was a carpenter and cabinet maker, and the doors and pulpit of Bethel Church were made by him of select ash lumber. After his wife's death he lived with John D. Groves on his Laurel Creek farm and built him a good house. His daughter, Harriet, married John McMillion, father of J. O. and Gus McMillion. The land records show grants of land in various parts of the county to Margaret Ewing, Elisha Ewing and James Ewing. A deed of record shows a conveyance of a lot for the Methodist Church, at Mount Vernon, to John H. Rader and others, trustees. This conveyance is dated in 1870, and was made by John Ewing.

The Ewings came from Greenbrier County where they were pioneer settlers, and large landholders. The relationship of the Ewings named in this county does not appear of record only as stated.

FITZWATER, *Norman-French*. Captain George Fitzwater came to what is now Nicholas County from Virginia with a company of surveyors and hunters soon after the Revolutionary War. He returned to Virginia, but soon came back with a man named Stockwell and made a number of land surveys along Gauley River from the Cross Lanes section to the Panther Mountain. He and Edward McClung were living together in a cabin on what is now the Hamilton farm at Cross Lanes at the time of the Morris Massacre. He was well informed, had a library of books brought with him into the wilderness. He built the first grist mill in the county on Meadow Creek, and was captain of the local militia. His sons were George, Isaac and Thomas. Thomas lived on Laurel Creek on land granted to his father, was an excellent blacksmith, and a leader in Bethel Methodist Church. He had one son, Augustua, and two daughters, Nancy and Amelia.

Thomas Fitzwater and John Fitzwater, twin-brothers and relatives of Captain George, followed him to the new country. Thomas Fitzwater had a family of nine children. A son of his, Thomas, settled on Little Beaver Creek. His sons, Clark, Orin D., Vaught and Homer, were well known citizens of that community.

John Fitzwater, brother of Thomas, who had located on Sammons creek, a few years before, had a family of eleven children—three sons, Charles, John and Squire, and eight daughters. Lewis and John Fitzwater, grandsons of John Fitzwater, had farms on McKees Creek. Rev. John R. Fitzwater is a son of Lewis Fitzwater.

Space forbids further listing of prominent members of this sturdy pioneer family.

FOCKLER, FAWKLER, FALKLER, *German*. Jacob Fawkler, the first of the name on our Land Books, in Nicholas County, purchased two tracts of land on Muddlety from John H. Robinson in 1836. In his will he names Cutlip and Daniel as his sons, and Catherine Hawver, Jane Chapman, Jemima Bell and Mary Bell, as his daughters.

Cutlip Folkler in his will names John, George and Samuel as his sons, and Elizabeth and Lanty as children of Samuel, deceased.

John Fockler and George Fockler were farmers in this community and respected citizens.

John Fockler married Mary Robinson; George Fockler married Susan Cox.

Okey and Arnett Fockler are sons of John Fockler; and Fay Fockler is a son of George Fockler. They are great grandsons of Jacob Falkler.

FOSTER, *Scotch-Irish*. Isaac Foster, ancestor of the family in Nicholas County, came from Monroe County in 1798, and located on what is known as the John R. McCutcheon place near Cross Lanes. His four sons, Isaac, Nathaniel, James and Nimrod, came with him. Isaac and James soon went West. Isaac senior, and his son Nathaniel, bought land in the Bend of Gauley, where Nathaniel cleared out a large farm. He was twice married—By the first marriage there were two sons: Isaac and John. Isaac moved west, John located on what is now the Crawford farm. He had two daughters, Elizabeth Duncan and Sarah Crawford. He owned the Foster Mill on Meadow Creek, and by his will gave it to his grandson Andrew W. Duncan.

By his second marriage Nathaniel had seven children, four girls and three sons: Sarah, the youngest daughter, married David R. Hamilton. Andrew B. Foster, his son, located on McKees creek; his son Creed V. Foster, lived on the home place until his death; a son of Creed, Albert, still resides there. Redmond G. Foster had no children. For many years he lived on the mill lot and operated the Foster mill. James A., the other son of Nathaniel, moved to Colorado.

Nimrod Foster, located on the farm owned by Edward

Pioneer Families 319

Hughes, later known as the John D. Groves place. He was a consumptive; and the records show he was released from work on the roads.

Nimrod Foster's will names Turly, Isaac, John, Paton, Presley and Sandy as his sons.

Many of the descendants of Isaac Foster remain in Nicholas County.

FRAME, *Scotch-Irish*. David Frame, Thomas Frame and James Frame settled on Elk River before the county was organized. On April 7, 1818 at the organization of the county, David Frame was qualified as a justice, and as such was a member of the first County Court. He resigned at the May term, 1821.

Thomas Frame was granted the right to build a dam and erect a mill on Elk River in 1821. Frametown still commemorates the early location of the Frames in Nicholas County. In 1830 David Frame conveyed a tract of 271 acres of land to his sons, Andrew Frame and John Frame. William Frame, son of John Frame, the only one of the name that leaves a will of record, names Andrew P. Frame, James T. Frame and Tyburtus Frame as his sons.

Dr. Ellis Frame, Guy Frame, Orville Frame and Roy Frame, sons of Tyburtus Frame, are well known citizens. Dr. Ellis Frame, who practiced as a physician in this county for many years, now lives in Webster County, where he continues his practice. Guy Frame is postmaster at Hookersville; Orville Frame and Roy Frame are business men at Birch River.

Frank Frame, a lawyer of Braxton County, married

Kate Bell, daughter of Samuel Bell of Nicholas County, and practiced his profession in this county.

Many descendants of this pioneer family live in Nicholas and adjoining counties.

GIVEN, *Scotch-Irish*. John, James and William Given, probably brothers, came from Bath County to what is now Nicholas County, several years before the county was organized.

William, who located on Peters Creek at the mouth of Pine Run, was appointed Commissioner of Revenue, at the first term of the County Court in 1818, and held this office for ten years.

James and John were both carpenters. They owned land on Elk River near the mouth of Birch River and in the Birch River and Strange Creek vicinity. James Given was one of the first justices and as such a member of the first County Court. He was employed to build the first Court House at Summersville, and was more than two years in completing it. The lumber for the court house was cut by whipsaws or hewed out by hand, and was furnished by John G. Stephenson and his brother Joshua from their lands near Gilboa.

Adam Given, a descendant of the pioneer Givens, was a celebrated minister in Nicholas and adjoining counties.

Many descendants of the Given family still are citizens of Nicholas and adjoining counties.

GRAY, *Scotch-Irish*. The Grays were pioneers in Monroe County. Archibald Gray of Monroe County was commissioned a Captain in the second Regiment of Infantry in the regular army of the United States, on the 27th day of January, 1801. His Commission, signed by

President John Adams is in possession of Mrs. Mary Rutledge, of Poe, widow of Lanty Rutledge, who was a great-grand son of Captain Archibald Gray. George Washington Gray and Charles Marion Gray, sons of Captain Archibald Gray came to Nicholas County from Monroe about 1840. In 1842 Thomas B. Morris conveyed 100 acres of land on Peters Creek to George Washington Gray. He was a prominent citizen and served a term as assessor. John Gray and Sinnett Gray were sons of George Washington Gray. In 1861 Charles Marion Gray bought 100 acres of land from John C. Dunbar, on Laurel Creek. It was on this land that the Methodists had their old Camp Meeting Grounds. Walter Gray and Gilbert, sons of John Gray, and grandsons of Marion, inherited this land. Marion Gray's children were John, Charles, Lucy and Peggy.

Charlie Gray had a family of twelve children. His son, Henry Gray is the father of eight children. His children are great-great grandchildren of Captain Archibald Gray.

GROSE, *German*. Samuel Grose whose name first appears on the records, came from Bath County in 1814 and located near the Koontz brothers, Jacob and John, on Line Creek.

John Grose, Jefferson, James, Samuel and William, were sons of Samuel. His son William Grose was born in Bath County, and later followed his father to Nicholas County. He married Susan Koontz and bought the Hess farm in 1838, now owned by the heirs of A. J. Legg. Their sons were William, Franklin, Andrew J., Washington, Covington and Wesley. William married Rebecca Ann Stephenson and located on Hutchinsons Creek. Rev. Logan S. Grose, a prominent Methodist preacher, and Walter R. Grose, a well known school man, are sons of this William.

Franklin Grose had one son, Andrew D. Grose, who was the father of the Bishop George R. Grose.

Covington Grose married Nancy Walker. His three sons, George, Clark and Joseph Tyler were prominent citizens. Samuel Grose, son of pioneer Samuel, settled near Cross Lanes. U. S. Grose, Dr. E. J. Grose and Waitman T. Grose, his sons, are well known.

John Grose, another son, lived on Laurel Creek; James and Jefferson, his brothers, settled on Line Creek.

Wm. O. Grose, son of John McD. Grose the saddler, lived in Summersville. His sons, John A. Grose and David O. Grose were in turn editors of the Nicholas Chronicle.

Many descendants of this family reside in Nicholas and adjoining Counties.

GROVES, *English*. John Groves, ancestor of the family in this county, was born in Botetourt County, Virginia. His father died, leaving his mother with three children, John and two daughters. She married Robert Martin of Virginia, who brought the family to this county in 1804. He settled on Camp Fork near Thomas Bailes, built a small mill which he operated for a short time, then left his home and was never afterward heard of. The son, John Groves, first located on McMillion's Creek, but sold to John McClung and moved to a farm near Summersville. His "open-faced camp" stood where H. D. Walker now has an orchard. Later he built a large log house on the land now owned by his grandson, Harrison Groves. Here court was held from 1819 to 1924. His active part in the organization of the county is of record in "County Order Book A".

His sons, Jackson, John, Nathan, William, Alfred, Mansfield, Alexander, Harrison and Austin all located in the county, with the exception of Jackson, who went to Illinois.

John Groves, Jr., was the father of John D. Groves, David R., and Alfred T. John D. Groves was a Federal soldier and a member of the Legislature. His daughter Laura was the mother of former Gov. Okey L. Patteson. David R. Groves was a farmer; his grandson Clide Groves is a member of the County Board of Education. Alfred T. Groves was a prominent teacher and a member of the County Court. The sons of William Groves were Jackson, Washington, Harvey, Franklin, John and Thomas and Cherington. They were all well known farmers. Joseph Groves was a son of Alexander, and his sons were Milton and Alexander. George Allen, Hill and Homer were sons of Mansfield Groves. Arnett Groves and Leonard are sons of Hill Groves and are merchants in Summersville.

Harrison Groves was the father of Henry, Alexander, Harrison and Alfred. Harrison was a teacher and County Superintendent of Schools.

Buhren H. Groves and Austin Groves were sons of Austin, Sr. Homer D. Groves, son of Harvey, was a prominent teacher and one time principal of Nicholas County High School. Sterling Groves of Nicholas County Bank, is a great-great-grandson of Pioneer John

Goves. The sixth generation of this family is made up. of hundreds of great-great-great-grandchildren of the pioneer.

HALSTEAD, HOLDSTADT, *Dutch.* The Halsteads trace their ancestry to Holland. Benjamin C. Halstead came to what is now Raleigh County at an early but uncertain date. A son, Mordecai, was born March 12, 1812, located in what is now Fayette County, married Margaret McClung of Nicholas County February 20, 1834. He lived until August 26, 1863, and was father of ten children: eight sons, John J., George Newman (died in infancy), William Amos, Joseph, George Alderson, Lewis Osborne, Simpson, and Benjamin Dickinson; and two daughters, Minerva and Mary.

John J. Halstead was born October 27, 1837, at the home of his mother's father. Soon after the opening of the Civil War, he enlisted in the Confederate Army and held a Commission as an officer, and later was made Captain of a company enlisted in Nicholas County. He was engaged much of the time in a guerrilla war waged with Captain J. R. Ramsey of "Home Guards" of the Union forces. After the war he married Virginia Dotson and located in Nicholas, served a term as sheriff, and was active in politics. His children were Edgar, Floyd, Squire, Quinten, Annie, Ada and Maggie. Squire, Floyd and Quinten still live in the county.

W. D. Halstead, son of Lewis Osborne, and W. A. Halstead, son of William Amos, lives in the Wilderness District. W. D. Halstead is prominent in the public life of the County; and W. A. Halstead is a farmer at Pool and has made a specialty of potato growing.

HAMILTON, *Scotch*. John Hamilton, first of the name in the county, was born in Pennsylvania in 1747. He came with his parents to Rockingham County, Virginia, was married there. With the aid of friends in the new country he purchased land in what was then Kanawha County. In 1805 he came with his family of seven children to the tract of land near Cross Lanes, where he had a house prepared for his residence. The estate has continued in the possession of his descendants and is now owned by Ralph Hamilton, a great, great grandson. He was a man of means and at the time the wealthiest man in the community. It is said that he brought the first wagon to Nicholas County.

In 1818 the county was organized at his home. He died in the Autumn of that year. His brothers, William and John McKee Hamilton were officers in militia. His son Robert was the first clerk of the County Court and held the office until his death in 1863. His son, David R. Hamilton married Sarah Foster. His sons, Augustus Hamilton and Andrew Hamilton were farmers in the community. David Hamilton, son of Augustus, lives on the home place of his father. John A. Hamilton, brother of David R. Hamilton, married Ann Peck. He succeeded his father as clerk and held the office till his death in 1902. His sons were Robert, Edwin and Samuel. Robert lives in the State of Washington. Sarah Hamilton, only child of Edwin Hamilton, is a deputy clerk in the office of the clerk of the county court. She is a great, great granddaughter of pioneer John Hamilton. Price Hamilton, son of Samuel Hamilton, occupies the old Hamilton home. John McKee Hamilton's children were Peyton,

John M. Lee, Charles, Alvin, Martha Hamilton Hanna, Rebecca Hamilton Fitzwater and Orinoco Hamilton Rader. John M. Hamilton, son of John McKee Hamilton was a prominent educator in Ohio. He was principal of Hughes High School in Cincinnati for several years.

HAMRICK, *Scotch-Irish*. The Hamricks were settlers in Nicholas before the county was organized. Benjamin Hamrick and his brother William first located on Elk River. Later they came to what is now Nicholas County. Benjamin Hamrick located on Beaver Creek. He was a Revolutionary soldier and his application for a pension states that he enlisted in the Continental Army in 1775, and was in the battles of White Plains, Trenton, Princeton, Germantown, Brandywine and Monmouth, and was present at the surrender of Cornwallis at Yorktown. He received his discharge in 1780. William Hamrick owned land and lived for a time on Laurel Creek. He was active in the Methodist Church at Old Bethel. He married Betsey Brown, a daughter of Alexander Brown, and removed to his old locality on Elk River. Joel Hamrick, relation to William unknown, located on McMillions Creek in 1810. The title to his land there proving defective he moved to Peters Creek in the neighborhood of the Keenans. He was a local Methodist preacher and was active in the organization of a Methodist Church in the vicinity of the present "Twin Churches". His son, Enoch Hamrick, was also a local preacher in the Methodist Church. He lived on Enoch's Run which still bears his name.

The descendants of the Hamrick family now live in Clay, Braxton and Webster Counties.

HANNA, *Scotch-Irish*. David Hanna, ancestor of the Nicholas Hannas, married Rebecca Hutchinson. He bought 1,000 acres of land at Welch Glades, now in Webster County, where he raised a large family. His son, William, was the father of Renick Hanna, who married Betsey Rader and was a successful teacher for many years in the County. Some of his descendants still live in the County.

Robert Hanna whose relation to Renick Hanna is not known was father of "Bud" Hanna and Joe Hanna. His daughter, Alice, married Theodore Dorsey, another daughter, Florence, married Emmett Baughaman, his daughter, Mintie married Homer Summers, and his daughter, Dolie, married Joe Tinnell.

Mark Hanna and Joseph Hanna are sons of "Bud" Hanna.

HARDWAY, *German*. George Hardway, first of the name in the county, came from Pendleton County in 1813 and bought land from Jesse James on Line Creek. Later he purchased land from Henry Morris and moved to Otter Creek.

His son, John Hardway, lived on the home place and kept a favorite place of entertainment on the Gauley Bridge Turnpike, known as the "*Half Way* Place". Lyonsville is now a village at the old "Half Way Place". Peter Hardway, grandson of pioneer, George Hardway, was a teacher and minister of the Baptist Church.

John E. Hardway, a descendant of George Hardway, lived on Peters Creek and was the father of a large family.

L. P. Hardway, a son, was a teacher. A daughter, Lenora, taught many years in the Charleston schools.

J. E. Hardway, another son of John E. Hardway, went to Texas and had a distinguished career as a lawyer in Houston.

HENDERSON, *Scotch.* The Hendersons trace their family to Sir James Henderson who was killed at the battle of Flodden Field, in 1513. Three brothers, descendants of the Highland clan, John, James and Samuel Henderson, came to Augusta County, Virginia about 1740. The Nicholas Hendersons are descendants of Robert Henderson, son of James. Shelton J. Henderson, son of Robert, bought land on Beaver creek, but did not locate on it. Joseph and Nicholas K. Henderson were first to settle in the county. Joseph's sons were Robert, Samuel G., William H. and Shelton; one daughter, Hester Henderson Wilson, who is the great grandmother of Dr. L. N. Strickland, lived in Summersville, and is buried in the Methodist cemetery. William H. and Shelton Henderson, were in the battle at Carnefix under the command of McCousland.

Samuel G. Henderson's three sons are Charles J., John M. and Farley F. Henderson. His daughter, Clia Henderson Morrison, lives at Richwood. Farley lives on his farm at Delphi. William Henderson's only son, M. K. Henderson, lives in Florida. Shelton Henderson located in Clay County. Walter S. Henderson, son of Nicholas K. Henderson, was prominent as a teacher and superintendent of schools in Nicholas County. He lived most of his life on his farm near Delphi; his children, Verta

Henderson Rogers, lives in Florida and his son N. R. Henderson lives in Kanawha.

Walter S. Henderson spent the last years of his life with his son Ray, who served a term as sheriff of Kanawha County.

HEREFORD, *English.* Dr. M. R. Hereford was born in Prince William County, Virginia, and came to Greenbrier County as a young man. He practiced as a physician there for a time and then moved to Braxton County.

In 1845 he located in Summersville and married Mary Ann Hamilton. After her death he married Ann C. Duffy, who lived only a short time. A daughter of this marriage, Mary Hereford, married James Thornton. Dr. Hereford's third wife was Frances McClung. The sons of this marriage were Rush, Andrew B., Newman and Frank. The daughters were Martha Suthern, Margaret Rippetoe and Elizabeth Brock. Andrew B. Hereford married Mary Alderson, daughter of Joseph A. Alderson, Sr. Frank Hereford married Annie Smith, who now resides at the old Hereford home. She was a daughter of Rev. Joseph L. Smith. Frances, oldest daughter of Andrew B. Hereford, married John Duffy, son of John Duffy, Sr.

Annie Louise, daughter of Frank Hereford, married H. G. Stout of Summersville, and they also reside at the old Hereford place.

HEROLD, *German.* The Herolds came from Germany to Pennsylvania, probably in the great wave of German emigration in the early 1700's.

Christopher Herold, ancestor of the family in Nicholas County, came from Virginia to Pendleton, and later to

Pocahontas County. He had a family of ten children: Henry, Peter, Benjamin, Charles, Christopher, Andrew, Josiah, Susan, Jane and Elizabeth.

Henry S. Herold, the oldest son, born in 1800, came to Nicholas early in its history. His children were, Anderson C. Herold, Washington L. Herold, Elizabeth M. Herold, Martha J. Herold, Charles A. Herold, Virginia L. Herold, Susan E. Herold, Henry B. Herold, William J. Herold and Mariah J. Herold.

Three of Henry S. Herold's sons are prominent in the history of the county: Anderson C. Herold, William J. Herold and Henry Benjamin Herold.

Anderson C. Herold, who married Talitha McClung, was the father of six sons: Lanty W. Herold, John M. Herold, Henry W. Herold, George A. Herold, Fielding D. Herold, and Charles F. Herold, all of whom settled in the Muddlety Valley.

Lanty W. Herold married Belle McNutt, daughter of John McNutt. He resided on the home place, was a teacher, member of the County Court, and successful farmer. George Dana Herold, a son, is a lawyer and former prosecuting attorney. Henry W. Herold, taught school, was sheriff of the County and active in politics. A son, Clarence Herold, resides at the home place of his father.

William J. Herold was the father of H. Lee Herold of the Herold & Herold hardware store in Summersville.

George A. Herold moved to Webster County and represented that County in the Legislature.

Porter Herold, son of Fielding D. Herold, is a banker

and merchant in Summersville. Other members of the family are prominent citizens of the county.

HICKMAN, *German*. Andrew J. Hickman, first of the family on the Land Books of the county, purchased a tract of 363 acres of land from William Rader in 1842, and later acquired other lands.

Arthur Hickman was conveyed a tract of land, consisting of 540 acres situated on Glade Creek, by Thomas Bright. Andrew A. Hickman owned land in Beaver District. His wife was Amanda Fitzwater. Harvey R. Hickman, who married Nancy Alice Huff, and Stuart T. Hickman owned land on Persinger. Milton Hickman and J. Scott Hickman were farmers in the Persinger community. J. Scott Hickman married Marie Crookshanks, a sister of W. M. Crookshanks, and reared a large family, many of whom still live in the county.

Bert H. Hickman, son of Reed Hickman, and grandson of Stuart T. Hickman, lost his life in World War I. The Richwood Post of the American Legion is named in his honor.

The Hickmans are farmers, respected and industrious citizens, and are related to many of the pioneer families of this county.

HILL, *English*. Spencer Hill, first of the name in the county, bought the farm of Jesse Childers on Twenty Mile Creek near Belva, in 1816. His son Moses Hill was the father of David Hill and Martin Hill. David spent his life on the home place of his father and grandfather. His sons, Henry and Luther, also lived there. Cynthia, a daughter of David, married C. D. Backus. Martin Hill purchased the farm of Silas Morris at the mouth of Line

Creek and spent his life there. His sons were, Henry C. Hill, Joseph R. Hill, Martin Hill, Benjamin F. Hill, Charles I. Hill, Schuyler Hill and Moses Hill. Henry C. Hill was a teacher and later practiced law. Joseph R. Hill was a farmer on a portion of his father's estate. Benjamin F. Hill was a Methodist preacher, and Charles I. Hill a teacher.

Another Hill family, whose ancestor in Nicholas County was William Hill, came from Pocahontas County and located in the Muddlety Valley. This family seems to have first located in North Carolina and southwestern Virginia. Hillsville, just over the North Carolina line in Virginia, was named from the settlement of the Hills there before the Revolution.

John Hill, James Hill and Joseph Hill were sons of William Hill, and were farmers and stockmen. John Hill's son, Otis, was a doctor; his daughter Viola married George Herold and Agnes, another daughter, married Dr. Dan P. Kessler. A son of Dr. Otis Hill, Dr. George Hill, is a successful physician in Webster County. Joseph Hill was a member of Nicholas County Court and lived beyond the century mark. His son, Ira E. Hill, is Clerk of the County Court.

Abram Hill, brother of William, was the father of Rev. Nelson Hill, one time pastor of the Summersville Methodist Church.

HINKLE, *German*. In 1827 Abraham Hinkle, first of the name on our Land Books, bought a tract of land near the present Town of Richwood, from James Yates. John Hinkle, son of Abraham, was a farmer in the same locality. Philip Hinkle, son of John, was a well known farmer, and he served as member of the House of Delegates. His son, A. L. Hinkle, farmer and lumberman, was a popular sheriff of Nicholas County. His father, Philip, while campaigning for the State Legislature, dressed in homespun, and riding a pack saddle cushioned with sheep skin, made a tour of the county. His opponent ridiculed him as a "backwoodsman", but the voters recognized his sterling character, and he was elected. In the Legislature he soon commanded attention for his practical common sense and frank honesty.

Millard Hinkle, son of A. L., and grandson of Philip, is a successful business man in Richwood.

Many of the descendants of Abraham Hinkle are still residents of the area and are well known and respected citizens.

HORAN, *Irish*. P. C. Horan came from Ireland to the United States some time prior to the Civil War. In 1857 he married Mary C. Duffy and located near Summersville. He was a teacher, and for several years was the only teacher in the county holding a first grade certificate. His children were, Theodore B. Horan, Andrew J. Horan, Thomas O. Horan, Pat C. Horan, Beirne Horan, Robert Emmett Horan, Margaret and Minnie.

Theodore B. Horan, Andrew J. Horan, Thomas O. Horan and Robert Emmett Horan were lawyers.

Theodore B. Horan served terms as prosecuting attorney in both Webster and Nicholas Counties. His children were Bronson, John, Dana, Alice, Daisy, Irene and Grace. Andrew J. Horan was long a partner of John D. Alderson, later he removed to Fayette County and finally to Kanawha County. He had no children.

Thomas O. Horan moved to Clay County and practiced law there. Pat C. Horan served a term as postmaster at Summersville. Robert Emmett was also postmaster at Summersville, and served a term as prosecuting attorney of Nicholas County.

None of the family now reside in the County, but Dana, son of Theodore, owns land in the county and has a summer home on his father's old home site. Miss Alice Horan and Miss Grace were successful teachers in Kanawha County, now retired.

HUFF, *German*. Lewis M. Huff came from Botetourt County, Virginia, in 1860 and purchased a tract of 316 acres of land on Persinger Creek from A. J. Nebergall. His sons, Robert Huff, William D. Huff and John A. Huff, were prominent in public life. William D. Huff acquired extensive real estate holdings, was a farmer, and also engaged in the mercantile business at Craigsville. In 1905 he was a member of the House of Delegates in the Legislature. He had a family of fourteen children. His daughter, Elizabeth, married Dr. F. H. Brown, and Gladys married L. J. Burr; a son, Randall Huff, lives in Summersville. John A. Huff was a farmer and justice of the peace in Beaver District. His children, Harry Huff and Minnie Huff, located in Braxton County. Robert Huff's son, W. C. Huff, who lives in Charleston, was for a time on the State Police Force. Lewis M. Huff had three daughters, Zerilda, who married Scott Bobbitt, Lumina, the wife of Clark Rader, and Nannie who married Harvey Hickman. Randall Huff, Harry Huff and W. C. Huff are grandsons of pioneer Lewis M. Huff.

HUFFMAN, HOFFMANN, *German*. Joseph Huffman and William G. Huffman, brothers, came from Monroe County in 1852 and located near Mt. Nebo in Wilderness District. Joseph purchased a tract of 281 acres from John Alderson Sr., and William G. Huffman bought a tract of 200 acres nearby from James McClung. Both acquired other lands and became owners of some of the best farm land in the community. George R. Huffman and Henry C. Huffman, sons of Joseph, located on farms in the vicinity. Allie E. Huffman, George W. Huffman and Haymond W. Huffman, sons of W. G. Huffman, also owned good farms nearby. Albina, a daughter of William G. Huffman, married George H. Alderson. Roy Alderson of Summersville is a grandson of William G. Huffman. Elizabeth, a daughter of Joseph Huffman, married Allen N. Boley, and Emma, another daughter, married J. E. Duncan. Verna Boley Odell and Sheriff L. W. Boley are grandchildren of Joseph Huffman. Lawrence Huffman and Lester H. Huffman are in business in Charleston. Other descendants of the Huffmans reside in the county.

Lewis R. Huffman came from Botetourt County after the Civil War and purchased a tract of 375 acres in Wilderness District from John D. Alderson. He is not a relative of the pioneer Huffmans.

HUGHES, *Scotch-Irish.* Thomas Hughes, a Revolutionary soldier, came from Prince William County, Virginia, soon after the Revolution, and aided in building the fort at the mouth of Hughes Creek, named for him. He built the first cabin on Laurel Creek, near where old Bethel Church once stood. Here he had a hunting camp. He died at the fort at Hughes Creek in 1794.

Edward Hughes, son of Thomas, made the first improvement on the McCutcheon farm at Cross Lanes. He had a large family and patented large tracts of land in different parts of the County. One tract of 1,000 acres lay along Gauley River above and below Hughes Ferry. William McClung of Greenbrier was granted a tract of 43,000 acres on the opposite side of the river and the closing line from Dogwood Gap to the beginning corner near the ferry was protracted, but found to actually cross the river. A famous law suit followed between McClung and Hughes, which ended after about fifteen years when the Supreme Court of Virginia held the river should be the dividing line. His two sons were William and Madison. Madison owned and operated the ferry all his life. His sons Mathew and Virgil and their numerous descendants are well known.

Judge Guthrie, formerly of Kanawha Circuit Court, was a grandson of Edward Hughes.

Bishop Edwin Holt Hughes and his brother, Bishop Matt Hughes, are relatives of the Hughes family in this County.

HUTCHINSON, *Scotch-Irish.* Jacob Hutchinson, ancestor of the family in Nicholas, bought a tract of land in 1798, on Muddlety from John Wooden. Jacob and his brother, William, came to the County from Greenbrier with C. W. Cottle. His wife was Hanna McMillion. William soon went to Ohio, but Jacob lived on his farm and was the father of four sons, all of whom settled in the County. His son, Joseph, was the father of James Finley Hutchinson and Anthony Hutchinson. John M. Hutchinson, the most distinguished of Jacob's sons, was a surveyor and had intimate knowledge of the land titles of the pioneer settlers. Some of his records are still to be found in the office of the circuit clerk. His wife was Nancy Rader. His son, J. M. Hutchinson, operated a store in Summersville, and later moved to Charleston. Two of his daughters, Daisy Kyle and Nita Kincaid live in Charleston.

Both James Finley Hutchinson and Anthony Hutchinson lived and died in the county, and some of their descendants still survive.

Samuel Hutchinson, the surveyor, who gave his name to Hutchinson's creek where he lived for a time, and Archibald, his brother, who lived on Muddlety when the county was organized, were of English descent, and no relation of Jacob's family. They soon left the County and moved to Greenbrier.

HYPES, *German*. The Hypes family came to Montgomery County, Virginia, in the Mennonites migration, some time before the Revolution.

The emigrant, Nicholas Hypes, was a wagon maker, and built wagons for the Continental Army. His son, John Hypes, was the father of Abram Hypes, Samuel Hypes, John Hypes, Joseph Hypes and Harvey Hypes. There were also several daughters. Joseph Hypes who married Susan Keifer in Christiansburg, Virginia, located on a farm on Sinking Creek, in Giles County, Virginia. He was involved in debt, and lost his farm to creditors. In 1855 he came to Nicholas County, but at the opening of the Civil War moved to Meigs County, Ohio. Some time after the war he returned to Nicholas County. The last days of his life were spent at the home of his son, Madison.

Joseph Hypes was the father of Madison Hypes, John Hypes, William Hypes, and Washington Hypes. His daughters were Malinda Backus, Arminta Brown, Mary McGraw and Jane Moore. Samuel W. Hypes, John Hypes, James Hypes, Joseph Hypes, Rupert Hypes, and Jacob Hypes were sons of Madison. His daughters were Martha Stone, Catherine Gray and Jane Eskew. Their descendants are well known. J. Lowell Hypes, son of Samuel W. Hypes, is Dean of the University of Connecticut. Hobart Hypes, another son, is a former teacher and businessman in Summersville.

Rev. Kermit Hypes, son of Joseph Hypes, is a minister of the Methodist Church.

Rev. W. R. Eskew, great grandson of Joseph Hypes, pioneer, is a well known minister of the Methodist Church.

JOHNSON, *Scotch-Irish*. William Johnson, a Revolutionary soldier, came from the Eastern Shore of Virginia, about 1798, and settled with his family near Henry Morris on Peters Creek. His family consisted of two sons: Rev. John Johnson and James Johnson; four daughters: Polly, who married Benjamin Darlington, Nancy, who married Peyton Foster, Amy who married Turley Foster, Elizabeth who married Presley Foster. He died in 1805 and his grave, marked by the D. A. R., is on Peters Creek, below the mouth of Otter Creek. Rev. John Johnson was the father of William Johnson, junior, a local Methodist preacher. James Johnson was the father of James A. Johnson, John A. Johnson and Marion Johnson. These members of the Johnson family were all active members of old Bethel Church. James A. Johnson married Ruhama Grose and located on Laurel Creek, and later moved to Wilderness District near Mt. Nebo. John A. Johnson's sons were James, Jarrett and Andrew M. Johnson. James Johnson married Elizabeth Dunbar. His son Homer Johnson, was a prominent business man. Arley M. Johnson, son of Andrew M. Johnson, is a member of the County Court and a business man in Summersville. His children are great, great, great, great grandchildren of the Revolutionary soldier, William Johnson.

Many of the descendants of William Johnson settled in Fayette and Kanawha Counties. W. S. Johnson, a great grandson, was superintendent of schools in Fayette and a State Senator. In the Senate he was the author of the present law on carrying concealed weapons, and was often called "Pistol Bill". He was State Treasurer for several terms and a popular political leader.

Mrs. W. S. Johnson, widow of W. S. Johnson, is an authority on pioneer history of the Morris, Johnson and Young families. She is a great, great granddaughter of Conrad Young.

JONES, JOHNS, JONAS, *Welsh*. Henry Jones, first of the name on our land books, bought a farm of 380 acres on Muddlety Creek in 1829. This land included a mill site where James Boggs had built a small grist mill about 1810. Henry Jones enlarged and improved the mill and operated it for a number of years. His son, Andrew J. Jones succeeded to the property. Perry and Fillmore, sons of

Andrew J. Jones, were located on part of this land by their father, and were farmers.

John W. Jones in his will dated 1846 names John W. Jones, William D. Jones, Charles N. Jones and Caleb W. Jones as sons. This family lived on the south side of Gauley. Caleb W. Jones in 1846 purchased a tract of 200 acres of land from John Brown, Commissioner of School Lands. Numerous descendants of this family located in Kentucky and Wilderness Districts.

Eldredge Jones of Beaver District was the father of J. Ed Jones, who was for many years actively engaged in manufacturing and marketing lumber. He lived in Richwood and was a large property owner.

John A. Jones, who lived on Twenty Mile, was not related to these pioneer families. His son, John A. Jones, is engaged in business in Clay Court House where he deals in coal and lumber. At least two other families of the name, later came to Nicholas County. It is not possible at this date from the records and scant family tradition to fix the relationship of the five or six Jones families in the county. The names Jones and Jonas seems to be just different forms of the original Welsh surname.

KEENAN, *Scotch-Irish*. The Keenans were early settlers in Monroe County. Edward Keenan was a prominent member of Rehoboth Methodist Church, the first of that denomination built west of the mountains.

Robert Keenan, son of Edward, came from Monroe in 1823 and bought a tract of 150 acres of land from Joel Hamrick, on what is now known as Keenan Branch. He soon acquired other lands and in 1831 he conveyed a tract of 100 acres to Andrew Keenan. Charles Keenan and A. P. Keenan, sons of Andrew, located in the community. A. P. Keenan was a fine carpenter and was for many years song leader in his community. Philip Duffy Keenan, son of Andrew Keenan, was the father of A. M. Keenan, a teacher and land surveyor. A son of A. M. Keenan, Burke, lives in Boone County, and his son, Eugene P. Keenan, is a lawyer.

Pioneer George Keenan was the father of David, William, Edward and Robert Keenan.

George H. Keenan and A. R. Keenan, sons of W. W. Keenan, are farmers and own the J. E. Renick farm in the Panther Mountain Community.

KESSLER, KESTLER, KETTLERS, (Kettle-makers) *German.* The Kesslers came from Hesse-Darmstadt, Germany. There were also soldiers of that name in the Hessian Army who were given grants of land, and settled in Maryland. In the early history of the county Jacob Kessler, and brother Frederick, settled in what is now Mountain Cove District in Fayette County. Frederick purchased 250 acres of land from Joseph Malcolm in 1827. In 1850 his widow and heirs conveyed to John R. McCutcheon, who had married Sally Kessler, the tract since known as the John R. McCutcheon farm.

Fred Kessler, Junior, married Mary Groves and located in Kentucky District. In 1853 he and John R. Vaughan established a store at the intersection of two county roads passing the John Hamilton farm. The postoffice located there was named Kesslers Cross Lanes. Descendants of these pioneers settled in Nicholas and Fayette Counties.

In 1795 Christopher Kessler came to Philadelphia from

Germany and eventually located in Botetourt County, Virginia. He had two children, Archie and Elizabeth. Archie married Catherine Peck in 1853, and as he was opposed to slavery he was compelled to leave there in 1860. He and his wife and two children, after many hardships, reached the "Promised Land" in Kentucky District and resided there until after the end of the Civil War, when he moved to Greenbrier County and spent the remainder of his life there. He had a family of twelve children, of whom four were doctors. Dr. Dan, Dr. Kent and Dr. Mart Kessler were born in Nicholas County; Dr. Joe was born in Greenbrier County. Dr. Dan andIzed Dr. Kent first located in Nicholas County, and are credited with performing the first major surgical operation in this county, by removing a large tumor from a man named Spencer at his home where Richwood is now located. James Kessler, a brother of the doctors, maintained a jeweler's shop in Richwood for many years. His son, Joseph Kessler, is prominent in the business life of Richwood, and another son, Herschel S. Kessler who lives in Elkins is a teacher. Many of our older citizens remember Archie Kessler when he lived in Nicholas County.

KINCAID, KINGCADE, *Scotch-Irish*. James Kincaid and his brother John Kincaid, who located near the mouth of Gauley River and operated a ferry over Gauley there, are the first of the name on our records. John Kincaid was the first constable appointed for Nicholas County, at the first meeting of the County Court in 1818. The descendants of James and John Kincaid settled mainly in what is now Fayette County. Kincaid post office in that county takes its name from the colony of Kincaids in that community. They have been a prominent family in that locality. W. L. Kincaid and Charles A. Kincaid were students at Summersville Normal School and successful teachers in their county. Charles A. Kincaid married Nellie Alderson, daughter of George Alderson.

William Kincaid, in 1839, settled on Laurel Creek in Nicholas County, and acquired several large tracts of land there. He was active in the Methodist Church, and a trustee of the Methodist Camp Meeting ground near Bethel Church. Several of his descendants settled on Twenty Mile Creek. James Kincaid and Jonathan Kincaid of the number were well known citizens. Jonathan purchased the A. N. Rippetoe farm and his son, Frank Kincaid now lives there.

Robert A. Kincaid, an attorney and one time prosecuting attorney, who came to the county just after the Civil War, was not related to the pioneer family of that name.

KING, *Scotch-Irish*. Charles W. King came from Wythe County, Virginia in 1810 and purchased land from Captain George Fitzwater in the Panther Mountain locality. He was well informed and taught school for a short time, but gave most of his time to farming. His sons, William, Joshua and David were farmers. David settled in what is now Clay county, where some of his descendants still live.

William King married Sarah Pierson and lived on Whitewater. He had a large family. His daughter Alice married Emerson Brown. After his wife's death William

King lived with a son, Fred King. Joshua King married Ester Pierson. The record is not clear where he lived, and little is known of his family. Lawrence Brown, son of Emerson, is a great grandson of Charles W. King.

Charles King and William King, no relation of Charles W. King, were early settlers in Wilderness District. James M. King's widow, who owned a farm near Mt. Nebo, was the mother of James C. King and Stuart R. King. James C. King was an up to date farmer. His family is well known. Stuart R. King was an attorney and served a term as prosecuting attorney of the county.

KOONTZ, KOONS, KUNTZ, *German.* The Koontz family came to Monroe County from Pennsylvania soon after the Revolution. Jacob Koontz and his brother John were early settlers. They came from Monroe and purchased John Bird's tannery on Line Creek and carried on an extensive business as tanners and shoemakers for several years. Later they moved to Fayette County where their descendants still live.

In 1816, Henry Koontz, another of the Koontz brothers came from Monroe and purchased a farm from Edward Ryan, now owned by Arthur B. Koontz, a great grandson of Henry Koontz. James Koontz, son of Henry Koontz, in his will names three sons, Samuel B. Koontz, John Koontz and Middleton H. Koontz and five daughters, Nancy Summers, Hannah Nicholls, Janetta Rader, Eliza Legg and Sarah Koontz. Samuel B. Koontz married Rebecca Rader, was a surveyor of the county and the father of Joseph Koontz, James Koontz, John Koontz and the twins Homer and Haymond. His daughters were Eugenia L. Groves, Mary Louella Keenan and

Pioneer Families 345

Lenora Bell Groves. John Koontz was a successful farmer and a sheriff of the county. His sons were Louis K. Koontz, John W. Koontz, Luther V. Koontz, Arthur B. Koontz and Pat D. Koontz, all active in public life. Arthur B. Koontz, only surviving son, is a prominent lawyer and business man in Charleston, Democratic National Committeeman and for several years member of the Board of Governors of the State University. C. H. Koontz, son of James M. Koontz, served a term as State Tax Commissioner.

John Kuntz and Henry Kuntz are sons of the Swiss emigrant, John Kuntz, leader in the settlement of the village of Swiss.

KYLE, *German*. John Kyle came from Virginia about 1835 and located on a tract of 123 acres on the head of Whitewater Creek. He bought the land from the heirs of John Hamilton; the tract is still known as the "Kyle Place." His son, Andrew Kyle, was born there in 1830, and appears to have lived with his father until after the Civil War. In 1865 Andrew Kyle moved to a farm in Wilderness District near Snow Hill. In addition to his farming he was a wagoner, transporting farm products and goods for merchants of the county. His children are: J. O. Kyle, Charles C. Kyle, John A. Kyle, Homer Kyle, Luverna Kyle Amick and Pearl Kyle Nutter. Charles C. Kyle lives in Summersville, but most of the Kyles still live in Wilderness and Kentucky District. Grandchildren and great grandchildren of John Kyle are residents of the county.

KYER, KIRE, *German*. The Kyers were among the first settlers in Nicholas County. They came with the

Cottles, Cutlips and others from the South Branch of the Potomac across the mountains and down Gauley River to the Glades along that river. They are listed among the refugees that fled to Donnally's Fort in Greenbrier at the time of the massacre of the Stroud family by the Indians. John Kyer, Augustus Kyer, and Nicholas Kyer are among the first of the name on our early records.

In 1855 W. D. Cottle conveyed to Charles W. Kyer a tract of 200 acres in the Cottle Glade locality.

Cottle B. Kyer, for many years a prominent teacher of the county, and James A. Kyer, a farmer and well known citizen, are lineal descendants of this pioneer family.

LEGG, *English*. The Leggs were early settlers in colonial Virginia. William Legg came from Monroe, in the early days of the county, married Elizabeth Ramsey, daughter of Bartholomew Ramey, and settled in what is now Fayette County. Many of his descendants still live in Fayette County. Charles Henderson Legg, son of William, married Harriet Jane Grose, daughter of William Grose and settled in the Panther Mountain Community. There were eight children of this marriage: A. J. Legg, Ermina Legg Cavendish, William M. Legg, Ira W. Legg, Susan Legg Mason, G. C. Legg, Gideon Legg and Lilian Legg Hawkins. Charles H. Legg's second wife was Serena Hull. To this marriage was born seven children: Ruby Legg Bowers, Clinton Legg, Clarence Legg, Lawrence Legg, Georgia Legg Crawford, Ava Legg Crosier and Francis Legg.

A. J. Legg, son of Charles H. Legg, was a teacher and writer. In 1930 he wrote a brochure: "A History of Panther Mountain Community", which was published by the Agricultural Extension Division, Morgantown, West Virginia. He married Elizabeth Burdette and they reared a family of two sons and six daughters. Lowell Legg, son of William M. Legg is a Methodist minister. Another William Legg, uncle of the above named William, was the father of six sons and two daughters. His son Eli Legg, lived on Pattersons Creek and was the father of John Legg, Vincent Legg, Franklin Legg and "Tip" Legg. His daughter Fanny married Hiram Walker and Leah married Jonathan Dunbar. John Legg's sons, Mansfield, Edward and Austin all lived in the community. Rev. L. M. Legg, a well known Methodist minister, is a son of Mansfield Legg. As many of the descendants of Eli Legg located on Patterson Creek, a branch of Laurel Creek, it became known as "Legg's Branch."

Many of the descendants of this William Legg live in Clay County.

LEMASTERS, *French*. Benjamin LeMasters, a Revolutionary soldier, enlisted in Pennsylvania, after the war came to Augusta County, Virginia, and later settled on Hutchinsons Creek in Nicholas County, about the year 1790.

He was wounded in battle, was with Washington at Valley Forge, and at times served as a courier for General Washington. In June 1818, he filed his affidavit for a pension as such soldier; and the County Court in its certificate to the War Department gave the name *LaMasters*. The certificate was returned by the Pension Department and the name was corrected to *LeMasters* as it appeared on the Army Rolls. He had a large family of ten daughters: Polly Boggs, Nancy Boggs, Jane Boggs,

Rebecca Rader, Elvira Rader, Agnes Frame, Kezia Campbell, Catherine Given, Charity Stephenson and Elizabeth Robinson. He left no son to perpetuate his name, but numerous descendants of the daughters still live in the county. He lived to a good age and lies buried on his old farm land.

LILLY, *Scotch-Irish*. David Lilly, first of the name on our records, was living on Twenty Mile when our county was organized. In 1820 he was appointed overseer of the road up Twenty Mile from its mouth to the mouth of Robinsons Fork and across the mountain and down Jerrys Fork to Peters Creek.

William Lilly, relation to David unknown, came from Botetourt County with a large family about 1810 and settled on Laurel Creek for a short time. He is credited with clearing the first land on Backus Branch. The field known as the "Lilly Field", is on the farm owned by H. E. Backus. He moved to Twenty Mile from Laurel Creek and settled at the mouth of Lilly's Branch, which is named for him, about one mile above Vaughan.

William Lilly was a Revolutionary soldier but lies in an unmarked grave near Vaughan.

The Lilly family has numerous branches in the State but few of the descendants of the Nicholas pioneers live in the county.

MALCOLM, MACOMB, *Scotch*. Samuel Malcolm of Monroe County, in 1824, purchased a tract of land of Alexander Reid of Nelson County, Virginia, located on Meadow Creek near Cross Lanes. It does not appear that Samuel Malcolm ever lived in Nicholas County. In 1814 Joseph Malcolm purchased a part of Joseph

McNutt's farm on Meadow Creek. His sons were John S. Malcolm, and James Malcolm. John S. Malcolm's sons, Addison Malcolm, John G. Malcolm, Ephraim S. Malcolm, Samuel Malcolm, and Dr. Michael Malcolm. John G. Malcolm was sheriff of Nicholas County for one term, owned a store at Cross Lanes, operated a large farm and was prominent in public life. Ephraim S. Malcolm, a farmer in the same community. His daughter, Dena Malcolm Jackson, was a teacher. Dr. Michael Malcolm owned land in the county, but located in Fayetteville and practiced medicine there for many years. John G. Malcolm's three sons, Melvin G. Malcolm, Chando Malcolm and Kelly Malcolm, all located in Kanawha County. Melvin and Chando were physicians; his daughters, Blanche Malcolm Coleman, Lida Malcolm Blume and Maude Malcolm Gill, live in Fayette County. James Malcolm's sons, Henry Malcolm, Clark Malcolm and Mitchell Malcolm, all farmers, lived in the community and were well known citizens. Clark Malcolm spent his life on the old home place. Homer Malcolm, son of Henry Malcolm, resides on the James Malcolm home place. He is a great grandson of Joseph Malcolm.

MARTIN, *Scotch-Irish*. Robert Martin, who had married the widow Groves, in Augusta County, came with his family, about 1800, and settled near Thomas Bailes on Camp Fork of Peters Creek. He built a mill there about 1805, and also operated his farm. Some years later he deserted his family and disappeared. His wife was the mother of pioneer John Groves, and Robert Martin was her third husband. Two sons, Robert and Samuel Martin, and two daughters, Polly and Susan, were born of this marriage. In 1821 Samuel Martin was commissioned as ensign in the company of John G. Stephenson of the 126th Regiment of the Virginia Militia. In 1822 he was appointed a constable.

Robert Martin owned several tracts of land in the county. In his will he names his children, one of whom, Robert, third of the name of record, died intestate. In 1881, his children and grandchildren, by agreement of record in Deed Book 16 at page 13, in the County Clerk's Office, provided for the partition of his farm on Peters Creek. The farm was divided into ten lots and the heirs named are Judson E. Martin, Harry C. Martin, Rebecca J. Martin, Eliza E. Martin Edna F. Martin, James E. Martin, Allen M. Martin, Kesia Baker, Nancy Shaver's heirs, and Mary Shaver's Heirs.

Walter T. Martin and his brother, George Martin, grandsons of Robert Martin, still live on the old homeplace and are the sole survivors of this branch of the Martin family in the County.

Other Martin families came into the County later, and their descendants are citizens of the County at this time.

MASON, *English*. John R. Mason, first of the name on our records, came from Wythe County, Virginia, about 1825, and married Elizabeth King, daughter of Charles W. King. It seems that Mason came from the same locality in Virginia where King had lived. He was a teacher but gave most of his attention to farming. He obtained land from his father-in-law and settled on what became known as "Mason Branch". His sons were Henry Mason, Marion Mason and Randolph Mason.

Henry married Caroline Walkub and moved to Fayette County and reared his family there. Marion married Jane Spinks and spent his life as a farmer on the Mason home place. His sons were John Floyd, Martin Bibb, Charles Doyle, Augustus L., and Omar W. Mason. His daughter, Ann, married Martin Hill and lived in Fayette County. The oldest son, John Floyd, was murdered and robbed in Ohio. Martin Bibb married Elizabeth Dorsey and lived on the Charles Drennen place on Peters Creek. He had a large family. His son, Robert, lives on the home place. Randolph Mason married Betty Woods and lived for a time on the John R. Mason land, then moved to Mason County where he spent his last days. His sons live in Pennsylvania. Charles Doyle Mason married Jennette Stephenson and lived near his father's home. He had one son, Wiley, and a daughter, Lena. Wiley is a veteran of World War I, lives in Summersville and has been twice elected mayor of the town. Omar W. Mason married Emma Grose, daughter of Clark Grose. He now owns and lives on the farm where his wife was reared. His sons, Howard and Edward, are in business in Summersville. A daughter, Ethel Hagerman, lives in Fayette County.

MILLER, *Scotch-Irish* and *German*. *David Miller* and John Miller of Scotch Irish lineage, came to Nicholas from Monroe County about 1820. David bought land from Captain George Fitzwater, on Laurel Creek but soon moved to Twenty Mile. John married a daughter of Samuel Neil, acquired several tracts of land, and settled on Jones Fork of Peters Creek.

John Miller's sons settled near on lands from their

father. He and his son, James S. Miller, were trustees of Salem Baptist Church and active members. Other sons, Andrew T., John, Clark and Thomas S., were well known citizens. Their descendants have disposed of their inherited lands and moved away.

William Miller, of German nationality, bought land of Samuel Malcolm and others on Coopers Creek in 1833. His son, Isaac C. Miller, succeeded to his father's farm, 1845, and later the land passed to Isaac's son, James R. Miller. James R. Miller married Virginia Campbell, a daughter of Abram Campbell.

James R. Miller died in early life, and the widow remained on the farm and reared a family of two sons and four daughters. Jesse, the oldest son, died in early life. James I. Miller, the other son, married Maggie Halstead, daughter of J. J. Halstead, and moved to Colorado. Emma, the oldest daughter, married Andrew A. Hamilton; Nora Miller married Homer Summers. Flora Miller married William H. Craig. Susan, another daughter, was a teacher.

MORRIS, *Scotch-Irish.* William Morris, father of Henry Morris, came to the Kanawha Valley in 1774. Henry Morris was first of the name to come to Nicholas County. He and his brothers had fought with General Lewis at Point Pleasant. His wife was Mary Bird who had been a captive of the Shawnee Indians for seven years. They had a family of eight children: one son, John, and seven daughters: Leah, Catherine, Peggy, Polly, Betsey, Sarah and Fanny. About 1790 the family moved to a cabin on Peters Creek, where Henry had marked off a tract of 600 acres some years before. In the spring of 1792 Peggy and Betsey were killed by Indians. Henry Morris lived till 1824, and lies buried on his home place. Catherine married William Bird who settled on Sycamore; Polly married Jesse James and lived on Otter Creek; Sarah married a neighbor, Conrad Young; Leah married Arch Price; and Fanny married Abram Farmer. John Morris married Jane Brown, daughter of Alexander Brown. Their family of twelve children were William, Banjamin, Edward, Thomas, Silas, Leonard, Ernest, Alfred, Jane, Martha, Margaret and Mary. William Morris was a doctor, Alfred, a Baptist minister; Jane married Rev. A. N. Rippetoe; Martha married William B. Summers, and Margaret married Andrew Nebergall. Alexander Morris, son of Dr. William, married Isabel Brown, daughter of Alexander Brown, junior. Clark Morris and Floyd Morris were sons of Alexander. Alfred Morris, son of Clark, is a great, great, great grandson of Henry Morris. William B. Summers owned a part of the original grant of Henry Morris which passed to his son, Paul Summers. Daisy Summers Long and his sister, Gladys Summers, now own and reside on the home place of their father, Paul Summers. Their home is near the site of the old Henry Morris cabin. They and their brother, Professor Festus P. Summers of the State university, are great, great grandchildren of Henry Morris.

Many descendants of Henry Morris live in Nicholas and adjoining counties, and a number of the oldest pioneer families of the county are connected by marriage with this famous family.

MORRISON, *Irish*. Andrew Taylor Morrison, first

of the name in this county, was the grandson of Andrew Morrison, an Irish emigrant, who was a Revolutionary soldier, reported killed in the battle of Brandywine, September, 1777. William Morrison, his grandson, was the grandfather of O. J. Morrison, the celebrated merchant.

Andrew T. usually called "Dad" Morrison by his neighbors, was twice married. His first wife was Sallie Littlepage. A daughter of this marriage married James Blizzard. His second wife was Betty Williams. A daughter, Isabel, married Andrew Odell. After his second wife's death he went to Ohio and spent the last years of his life with his son, John Morrison.

Andrew B. Morrison who lived on Persinger in Nicholas County, was a grand nephew of Andrew T. Morrison. Andrew B. was a local preacher in the Methodist Church, and an ardent Prohibitionist. His family is well known.

The Morrisons of Braxton County are relations of "Dad" Morrison.

McCLUNG, MacLUNG, *Scotch*. This most populous and widely connected family in the county looms largely in the history of our early settlements.

Edward McClung with his family of three children was living in a cabin at what is now Cross Lanes, at the time of the Morris massacre. He was drowned in the Kanawha River in 1794 and his family returned to this county. The oldest daughter married John Groves, the other daughter married William Smithey and his son Edward located in Kentucky District, where some of his descendants still live. C. W. A. McClung is a great-great grandson of Edward.

John McClung and Samuel, his brother, came from Greenbrier to Cherrytree Bottom, about 1798. In 1815 John McClung moved to McMillions Creek and bought a farm of John Groves. Descendants of this branch of the family are well known citizens.

William McClung, an early settler in Greenbrier, and his partners were speculators in Nicholas County lands, south of Gauley River. William McClung operated the first ferry over Gauley River, later known as Hughes's Ferry. His son, Alexander, located on a part of these lands near Meadow River. His son, A. J. McClung, was prominent Baptist minister. Charles A. McClung, son of A. J. McClung, was a successful teacher. Draper McClung, a business man in Summersville, is a great-great grandson of William McClung.

Dr. James McClung and his brother, Dr. Dennis, were among the first physicians locating in Richwood. Dr. James founded the McClung Hospital, now under the management of his sons, Dr. Bill and Dr. James McClung. Dr. James McClung found time from his duties as a busy physician to take an active part in politics. He was a senator from the Ninth Senatorial District 1913-1917.

Other members of the McClung family have come from Greenbrier County to Nicholas County from time to time, but their relationship is not known.

McCOY, *Scotch-Irish*. The McCoys were among the early settlers of Greenbrier County where many of their descendants and relatives still live.

David McCoy, first of the name on our records, came

to Nicholas County, then a part of Kanawha County, and was commissioned a captain in the Virginia Militia in 1815. In 1821 he was given a commission as justice of the peace in the new County of Nicholas, and his name occurs frequently on the early records. He owned a tract of land on Muddlety Creek that includes what is now the Peck Farm, two miles from Summersville.

Andrew H. McCoy, whose relation to David McCoy does not appear, came from Greenbrier County in 1844 and purchased a large tract of land on Brushy Fork of Muddlety from John Brown, Commissioner of School Lands. Ownership of part of this land passed to his son William McCoy. William H. McCoy, son of William, inherited land from his father, and Rebecca McCoy, his widow, in her will names as children: Walter McCoy, Ann McCoy Bryant, Margaret McCoy Green, Andrew McCoy, Lillie McCoy Rapp and Richard S. McCoy. A daughter of Richard S. McCoy, Blanche McCoy, married Haymond V. Summers and is a teacher in Nicholas County High School. Andrew H. McCoy, brother of Richard S. McCoy, was a farmer on Muddlety Creek. His sons, Howard McCoy and Otto McCoy, are great-great grandsons of Andrew H. McCoy, Senior. Howard McCoy is a businessman in Charleston. Otto McCoy lives in Williamson, West Virginia.

Only a few of the descendants of the pioneer McCoys now live in the county.

McCUTCHEON, *Scotch*. Jonas McCutcheon and family came from Scotland to Fayette County. In 1851 his son, John R. McCutcheon, located on a farm of 216 acres purchased from Frederick Kessler and located near

Kesslers Cross Lanes. John R. McCutcheon's first wife was Sally Kessler. He was a delegate to the First Constitutional Convention of West Virginia. His children were Sally Fitzwater, Elizabeth Knox, and Allen McCutcheon, Henry, Dr. Rufus, Newton and Rev. John L. McCutcheon.

Jonas McCutcheon and Robert McCutcheon, who settled on McKees Creek, were descendants of pioneer Jonas. Thomas, Arthur and Floyd, sons of Jonas were well known farmers in the McKees Creek area. Effie McCutcheon Odell is a daughter of Thomas McCutcheon, and I. Ray, former county superintendent of schools, is a son of Arthur McCutcheon.

Robert McCutcheon, not related to pioneer Jonas, came from Pocahontas to Greenbrier, and then about 1820 purchased land and located near Hominy Falls. His son, Isaac J. McCutcheon, married Jane Hendrick in 1844. They had a family of thirteen children. A daughter, Nancy Elizabeth, married Nicholas Wiseman, father of P. N. Wiseman. Dr. I. G. McCutcheon was a son of Isaac. Bernard N., another son, was the father of Dr. L. N. McCutcheon, Dr. Leonard D. and Dr. Lester G. McCutcheon. John H. McCutcheon, an attorney, is a son of Dr. Lester C., and Bernard N. McCutcheon, Cashier of Nicholas County Bank, is a son of Dr. L. N. McCutcheon.

McMILLION, *Scotch-Irish*. The McMillions were among the early settlers of Greenbrier valley. About 1812-14 James and Joseph McMillion, brothers, came from Greenbrier to what is now Nicholas County. Joseph settled on Williams Creek, and James acquired several tracts of land in various parts of the county. When the Town of Summersville was laid off he purchased several town lots. At the February Term of the County Court in 1825 James was appointed deputy to Samuel Hutchinson, the county surveyor. In the course of his work he had the name of Williams Creek changed to McMillions Creek in honor of his brother Joseph.

About 1873, Joseph McMillion, Jr., son of Joseph, settled near Summersville. James Alexander McMillion, his son, operated a blacksmith shop in Summersville for many years. Joseph M. McMillion is a son of James A. McMillion. A. Houston McMillion, another son of Joseph McMillion, was a farmer near Summersville. His family is well known.

John F. McMillion, a cousin of Joseph, was a farmer. His oldest son, Bedford McMillion, is the father of Frank McMillion and Coleman McMillion, prominent businessmen in Summersville. Joseph O. McMillion for many years a justice of the county is a son of John F. McMillion. Many other descendants of the pioneer brothers live in the county.

George W. McMillion, a distant relative, came from Greenbrier County and located on the farm of Mathew McClung, his uncle, on the Wilderness Road. He was interested in education and for many years was Secretary of the Board of Education of Wilderness District. Holt McMillion is a son of George W. McMillion.

McNUTT, *Scotch-Irish*. Joseph McNutt came from Rockbridge County in 1803 and located near Cross Lanes. About 1812 he sold his lands to Joseph Malcolm and William Miller and moved to Rich Creek. The story is

Pioneer Families 359

told of his runaway slave, who for a time hid in a cave on the mountain west of John Dorsey's home on Twenty Mile. At night she would forage for food in the neighborhood. One dark night, attempting to get some meat from an out house of Dorsey's, she was driven by his bear dogs to take refuge on a drift heap in the creek. John Dorsey awakened in the night by the baying of his dogs, in the darkness, and mistaking the object on the drift heap for a bear, shot and killed her. Her grave is still to be seen on the land of Landon Backus on Twenty Mile.

John McNutt, son of Joseph, was a "49'er", and had some success in his hunt for gold. He was a citizen of the county and large land owner for several years. His son, B. C. McNutt, located in Braxton County, and was at one time sheriff of the county. A daughter, Belle McNutt, married L. W. Herold. The children of L. W., and Belle Herold, have been prominent in public life. George Dana Herold is an attorney of the county and has served as prosecuting attorney. A daughter, Laura, married John M. Wolverton. His son, James Wolverton, succeeded to his father's law practice. He is a great grandson of pioneer Joseph McNutt.

McCUE, *Scotch-Irish*. David McCue and his son, David, Jr., came to Nicholas County several years before its organization, and located on Beaver Creek. Later they sold their land to John McClung and moved to Missouri. David Junior is said to have been a soldier in the Confederate army and taken prisoner at the capture of Vicksburg. His sons were John, Wm. D. and Fielding. K. B. McCue, son of John McCue, located near his father and was prominent farmer and cattleman. He also was an extensive dealer in real estate and was well and favorably known. He had a large family of children, but only his son John McCue now lives in the county. He owns and operates the old home farm.

William D. McCue was a farmer and served a term as Commissioner of the County Court. His sons, Price McCue, Allen McCue and Ottmer McCue are well to do farmers.

Fielding McCue was a farmer. His son, Arnold McCue is also a farmer and resides on the farm owned by his father. Anthony F. McCue, the other son of Fielding, was a distinguished lawyer living in Clarksburg.

Arnold McCue served a term as Commissioner of the County Court. All the McCues living in the county are descendants of David McCue.

MURPHY, *Irish*. David Murphy settled on Muddlety in 1816 on what was later known as the Anderson Herold farm. William H. Murphy, relation to David Murphy unknown, also settled on Muddlety about 1832. He was prominent in establishing a church building there. John M. Hutchinson, in his letters on the early settlements, published many years ago, says: "William Murphy, the Hutchinsons and McCoys were members of a Methodist society, and a little log church was built about 1834 on the site of the Twin Churches. A man by the name of Armstrong built the church and it was called Armstrong Chapel. Later Anthony's Chapel, named for Anthony McClung, was erected".

John Murphy and James Murphy, probably not related to William, located on Birch River and Strange

Pioneer Families 361

Creek about 1835. Many of their descendants still live in Nicholas and Clay Counties.

Michael Murphy, who bought land and settled in the Anglins Creek section of Wilderness District, was not a relative of the pioneer Murphys.

His sons, John W. Murphy and Jerry Murphy were well known citizens. Carl Murphy, a business man of Summersville is a son of John W. Murphy.

At this date it is impossible from the record to trace the relationship of the Murphys now living in the county.

NEIL, NEAL, *Scotch-Irish*. Samuel Neil, came from Augusta County, Virginia in 1809, and purchased Conrad Young's land on Peters Creek. He was a wagon maker and owned the second wagon used in the County. He was commissioned a justice of the peace for Kanawha County two or three years before the organization of Nicholas County. For many years he was prominent in the affairs of the county. He names in his will his sons, James G. Neil, Samuel Neil, Andrew Neil and Robert G. Neil.

Robert G. Neil was given the home place: His sons, Middleton, Harrison, Nathan and Grimes, by his first wife, and Van Pelt by his second wife, were given the home place by partition deeds, and all located on their farms, except Middleton, who went to Missouri. John Neil, son of Nathan, served a term as member of the County Court. Andrew Neil patented a tract of land on Little Elk. His son, James G. Neil settled on Peters Creek. Franklin Neil, a son, was a skilful mechanic, made wagons, spinning wheels, etc. His son, James G., was also a mechanic, and the skill of his ancestors is still alive in Newman Neil, a great great grandson of pioneer Samuel, who still carries on the trade as blacksmith and wagon maker.

John Neal, a son of the Revolutionary soldier, Jerry Neal, who never came to this county, settled on Twenty Mile in 1819. His son, Jerry Neil married Peggy Brown, daughter of Alexander Brown. His sons, William and John spent their lives on Twenty Mile and raised large families, none of whom now live in the County.

The two ancestors, Samuel Neil and John Neal were not related.

NUTTER, *German.* David Nutter came from Monroe County in 1814 and settled on Laurel Creek, on the farm afterwards owned by Rev. A. N. Rippetoe. He was active in the local government of the county. Later he moved to the Robert Foster farm in the Bend of Gauley where he spent his life. After the death of his first wife, he married Christina Odell, daughter of Jeremiah Odell, the Revolutionary soldier. She lived to a great age and was known by relatives and neighbors as "Aunt Teeny". Her sons were Grandison Nutter, John Nutter, Levi Nutter and Joseph Nutter. Two of David Nutter's sons by his first marriage, David, Junior, and Elijah, lived in the Cross Lanes community.

Isaac Nutter, son of John Nutter, was prominent as a surveyor of lands, and for many years looked after the lands of Gauley Coal Land Company. Henry Nutter, Marshall Nutter, Felix Nutter and Newman Nutter, grandsons of Levi Nutter, were all teachers and the three last named were ministers of the Methodist Church.

Henry Nutter went to Arkansas in early life and was a successful teacher.

Levi Nutter married Polly Backus, daughter of Joseph Backus. His sons were Pascal, Van and John. John was a teacher and moved to Oregon.

Johnnie Nutter of Summersville, is a great-great grandson of David Nutter. His father, Algerine Nutter, was a son of Grandison Nutter.

Many descendants of David Nutter live in Nicholas and adjoining counties.

NICHOLLS, *Scotch-Irish*. James Nicholls, first of the name on the records settled near Cross Lanes before the County was organized. In 1821 he sold his farm to Bedford Foster and moved to Bell Creek. In 1824 he was overseer of the road from the mouth of Gauley to Little Elk Creek. His sons, Frank Nicholls and Marshall Nicholls succeeded to their father's estate. Willis Nicholls, whose relation to pioneer James Nicholls is unknown, was a farmer. His wife was Hannah Koontz.

Alexander Nicholls lived on White Water, was a farmer and also a gunsmith. He was active as a member of Bethel Methodist church. Isaac R. Nicholls, a son, was a soldier in the Union Army. Anderson Nicholls, a relative of Alexander Nicholls, was a Methodist preacher.

Robert Nicholls is a farmer on Line Creek.

Cecil Nicholls is a business man in Summersville.

ODELL, *Irish*. Jeremiah Odell and his brothers Sylvanus and Jacob, came from Shenandoah County, Virginia to Nicholas County sometime before its organization. Jeremiah was a Revolutionary soldier of a restless disposition. He first settled on Hominy Creek then moved to Twenty Mile, back to McKees Creek and then to Hughes Ferry. Later he made two or three settlements on the Wilderness Road, the last being about six miles from the ferry. A son, Jeremiah, who was a Justice of the Peace for several years, inherited this place. A son of Jeremiah, Jr., Perry Odell, was also a Justice. Rev. A. E. Odell, son of Perry, was a popular minister of the Southern Methodist Church.

Sylvanus Odell bought land of Captain George Fitzwater near Cross Lanes, and his son John Odell inherited the farm. John's son, Addison C. Odell, continued on the same land.

Felix Odell, John B., and Andrew, all prominent citizens, were nephews of pioneer Jeremiah.

Granville Odell, another nephew of Jeremiah, was a member of the County Court and a merchant at Hominy Falls.

Thomas Odell, a recent Sheriff of Nicholas County, is a son of Samuel Odell, who was a son of Jacob Odell.

Dock L. Odell, former Assessor of Nicholas County, is a great-great grandson of the old soldier, Jeremiah.

The numerous descendants of these pioneers form one of the largest family groups in the county, and are related to many of the oldest families of Nicholas County. The Odells have been prominent in the civil and political life since the county's formation.

PATTERSON, *English.* Henry Patterson came from Virginia about 1850, married Mary Ann McVey, and in 1855 Henry O. Middleton conveyed to Henry Patterson and Mary Ann Patterson a tract of 220 acres of land on the north side of Gauley River opposite the mouth of Meadow River. On this land Henry Patterson located and cleared out his farm. His sons were, W. H. Patterson, Augustus Patterson, John B. Patterson, Leonidas C. Patterson, Milton Patterson and Alexander M. Patterson. W. H. Patterson and Augustus Patterson occupied the home place on the south side of Gauley River at the ferry, improved the Carnefix mill property and operated the ferry over Gauley River. W. H. Patterson married Ritta Walker, daughter of Marion Walker; Augustus Patterson married May Groves, daughter of David R. Groves; Leonidas C. Patterson married Lola Groves, daughter of John D. Groves and located at Mount Hope in Fayette County. He wrote his name Patteson in his business there. His son, Okey L. Patteson, was governor of the State from 1949 to 1953. Alex M. Patterson married Vergie Groves and moved to Fayette County.

The Battle of Carnefix Ferry was fought on the Henry Patterson farm. In 1935 the State purchased the portion of the farm on which this battle occurred, and by act of the Legislature established Carnefix Battlefield Park.

None of the Patterson family now lives in Nicholas County.

PERKINS, *German*. David Perkins, first of the name on the records of Nicholas County, was the first blacksmith to locate in the town of Summersville. He was the owner of several lots in the new town. These are in the Land Books of 1825-32.

David W. Perkins, presumably a son of the blacksmith, was also the owner of land in several localities. In 1850 he conveyed a tract of 145 acres on the south side of

Gauley to John Perkins. John Perkins was the father of Holley and Maston Perkins, prominent citizens of Kentucky District, and leaders in Church work. Holly Perkins was a soldier in the Civil War, on the Confederate side. His son, Clay G. Perkins, was Deputy County Clerk under Joseph A. Alderson. Another son, Rev. C. C. Perkins, is a minister of the Methodist Church. A. H. Perkins, son of Maston, was also a preacher. Shawver Perkins was also a son of Maston.

Floyd C. Perkins, son of H. H. (Dick) Perkins, was Assessor of Nicholas County, and later served a term as Sheriff. His son, Brady Perkins, lives in Summersville and is in business.

David H. Perkins, a teacher and later a preacher in the Methodist Church, was a son of James Perkins, and a great grandson of the pioneer David Perkins. Many descendants of David Perkins still live in Nicholas County and are prominent in public life.

PIERSON, *Scotch-Irish*. Joseph Pierson, pioneer of the family in Nicholas County, came from Monroe County in 1823, and purchased a tract of 100 acres from Mathias Young on Peters Creek. He acquired other lands on White Water. His brother Hiram Pierson was a prominent citizen of that locality and served as a Union soldier in the Civil War. He spent several months as a prisoner of the Confederates in the war prison at Salisbury, North Carolina.

Hiram Reed Pierson, John Alexander, David, Jonathan B. and Bing Pierson were sons of Hiram Pierson.

David Pierson married Mary Brown, daughter of

pioneer Alexander Brown. One of his sons, Hanson Pierson, was a teacher and surveyor of lands.

Blaine Pierson was a son of John Alexander. Fremont Pierson was a farmer of the community and a son of Hiram Reed Pierson.

Jonathan B. Pierson was a soldier in the Union Army. He married Mary A. Renick and raised a large family, none of whom now live in Nicholas County. Many of the descendants of the pioneer Piersons still live in the county and are respected, useful citizens.

PITTSENBARGER, *German*. In 1841 Jacob Amick sold a tract of land to Peter Pittsenbarger, ancestor of the family in Nicholas County. William Pittsenbarger, a son of Peter, continued on the home place after his father's death. James Pittsenbarger, a son of William, continued to live on the farm of his father. He had a son, Henry, who lost his life in World War I. Another son, William, is a farmer living on a part of the old home place. Louis, a brother of William, resides in Summersville. His son, Henry, is a teacher in Nicholas County High School.

A number of the descendants of pioneer Peter Pittsenbarger still live in the County.

RAMSEY, *Scotch*. Bartholomew Ramsey, ancestor of the Nicholas County Ramseys, was born in Pennsylvania about 1777. His wife was Margaret Wiseman. He came to Monroe sometime after the Revolution, and in 1819, moved to Nicholas County and settled near Leander, now Fayette County. His sons were William, Richard, Isaac, John W., James Riley, Abner and Charles. His daughters were Elizabeth Legg and Ludy Neal. Captain James

Riley Ramsey moved to Nicholas County in 1851 and purchased land from William McClung. His wife was Jane Legg, daughter of Thomas Legg. He died at a son's home in Ohio, in 1887. His sons were, Thomas, Addison, John Reed, Edmund Cassett, Wesley Marion, Nicholas Hance, Wallace Cromwell, William Harrison, Jacob Koontz and James Clark. Just after the Battle of Carnefix Ferry, William Hance Ramsey was killed by bushwhackers, and lies buried where he fell by the roadside. His son William Hance Ramsey was a sheriff in Fayette County. James Clark Ramsey, the youngest son of Captain Ramsey, published a history of the Ramsey Family in 1933. E. F. Ramsey, son of Wesley Marion Ramsey, was a teacher and a member of the house of Delegates from this county in 1921.

William Ramsey and Richard Ramsey, who lived on Bell Creek, were brothers of Captain Riley Ramsey. Jackson Ramsey and William, junior, were sons of Richard Ramsey. David Ramsey was a son of William Ramsey. George Ramsey who settled on Twenty Mile, is a son of David Ramsey.

Many descendants of Bartholomew Ramsey live in Fayette, Clay and Nicholas Counties.

RADER (READER), *German*. George Rader, pioneer of the name, settled on Bucks Garden in 1800. He was a farmer and blacksmith. He divided his farm between his sons, Anthony and Sinnett. Dr. Anthony was a successful country doctor and politician. His large family and their descendants are well known.

A. F. Rader, son of Sinnett, served as Recorder and

Pioneer Families 369

later Clerk of Nicholas County. His sister, Eugenia, was the wife of John D. Alderson.

William Rader owned a farm on Camp Fork adjoining Samuel Bell.

John Rader, Sr. names Allen, John Mc., Benjamin L. and Joseph as sons. Joseph Rader was the father of Michael L. Rader; and two daughters, Elvira Groves and Rebecca Koontz. Dr. J. E. Rader was a son of Michael Rader.

The sons of "Big Anthony" Rader, Michael, John H., Samuel, William, Clark, Robert and Harvey were farmers on Persinger and Glade Creek. John H. Rader was the father of A. B. Rader, who served a term as Surveyor of the county. Clark Rader was the father of a large family, all well known citizens.

William Rader's sons are, Scott, Howard, Joseph and Henry. Henry was a popular hotel man in Summersville for many years.

Feamster Rader owned land in Kentucky District. Allen Rader, who also lived in Kentucky District, was the father of a large family and many of his descendants still live in the district.

Members of this numerous family have been prominent in public life in the county since its settlement.

RENICK, *German*. William Renick was a pioneer settler of Greenbrier County. James Avis Renick, a step-son of Willis Martin, came with his step-father to Nicholas County in the early days of the county. Martin purchased the Thomas Legg farm in the Panther Mountain community, and some time before the Civil War, left the farm to James Avis Renick and moved to Illinois.

James Avis Renick married Margaret Grose, daughter of William Grose, Senior. They reared a family of three sons, William, James E., and George; and five daughters, Lydia Malcolm, Mary Ann Pierson, Margaret Harrah, Elizabeth Starbuck and Lenona Drennen. William Renick was one of the first group of teachers in the new State of West Virginia. He located in Fayette County. His son, A. J. Renick, was a teacher and later a minister of the Methodist Church. A grandson of William Renick, Myron Renick, is a prominent attorney in Fayette County and active in politics. James E. Renick engaged for a time in the mercantile business in Fayette County, then sold the farm he had inherited from his father and moved with his family to Arkansas many years ago. He and his brother, George, died there, and some of children still live in that state.

Eugene Drennen and Fred Drennen, sons of Lenona Renick Drennen, who married Thomas Drennen, are grandsons of James Avis Renick. None of the family name now live in the county.

RIPPETOE, *French.* Alexander N. Rippetoe, James H. Rippetoe, Andrew Jackson Rippetoe and Calvin Rippetoe, four brothers, came to Nicholas County and bought land on Twenty Mile and Bell Creek, in 1853. Andrew Jackson Rippetoe married Mary Backus, daughter of Pascal Backus, and located at the mouth of Camp Fork of Twenty Mile. His family consisted of two daughters, Ann, who married Thomas C. Brown and Elizabeth who married Webster Brown.

James H. Rippetoe married Hanna Backus, daughter of Pascal Backus. His sons, Lewis, Clark, Pascal and

George, were well known businessmen in the community. Later they located in Charleston, where many of these descendants now reside.

Alexander N. Rippetoe married Jane Morris, a daughter of John Morris, and located on the farm near Cross Lanes, where he spent his life. He was a successful minister of the Baptist Church. His family consisted of three sons, Wyatt, the well known teacher of vocal music, Hansford, and William; two daughters, Bettie Thurmond and Sarah Paulina Vaughan. Hansford married Maggie Hereford; William died in early manhood.

Calvin Rippetoe was a Baptist minister and lived in Fayette County.

ROBINSON, *Scotch-Irish*. David Robinson, first of the name on our records, came from Augusta County with a party of surveyors soon after the Revolution. It is a family tradition that he was a son of John Robinson, who had served as president of the House of Burgesses in Colonial Virginia. About 1790 he located with his family on Hutchinsons Creek. His son, James Robinson, who was one of the justices of the peace that constituted the first County Court, had a residence near the home of Glen Herold in Summersville. County and Circuit Courts were held at his house, after the organization of the County at Cross Lanes, until moved to the home of John Groves. In his will he names six daughters: Cynthia Collison, Rebecca Hamilton, Peggy Perkins, Miriam Robinson, Agnes Robinson, and Elizabeth Robinson, a son, John H. Robinson, who in his will names James Robinson, J. Haymond Robinson, Ben H. Robinson, Samuel H. Robinson, Elizabeth Robinson Rader and Juliet Robinson, as his children.

J. Haymond Robinson located on Muddlety. He was three times married and the father of ten children. He served two terms as County Superintendent of Schools, and was also a surveyor. His sons, Omar G. Robinson and Oscar K. Robinson are great-great grandsons of David Robinson.

SEBERT, SEYBERT, SEIBERT, *German.* The Seiberts came to the South Branch of the Potomac about 1740. They had come to Pennsylvania in the Mennonite emigration from the Palatinate in Germany. The spelling of the name was gradually changed to the present form. About 1750, Captain Seibert built a fort on the South Branch about 12 miles from Franklin. In 1758 Indians under the Chief, Killbuck, captured the fort and killed Captain Seibert and twenty others. They are buried there in one grave. The story is told in Kercheval's "History of the Valley".

Abraham Sebert, a descendant of Captain Sebert, came from Pendleton County in 1839, and bought land of Noah Davis. His sons were John J. Sebert, Samuel E. Sebert, William Sebert and Adam Sebert. Adam died without a family. John J. Sebert's sons, Ellis Sebert and Joseph F. Sebert, were farmers. Dana, Lloyd and Lee Sebert are sons of Ellis and great grandsons of Abraham Sebert. Samuel Sebert's sons were Kyle Sebert and Hunter Sebert; his daughters, Elsie and Bertha. Bertha married O. G. Robinson. Jacob F. Sebert, Abraham Sebert, John Sebert and Samuel Sebert were sons of William Sebert. Jacob Sebert's sons were Ellis and Alva. Russell

Sebert, son of Joseph F. Sebert, is a farmer living on his father's home place. Lloyd Sebert, son of Ellis, is a businessman in Summersville.

Descendants of the pioneer Seberts and their relations still live in Pendleton County, West Virginia, and Montgomery and Highland Counties, Virginia.

A Mr. Ferdinand Lair now owns the site of Seybert's Fort and traces of the old fort can still be seen, with the graves of the murdered inmates nearby.

SHAWVER, *German*. Boston Shawver, first of the name as a landholder, came from Greenbrier County in 1822 and purchased two 100 acre tracts of land on Anglins Creek. Nothing in our record shows his family history.

George W. Shawver (known as "Brother" Shawver) was a farmer in the neighborhood. He was somewhat eccentric but a good religious citizen. He was a constant attendant at revival meetings, and uniformly addressed every one as "brother" or "sister" as the case might be. The habit was so strong that he addressed his workhorse as "brother" as they cultivated his crops. His sons were John, Thomas, Henry, and Felix, and his daughter, Teena. Arthur V. Shawver, a citizen of Summersville, is a son of Thomas Shawver; and G. W. Shawver, usually called "Billy", was a son of Henry Shawver. "Billy" Shawver was sheriff of Nicholas County for the term 1925-29. He lived in Richwood where he was an extensive property owner. His wife, Malinda Groves Shawver, survives him and resides in Richwood with members of her family.

Thomas H. Shawver, whose relation to George W.

Shawver does not appear, purchased a tract of land from Dickinson McClung on Meadow River, built a mill and erected a bridge across the river at his place. He was given license by the County Court to collect toll on this bridge which led across the river to the rough mountain road used for several years as a connection between Fayette and Nicholas Counties.

George W. Shawver, a son of Thomas, attended Shelton College at St. Albans and prepared for teaching but did not follow the profession, and later moved to North Carolina.

The family still has a number of representative citizens in the county and in adjoining counties.

SHELTON, *Scotch-Irish*. Winston Shelton, ancestor of the Sheltons of Nicholas County, bought two tracts of land from William Hamrick, on Laurel Creek, in 1845. Later he purchased a tract of land on Peters Creek where Ed Ford now lives, located there and operated a store and postoffice, named Winston. He was the sheriff of Nicholas County under the government of Virginia. Under the new state of West Virginia, he represented the county as a member of the House of Delegates and also as a State Senator. His sons, William Shelton, John Shelton, and Samuel Shelton all located in the county, but his youngest son, Richard Shelton settled in Clay County. Benjamin Shelton, son of William Shelton, was a lumberman. His son, Frank Shelton, is a successful businessman living at Swiss. Ed Shelton, son of John Shelton, is a well known and respected citizen of the Lockwood community.

Pioneer Families 375

A number of descendants and relatives of Winston Shelton live in Nicholas and adjoining counties.

SIMMS, *English*. The Simms family was among the earliest to settle in the colony at Jamestown in Virginia. Numerous descendants in the three centuries since make it impossible to trace relationship now. James Simms, the first of the name to come to Nicholas County, came from Bath County in 1787 and located at the mouth of Little Elk Creek on Gauley River. He was a gunsmith and the Simms rifle was praised for its accuracy. He had two sons, William and Martin, both gunsmiths. William's sons were Miletus, John and Frank. Miletus lived on the old home place and kept public entertainment. Elbridge, Eugene and Walter were sons of Miletus. Walter was a merchant and postmaster at Swiss. John Simms lived on his farm near Summersville. His sons were John, Henry and Frank. His daughters, Emma and Betty; Emma married John Fitzwater. John had a large family; Henry Simms's son John is a prominent businessman in Summersville. Frank Simms who lived on a farm near Belva, was the father of a large family. A son, Meredith, lived in Fayette County, and was a local politician and served as a member of the county court.

John T. Simms, who belongs to another branch of the family, was born and reared in Fayette County. He attended the Summersville Normal School, married Ada Alderson, daughter of John D. Alderson, and thus became identified with the people of our county. He was a teacher, became a prominent lawyer and judge of the Criminal Court of Fayette County. Later he moved to

Charleston and was prominent in the social and political life there.

SIERS-SEARS-SEERS-SAWYERS, *German*. Reuben Siers came from Monroe County and purchased 500 acres of land from Samuel McDowell Moore on Hominy Creek in 1850. His sons were William A. Siers and Reuben S. Siers. In 1880 Reuben Siers conveyed part of the 500 acres to William A. Siers, and William conveyed a tract of 48 acres to Henry Britton Siers. Henry Britton Siers and his wife Clementine Siers acquired other lands adjoining. After her husband's death Clementine Sears made conveyances to Charles Wesley Sears and H. B. Siers. Charles Wesley Siers was the husband of Melissa Siers, who still resides on the home place. She recently made a conveyance of a lot to her son, Tilden Siers, who resides there. The Siers family is related to many other families in the community.

It appears from family tradition that the varied spellings of the name as given above, are abbreviation of the name Sawyers. Relationship of the Siers family to the Sawyers family in this county is claimed by Mrs. Melissa Siers. The members of this family have usually been farmers and they have the reputation of industrious and law-abiding citizens.

SKAGGS, SCAGGS, *German*. Members of this family were early settlers in Greenbrier County. In 1818 Joseph Skaggs and his brother, James, bought two large tracts of land on what was then called the "Kanawha" road, near the present site of Ansted. In 1821 the James River and Kanawha Turnpike was located through their lands. In 1845, John Brown, Commissioner of School

Lands, conveyed to Alexander Skaggs of Greenbrier, an undivided interest in the 5,687 acre grant of William McClung and others, situated in Kentucky District. About this time, members of the family from Fayette County settled in the Wilderness District of Nicholas County. Isaac M. Skaggs from Greenbrier located in the county. Isaac Skaggs was not long a resident of the county, but J. W. Skaggs spent his life on his farm near Spinks Postoffice. His son, Herschel Skaggs, is a businessman in Summersville.

E. W. Skaggs, son of Henry Skaggs of Fayette County, atended Summersville Normal School, became a teacher, married Goodie Spinks, daughter of Joseph Spinks, and located in Summersville. Later he taught in the Normal School and was elected County Superintendent of Schools for the county, but resigned after about one year and moved to Ansted in Fayette County. His children were Glenn Skaggs, who located in Florida and Thelma Skaggs Shaw, who lives in Fairmont.

SMITH, *Scotch-Irish*. Thomas Smith, in 1795, settled on the Edward Hughes place near Cross Lanes. His son, John Smith moved to Twenty Mile, and was the father of Miletus Smith and Alexander Smith. Miletus cleared out and cultivated a large farm on Bell Creek, partly in Fayette County. For many years he operated a grist mill and store.

Alexander Smith, his brother, was very eccentric. Upon the death of his wife he placed her body in a closed box and kept the box under a cliff by the road side for several years, and until he was compelled by his neighbors to bury the body.

Miletus Smith's sons were Green Smith, John Smith and Walter Smith.

Green Smith married Lydia D. Johnson. Their children were, Hulbert, Agnes, Verla, Dadah and Kathleen.

Verla Smith married W. D. Long and she and her husband died, leaving an infant son, W. D. Long II, who was reared by his grandmother, Lydia D. Smith. He was a great-great grandson of pioneer Thomas Smith.

John Smith married Betty Morris and located on the home place of his father.

No other members of the family live in the County.

Major Frank B. Smith, who came to Summersville after the Civil War and practiced law there, was not related to the pioneer Smith family. He married Margaret Duffy and his family consisted of his sons Powie Smith and Pat D. Smith. Powie Smith was a printer and assisted in the publication of the Nicholas Republican. Pat D. Smith married Runa Rader, daughter of John H. Rader and after residing in Nicholas County awhile he went to Fayette County where he operated a store. A daughter, Margaret Smith was the wife of Luther Stephenson. For a number of years she was a prominent teacher in the schools of the county.

SPARKS, *Scotch-Irish*. James Sparks, first on our records, came to Glade Creek sometime before 1818. He was appointed overseer of a road from the east side of Muddlety at the bridge to the head of Persinger Run in 1825.

John Sparks settled on Philips Run in 1833. His sons, Joseph Sparks and James E. Sparks lived on adjoining farms on Persinger.

Noah F. Sparks was a local merchant on Persinger for several years.

Bing Sparks operated a mill near where the church stands. The church was named "Sparks Chapel" in honor of James E. Sparks. He was the father of J. Calvin Sparks and the grandfather of Colbert K. Sparks, merchant and postmaster at Persinger. Madge Sparks, a teacher in the public schools, is a daughter of J. Calvin Sparks.

Isaac Sparks purchased land from Joseph Copenhaver and his sons, Rush Sparks and Joseph Sparks settled in the community. Joseph Sparks operated a store and was postmaster at Sparks, the office which bears his name.

Many descendants and relatives of this family live in the county.

SPENCER, SPINCER, *German*. Abraham H. Spencer, first of the name on our Land Books was conveyed 129 acres of land on the south side of Gauley by Joseph Cavendish in 1845. Later Abraham D. Spencer and Allen Spencer located in Kentucky District.

Another Allen Spencer was living at the Fork of Cherry River at the beginning of the development of the lumber industry and the founding of Richwood. The relation of the Spencers that settled in Kentucky District and those that settled in Beaver District does not appear of record from the deeds and wills of the Spencers.

Many descendants of the two Spencer families live in the county, and are connected with prominent pioneer families.

SPINKS, *Scotch-Irish*. Alexander Spinks, first of the name on our records, was appointed a deputy for Samuel

Hutchinson, Sheriff, at the September Term of Court 1824. In 1825 he was employed to build the stone jail building that was in use till the present structure was finished in 1905.

His son, Joseph Spinks was a prominent farmer and the father of Bowd Spinks, Homer H. Spinks, Arthur Spinks, Tressie Herold, Rebecca Atwood, Goldie Skaggs and Mattie Woods. Homer was a teacher and later operated a hotel in Summersville. Arthur Spinks was a doctor. None of Joseph Spinks' immediate family live in the county. John Spinks, a brother of Joseph, was the father of James Spinks, Julia and Maggie by his first marriage, and his second wife was Caroline Johnson. Sarah Ann Spinks, a daughter of this marriage, was the wife of A. L. Brown. Jane Spinks, a sister of Joseph Spinks, married Marion Mason; another sister, Elizabeth Spinks, married Harrison Neil.

Descendants and relatives of Alexander Spinks still live in the county.

STANARD, *Scotch-Irish*. James M. Stanard, first of the name on the records of Nicholas County, came from Virginia before the organization of the County. He was clerk of the Circuit Court in the term of Judge E. S. Duncan, and also Commissioner in Chancery. About 1839 he returned to Virginia, to settle up his wife's estate. He conveyed all his property, both personal and real, to Lawrence Stanard, whose relation to James M. Stanard does not appear. Lawrence Stanard, conveyed the Muddlety land to Fielding McClung, and later acquired land on Camp Fork of Peters Creek. His sons, Walter and William, were well known citizens of the community. William remained on the home place, and reared a large family, some of whom still live in the County. Walter located at Webster Springs, and was a prominent citizen of that County.

Mary, the only daughter of Lawrence Stanard, married R. M. Bryant.

STEPHENSON, *German*. John G. Stephenson and his brother, Joshua, were early settlers on Birch River. They soon moved to Peters Creek and acquired lands where their descendants still reside. Both were active in the early history of the county. The lumber used in construction of the first courthouse was furnished by them. The frame timbers were hewed out and the boards cut with the whipsaw. David Stephenson moved to Peters Creek some years later.

In 1824 John G. Stephenson was commissioned Colonel of the 126th Regiment of Virginia Militia, and his brother, Joshua, was a lieutenant in the militia. John G. also represented his county several times as a delegate to the General Assembly at Richmond. His sons, John G. Jr., Cortez, and Joshua were well known citizens. "Big John" Stephenson was a son of Joshua. Samuel and Madison, who located in what is now Clay County, were sons of Joshua.

Alex M. Stephenson, teacher and merchant, was a son of George Stephenson. He operated a store for many years at Gilboa and then moved to another state.

Charles E. Stephenson, son of Cortez, served two terms as Circuit Clerk of Nicholas County.

Frank and Curt Stephenson were sons of John G. Stephenson. Bud, son of Frank, is a merchant at Drennen. He is a great-great grandson of John G. Stephenson.

STICKLER, *German*. William Stickler, first on the Land Books of Nicholas County, came from Monroe County and purchased 278 acres of land from Isaac Wiseman in 1856.

Harvey B. Stickler, a son of William, located on a farm on Anglins Creek, purchased of John Caraway.

His sons were Calvin M., George A., W. G. Stickler and D. T. Stickler. Calvin M. was prominent in public life, and served for a number of years as Jury Commissioner under Judge McWhorter. George A. located in Fayette County and his daughter, Lolita J. Stickler became a missionary of the Baptist Church to the Indians of the Southwest.

The widow of D. T. Stickler still resides on the farm left by her husband on U. S. Route 19, on the waters of Anglins Creek.

SUMMERS, SOMERS, *Dutch*. Jehu Summers, ancestor of the family in Nicholas County, came from Pendleton County in 1803, and bought land from James Shirkey on Twenty Mile. He was twice married and the father of twenty-one children. He was appointed with Joseph Backhouse and others to locate the first road up Twenty Mile from Spencer Hill's farm to the residence of David Miller.

William B. Summers, son of Jehu Summers, married Martha Morris, a granddaughter of Henry Morris. They spent their lives on a part of the Henry Morris 600 acres grant. Paul Summers and Silas Summers were sons of William B. Summers.

Professor Festus P. Summers, son of Paul Summers, author and historian, is a member of the faculty of the State University. Daisy Summers Long and Gladys Summers, daughters of Paul Summers, own the home where their father located and their residence is near the site where Henry Morris built his cabin in 1792.

Homer Summers and Joseph Summers are sons of Christopher Summers. Haymond Summers, son of Joseph Summers was Clerk of the Circuit Court from 1939 to 1945. Jennings J. Summers was Clerk of the Circuit Court from 1909 to 1921. Festus P. Summers and his sisters Gladys and Daisy are great, great grandchildren of pioneer Henry Morris.

TYREE, *Scotch-Irish*. The Tyrees were early settlers in that part of Nicholas now in Fayette County. The old Tyree Tavern, still standing in the Town of Ansted, was a station on the James River and Kanawha Turnpike. Colonel Tyree, who lived there after the Civil War was an officer in General Stonewall Jackson's brigade. He erected a memorial stone at Jackson's mother's grave in the cemetery at Ansted.

John Tyree in 1845 bought a tract of 560 acres on Muddlety from James M. Stanard. His sons, John R. Tyree and F. M. Tyree, lived and operated good farms there for many years. Both were well known citizens and John R. Tyree served a term as assessor of the county. He married Margaret McClung, a daughter of Allen McClung. George E. Tyree, Hudson Tyree, Marshall L. Tyree and Richard F. Tyree were sons of John R. Tyree; and his daughters were Rebecca Groves, Mary Ella Groves and Arminta Groves. F. M. Tyree married Susan Davis, a daughter of David Alfred Davis. Edward Tyree and Otis Tyree are sons of F. M. Tyree. His daughters were Florence, who married Scott McClung and Mary who married ...... Bostick. The relationship of the Tyrees of Fayette County and the Nicholas County family does not appear from the record.

VAUGHAN, *German.* About 1829 Clement Vaughan came to Nicholas County and purchased the property of Philip Metzker, who was a tavern keeper and postmaster at Metzker postoffice on James River and Kanawha Turnpike, a short distance east of the present town of Ansted. The postoffice was later named Mountain Cove.

In 1853 John R. Vaughan, son of Clement, came to Cross Lanes and purchased a tract of twenty acres of land from David R. Hamilton. In partnership with Frederick Kessler he opened a store there, and on April 19, 1854, he was appointed postmaster of Kesslers Cross Lanes. He married Euphenia Loving and for many years conducted a successful mercantile business there and continued as postmaster.

His children were Arthur L., Edgar, and Florence Vaughan. Florence married Dr. Joseph E. Rader. Arthur married Sarah Paulina Rippetoe, daughter of Rev. A. N. Rippetoe, and operated a store on Twenty Mile at Vaughan postoffice named for him. After his father's death he continued the mercantile business at Cross Lanes, and engaged in real estate business. His sons were Van, Dyer and Guy. Guy Vaughan is in the active ministry of the Baptist Church. The daughters were Gay, Goldie, Willie, Gladys, Eloise and Norine. Van, Dyer, Mrs. Gay Peyton and Winnie Vaughan are deceased. Goldie married E. C. Echols and lives in Virginia. Eloise married Carl Paller, a civil engineer, and lives in the mansion house built by her grandfather a century ago. Miss Gladys, a popular columnist writer, also has her residence at the family home, but spends some time at Staunton, Virginia, with her sister Mrs. Goldie Echolls.

VANBIBBER, VANBEBBER, *Dutch*. John, Isaac, Peter and Brigetta VanBibber came to Virginia not later than 1770. Peter located for a short time at the fort on Wolf Creek in Greenbrier. In 1773 John and Peter, while surveying, camped under a cliff at Kanawha Falls, and John VanBibber's name was cut on a wall of the cliff. The three brothers were at the Battle of Point Pleasant where Isaac was killed. After the battle, John and Peter located at Point Pleasant. In 1787 the Indians killed Isaac Robinson, husband of Brigetta, and took her prisoner. Later John VanBibber's daughter, Rhoda was killed and Joseph and Jacob, sons of Peter, taken prisoner. Virgil A. Lewis, in his history says that Rhoda had beautiful red hair and that her scalp was sold to the British at Detroit for $60.00.

Peter VanBibber, ancestor of the Nicholas VanBibbers, was born in Maryland in 1733, and died at Point Pleasant in 1796. His son, Mathias, was born in the fort at Wolf Creek in 1772 and died in Nicholas County in 1827. He was an associate of Daniel Boone in Kanawha Valley, went with Boone to Missouri but soon returned east. His first wife was Margaret Gardner, his second wife, Peggy Hutchinson, daughter of Samuel Hutchinson. His daughter Felicity married Moses Hill, Marjory married Noah Davis and Olive married Robert Keenan. His sons,

David C. R. VanBibber, Mathias VanBibber, Moses VanBibber, James VanBibber, Donally VanBibber, Nathan VanBibber, John VanBibber and Davis VanBibber, were well known citizens of the county. Donally was the father of Margaret, wife of James Carden; John was the father of George VanBibber, last of the name to live in Nicholas County; James was the father of Frances VanBibber Hankemeyer, who has compiled a genealogy of the VanBibber family. D. L. "Montie" Carden, son of James Carden is a great-great grandson of Peter VanBibber. Mathias VanBibber is buried on the old VanBibber farm now owned by the heirs of Frank Grose.

> NOTE: The story of "VanBibber's Leap" is pure fiction. Its origin was a story printed in "Youth's Companion" in 1881, by a writer named Harding. One name given to the hero of the story is Hiram, another version names him as Reuben. No such names are found in the family history.

WALKER, *Scotch-Irish*. Elverton P. Walker, first of the name on the Land Books of the County, came from King George County about 1806, married a daughter of Michael Baker and located on the John Hess farm on Laurel Creek. He had a family of fourteen children. Some of his sons went west, but Hiram, Jackson and James located on Laurel Creek. Hiram married Fanny Legg, daughter of Thomas Legg, and their sons William Mack, Levi, Madison, Marion, Doyle, Taylor, Clark and Irvin all located in the county. William Mack married Eliza J. Neil and operated a pottery and brick yard at Summersville for many years. His sons were Floyd, James, Augustus and DeVolle; his daughters, Maggie and Minnie.

Marion Walker had a store at the present location of Tipton. His son, Charles N. Walker, was a teacher, owned a farm on McKees Creek, and later moved to Summersville. Arthur E. Walker, son of Charles N., is an attorney in Morgantown.

Robert L. Walker, son of Marion, was a member of the House of Delegates.

James Walker, son of William Mack, located on a farm near Beaver Mills. His children are all well known citizens. Mrs. Edith Morris of Summersville is a daughter of James. Floyd and Augustus had no children. DeVolle lives in Summersville and with his family operates a store, and owns the Walker Addition to the old Groves Cemetery.

Jackson Walker, son of Elverton P., married Charlotte Nicholls, and spent his life on his farm. His sons were Lewis, Hansford and Marshall. He and his brother, Hiram, were active members of Old Bethel Church. James Walker, brother of Hiram and Jackson, was the father of John A. and Scott Walker. John A. Walker's sons, Dick and Logan, were merchants. Grover Walker, son of Lee Walker, is a grandson of Madison.

William L. Walker, a great grandson of Elverton P. Walker, married Rebecca Jane Backus, a sister of George W. Backus and lived at Vaughan. He was active for many years in local politics.

The Walker family is related to many pioneer families now living in Nicholas and adjoining Counties.

WHITMAN, *German.* Robert Whitman, ancestor of the family in this county, bought 300 acres of land from Alexander McClung, on Hominy Creek, in 1841. William Whitman purchased 100 acres in the same locality from John W. Jones in 1843. Andrew M. Whitman was conveyed 600 acres by William Groves in 1846, and he conveyed this tract to Holly J. Whitman in 1853.

The Whitmans were prominent farmers in the early days of the county, but the family name is not borne by many descendants at this date.

WILLIAMS, *Scotch-Irish*. The Williams family came largely from Greenbrier County, where they were early settlers.

William Williams was an early settler on upper Twenty Mile. His sons were Alexander and Sheldon P. Williams. Sheldon P. Williams married Susan E. Dunbar and lived for a time on the Dunbar farm on Laurel Creek.

Another Alexander Williams located on the southside of Gauley. In his will he names as children, Alexander, James G., Austin H., Rebecca J. Fitzwater, Margaret O. Williams, Virginia Craig, Roxana Bryant and Ledona Carnefix.

S. H. Williams owned a farm on Beaver Creek. His sons were Orlando F. and Averill A. Williams.

Austin H. Williams was a prosperous farmer of Kentucky District and reared a large family.

L. C. Williams, who came from North Carolina, was a dealer in real estate and active in politics. He was not related to the pioneer Williamses. Arthur J. Williams, a son of L. C. Williams, was a farmer and extensive dealer in real estate. His son, Lee Williams, operates a store at Lockwood.

Lee Williams and Thomas Williams, brothers, owned and edited the Nicholas Chronicle for several years.

WISEMAN, *English*. Isaac Wiseman leads the record of the "Wiseman Family in America," published by Dr. B. W. S. Wiseman of Indiana in 1910. According to this record Isaac Wiseman came from Pennsylvania to Rockingham County, Virginia, soon after the Revolution, then to Monroe County. He and his wife, Elizabeth, were buried in Rehoboth Churchyard near Union. His son, John, was ordained a Methodist minister by Bishop Asbury and was in the Continental Army with Washington at Valley Forge. William, a son of Isaac, seems to have remained in Monroe. He married Mary Ramsey. Isaac Ward Wiseman, son of William, was raised in the family of Bartholomew Ramsey. He was a soldier in the company of his cousin, J. Riley Ramsey, in the Civil War. He married and lived in Nicholas County near Mt. Nebo for several years, but died at the home of his daughter, Rebecca Hawkins, in Fayette County. His son, William Wiseman, married Barbara Odell, daughter of Jacob Odell. He had two children: Nicholas Wiseman and Rebecca Ann Bailes. Nicholas Wiseman married Nancy Elizabeth McCutcheon. His two sons, William Johnson Wiseman and Perry N. Wiseman, are well known as citizens of the County. Wm. Johnson Wiseman served a term as Assessor of the County. Perry N. Wiseman was a successful teacher, Clerk of the County Court, and State Senator from his district.

Samuel Wiseman, grandson of pioneer Isaac, was born in Monroe County, came to Nicholas County and commissioned a justice in 1822. Two of his sons, Alexander and John N., were born in Monroe County but came to Nicholas County and were well known citizens. A daughter of Samuel, Isabel Jane, married Matthew Hughes; another daughter, Margaret, married Perry Odell.

The Wiseman family is related to many of the early families of the County.

WOODS, WOOD, *English*. This family name appears among the earliest settlers in Colonial Virginia.

Stephen Woods came to Cottle Glades before the county was organized. Colonel Edward Campbell notes his settlement and says: "From him came all the Woodses who live in Nicholas County."

Isaac Woods, the only one of the name with a will of record, owned several tracts of land, and in his will names John S. Woods and Elizabeth Schindel as his children.

M. Dyer Woods and Milton Woods were sons of John S. Woods.

Alexander Woods, who owned land on Beaver, was the father of William H. Woods and John Woods. William Woods was a teacher and lived at Beaver Mills. Betty Woods, a daughter of Alexander Woods, married Randolph Mason.

Cornelius Woods, who lived on Twenty Mile, owned several tracts of timber lands in that vicinity, and was a dealer in land.

Ferguson Woods, who owned land on Little Mountain, was brother of Van Woods who lived on Buffalo.

Others of the name are listed on our land books, but from the records nothing appears to indicate their relationship.

YOUNG, *German*. Conrad Young came to Peters Creek about 1791 and built his cabin just above Morris on what was later known as the "Neil Place". He had three grown sons at the time of the settlement: Mathias, Charles and Henry. Mathias traveled through the woods eight miles to the cabin of Edward McClung and Captain George Fitzwater the night after the Morris children were killed to warn them of the danger of Indians and assisted McClung to take his wife and children to the fort at Hughes's Creek next day. Charles Young was a noted hunter but owned no land. Mathias located land on Laurel Creek but sold to Jonathan Dunbar and went with his brothers and father to the Elk River settlements in 1809, when Samuel Neil purchased the Young land. Conrad Young was married three times and had several other children but no record of them is found in Nicholas County. A daughter of Conrad Young married Thomas Smith, an early pioneer, who first settled on the Edward McClung land and later moved to Twenty Mile Creek. Descendants of Conrad Young still live in the Elk River Valley.

Rev. George Wellington Young, a distinguished Methodist minister, who married a daughter of John Groves of the Cross Lanes community, was not a relative of Conrad Young. His ancestors came from Madison County, Virginia.

CHAPTER XII

Products, Future Possibilities

IN HIS HUMOROUS lecture on the State of Maine Josh Billings said: "The principal product is its men and women". The principal product of Nicholas County is its men and women.

The character of a people is determined chiefly by heredity and environment. The heredity of the pioneers of Nicholas County, which descends to the present generation, has been exhibited in preceding chapters. The basic elements of environment are: *geographic*—climate, soil and products; *political*—government and laws; *social* —educational and religious institutions. In this chapter the geographic and topographical situation is presented. The other conditions have been shown in previous chapters.

The 420,333 acres comprising the area of Nicholas County falls into three types of land: forest or mountain land, marginal land and arable or agricultural land. In 1932 the United States Department of Agriculture in cooperation with the West Virginia Agricultural Experiment Station, published Bulletin 303, in which the topography of the county was described and the location of the three types of land with maps and statistics pertaining to each was produced. It appears by the census of 1930 that there were at that date 1800 farms in Nicholas

County, with an average of 148 acres, of which about one-half was forest land. The total forest land as of that date was estimated to cover about 83% of the area of the county, this included about 1200 acres estimated as the water surface of the main streams. The forest surface was about 339,000 acres, leaving a little less than 82,000 acres of agricultural and marginal land in the county. It was further estimated that of this amount, about 27,000 acres was marginal and 55,000 acres agricultural land. From the maps it appears that the central part of the county, extending from the Fayette county line to Webster county in a northeasterly-southwesterly direction is a belt of the terrain known as the plateau region of West Virginia, and is that portion of the county best suited to successful farming. This area includes the western portion of Wilderness and Kentucky Districts, the eastern portion of Grant and Summersville Districts and the part of Beaver District north of Gauley River. The farms around Mount Lookout, Canvas and Craigsville are typical of this area. The western portions of Jefferson, Grant and Summersville Districts, extending from the valley of Peters Creek to the Clay County line is classed as Mountain land. Twenty Mile Creek flowing south through this area has a narrow valley from which ridges on either side rise to a height of 800 to 1500 feet with narrow rocky crests. The same type of terrain lies west of the Muddlety valley in Hamilton District. The southeastern portion of the county in Wilderness, Kentucky and Beaver Districts rises in forest lands to the broken ridges and knobs on the Greenbrier line to heights varying from 2500 to more than 3500 feet.

About one-half of the forest lands belongs to the citizens, mainly in surface ownership, and the residue is in the possession of corporate interests, except the overlap of the Monongahela National Forest, in Beaver District, lying mainly between Gauley River and Cherry River and Big Laurel, and having an area of 23,434 acres. The mountain or forest lands consist of the "cut-over" virgin forests and the "old-field" growths on abandoned farm lands. The virgin forest no longer exists in Nicholas County.

The soils of the county are roughly classed as residual or upland soils, derived from the weathering of imbedded shales and sandstone; and alluvial soils composed of materials washed down from the uplands; these soils vary from the fine silt loam to sandy clay.

The climate is temperate and weather conditions conducive to health. Late spring, summer and early fall are pleasant with only occasional hot spells, with cool nights throughout the warm season. The temperature varies with the great diversity of elevation. On the high ridges the winter is longer and there is more snow. Often the lower elevations will have light rain and the higher regions heavy snow. State Route 39 leading from Belva through Richwood to the county line, rises from 675 feet at Belva to about 2300 feet, and is a fair index to the climate and weather variations. At Holcomb, with an elevation of 2042 feet, observations for the past fifty years show the last killing frost is about May 15th, and the first about September 25th, giving a growing season of four and one-third months. In the Belva area the growing season is almost a month longer. It is difficult to give an average annual temperature in such a variety of elevations, but it may be approximated as about 55 degrees, with a maximum of 95 degrees and a minimum of 20 degrees below zero. Only in occasional years are there sub-zero temperatures. The rainfall is also variable but averages about 50 inches annually. The drainage of the county is good except in the glades as in the meadows of Cross Lanes, Muddlety and Beaver.

For the first one hundred years the chief occupation of the county was farming. This progressed from the rude manual labor that opened clearings with axe and fire to give small cornfields, to the clearing and fencing of grainfields and meadows by the time the county was organized. Corn was planted on the rough unplowed land amid stumps and log heaps by digging hills and dropping by hand and covering with hoe. Cultivation was simply keeping the weeds from overwhelming the plants. Later when horses and oxen were had the corn ground was plowed and laid off in furrows, the grains dropped by hand and more attention given to cultivation. Wheat was not grown until the cornfield was in condition to receive the grain and at first was sown between the corn rows by hand. The farm implements were of the crudest kind and were of domestic manufacture. Very little improvement was made in farm implements prior to the Civil War. Clothing was "homemade" from the wool of sheep, after they were introduced about 1810, and from flax. Yet with the crude and laborious method in growing corn more corn was grown in the decade from 1850 to 1860 than has been produced since in any like period. Cattle were the first livestock product to have a cash value. Most of the settlers at the time the county was organized would have two or three calves to sell to their more prosperous neighbor who might be collecting a small drove of yearlings to be raised for the market. Drovers would purchase from these local herds two and three year olds and drive them on foot over the James River and Kanawha Turnpike to eastern markets. Hogs and sheep, but in less quantity, were also produced for the eastern markets. C. W. Cottle, who had settled near Cottle Knob, in what was afterward known as Cottle Glade, had cleared out and maintained the first stock farm in the county. With abundant pasture and forage from the wild meadows he sometimes wintered as many as 200 head of young cattle. He was thus employed at the time the county was organized. The only drawback in cattle raising was the difficulty in producing winter feed. The wild grasses in the glades and along the streams supplied abundant forage except in the winter season. Few farmers had any winter feed for livestock except the fodder from their cornfields. Meadows and pastures were slowly developed. Often the settlers were obliged to keep their cows alive after the limited amount of fodder was consumed, by "browsing" their cattle. This was done by cutting down saplings and small trees, such as birch, maple and linn that would give roughage from the budding twigs and branches that the animals found edible.

Corn was the staple product of Nicholas County until the Civil War and even later. To produce this life-giving product the pioneer must cut down the fine trees on the fertile bottom lands and on the rich coves and hillsides. There was no alternative. He could not eat the trees, so he cleared land for his corn year after year till the timber was taken from the most of the level and fertile land. Thus much land was cleared that should have been left in forest to conserve the timber and prevent erosion. Even had the pioneer's *foresight* equalled our *"hindsight"* he had no other choice. Crop after crop was grown until in a few years the soil was exhausted and the clearings abandoned for new ground. Little or no attempt was made to maintain the fertility of the soil; indeed little could have been done as commercial fertilizers were not in use until about 1880; and at that time could not be had in Nicholas County. The only method of fertilizing the soil prior to this time was by the use of stable manure and wood ashes, which was limited chiefly to gardens and truck patches.

Wheat was grown only in a small way before the organization of the county. It like the other grains and grasses could not be successfully cultivated on the raw new ground, and it was at first sown in cornfields after the wild nature of the soil had been removed by a few crops of corn. Potatoes, beans, pumpkins, and other common vegetables were supplemented by the forest products. Wild grapes, blackberries, huckleberries, mulberries, service berries, persimmons and pawpaws were abundant in season, and were gratefully accepted. Gradually seedling apples and peaches were found around the cabins, and currants and gooseberries were brought in from the older settlements.

Slow progress was at first made in methods of farming. As horses and oxen came into use the labor of clearing and cultivating the land was lightened; shops and mechanics produced better farming implements and grain fields, pastures and meadows began to appear in all parts of the county. In a few years grain cradles replaced sickles and the "chaff-piler' threshing machine operated by horse-power took the place of flails and threshing-floor. In the 1880's hand cornplanters, grain drills, mowing machines and steel turning plows came into use, and wheat and corn were produced in greater quantities than since that period.

The increase in grain production led to better mills. One of the important mills was at Woods Ferry, another at Carnefix Ferry. These two mills never lacked for water power, and in failure of water in the smaller streams were patronized by the farmers of Nicholas, Webster and Fayette counties. Many local mills on smaller streams were fitted to produce flour and meal of good grade. In the bread stuffs from these mills no vitamins were lost, and there was no call for "enriched" bread.

At this period the production of the farms was largely consumed at home. In addition to flour and meal, beef, pork and mutton were in abundance. Clothing was a home product, but the carding machines now prepared wool into "rolls", in place of the hand carding-combs, and woolen cloth was manufactured with less labor. Almost every community had its blacksmith and in his shop he produced plow points, mattocks, hoes and other farm tools, shod horses from shoes and nails made on his anvil from iron sheets and bars. He also prepared "irons" for the wagonmaker, and wagons were made at a cost of as low as $25.00. Oxen were trained for plowing and other farm work, but horses were in general use on the roads. One important item produced for home consumption was sorghum molasses. The cane was grown and the molasses made on almost all the farms. The castiron cane mill came into general use for this product. Another product of the period for home building came with the portable steam sawmills. Lumber cut from choice oak and poplar lumber was on the local market at $5.00 to $10.00 a thousand feet. As a result of this low priced lumber, that replaced the product of the broadaxe and whipsaw, the old loghouses were replaced with neat frame buildings or the loghouse "weatherboarded" with the dressed lumber and painted. Several such structures are found at this time. As late as 1881 the residence of George W. MacMillion on the Wilderness Road was the only "white house" in the District.

Orchards of improved fruit were now found, and a better grade of cattle began to replace the "natives" and "scrubs". Cattle was still the chief cash product but sheep and hogs were raised for annual sale. The sheep were produced with little cost as they could subsist in the woodlands without much attention except to be occasionally rounded up and given salt. Hogs were also allowed to subsist on the abundant mast from the chestnuts, oaks and beeches of the virgin forest. In mountain sections especially, large droves of hogs were kept in this way. They often became so wild that it was necessary to hunt them for butchering in the way wild game was taken. In 1884, the writer teaching on Twenty Mile Creek, boarded with a farmer who had some forty or fifty hogs slaughtered in this way. He would prepare for the "killing", and two or three men with rifles and dogs would hunt and bring in the slaughtered animals on a rude sled. The meat not wanted for immediate home consumption, was taken to the Kanawha market, or carefully salted and cured for future use or sale. So abundant was mast in those days that hogs fattened without other food and "wintered" in the woods. In the late 1870's, the industries being established in the Kanawha Valley provided a steady market for all farm products. The coal mines and salt furnaces were employing a large number of laborers with families who were largely dependent upon the products of the country farms for their food. They cultivated no gardens and the farmers in the Valley, engaged in growing grain and raising cattle and horses, could not furnish these workers needed supplies. Nicholas County reached by the Gauley Bridge and Weston Turnpike thus became the principal source of supply. Quickly the mountain farmers took advantage of this situation. They could sell to the stores that wanted their products only at a price that gave the merchants a profit and must take goods from the stores at a high price. Many farmers at least once a year, usually in the late autumn, took their own productions to Kanawha, and thereby obtained a good price in cash instead of goods from the country stores. In preparation for the trip a covered wagon was carefully stocked with the items for sale and outfitted with food for driver and team and bedding for camping, sufficient for the week necessary to go and return.

From the coal mines at Cannelton and Coal Valley as

Products Future Possibilities

Montgomery was then named, the market extended to Malden. All along this way eager housewives watched for the "Nicholas peddlers". Apples, potatoes, butter, eggs, chickens, pork, beef, sorghum molasses and any farm product that was edible was salable. Boys gathered chestnuts and walnuts and earned pocket money on these trips.

At Malden, then the center of the salt manufacturing, an enterprising merchant by the name of Putney established a large general store that monopolized the Nicholas County trade. He acquainted himself with the character and kind of goods that the mountaineers would purchase and gave them special attention. Rarely did they go on to Charleston to trade.

As demands for the farm products grew and prices advanced, some of the coal companies established stores to supply their employees, and in a few instances operated weekly conveyances to gather the supplies direct from the farmers. John R. Vaughan at Kesslers Cross Lanes, Thomas Drennen and others also engaged in buying and collecting from the farms and supplying the company stores on regular contract.

For more than a generation this method of marketing farm products continued. By 1890 farm products of all kinds began to reach the Kanawha Valley from Ohio farms. This in time took the produce market largely from Nicholas County. The railroads and steamboats brought these western products in great quantities and at lower prices, and with the more systematic trade superseded the somewhat irregular traffic from the mountains. Today the situation is reversed and Nicholas County farmers are buying the western farm products and neglecting their opportunity to grow and sell their home grown grains, fruits and vegetables.

The agricultural possibilities of Nicholas County have never been fully presented to our people. Generation after generation has drawn on the natural resources with little thought of conserving and developing them. The present generation is just awakening to the problems they must solve and are trying to adjust themselves to the change that must come from outmoded conditions in our country life. Nicholas can and should produce its own farm products needed for home use.

It has been demonstrated that wheat can be grown on our lands with a yield of at least thirty bushels to the acre. Corn now averaging forty bushels can be made to produce one hundred bushels per acre.

In 1911 the State Department of Agriculture was established with a Commissioner of Agriculture. The West Virginia Experiment Station in connection with the State University was organized and the era of scientific farming was dawning. Up to this time modern agricultural science had played no part in our farming operations. From this time both State and Federal laws have concurred to bring farming to the status of a profession. Could we have had the training and assistance in agriculture now offered to every farmer in the land, three generations ago, the tremendous task now before us of restoring exhausted soil, conserving our forests and clearing up our polluted water courses would not burden us.

The study of our history shows a gradual decline of live interest in the farm and a gradual decrease in farm products. As late as 1890 farming was the occupation of our people. In 1880 the census shows 1,115 farms with an average acreage of 198½. Fifty years later the census of 1930 shows 1,800 farms with an average of 148 acres. In 1950 we have 1,807 farms with an average of 68 acres. In this report a lot of three acres is listed as a farm; more than one-half of the 1807 farms are less than 50 acres in area; only eight farms are given an area above 500 acres; and the areas given include arable, marginal and forest land. In the period of 70 years given the decrease in farm production has constantly fallen off in production by the acre and in the total production. This is shown in the 1950 agricultural census by a comparison of production in 1944-45 with that of 1949-50.

Comparison of Farm Products and Farm and Home Equipment Shown by Census Reports for the Five Year Period

Farm Crops:

Corn......1944, 213,905 bushels, 1949, 195,204 bushels
Wheat....1944, 15,906   "   1949, 14,215   "
Potatoes...1944, 119,093 "   1949, 70,400   "
Apples....1945, 68,052 trees,   1950, 39,572 trees
Peaches...1945, 15,280   "   1950, 7,101   "
Cherries...1945, 6,955   "   1950, 3,611   "
Grapes....1945, 4,300 vines   1950, 2,706 vines

Farm Animals:

Horses and Mules......1945, 1,848, 1950, 1,630
Cattle.................1945, 9,564, 1950, 7,773
Sheep..................1945, 7,846, 1950, 3,357

Hogs..................1945, 4,134, 1950, 2,795
Chickens.............. 1945, 76,784, 1950, 59,772
Turkeys...............1945, 1,675, 1950, 1,270

Farm and Home Equipment

Equipment:

Electricity......1945, 634 farms, 1950, 1,321 farms
Telephones.....1945, 112   "   1950, 195   "
Tractors....... 1945, 77   "   1950, 150   "
Autos..........1945, 621   "   1950, 650   "

The farms are classified in districts by the U. S. Agricultural Department, as follows:

A—whole time given by owners.
B—owner working out in winters.
C—operated by family, owner working out.
D—used for garden and residence only.
E—operated with neighboring farms.
F—neither land nor buildings used in farming.

Greatest number of "A" farms in Wilderness, least number in Jefferson;

Greatest number of "B" farms in Hamilton, least number in Summersville;

Greatest number of "C" farms in Hamilton, least number in Jefferson;

Greatest number of "D" farms in Kentucky, least number in Grant;

Greatest number of "E" farms in Beaver, least number in Grant;

Products Future Possibilities 405

Greatest number of "F" farms in Kentucky, least number in Beaver.

The total farm income for 1944 was $593,391.00; for 1949 the total income was $705,691.00.

Under present conditions the "Class D" farms can produce good living, though situated in the marginal or forest lands if but five or six acres of arable land is found on which to grow grain and vegetables. Fruit and pasture can be had on the hillsides of the mountain land. The other classes of farms in the agricultural areas can produce grains, and support livestock. Potatoes are an important crop in this area. The soil at an elevation of 2,000 feet and upward, in Wilderness and Kentucky Districts is especially good for producing a fine grade of potatoes. Potatoes grown here are equal in quality to the much advertised Maine and Idaho potatoes. Floyd H. Champe, R. A. Halstead, B. A. Wiseman and others are successful growers in Wilderness District. Mr. Champe equipped with up-to-date machinery and using modern methods estimates that 300 bushels on an average, with a possibility of 450 bushels to the acre can be produced in his vicinity. He estimates the cost of production to vary from $90.00 to $110.00 per acre. His "Nicholas County Potatoes" marketed in bags is by actual test equal to the vaunted Maine and Idaho product and can be sold at a fair profit for much less than the imported potatoes.

Fruit, especially apples, cherries and all small fruits can be grown successfully in the county. Wilderness and Kentucky Districts have soil especially suitable for fruit growing. Cherries have been grown in the Mount

Lookout neighborhood for more than a century. Strawberries can be grown in this county as successfully as in Upshur, which is making a reputation for its berries. The apple and peach trees once found on almost every farm in the county have gradually disappeared as shown in the last census. A fine apple orchard on the farm of June Eakin in the Cross Lanes community proves that Nicholas County can produce good apples. A product once common in the county is sorghum molasses. The soil and altitude of the county is favorable to growing a fine quality of sorghum cane. This product is in constant demand and has become an important item of farm production.

Outside of agricultural products we have coal and gas, now in commercial production and with prospects of greater development. The clays of the county are suitable for brick and pottery making. Gauley and its principal streams have potential water power for generating the electricity needed in the future.

Nicholas County now offers attractive country life as never before. Good roads give transportation from almost every farm to church, school and market. Farm life is no longer lonely and unattractive. Modern machinery enables one man to do the work of ten in pioneer days. Modern furniture and household equipment gives the housewife relief from the drudgery of her mother's days.

The State and Federal Governments with the Agricultural Extension Service, the Farm Bureau, the Agricultural and Home Demonstration Agents, The Conservation Commission, and the local Farm Women's Clubs, Future Farmers, 4-H Clubs, the Cooperative Associations and various other groups, combine to make farming a real profession.

The County has made progress in setting up these local organizations. Results are appearing in methods of farming. The marginal lands are being made agricultural by contour cultivation, seeding to pastures and tree planting. Artificial ponds furnish fish and can be used for the irrigating of gardens. The latest scientific methods dealing with all features of farm life comes in attractive bulletins without cost and actual demonstrations in farm and home subjects are given by trained agents.

When our people are led to see the opportunities now offered on the farm; when attractive farm homes are found to have the same utilities—telephones, daily mails at the door, electric services of all kinds, with the added beauty of natural surroundings; when markets are provided for all farm products and the farm income equals or exceeds the salaried position, the goal of farm organization will become a reality.

Markets established by cooperation with the local merchants, roadside markets along the main highways offering tourists farm products in attractive form, are future prospects in Nicholas County.

In conclusion it must always be kept in mind that *men* and *women* are the principal products of our county, and no better training ground than the farm home has yet been found for the young. There, busy with daily chores, they learn industry; in contact with animals and vegetable life they observe and think as in no other surroundings. Histoy demonstrates this in the lives of our greatest men and women.

Time will come when our coal, oil and gas will be exhausted, but our fertile lands made more productive each year, will furnish grains, fruit and vegetables in the current of health giving mountain air.

MORRIS MONUMENT, 1916

APPENDIX

Historical Address

(Delivered by W. G. Brown at the unveiling of the monument to the memory of the Morris Children, on the Court House Lawn November 1916).

Ladies and Gentlemen, Citizens of Nicholas and Children of the Pioneers:

Today we turn to the past and pause a moment to scan a few dark pages of the Book of Pioneer Life; that grim and iron-bound volume wherein we read how our forefathers won the wide lands that we inherit. Scarcely a leaf that is not blood-stained, but through the darkest blot of savage massacre we see the finest heroism and the noblest sacrifice, the daring and resolution of men, the bravery and patient endurance of women. It shows us a stern race that toiled hard, endured greatly and fronted every adversity fearlessly. Its virtues may seem rough and coarse to the mild-eyed youth of today who is almost overcome with the story of its struggles, but I would that we so prized strength of body and mind, courage, good faith, generosity, hospitality, and loyalty to friends as did our forefathers in the pioneer days.

A century and a quarter ago where we now stand in the shadow of these public edifices, surrounded by the conveniences of our wonderful civilization, there lay the gloomy shades of the primeval forest, like a vast unrent mantle, where never ending woodlands were almost impenetrable, save where a few Indian trails gave a meager passage to the sometime hunter. From the Greenbrier to the Ohio, a few daring settlers, here and there, miles apart, had built their rude cabins in their small, stump-dotted clearings. What is now West Virginia was then divided into ten counties, the largest of which was Kanawha, extending from Greenbrier to the Ohio and bordering on that river from the mouth of the Big Sandy to the Little Kanawha, a distance of more than one hundred miles. In this large territory, covering one-fifth of the present area of the state, were but few settlers. Daniel Boone, a member of the General Assembly of Virginia from Kanawha County, wrote Governor Henry Lee, on December 12, 1791, that there were only sixty-eight men able to bear arms in the county, and nearly all of them lived between Fort Clendenin, now Charleston, and the mouth of Paint creek, then known as the "Boat Yards". Among these hardy frontiersmen were Leonard Morris and his brothers, William, Joshua, Benjamin and Henry, three of whom at least, fought with Lewis at Point Pleasant, in 1774. Shortly before this battle, Leonard had built his cabin where Marmet now stands, and the creek flowing into the Kanawha there is still known as "Len's Creek". Not long afterwards Henry Morris, who had wandered up into the mountains of what is now Nicholas county, accompanied by Peter, who was either his negro slave or an indentured servant, built a brush camp on the bank of a large creek, flowing into Gauley river. Returning in the late fall to the Kanawha settlement for supplies, Morris left Peter alone, and for some reason did not return until spring. Old Peter spent the winter alone in the camp, subsisting on a bear he had killed and what he could gather from the forest, thus giving his name to the creek. Later Morris brought his family to the Peters creek cabin to live. He had married Mary Bird, a pioneer girl who had been captured by the Shawnees when seven years old and had lived in their wigwams until she was fifteen. Among their children were two daughters, Betsey and Peggy. Born and bred to hardship the family lived quietly for some time in their rude dwelling place, from whose door sills stretched leagues on leagues of solemn, mysterious, wolf-haunted woodland. The first neighbors were eight or ten miles away on McClung's Meadow creek, near the Cross Lanes community, where Edward McClung and Capt. George Fitzwater had erected their log huts and moved their families a year or two before Morris had settled on Peters creek.

The daring of Henry Morris in settling in this lonely wilderness can only be realized when we note the condition of the frontier at that time. To the eastward was a small settlement in Greenbrier; to the west a few settlers lived on the Kanawha; to the north the nearest neighbors lived on the West Fork and Buckhannon rivers; and to the south no white man could be found till you reached the cabins of Tennessee and Kentucky.

Fort Savannah stood on the present site of Lewisburg, and Fort Donnally was ten miles to the northwest of Fort Savannah. Fort Clendenin was at the mouth of Elk River where Charleston now stands, and Fort Randolph at Point Pleasant. The nearest road to the Morris cabin was the rude passway hewed out by the axmen of General Lewis down the New river on their way to Point Pleasant in 1774 to meet Cornstalk.

While the battle of Point Pleasant had checked the Indian raids for a time, the defeat of General Harmar in 1790 and of General St. Clair in 1791, had so emboldened the Indians that small parties of revengeful savages overran the defenseless frontier, carrying death and destruction to many a lonely home.

Such was the condition of the scattered inhabitants of the county of Kanawha in the year of our Lord 1792; and while only three years were to elapse until "Mad Anthony" Wayne should humble the northwestern Indians at Fallen Timbers, yet at this date the frontiersman must rely on himself alone for protection from his lurking foes.

If on that fateful May day, 1792, one could have stood on the high ridge south of Peters creek, near where Paul Summers once lived and looked down on the little valley below, he would have seen a small clearing covered with stumps and girdled trees surrounding a little one-story cabin of unhewn logs, the roof of bark, held on with heavy poles and flat stones, with but one room. Its low, squatty chimney was built of sticks and clay and the cracks between the logs were "chinked and daubed".

It had no windows, but coming near you might have entered when the heavy puncheon door was unbarred from within and swung open on its deer-skin hinges. The solid earth was the only floor. Pegs of wood were driven into the walls to serve as a wardrobe; and buck antlers fastened to joists just over the door held the ever ready rifle, and in easy reach, was the keen-edged ax,

Dedication Address—Unveiling of Morris Monument 413

both weapon and tool. The table was a great puncheon set on four stout legs; there were a few three-legged stools, and couches of hemlock boughs covered with bear skins and deer hides. The huge fireplace made of undressed stones was filled with burning logs. Strips of venison hung about drying; a cake of corn bread on a smooth board was baking in the hot ashes; in the corner stood a cradle made of peeled hickory bark. Outside was a small field planted with Indian corn, with beans, pumpkins and melons growing in it, and surrounded by a small brush fence to keep out the cows that must range the woods for pasture. From the cabin door two young girls appear and pass through the clearing to the woods beyond—Peggy and Betsey. They are dressed in linsey-woolsey with short skirts, heads and feet are bare. A little way in the woods they stop as they hear the tinkling of a bell. The cows are near.

The next moment the branches part and two or three savages rush upon them. Betsey was killed at once, but Peggy quick as a flash speeds for the cabin, pursued by a red demon. Almost in sight of home she trips and falls, and is the victim of the merciless tomahawk. Morris just returning from hunting hears the screams of the children and their mother calling him, and in haste reaches Peggy lying in the path scalped and dying. Before he can avenge the death of his children the forest has swallowed up the treacherous savages.

Let us pass over the harrowing details of this fiendish outrage. The snows of one hundred twenty-four winters have covered the grave of the Morris girls where they lie buried near the place of their tragic death, and for years their resting place has been unmarked save by the lone dogwood tree that grows above their dust. Today it is well for us to recall the story of this tragedy; it is well to scan again the history of this family, for their toil and suffering has been repeated in almost every community of the county and state. The murder of the Morris children is not unique in our pioneer history, it is only typical. Three times were the settlements of Greenbrier wiped out by Indian massacres. Every settlement has its legend of savage atrocity. Strouds creek commemorates the bloody fate of an early settler of Nicholas county.

This memorial, while it enshrines the memory of the last victims of Indian treachery, in this county, also bears on its face, first touched by the morning light, a dedication to the pioneers of Nicholas county. These pioneers have long since ceased their labors. Their dust is sleeping in the soil we thoughtlessly tread today.

Through the untiring efforts of George H. Alderson, himself of old pioneer stock, and born on soil that was once a part of Nicholas, this fitting memorial stands here today.

As I look over this throng I see the descendants of the men and women who toiled and suffered that we might have their goodly heritage. More than eighty per cent of our county's population is directly descended from the old families that conquered the wilderness and bequeathed to us all that embellishes our lives in this generation. Do not we, their children, desire to keep green their memories and do honor to their achievements?

When the children of Israel had passed over Jordan, Joshua at the command of Jehova took twelve stones from the river's bed and built a monument therewith, saying, "That this may be a sign among you, that when your children ask their fathers in time to come, saying, 'What mean you by these stones?'", then they were to answer them with the story of their bondage and the history of the Exodus and the conquest of Canaan.

In like manner may this memorial forever keep in mind the deeds of our ancestors, and when children in time to come shall ask its meaning, let the story of the pioneers be told. How they faced their red enemies, lurking ever in the deep woods, wolf-hearted and hawk-eyed, and drove them on toward the setting sun; how the forests were felled, fields were cleared, and homes erected while contending with the numberless dangers of the wilderness; how with scant shelter they endured droughts, deep snow, cloudbursts and freshets. How, surrounded by forests, there was no protection from the swarms of deer flies, mosquitos and gnats in the hot weather; rattlesnakes and copperheads infested the woods, constant sources of danger and death. Bears and wolves continually destroyed their live stock, and panthers frequently attacked men as well. Their clothing was coarse and fashioned from the skins of animals, and from flax and wool which they produced and manufactured themselves. Their food was mainly the flesh of deer, bear, and smaller animals, supplemented by parched corn or coarse bread made from the corn crushed with pestle and mortar and run through a sifter of punctured deer skin stretched on a hoop. They suffered from wounds and disease without medical or surgical aid. They had few books and no newspapers. They had no stores and postoffices. Their only social pleasures came from their log-rollings, house raisings, flax-pullings, and corn huskings, where the community all united to assist some needy member, and concluded their toil with frolic and dance for the young people.

Again, I ask you, shall we allow the memory of these heroic men and women to perish? Shall we forget the obligations we owe them, and which can only be discharged by our emulation of their courage and virtues? This beautiful Monument answers, "No!" And when our children and their children's children shall ask "What means this stone", they shall hear the story of how our fathers, in the olden days, with rifle and ax, beat back the American savage and gave the forest to the sickle and the plow; and hearing they shall be thrilled with the mighty deeds of their forebears, and the pioneer blood sleeping in their veins shall be stirred to action, that they may keep unstained so glorious an heritage.

GAULEY RIVER

I have read in song and story
    Of the Old World's famous streams,
With their vine-clad castles hoary,
    Pictured oft in poet's dreams;

How the Tiber's turbid water
    Dashes high in yellow foam,
As he guards his ancient daughter,
    Proud, patrician, classic Rome;

SCENE ON GAULEY RIVER

How the Rhine from Alpine fountain,
   Rushes bold and clear and free,
Passing storied vale and mountain,
   Till it finds the German sea.

But no lay of Lord Macaulay
   Sketching some historic scene,
Could depict the limpid Gauley,
   Coursing giant cliffs between.

Whence the *name* no one remembers;
   Lost the reason for the same;
Mem'ry fire in dying embers,
   Throws no light on Gauley's name.

"To-ke-bi-lo-ke", named by Shawnee,
   In his tongue—"The Falling Creek",
As in flood its current tawny,
   Voiced the name its waters speak.

Gaul or Gallia in past ages,
   Gave its name to ancient France,
(Though now lost to Hist'ry's pages,
   Hence the river's name, perchance).

Coureur de bois adventure questing,
   May have heard the waters fall,
And in Gauley's canyons resting,
   Conjured up the name of Gaul.

Matters not by whom the christ'ning;
   Matters not the name or giver;

As I stand in rapture list'ning,
   To the music of my river.

High in Allegheny Mountains,
   Seven rivers burst from earth,
Here in crystal, cloud-fed fountains,
   Sylvan Gauley has its birth.

Thence from cloud-swept mountain fastness,
   Silvery streamlets, gurgling, well;
Bounding down neath leafy vastness,
   They unite in flowery dell,

Then from rocky basins leaping,
   Gauley's sparkling waters flow;
Now in shimmering eddies sleeping,
   Foaming next through shoals like snow.

Alternating depth and shallow,
   Onward swift the river glides,
Banks green-fringed with pine and willow,
   Where the wildflower coyly hides.

Mile on mile the scene's repeated;
   Towering forests stretch beside,
From whose shady depths secreted,
   Cool springs rise to join the tide.

In deep pools with waters brimming
   Over shoals in fleecy spray,
Gleaming fish from clear depths swimming,
   Dart and flash the livelong day.

Every eddy's Nature's mirror,
  Throwing back some thrilling scene,
Till the warm blue sky seems nearer
  Than the mountain's summit green.

Summer's change to Autumn's glowing
  Paints the trees in rainbow's hues,
Mirrored in the waters flowing,
  Frames a myriad radiant views.

Winter steals the regal pigment
  From the forest monarch's crown,
Leaving but a ghostly figment,
  As the dead leaves flutter down.

Still the hemlock's verdant sheen,
  Rhododendron, pine and holly
With their fadeless living green
  Robe the wintry shores of Gauley.

Beauteous now in novel brightness
  Gauley's trees are crowned with snow,
Garmented in ermine whiteness,
  Charms untouched by Winter's blow.

Mountain river, how I love thee!
  Pure and dashing, bright and free,
With God's smiling sky above thee,
  Teach thy lesson now to me.

May my life with true course given,
  Like thine own toward sunset sea,

Mirror back the tints of heaven,
   Till it meets eternity.

—W. G. Brown

(Published in the *Wheeling Intelligencer*, 1895)

BROWN WATERS OF GAULEY

The waters of Gauley,
Wild waters and brown,
Through the hill-bounded valley,
Sweep onward and down;
Over rocks, over shallows,
Through shaded ravines,
Where the beautiful hallows
Wild, varying scenes;
Where the tulip tree scatters
Its blossoms in spring,
And the bank-swallow spatters
With foam its sweet wing;
Where the dun deer is stooping
To drink from the spray,
And the fish-eagle swooping
Bears down on his prey—
Brown waters of Gauley,
That sweep past the shore—

Dark waters of Gauley
That move evermore.

* * *

Brown waters of Gauley,
My fingers I lave,
In the foam that lies scattered
Upon your brown wave,
From sunlight to shadow,
To shadow more dark,
'Neath the low-bending birches
I guide my rude barque;
Through the shallows whose brawling
Falls full on my ear,
Through the sharp mossy masses,
My vessel I steer,
What care I for honors,
The world might bestow,
What care I for gold,
With its glare and its glow?
The world and its troubles
I leave on the shore
Of the waters of Gauley
That move evermore.

—Thomas Dunn English, 1882.

The above poem was written by the famous author and poet during his residence in West Virginia. His beloved ballad "Ben

Bolt" is reputed to have been written in the old graveyard of the Methodist Church in Summersville. It is included in his volume "American Ballads".

TEACHING LOCAL HISTORY

"The study of local history properly adapted to the mind of the child will give a reality to the past, and fill its dim spaces with persons that move and live and feel".

History starts with homelife. The child begins his journey into life by becoming familiar with every detail of living around the house. His inquiring mind needs only to be guided in learning the meaning of family government, the purpose of church and school, and his duties to others in the home and social life around him. First impressions of his relation to the family, the church, the school and industrial life are fundamental. Prime responsibility for such impressions lies with the parents, but the teacher comes next in training a child for citizenship. There is no greater means of instilling a sense of pride and responsibility into a child's mind, than to awake in him the feeling of his belonging to the community, the pride of being a part of it through relationship to the forefathers who hewed out their homes in the early days when history was in the making.

A teacher who is in touch with the child's home life and has been trained in modern historical methods can present the many phases of the local history as a sound foundation for later studies in geography, civics, and broader fields of state, national and world history.

The record of pioneer families of the community, with written history and with legends handed down through the generations of those exciting days when the early settlers followed mountain trails to a chosen location, cleared forests, fought Indians and wild animals, built homes and schools, and constructed roads and bridges to give today's easy way of life, stir and delight children, and give them a realization of the way history is made.

Dr. James M. Callaghan, in his histories of West Virginia, stresses the importance of teaching local history in the grades, using it as the very foundation for educating our future citizens. *"History like Charity should begin at home"*, he says. This noted writer suggests more than a hundred subjects as a general outline for such study. He specifies: Oldest settlements, earliest settlers, wild animals they encountered; the type of homes they constructed and the way they were furnished; work and play of the settlers; their schools and churches, first stores and first postoffices. The names and histories of the first families and the history of early preachers and teachers are of interest.

Local history is made into a present day saga by materail available in old books, photographs, letters, deeds and wills, and by stories the older generation can tell of their way of life. Attics are storehouses of yesterday's mode of life. Old trunks give forth treasures of clothing and daguerreotypes, old literature and books of poems and song. Spinning wheels and sturdy looms, and candle moulds tell of diligent housewives, and in the smokehouse and old barns are the adz and whipsaw, the drawing knife, iron wedge and maul of log cabin days. Wooden grain cradles and flails are still found to tell of harvest time. The early homes in Nicholas employed the broadaxe, mattock, ox-yoke, pack-saddle, sidesaddle, flax brake, scutching knife, hackles, iron pots, chimney cranes, dutch ovens, pot-hooks, looms, reels, wooden tubs and grain measures, splint brooms, mountain rifles, and scores of other objects, the very names of which are not found in today's vocabulary. But the older generations can tell interesting stories to their grandchildren of their early home life, of the clothes they wore, the food they ate, their apple peelings and molasses making. Perhaps there is a blue and white coverlid woven by a forgotten housewife, or a cherished piece of walnut furniture, shaped and fashioned by an ancestor, that a child can speak of with pride. "Home-made" was an adjective applied to almost any article in the pioneer home. It was a word defining the independence and ingenuity of those early settlers. It meant they were capable of providing their own shelter, home, clothing, fuel and entertainment. This hardy way of existence trained our ancestors in the "American Way of Life". These "home-made" relics, now so eagerly sought for by museums and private collectors, speak to us of the skill, patient industry and independence of our forefathers which should be recalled with rightful pride.

In Nicholas County, at the Carnefix Battleground Park, near Cross Lanes, a museum is now under construction. This will house a collection of pioneer tools and articles used by the early settlers of the county, together with historical articles connected with the battle, fought there during the Civil War. Teachers, working with the

Battleground Commission could make an interesting school project in which the children would gather acceptable material to be added to the museum's wealth.

The museum in the Department of Archives in Charleston has much material of interest to Nicholas County schools. Old books and old records, and primitive furnishings and implements employed by our pioneer ancestors are seen there.

In the Nation's Capital there are historic statues and parks at every square, and the Smithsonian Institution and National Museum are so filled with historic objects that a student of local and national history has the whole story before him. As never before teachers are taking advantage of such concrete methods of teaching history, and classes from schools all over the nation are taken to their county-seats, their state capitols and to Washington, to teach our children what future citizens of America should know.

But the beginning of love of country, and a desire to be a useful citizen must begin in the home; must travel through the grades of school, if a full and satisfying knowledge of our origin and growth as a nation is to be accomplished. Just as the little rivulets from the wayside spring join with larger streams to form the mighty rivers, just so local history is the basis of national history.

Index *to* Pioneer Families

ALDERSON	282
AMICK	283
BACKUS	284
BAILES	286
BAKER	286
BAUGHMAN	287
BELL	288
BENNETT	289
BOBBITT	290a
BOLEY	290
BROCK	291
BROWN	292
BRYANT	295
BURDETT	296
CALLAGHAN	297
CAMPBEL	298
CARNEFIX	299
CAVENDISH	300
CHAPMAN	301
COPENHAVER	302
CORRON	302
COTTLE	303
CRAIG	304
CROOKSHANKS	305
CUTLIP	306
DAVIS	307
DIETZ	307
DODRILL	308
DORSEY	309
DOTSON	311
DRENNEN	312
DUFFY	313
DUNBAR	314
EVANS	315
EWING	315
FITZWATER	316
FOCKLER	317
FOSTER	318
FRAME	319
GIVEN	320
GRAY	320
GROSE	321
GROVES	322
HALSTEAD	324
HAMILTON	325
HAMRICK	326
HANNA	327
HARDWAY	327
HENDERSON	328
HEREFORD	329
HEROLD	329
HICKMAN	331
HILL	331
HINKLE	332
HORAN	333
HUFF	334
HUFFMAN	334
HUGHES	335
HUTCHINSON	336
HYPES	337
JOHNSON	338
JONES	339
KEENAN	340
KESSLER	341
KINCAID	342
KING	343
KOONTZ	344
KYLE	345
KYLER	345
LEGG	346
LEMASTERS	347
LILLY	348
MALCOLM	348
MARTIN	342

Index *to* Pioneer Families

MASON	350
MILLER	351
MORRIS	352
MORRISON	353
McCLUNG	354
McCOY	355
McCUTCHEN	356
McCUE	359
McMILLION	357
McNUTT	358
MURPHY	360
NEIL	361
NICHOLS	363
NUTTER	362
ODELL	363
PATTERSON	364
PERKINS	365
PIERSON	366
PITTSENBERGER	367
RAMSEY	367
RADER	368
RENICK	369
RIPPETOE	370
ROBINSON	371
SEBERT	372
SHAWVER	373
SHELTON	374
SIMMS	375
SIERS	376
SKAGGS	376
SMITH	377
SPARKS	378
SPENCER	379
SPINKS	379
STANARD	380
STEPHENSON	381
STICKLER	382
SUMMERS	382
TYREE	383
VANBIBBER	385
VAUGHAN	384
WALKER	386
WHITMAN	387
WILLIAMS	388
WISEMAN	389
WOODS	390
YOUNG	391

www.ingramcontent.com/pod-product-compliance
Lightning Source LLC
Chambersburg PA
CBHW030539080526
44585CB00012B/200